A First Course in Psychology

Third Edition

Nicky Hayes

Nelson

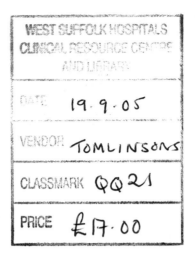
Thomas Nelson and Sons Ltd
Delta Place
27 Bath Road
CHELTENHAM
GL53 7TH
United Kingdom

© Nicky Hayes 1984
First published by Harrap Ltd 1984
(under ISBN 0-245-54058-X)
Second impression published by Thomas Nelson and Sons Ltd 1984
Second edition published 1988
Third edition published 1993

ISBN 0-17-448181-0
05 06 07 / 15 14 13 12

Printed in Croatia

Contents

Preface to the third edition

In the nine years which have elapsed since the debut of 'A First Course in Psychology', I have never ceased to be – to use the Merseyside colloquialism – 'dead chuffed' about the response it has received. I am delighted that so many teachers and students have let me know, both in person and by letter, how much they have appreciated it, and I'd like to thank them for their trouble. At the risk of sounding pretentious, I must say that such tributes make everything worthwhile.

One thing which has been apparent from these messages is that 'A First Course in Psychology' has a readership which goes far beyond the constraints of the GCSE psychology syllabus. It is used on a wide range of courses, at many levels. Some of the additions which have been made in this third edition are an attempt to address the needs of this wider readership. For example, GCSE psychology students don't need full academic source references, but many other students do, so in response to requests, a full reference listing has been included.

The third edition has continued the work of the second, extending the range and relevance of the book by including chapters on areas of psychology which were not previously covered. Cognitive psychology, for example, is now more fully represented (some would say not before time) through an extension to the previous 'Perception' chapter and a new chapter on 'Thinking and Remembering'. A new chapter on 'Measuring Mental Characteristics' takes up some of the issues which are raised in the chapter on 'Intelligence', and discusses how they apply to a wider range of psychometric tests, including personality and occupational tests. And a chapter on 'Social Perception' augments the book's coverage of social psychology by discussing the psychology of social explanations, attitudes and prejudice.

The rest of the text remains for the most part untouched, apart from the inevitable minor alterations to bring it more up to date. As a teacher I have experienced the frustration of discovering that a familiar and useful chunk of content has disappeared in a new edition of a textbook, as a writer replaces well-established information with accounts of modern research. There are useful lessons to be learned from the development of ideas in psychology, and in my view it is important for a new edition of a textbook to continue to cover these, while at the same time it is important that it should reflect more recent developments within the discipline. Carried to logical conclusions, of course, this argument implies that a textbook will grow ever-larger with each new edition. There must be some top limit to this, but 'A First Course in Psychology' has not reached it yet. The new edition is therefore bigger, and I hope better (more comprehensive, anyway), than the previous one. I hope you find it useful. And, just as importantly, that you enjoy it.

Nicky Hayes
Spring 1993

Acknowledgements

My sincere thanks are due to all the psychology teachers whose comments have been so valuable in guiding the changes of this edition. I am also grateful to Philip Banyard and Peter Stratton, for their useful, if at times throwaway, comments. I'd like to express my appreciation, too, of Julia Cousins at Nelson, whose enthusiasm for the new edition has been so inspirational, and with whom it has been a pleasure to work. I remain deeply grateful to Pyrrol McKone, whose support was so essential during the initial preparation of A First Course in Psychology. And most of all, I am grateful to those teachers and students whose consistent adoption of this text convinced my publishers that a new edition was a Good Thing.

Fig 14.1 is taken from 'The Origin of Form Perception' by Robert L. Fantz, *Scientific American*, May 1961, p. 66, by permission of David Linton; Fig 14.4 is taken from 'The Visual Cliff' by Eleanor J. Gibson & Richard D. Walk, *Scientific American*, April 1960, p. 65, by permission of William Vandivert. Fig 16.8 is by permission of Pete Ward

Chapter 1

About psychology

On picking up this book your first question may well be: 'What exactly is psychology anyway?'. There are many possible answers to this question – I hope that by the time you have finished this book you will have some ideas of your own. Perhaps the best way to start, though, would be to try to define psychology in some way.

When psychology first started, it was thought of as an attempt to study the mind, or mental life. The earliest psychologists were often philosophers who had become interested in how human beings work – what makes them 'tick'. So they spent a great deal of time trying to analyse their own reactions, and to develop ideas about people based on their own experiences, and on examining other people's experiences. Trying to analyse your own, personal experience and reactions is known as _introspection_.

But there are problems with introspection as a way of finding things out. One of the main ones is that we are often unconsciously biased – we don't notice things because we don't expect them to be there, or we don't think they are important. And, because our biases are often unconscious, it is very difficult for us to control them. Another problem with introspection as a way of finding things out, is that it is not possible for other people to check our observations; that is, we cannot develop any _objective_ way of looking at a person's personal experiences and reactions.

So it gradually became clear that introspection, though very interesting as an approach, was not really enough if we wanted to find out about human beings. There were problems, too, with defining psychology as 'the study of the mind', as many people did. One of these problems is that, while we all know what we mean when we talk of the 'mind', it is very difficult to know if other people mean the same thing. For example: I might talk about my 'mind', and be thinking of that part of myself which engages in thinking and remembering; while you might talk about your 'mind' and be thinking, not just of those parts, but also of your emotions and feelings as well. So although we would be using the same words, we would be thinking of different things, and we would therefore be likely to disagree with what the other person said.

Another problem with talking about the mind – the main one, even – is that we cannot see or touch it; in fact, we have no outward sign that it exists at all, except as it shows through people's *behaviour*. I cannot know what you are thinking, but, if you smile at me and nod your head when I am talking to you, then I may judge that you agree with what I am saying. But the information that I have used to work this out was your behaviour – smiles and head-nodding.

Because of this, there was a change in psychology at the beginning of this century. Psychologists began to concentrate much more on studying behaviour, as a way of finding out about people, than on 'introspection'. Information about people was obtained by studying what they did, their actions, speech, and so on. Behaviour is anything which people do that can be observed by someone else; talking, for instance, has been called 'verbal behaviour', and we can also talk about things like 'social behaviour', or 'aggressive behaviour'.

But there are problems, too, with simply studying behaviour. There is more to people than just the behaviour which they are engaging in at any particular time. We all have many memories that may affect the things that we do: we have learned from our *experiences* since we were very tiny. Although it isn't possible for someone else to see our experiences, they do have an influence on how we act – on our behaviour. So the definition of psychology changed: from being the study of the mind, or the study of mental life, it had now a new definition:

Psychology is the study of behaviour and experience.

This is a much better definition than simply talking of the study of the mind, but it isn't perfect yet! For example: if I were to tell you an amusing story about a five-year-old child that I know, I would probably be describing experience and behaviour. But would you think that you had learned about five-year-olds *in general* from it? Probably not – you would be well aware that five-year-olds are different from each other, and that just because little Jane acted this way, it doesn't mean that little Catherine would also act in this same way. Yet I would still have been describing behaviour and experience. But if I were to tell you about a careful study of many different five-year-olds, living in many different types of homes, that would be different. You might well think that you could learn something about five-year-olds in general then. So we need to include another word in our definition:

Psychology is the *scientific* study of behaviour and experience.

By including the word scientific, we are saying that our study must be serious and systematic; and also, that we should be able to apply our findings to others, as well as to the people we are studying.

Gradually, psychology became more and more concerned with how experience and our understanding of the world around us influence behaviour. In particular, psychologists became interested in *cognitive processes* – how we interpret the information that we receive through our senses, and how we memorise it or use it to solve problems. This 'cognitive revolution' meant that the study of the mind became popular again in psychology: but not in the old introspectionist way. Rather, cognitive psychologists adopt more objective and scientific ways of studying how cognitive processes work, so that they are less likely to be taken in by unconscious bias.

How do we find things out in psychology?

Throughout this book, you will find references to studies which people have done, to find out why something happens, or to test an idea which they have had. Finding evidence is a vital part of modern psychology.

There are various stages to doing a systematic study, all of which are important in their own right, and which we will look at. Perhaps the first stage will seem obvious, but it's still important. This is sorting out exactly what the study is *for*. Suppose you were interested in the effects on children of watching television. It's no good just saying 'Oh, I'm interested in what effects it has', because that won't get you anywhere – how are you going to start looking for the effects? As I said at the beginning of this chapter, we need to have a *systematic* approach if we want to find things out which will apply to everyone; it's not enough just to rely on anecdotes, because people are individuals, and can behave very differently.

So we need to narrow it down, until we are asking a definite question, which we can test out in a systematic fashion. You might say something like: 'Does violence shown on television affect children?' Now, at least, we know what we are looking *at* – violence on TV – but we still aren't very sure what sort of effects we will look for. Do we mean 'Does it upset children?'. That would be one effect which we could look for. But I don't think it would really be the one which we had in mind when we first asked the question. That would be more like 'Do children behave more violently to each other, when they've been watching violent TV?'. Whatever it is that we are interested in, we have to make sure that we are asking a question which will tell us that answer, and not the answer to an entirely different question! This process of narrowing down the questions to which we want answers is a part of the way that we develop the *hypothesis* for the study.

Most studies are designed to test a hypothesis. In our example, the hypothesis which we would be testing could be: 'Children who watch violent TV will show more violent behaviour than children who watch non-violent TV.' That would be a kind of statement which we make and then test to see if it's really true. The test, of course, is the study which we now go on to design, but the kind of study we design *depends* on the hypothesis which we are testing – a different hypothesis would need a different method of study. For instance, we might decide that our hypothesis would be 'Teenagers who are violent watch more violent TV than teenagers who are not violent', in which case we would probably do a totally different kind of study to investigate the hypothesis.

There are three main standards which a good psychological study should live up to. The first is that it should be possible to *generalise* from the results. There's no point studying people or animals in detail if we can't hope to find out about people or animals in general from it; that wouldn't be much better than an interesting anecdote. It's only if we feel that a study has something more to say, about others as well, that we count it as good evidence.

A second standard is that an experiment should be *replicable*. That means that it should be possible for someone else to copy exactly what the first investigator did, and to get exactly the same results. If we can't do that, then we would say that it's not really very good evidence – the results might just have happened because of some problem in the way that the study was designed, or because the experimenter happened to get very unusual subjects.

The third standard is that whatever is used to assess the effects in the study – the measure – should be *valid*. That means that it really should be measuring what it is trying to measure. For instance, if we were looking at whether violent TV caused violence in children, and we just measured whether they got upset or not, it wouldn't really be valid, because being upset is not necessarily the same as getting violent. So we need to make sure that the study is as realistic and valid as possible.

There are several different methods that we can use to find things out in psychology. Each of these methods is useful for finding out different types of things, but also each of them has its own problems which we have to be very careful about. We will look at some of these methods in turn, and also at some of their problems.

Experiments   Experiments are what we do when we are trying to find out if one thing *causes* something else. Because of this, when we are doing an experiment we have to make sure that the results we have got could not have happened in any way other than the one we are trying to investigate. For example: suppose we were trying to find out if students did better at arithmetic tests when they were sitting in a cool room, than when they were sitting in a hot room. Obviously, we would have to test students in a hot room, and also in a cool room. But there are other things we have to take into account too – was it the same room? Perhaps one of the rooms was more comfortable than the other one. The students might have felt more relaxed, and so performed better in the test. If that happened, then we might think that our results showed that the cool room was better than the hot room, but they might really be showing that a comfortable room was better than an uncomfortable one!

There are lots of factors like this which can influence experiments. A good experiment needs to be *well-controlled*; that is, all these possible influences need to have been noticed and prevented. For example, you could prevent that last problem by making sure that you always used the same room, but heated it differently.

Another factor that we need to be very careful about is the way that our subjects are selected. (This is true of all psychological studies, not just experiments.) A study by Orne, in 1972, showed that volunteer subjects would be much more co-operative and helpful if they knew they were taking part in a psychological experiment, than if they were just being asked to do something in their normal life. Orne asked subjects to add up pairs of numbers on a piece of paper, and then to tear it up. People would refuse to do this after a while unless they thought it was part of an experiment. If they thought that, then they would do it time and time again!

What this means, then, is that we have to be sure that our subjects are acting realistically, and with many laboratory experiments it isn't possible to be certain of this. Since we also need to make sure that our subjects don't try to be too helpful, and give us the results that we want to get, most experiments will use a *single-blind control*. This means that the subject doesn't know what the hypothesis of the experiment is, so they can't mess it up by trying to be too helpful!

In experiments it's important to be really careful about subjects guessing the hypothesis. For instance, if we were testing a new type of drug, our subjects might get clues about what we were expecting by little things, like the way that we asked the question, and whether we seemed more interested in some answers than in others. In studies like these, this problem is

often coped with by using a *double-blind control*. This means
that neither the subject nor the experimenter knows what the
hypothesis is. The experimenter is just someone who is working
on the experiment but who isn't fully informed about it, so
they can't pass on unconscious 'clues' to the subject.
Standardised procedures can also be used to prevent these
kinds of *experimenter effects*. This means that every step of the
experiment is decided beforehand, so that all the subjects get
identical experiences. This ensures that the experimenter
doesn't unconsciously influence the results by varying the
experiment slightly.

Standardised instructions are used when subjects might be
affected by the way that they are told to do something. So
everything that the experimenter says to the subject is decided
beforehand, making sure that all the subjects are given exactly
the same information.

There are many other ways in which experiments can be
influenced, and as I said, a good experimenter will have
controlled them – so that the results could not possibly have
been caused by anything else. As you read through this book,
you will find many accounts of experiments: always ask yourself,
each time you read about one: 'Could these results have come
from anything else?' If they could, then we can't take the
experiment to be convincing proof of what it was trying to look
at.

Observations   Many subjects in psychology are not suitable for investigation
by means of experiments. If we wanted to find out about young
children and their playing, for instance, we could not do
experiments on the children, for fear that restricting them so
much might harm or change their development. So we find out
about their playing by *observation* – by watching them carefully,
and seeing what we can learn from that.

Again there are problems with relying on observation to find
things out. One of the main problems is that, because there are
lots of things going on at once, it is very difficult to sort out
which thing *causes* the other. The behaviour we are interested
in might be caused by several different factors all working
together, or it might arise from something that happened
before we started watching, and so on. So we have to be content
with describing what is happening, and trying to work things
out from that.

Other problems, too, arise from possible biases in the
observer – especially if they know what the observational study
is interested in. For instance: suppose the study was to find
out if children in crowded rooms played more aggressively than
children with plenty of space. The observer has to note down

all the behaviour which the children engage in, and especially aggressive behaviour. But quite a lot of actions that children do can be read two ways: if a child lifts its hand and there is another child standing close by, it could be a threatening action. On the other hand, it might not be – the child might be pointing or even just stretching! But if the observer is expecting the child to be aggressive, then it could be noted down as an aggressive action, even though it wasn't. So observers need to be carefully trained, and it is better if they don't know what the study is about.

Perhaps one of the biggest problems of observational studies, with both humans and animals, is our tendency to act differently if we know that we are being watched. If we go back to the 'children and TV' study, for instance, it's unlikely that we could really get an idea of how violent a particular child or teenager was, just from observation. After all, most violence occurs when people *aren't* watching, not when they are!

But, also, it's very difficult to act naturally when you are aware that someone else is watching you. Try it sometime! So what the psychologist sees may easily not be valid – it may have become unrealistic from the very beginning, just by the way it is being studied.

There are three ways that psychologists try to get round this problem. The first one – perhaps the most common – is to try to get the subjects *accustomed* to the observer, so that after a while being watched won't bother them as much, and their behaviour will become more natural. Although this can take a bit of time, it's a method that's quite often used, because it doesn't affect other aspects of the study too much.

Another method is to *conceal* the observer from the subjects – for instance, by using two-way mirrors, or hidden video cameras. But this means that whatever behaviour is being observed has to take place in that particular room or area – if the subjects move away, or just turn their backs to the mirror or camera, the observer isn't able to get a clear view of what they are doing. So this affects the way that the study has to be designed; you couldn't do a very 'natural' study like this.

The third method is known as *participant observation* – where the observer joins in with the group that is being observed. Although this means that the study is often more realistic, it can also mean that the observer gets too involved with what is going on, and so is not as objective as he or she could be. And, also, it isn't very easy for another person to check what the observer is studying, or to replicate it.

Case studies Rather than trying to collect information from a whole mass of people some studies have concentrated on just one or two individuals, and looked at their experiences and behaviour in detail. This is another useful way we can find things out about how people are influenced, and how different things develop. But case studies, too, have their problems. The most important one of these is the way that only one or two people can be studied at a time. Although this means that we can find out about them in more detail than we could have done otherwise, it also means that we have no way of knowing how *typical* these people are. It might be that the people we have chosen to study are really very unusual, and not like the rest of us at all! In that case, although we might find out interesting things about them, it wouldn't help as much in finding out about people in general.

Longitudinal and cross-sectional studies

A *longitudinal* study is where the same individuals are studied over a long period of time, so that the changes that happen to them can be recorded. For example: if we wanted to compare three-year-olds with nine-year-olds, we could do it by taking a group of each age and looking at them systematically. This would be a *cross-sectional study*. But we would have no way of knowing whether the present three-year-olds were acting in the same way as the nine-year-olds had when they were three. It could be that times had changed slightly – they might have been brought up slightly differently by their parents, or watched different TV programmes, and this could make a difference.

With a longitudinal study, we can control this sort of problem. By looking at the same children when they are three and again when they are nine, we can be sure that we have the same types of experience in both groups of children. Also, of course, the individual differences between the children don't matter so much either! On the other hand, as you can imagine, longitudinal studies take a long time to conduct, and are quite expensive too.

The problem of individual differences affecting experiments is one which can be very important. A cross-sectional study is an example of what is known as an *independent-measures design*. This is when we have different people in each of the conditions that we are studying: in this case, for instance, we have different people for our three-year-olds and for our nine-year-olds.

But this leaves us with the difficulty that I mentioned before. Experiences in the two groups may be different, and individual differences may affect our results. So if we have an independent-measures design, we need to study a lot of people in each group, in the hope that, with enough people, individual differences will be averaged out and won't affect the study.

One way we can control for individual differences, though, is to use a *repeated-measures design*. By doing this, we study the same people in the different conditions of our experiment. So any individual differences get cancelled out, and we can simply look at the differences between the results that the person had in one condition (like doing an arithmetic test in a hot room) and their results in the other condition (like doing a similar test in a cold room). A longitudinal study is an example of a repeated-measures design, because we are studying the same person at different ages.

Interviews Interviews are another way of collecting useful information to enable us to find out about people. There are many different ways to conduct an interview, ranging from casual chats with people to formal, standardised, set questions which have to be asked in a particular way. Iona and Peter Opie published a study of the rhymes and word-games that school-children use; they collected their data simply by going round school playgrounds and chatting with school-children. On the other hand, George Brown and Tirril Harris's study of depression in a group of London housewives was based on information collected through formal, standard interviews, because in this way it was easier to compare the different women's circumstances.

Each of these methods has advantages and disadvantages. Collecting information by casual, informal interviews means that often the information given is more spontaneous and realistic. But it can also make it very difficult to *generalise* – one person may talk about something so differently from the way that another person does, that it becomes almost impossible to compare what the two people said.

If we use formal, standard interviews, it is much easier to generalise from the results. But if people feel that they are being asked a set of routine and automatic questions from a list they often do not talk as freely as they would in a casual conversation. The interviewer needs to be thoroughly skilled and trained, to make it seem a natural and not an awkward, situation. This can mean that a formal interview study is quite difficult (and expensive) to conduct well.

Surveys Although surveys are often more useful to sociologists than they are to psychologists, they can nonetheless be very helpful. For instance, supposing we were interested in whether violent TV had effects on young people, we might decide to begin our study by a large survey of people's TV watching habits, and their preferred programmes. From the results of this survey, we could pick out extreme groups of subjects – some who watch very violent TV and some who never watch violent TV. Once we had found these people, we could investigate further by using a different method, maybe observations or experiments.

One problem with all psychological methods, but particularly with surveys, is that it matters a great deal just how the subjects are selected. If we are comparing two groups of people, or wanting to find out about people in general, then it is very important that we have a *representative sample* of subjects. If our sample is biased in some way (for example, only asking very middle-class people about their TV-watching habits), then we are not able to generalise from the results. And in some studies it may even distort the results completely.

In order to get a representative sample, we need to try to make sure that everyone has an equal chance of being chosen. There are two main ways that we can do this: random or stratified sampling.

Random sampling is when we try to make sure that our choice has not been influenced by anything about that person. For instance, if we stood in a busy street and asked people to answer questions, although we might think we were equally likely to approach anyone, unconsciously we would probably only go up to the ones who looked as though they might answer. But if we approached every seventh or tenth person, say, regardless of what they looked like, that would form a more random sample.

Stratified or quota sampling is when we try to select balanced numbers from different types of subjects. So, if we wanted to look at how people from different countries thought of English people, there would be no point in going up to every fifth person in the street. Instead, we would try to get a certain number of people from each different country, and ask for their opinions. In this way, our sample would be more representative.

Both surveys and interviews have the advantage that we are able to study very large samples of subjects fairly easily. However, they have the disadvantage that we cannot really go into things in much detail. Only the more obvious or apparent kinds of human behaviour can be studied using these methods.

Most psychologists use a combination of different approaches and methods, so that they can look at things from several different angles. There's no such thing as a perfect method of study in psychology, but by being aware of the problems, and controlling them as far as possible, we can collect some pretty reliable evidence for many of the questions we ask about human beings.

Ethical issues in psychology

Whatever method of investigation they use, psychologists need to make sure that they do not cause their subjects any distress or damage as a result of their investigations. In 1990, the British Psychological Society produced a set of ethical guidelines for psychological research with human subjects, which consisted of the following ten principles:

1 In all circumstances, investigators must consider the ethical implications and psychological consequences for the participants in their research.

2 Whenever possible, investigators should inform participants of the objectives of the research and gain their informed consent. If this is not possible, special safeguarding procedures must be followed.

3 Withholding of information or misleading participants is unacceptable if they might object or show unease once debriefing is over. Intentional deception should be avoided whenever possible.

4 In all studies where the participants are aware that they have taken part in an investigation, they must be fully debriefed, such that they are able to complete their understanding of the nature of the research.

5 Investigators must emphasise the subject's right to withdraw from the experiment at any time, should they so wish.

6 All data obtained must be treated as confidential unless otherwise agreed in advance.

7 Investigators must protect participants from physical and mental harm during investigations, or arising from them.

8 Studies based on observation must respect the privacy and psychological well-being of the people studied. Covert observation without prior consent is only permissible in situations where those observed would expect to be observed by strangers.

9 Investigators must exercise care in giving advice on psychological problems, and recommend professional advice where appropriate.

10 Investigators share responsibility for the ethical treatment of their subjects with associates, employers or students complying with these standards, and should encourage others to rethink their ideas if this is in question.

(Adapted from *Revised Ethical Principles for conducting research with human subjects*, British Psychological Society 1990.)

Why do we use animals in psychology?

As you read through this book, you will come across many studies which have been done using animals. Many of the findings about how learning takes place, for instance, have been discovered as a result of work with animals, but in the last section I talked about psychology as if it were simply the study of human beings.

There are several reasons why psychologists have used animals in the past; and in many cases work with animals has been quite useful in letting us find out important things both about human beings and about animals themselves. Ethological studies, for instance, involve studying animals in their natural environments rather than doing experiments on them, and they have often given us valuable insights into social interaction or mother-infant behaviour, and so on. In the next chapter, we will be looking at the theory of evolution, and how this implies that studies of animals in this way may help us to come to understand more about some of the basic psychology of human beings.

But there has also been a considerable amount of experimental work done with animals, which is more controversial. Much of the work in physiological psychology, for instance, has involved performing laboratory studies on animals, and these can present distinct *ethical* problems. (Ethical issues are issues which are to do with what is right and wrong, and modern psychologists are very concerned with making sure that the work that they do is ethically acceptable.)

Singer (1976) argued that animal experiments, particularly in psychology, are unjustifiably cruel, and involve considerable suffering on the part of the animals concerned. In addition, he argued, these experiments are often trivial and don't contribute anything much to our general understanding. And if we look at animal studies which have been performed in the past by psychologists, we can find several examples of what he meant – there are some studies which seem distinctly cruel, and which don't really tell us anything much at all.

But at the same time, many psychologists argue that to treat all animal experiments in the same way, and to prevent all of them, would be 'throwing the baby out with the bathwater'. For example: Gray (1985) showed how studies with animals had led directly to a better understanding of anti-anxiety drugs, which meant that they could be developed and used far more safely.

Archer (1986) argued that while it is undoubtedly true that psychologists in the past have misused animal experiments, that doesn't mean that all animal studies should be treated in the same way. He considers that it is important for very strict guidelines to be used, and for animal studies to be undertaken only for research which is 'high quality'; but he sees some animal studies as giving an understanding of psychobiological processes which can't be obtained in any other way, and which is directly beneficial to human beings.

The argument is a complex one, which has many sides to it. For instance, one argument that those who are opposed to animal experiments use, is that animal physiology is different from that of humans anyway – animals are very different from each other as well – and just because we find a mechanism which looks similar, this doesn't mean that it is the same thing at all. So studies of, for instance, brain structure or functioning in experimental rats won't necessarily tell us anything at all about human beings.

In part, the use of animal experiments in psychology originated with the behaviourists, who were mainly concerned with identifying the basic 'building blocks' of behaviour (we will be looking at this more closely in Chapter 18). Because they saw animals as being simpler than human beings, at least in the kinds of behaviour and learning that they showed, they thought that by studying animals they would be able to see the important features more clearly, in the same way that the components of a cell are clearer to a biologist studying a simple, one-celled animal. Also, they thought, animal learning wasn't complicated by human problems like memory or experience, but was a direct and straightforward reaction to the situation. (Many modern animal psychologists would disagree with this assumption too!)

Many developments in medicine and physiology had come from laboratory studies with animals, and as physiological psychologists began to investigate the brain and its mechanisms more and more deeply, they too used animals for their research. The most intensive time for such research with animals seems to have been the 1950s and 1960s – since then, psychologists have become increasingly concerned about the ethical aspects of animal experimentation, and such studies are not nearly as common now as they used to be. In the next chapter, we will be looking at some of the findings from ethological studies of animals, and at the theory of evolution which underlies all of the comparisons between animals and human beings.

Summary

1 Psychology may be defined as 'the scientific study of behaviour and experience'.

2 Collecting evidence in psychology is important. Formulating the hypothesis is a first stage in all scientific studies.

3 Experiments are performed to identify causes. But they have the disadvantage that attempts to control them carefully may make them become artificial or unrealistic.

4 Observations may be more realistic than experiments, but it is not possible to deduce causality from them. Also, observer effects may influence the results.

5 Case studies allow the psychologist to investigate things very deeply, but because of the small samples it may not be possible to generalise from the results.

6 Interviews and surveys allow us to study large samples of people, but they are limited in the kinds of thing they can investigate.

7 Many psychologists are very concerned about the ethical questions raised by both animal and human experiments in psychology.

Chapter 2

Inheritance and behaviour

How does it all
happen?
If we are going to look at how people and animals develop, then we need to start off by seeing how heredity works. To do this, we must look at the way that a creature develops from the very beginning.

If two creatures mate successfully, they will produce a fertilised egg, or *zygote*. This zygote is tiny – at first it only has about four cells, but these cells start to divide and multiply. As they do, the creature grows, and very gradually it will mature into a human being, or a cat, or an elephant, or whatever its parents are.

But how does it know what to develop into? When it starts life as a zygote it just hasn't got enough cells to be a miniature copy of its parents. So somewhere, these four cells have to carry instructions about the creature's future development, to tell it when some particular cells need to grow into a liver, or some need to become bone, and so on.

These instructions are carried in the nucleus of each cell. Each nucleus contains several pairs of thread-like structures called *chromosomes*, and each chromosome carries thousands of tiny *genes* that are responsible for the creature's development. Because of this, the study of heredity is called *genetics*.

Each gene has the instructions for the development of a special part of the body. For example, in mice there is a particular gene, on a particular chromosome, which controls the colour of the fur. If this gene is present, then the mouse's fur will be normal – mouse-coloured. But if it is missing for some reason, then the mouse won't have any pigment in its fur and it will be white. And its eyes will look pink, because it won't have any colouring pigment in its eyes either. (The pink comes from the blood vessels at the back of the eyeball.)

Working together, then, all these thousands of genes will tell the creature how to develop, and will direct when things should happen (like, perhaps, when the creature should develop lungs, or teeth). Some genes are responsible for more than one thing, while sometimes you can find several genes all working on one characteristic. When this happens, these characteristics are known as *polygenic* ('poly-' means many). Those psychologists who believe that intelligence is inherited, for instance, usually

believe that it comes from the action of lots of different genes.
We will be looking at intelligence more closely later on.

Each cell, then, contains all the instructions for how the
creature, or organism, will develop throughout its life. When
each cell divides, to make two new cells, the chromosomes
divide as well, so that there are two complete copies of these
genetic instructions. This process is called *mitosis*.

Scientists have made use of mitosis to develop what is known
as *cloning*. In order to 'clone' a creature, for instance a frog,
scientists take a few cells from anywhere in that frog, but
usually the mouth lining, and they grow these cells in a special
culture. As the cells divide and multiply, they gradually develop
into another, complete, living frog, identical to the first one.
This is only possible because each individual cell contains the
whole genetic pattern for the frog's development.

In cloning, though, there isn't any individual variation. Each
individual which grows like this is genetically identical to the
'parent' animal, so all its physical characteristics – colouring,
size, and so on – will be exactly the same (unless its growth
has been stunted through lack of food or something). But we
are not the same as our parents; although we might be like
them in many ways, there are also many ways in which we are
different from them. So it's clear that the process of mitosis
isn't enough to explain all genetic transmission; there has to
be a second process involved.

This second process is called *meiosis*. It's the way that we come
to inherit some things from our father, but also some things
from our mother, too. When the zygote is first formed, half of
its chromosomes have come from one parent, and the other
half of them from the other parent. So we get some of our
inherited characteristics from each of our parents.

What happens is this: I mentioned before that the cell
nucleus contains several pairs of chromosomes. In mitosis each
chromosome simply divides, but in meiosis, only one
chromosome from each pair goes into the new cell. So, in
order to get enough chromosomes to make a complete set, the
new cell has to join up with another cell containing a half-set
of chromosomes.

The reproductive cells – sperm and ova – each contain only
half the number of chromosomes. When they join together,
there are enough to make a completely new animal, of the same
species as the parents. Incidentally, each species has a different
number of pairs of chromosomes in its cells – humans have 23
pairs, mice have 20, crayfish have 100, rhesus monkeys have
24, and so on.

As we've seen then, we get one set of characteristics from one of our parents, and the other set through our other parent. But what happens if these genetic instructions contradict each other? Supposing the genes you inherited from your mother said that you would have brown eyes, while the genes from your father said that you would have blue eyes? How would your body know which you should have?

The answer is that some genes seem to be more 'powerful' than others. If you have one gene for blue eyes and the other for brown eyes, then you will develop the one which is more powerful – known as the *dominant* gene. Although you would still possess the other gene – the *recessive* gene – it wouldn't show in your body; but you might pass it on to your children.

In the case of eye colour, it is the brown-eyed gene which is dominant, so if you had one of each, then you'd end up with brown eyes. But, through meiosis, some of your children would inherit the gene for brown eyes and some would inherit the gene for blue eyes. If the child with the blue-eyed gene also inherited a blue-eyed gene from its other parent, then it would develop blue eyes. In other words, if a recessive gene shows up in your development, you must have inherited it from both parents. Sometimes, a gene may be faulty, or may cause you to develop some illness or disorder. In most cases if this happens, the faulty gene will be recessive, and the healthy gene on the other chromosome (chromosomes are arranged in pairs, remember?) will be dominant. So you will grow up perfectly healthy. But sometimes it's possible to inherit a faulty gene from each parent – in the same way that blue-eyed people have inherited a blue-eyed gene from each parent. If that happens, then you may develop the disease or disorder even though your parents are perfectly healthy.

There are some characteristics, though, which can't be sorted out by having dominant or recessive genes; in particular, the sex which we turn out to be. After all, if one sex-gene were dominant over the other, then we wouldn't get equal numbers of men and women at all – there would end up being far more of one than of the other. So it's clear that our sex must be decided by a totally different mechanism. In fact, one of our 23 pairs of chromosomes determines our sex – not just one single gene.

These special chromosomes are usually called the *X* and *Y chromosomes*, because that's a bit what they look like under a microscope. Everyone has at least one X chromosome; women have two, but men have one X and one Y chromosome. This means that when the reproductive cells are being produced, through meiosis, the ova will each contain one X chromosome.

The sperm, though, may contain either an X chromosome or a Y chromosome. If an X sperm fertilises the egg, the child will be a girl, but if a Y sperm fertilises the egg, then it will be a boy. So, if everything else works equally, we should have just as many boys born as girls.

In practice, though, everything doesn't work equally – for some reason there seem to be more boys born than there are girls. However, boy infants are much more prone to illness, or to miscarriage; over time, nature balances it out.

Sometimes, disorders may be linked to the sex chromosomes, so that they only show up in one sex – usually males. The reason for this is that the Y chromosome is much shorter than the X chromosome. Normally, if there is a defective gene on one chromosome, the healthy one on the other chromosome will 'cancel it out', so the individual grows up normally. But, because the Y chromosome is so short, if there is a defective gene on the X chromosome, in some places there just isn't a gene there on the Y chromosome to cancel it out. So a disorder can develop.

How can we study genetic influences?

As we saw in the discussion of 'dominant' and 'recessive' genes, a person can have the genes for two entirely different traits, but only develop one of them. We wouldn't be able to tell, simply from looking at the person, what genes they possessed. Also, the type of *environment* that someone is in may affect the way that they develop; for instance, if you are short of food as a child you're unlikely to reach your full growth, although you may have the genes to be much taller.

Imagine walking down the street, and seeing two medium-height, brown-haired, dark-eyed women together. By just looking at them, they might look pretty similar – the genetic characteristics that they have developed seem to be the same. We call this the *phenotype* – that is, those characteristics which someone has *actually developed* in their body.

But, genetically, although they look similar, those two women might be quite different. Suppose, for instance, that the first woman had the genes for average height, two brown-eyed genes, and two genes for brown hair. Nothing very surprising there. But the second woman might have genes for tall growth, (only she suffered from malnutrition during infancy and so didn't grow fully); one blue-eyed gene and one brown-eyed gene (so she developed brown eyes), and one gene for red hair and one for brown hair (brown-hair genes are dominant over red-hair genes). Although they may look similar, genetically the two women are completely different. The genetic characteristics which someone has are called the *genotype*. In this case, the two women have similar phenotypes, but different genotypes. But we can see from this that it's not a lot of use

trying to study heredity by observing how people have
developed – we wouldn't know what the genotype underlying
it was!

However, there is one case where we can know something
about the genotype of a person; that is in the case of identical
twins. There are two different types of twins: fraternal twins,
or 'dizygotic twins', and identical, or 'monozygotic twins'. We
usually call these MZ and DZ twins for short.

Fraternal twins (DZ) are like ordinary siblings (brothers and
sisters). They have come from two separate zygotes, and have
grown side-by-side in the mother's womb. Although they have
both inherited characteristics from the same parents, they are
different characteristics, in the same way that ordinary brothers
or sisters are not exactly the same. So with DZ twins we can't
tell anything much about the genotype.

But identical twins (MZ) have both come from the *same*
zygote. After it was fertilised, the zygote split in two, and
developed into two separate individuals. So in this case, we
know that they have the same genotype, because that was
settled before the zygote separated. This means, that by
studying MZ twins who have grown up in different
environments, we can see how much effect that environment
has had, as we know that it won't be due to a genetic difference
in the first place. So MZ twins can be very useful when we are
trying to study how much influence heredity has on behaviour.

**What about
inherited
behaviour?**
Until now I've been talking mostly about physical
characteristics, as being the sort of things that we inherit. But
other things can be inherited too – in particular, certain kinds
of *behaviour* can be inherited. Since, earlier, we defined
psychology as 'the study of behaviour and experience', it follows
that inherited behaviour will be one of the things that
psychologists are interested in. Inherited behaviour is the kind
of thing that used to be called 'instinct'. In the early days of
psychology, the idea of 'instincts' was used to explain all kinds
of different behaviour; people would talk about 'an instinct for
security', or a 'social instinct', for instance. These ideas would
be used as explanations for why people act as they do.

The problem with 'instincts' though, is that they don't really
tell you very much about what people actually *do* to reach these
aims. When we talk about 'an instinct for security', we are
talking about what the behaviour is *for*, but we haven't said
anything about what the behaviour actually *is*. After all, to some
people security might mean having lots of money in the bank,
while to other people it might mean being happily married.
And the kinds of things that people would do to get that
'security', would be very different. So although we might think

that we've explained the behaviour, by talking about 'an instinct for security', we still haven't explained what people really do.

On the other hand, it is clear that some kinds of behaviour – particularly in animals – are inherited, rather than learned through experience. And since this is similar to the old idea of instinct, in a way, we tend to call this 'instinctive behaviour', or 'innate behaviour'. But when we are studying this, we are most concerned with finding out what the behaviour actually is, rather than (at first) what it's for. (We can find out what it's for much better when we have a good understanding of it.)

Konrad Lorenz published a paper in 1958 in which he showed that many species had inherited similar behaviour patterns. He was particularly interested in the behaviour of ducks, and showed the way that, in the spring, these ducks would develop complicated 'rituals' of bobbing their heads and shaking their tails, which formed a kind of 'courtship display' – a way of attracting another duck for mating. Lorenz showed that several different kinds of ducks had very similar displays, and would perform the same actions in the same order. This was quite clearly inherited behaviour.

In particular, Lorenz showed the way that these inherited behaviour patterns were *stereotyped* – that is, they were always the same, and never changed about or varied. He called these *'fixed action patterns'*. This unchanging nature is one of the very noticeable things about inherited behaviour, whereas behaviour which has been learned through experience is often

Fig. 2.1 Stereotyped behaviour patterns shown by ducks

different from one individual to the next; for instance, we all
have slightly different handwriting. But inherited behaviour is
very much the same from one individual to another – it's fixed
and stereotyped. Even something as long and complicated as
a duck's courtship display could be set in a ritual pattern, which
was the same from one duck to another.

Lorenz also described some other ways that it should be
possible to tell whether a particular type of behaviour has been
inherited. One of these was that, if behaviour is inherited, it
should show up in an animal which has been reared with no
contact with other members of its species. Although it hasn't
been able to *learn* any behaviour from parents or others, it will
still have the chromosomes and genes which are typical of that
kind of creature. So if the behaviour is inherited – passed on
through genes and chromosomes – then it should still show
this behaviour even if it is brought up in isolation.

Another way of telling whether behaviour is inherited, comes
from the idea that inherited behaviour does not need to be
learned. So, according to Lorenz, the animal should not need
to *practise* it at all; instead, the behaviour should show up in
an animal which has been prevented from practising it, as long
as that animal was old enough. In the next chapter, we'll be
looking at some studies of behaviour which have used these
criteria for inherited behaviour, to see if something has been
inherited or not.

N. Tinbergen, in 1951, performed a complicated study on the
mating behaviour of sticklebacks. These fish have developed an
elaborate system of fixed action patterns, which results in a
kind of 'dance' which the male and the female do together,
each taking turns to do their bit, when it is mating time.

The male stickleback builds a nest, like a tunnel of weeds,
in the stream bed. When the nest is ready, if he sees a female
stickleback he swims towards her with a funny sort of zig-zag
movement. When the female sees this, she starts swimming
with her head and tail turned upwards. (This shows that she
has a swollen abdomen, full of eggs ready to be fertilised.)
The male then swims to the nest, and the female follows. When
the female goes into the nest, he prods her several times with
his snout, and then she lays her eggs. After this, she leaves the
nest and the male swims in and fertilises them. Then the
female is chased away by the male, and he is left to guard his
nest until the next female stickleback with eggs comes along.

All this is a well-developed ritual which these fish have
inherited, and will perform automatically. Tinbergen showed
that the stickleback will also behave like this towards a
convincing dummy – a model painted like a female stickleback.

(a) Male sees female and begins
    zig-zag dance

(b) Female shows her swollen abdomen

(c) Male leads female to nest

(d) Male prods female which
    stimulates her to lay her eggs

Fig. 2.2 Sticklebacks' courtship ritual

By developing these inherited behaviour patterns, the fish can
make sure that an approaching fish isn't an enemy, and does
belong to the same species: if the fish didn't respond properly,
the stickleback would chase it away.

One of the things about this kind of inherited behaviour, is
that it has to be 'triggered off' by something. In the case of
the sticklebacks, it is the male's zig-zag dance which 'triggers
off' the behaviour in the female, while it is the sight of the
female's swollen abdomen which 'triggers off' the male's
leading her to the nest. Each correct action becomes the trigger
for the next action.

Since this behaviour is inherited, it's important that the
'trigger' for it should be inherited as well. These have come
to be called sign stimuli, because they provide a signal which
releases the inherited behaviour which the animal has stored
in its genes and chromosomes.

A study by J. P. Hailman, in 1969, looked at the way young
herring gulls behave when their parents come to feed them.
These young gulls are fed regurgitated food by the parents,
and they get this food by pecking at the parent gull's beak.
Hailman was interested in how these young gulls 'know' that
this is what they should do. By experimenting with newly-
hatched gulls and cardboard models, he found that these young

Fig. 2.3 Hailman's herring gull study

gulls were pecking at a bright red spot on their parents' beaks. Also, he found that they wouldn't peck at a model with a red spot, unless he moved it from side to side in the way that the parent gull moves its head when it comes back to the nest. So in this case, it was the moving bright red spot which acted as the sign stimulus for the young gull's pecking behaviour.

Hailman also found that the young gulls showed a definite improvement with practice, over the first few days. At first, their pecking was random and inaccurate, but as the time progressed, they learned to peck more accurately, and therefore received food more easily.

Fig. 2.4 Tinbergen's 'Hawk-Goose' shape

An earlier study by Tinbergen, in 1951, had looked at the way that young turkey chicks in a farmyard will 'freeze' if a hawk flies overhead, although they ignore all other birds. He developed a cut-out model which he called his 'hawk-goose' shape. If it was pulled one way, it looked like a goose flying with its neck stretched out, but if it was pulled the other way it looked like a hawk with a long tail. Tinbergen found that the chicks would freeze if the shape was pulled in the 'hawk' direction, but not if it was pulled the 'goose' way. So this showed that the sign stimulus for the chicks' 'freezing' wasn't just the *shape*, but it was also the direction in which it *moved*.

Tinbergen's study was criticised because people said he hadn't taken the young chicks early enough. Although they were very young when he used them, they had still spent some time in a farmyard, and so they might have learned this behaviour from other turkeys around them. So in this case, instead of being inherited, the behaviour might have been learned.

The
nature/nurture
debate

Psychologists have often disagreed as to whether a particular item of behaviour has occurred through genetic factors – heredity – or through the animal's experience in the environment – learning. In psychology, this is known as the 'nature/nurture debate'. On the one side, we have those psychologists who believe that heredity is most important, and they are known as *nativists*. On the other side, we have those who think that learning and environmental influences are more important, and they are known as *empiricists*.

There have been quite a few studies on just how much influence the environment has on development, or just how much can be inherited. We will look at some of those experiments, and see what they can tell us about the nature/nurture debate.

In 1964, Marler and Tamura performed an experiment with a particular American sparrow – the American White-Crowned Sparrow. These birds have a very distinctive song, which is very similar all over the American continent. There are slight regional variations, but the basic song is always the same. If fledglings are brought up in the laboratory, so that they never hear any other sparrows, they will still produce this song when they are mature. So there is evidence that this is not learned, but arises through genetic maturation – once the bird is old enough, it will produce the song. Interestingly, the birds will pick up the regional 'accent' if they hear it during the first few months of their lives, even though they aren't old enough to sing themselves. But if they are brought up in isolation for the first four months, they don't pick up the accent, even if they hear other birds after that. So there does seem to be *some* environmental influence – on the accent – but the basic song appears to be genetically determined, and to appear simply through maturation.

A study by Levine, in 1960, showed that if very young rat pups are handled – something which they find very stressful – then they tend to develop earlier. Although they still go through all the same stages of development as ordinary rat pups, and in the same order, they seem to go through each stage a bit more quickly, and so they reach maturity a bit earlier. This shows that, even though development might be genetically determined, there can still be an influence from the environment: if it is very stimulating, then development may be faster.

A study which examined what happens if you breed animals selectively was performed by Broadhurst, in 1960. He had noticed, in his work with laboratory rats, that some of them appeared to be much more emotional than others. Empiricists would argue that this emotionality arose because of stressful experiences which the rat had gone through in its life; even in laboratory rats, experiences are never exactly the same from one rat to the next. On the other hand, nativists would argue that this increased emotionality was genetic, and passed on from the parents. So Broadhurst tried to breed a strain of specially emotional rats by breeding them together; and by breeding the most placid rats together he hoped to produce a very calm strain.

Broadhurst tried this selective breeding for 15 generations of rats, and then continued the study for another 5 generations, but this time letting the rats mate freely instead of always selecting the most emotional or the calmest. He measured emotionality in two ways: both by the 'open field' test. When rats are placed in an open, lit space, they tend to become alarmed, and this shows by how many droppings they produce – the more nervous the higher the number of droppings. So the emotional rats would be those with the highest defecation rate. The second measure which Broadhurst used was the 'ambulation score', in other words, how much they were prepared to wander round and explore the 'open field' area. The calmest rats explored more than the emotional ones.

Broadhurst found that he was successful in producing emotional and non-emotional rats. He called his two strains 'Maudsley Reactive' for the emotional ones, and 'Maudsley Non-reactive' for the calm ones (he performed this study at the Maudsley Hospital). In order to make sure that these were really genetic factors, and not simply learned by the infant from its parent, he practised 'cross-fostering'. Pups from reactive mothers were brought up by non-reactive foster mothers, and vice versa. Thus the pups could not have learned their behaviour from the mothers, and it did appear that emotionality was inherited. The reactive strain were much faster to escape from electric shocks, or underwater tunnels, and avoided open spaces. The non-reactive ones were slower on those tests, but they would explore open spaces more readily and seemed more curious and less timid.

The only argument which could still imply that the pups had got their emotionality from their environment, was put forward by S. Rose, who pointed out that the reactive mothers might actually have provided a different environment for their pups while they were in the womb! Stress produces changes in the hormones in the bloodstream (we'll be looking at this more closely later on), and these hormones may have affected the developing pups while they were in the mother, and might have influenced their development. If this were the case, then it would still be an influence from the environment, and not genetic. Rose called this process 'transgenerational transmission' – the way that an environmental factor can affect an animal before birth, so that it appears to be a genetic factor. So it appears that even here we can't really be *certain* that the emotional characteristic was inherited and not caused by the environment.

If we are going to use studies of animals, like this, in the hope that we can learn about ourselves from them, then it's important that we understand just *how* we are connected with other animals, and which animals are most similar to us. To do this, we have to look at the theory of evolution, and the phylogenetic scale.

How evolution works

The theory of evolution was put forward by Charles Darwin in the last century. What he said, essentially, was that a species would develop in certain ways as a response to features in its environment. This meant, for example, that a bird which lived mainly on seeds which were hard to crack, would tend to develop the kind of beak which would enable it to crack seeds easily – a thick, strong one.

The way in which this happens is, roughly, like this: imagine a group of birds living on an island, where the main food available is seeds. Seeds may be hard to crack open, but once opened they are very nourishing. Those birds which have the strongest beaks will be able to crack open the seeds more easily than the other birds. Because of this, they will get more of them to eat, and are likely to be stronger and healthier than the other birds. As they are stronger and healthier, they will be more likely to survive a hard winter, and they will be less likely to die from diseases. So they are more likely to breed than the other birds, and through genetic transmission they may pass on their strong beak (the 'survival characteristic') to their offspring. Since this means that their offspring, too, will be stronger and healthier than the other birds on the island, gradually, over many generations, the whole colony of birds will come to develop strong beaks.

Now, imagine another island, with the same type of birds on it, but this time the only available food on the island is insects, which hide under stones. Obviously, this time it won't be those birds with thick, short, strong beaks which are most successful; it will be those birds with long beaks which they can use to turn the stones over, so that they can get at the insects underneath. In the same way as happened on the other island, gradually, over several generations these birds will come to develop long beaks, since those who inherit them will be stronger and more likely to survive than those who don't.

Charles Darwin did, in fact, find this to be happening on a group of islands off South America, known as the Galapagos Islands. On each of these islands he found a slightly different kind of finch, but it was obvious that, although the birds on each island were different, at some time in the past they had all been the same, or rather, they had all had the same *ancestors*.

So we can see how the species will change, gradually, in response to its *environment*, the kind of surroundings which the creature lives in. Broadly, we can summarise evolution in two points:

1 *Individuals* in a species do not change. The change happens genetically, and occurs gradually over many generations.

2 The change which is produced is something which gives the creature an *advantage* (like being able to get more food) over other members of the species which do not have this feature.

So what does this have to do with humans?

By means of evolution, these small differences have become so great that whole species have evolved, from what we call 'common ancestors'. In other words, over millions of years, the difference between groups of creatures which were originally the same (like the birds in our example) has become so extreme, that the 'new' animal is considered to be a totally different *type* of creature to its ancestors. By looking at the evolutionary 'tree' shown in the diagram, we can see how whole groups of creatures have developed from what in the beginning were just simple, one-celled animals (protozoa). At the very top of the 'tree' (that is, the most recently evolved), we find the group of creatures known as 'mammals' and at the top of those, we find the order of 'primates', divided into monkeys and apes. This is the place where human beings belong on the diagram: we are apes, belonging to the same family as gorillas and chimpanzees.

Obviously I do not mean that we are the *same* as gorillas and chimpanzees – nor do I mean that we even look like them. (Although we do look more like them than, say, we look like frogs.) And I certainly don't mean that our proper 'place' is in the jungle, living in trees! But, at some time, millions of years ago, chimpanzees and humans shared a 'common ancestor'. Since then, as you can see, we have evolved quite differently.

But now, if I return to the original question, which was 'why

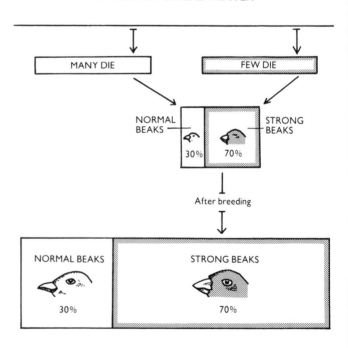

Fig. 2.5 How natural selection works
Although the number of birds with strong beaks actually falls slightly, the proportion increases greatly

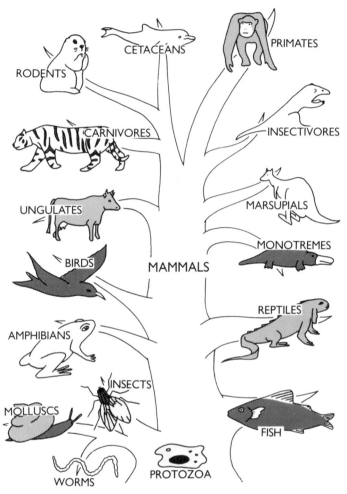

Fig. 2.6 An evolutionary tree

do we use animals in psychology?', I hope that you will be able to answer this for yourself. Since we, too, have *evolved* in the same sort of way as other kinds of animals, then we may share many kinds of characteristics with them. By investigating their behaviour we may come to learn more about our own.

But we are definitely not likely to learn much if we treat all animals as though they were the same. It is clear, I think, that we will learn most from those animals which are most like us, those which are *closest* to us on the evolutionary tree. So we use the concept of the *phylogenetic scale*, to express how highly-evolved a kind of animal is, and how close to humans it is. So

HUMAN

MONKEY

CAT

BIRD

FROG

Fig. 2.7 Brain development and the Phylogenetic Scale
The cerebral cortex is shaded in each figure

at the bottom of the phylogenetic scale we would put the simplest animals, like the protozoa, then we would put such creatures as fish, lizards, frogs, and so on. A bit higher up, we would have the birds, and then the first kinds of mammals, the marsupials. After that, we would place the different kinds of mammals, until we reached the top, with human beings. Of course, an attempt to represent evolution in a straight line like this is not really very accurate – there are many side-branches and so on, but if we talk of the phylogenetic scale we have at least got a way of saying how close an animal is to a human being, in evolutionary terms. And this is useful in psychology, particularly, because we would place more weight on a study of say, chimpanzees, than we would on a study of birds – at least if we wanted to know about human beings.

In particular, the brain becomes different as we move up the phylogenetic scale. And the difference is most strong in that part of the brain which is concerned with things like learning and remembering – the cerebrum. So when we move up the phylogenetic scale, we are also talking about more ability to learn and to remember things – and this is important in psychology too. Animals lower down the phylogenetic scale do not rely very much on learning, but rather on inherited behaviour, while those higher up rely much more on learning.

So much for animals – what about humans?

If we are trying to find out about the nature/nurture debate regarding human beings, we're obviously much more limited in the way that we can try to find things out. We can't try breeding certain humans together, and looking at what their children are like, for instance. But there have been a few studies which have tried to look at the question of how much development is genetically determined, and how much influence the environment has.

One of the first people to investigate this question in detail was Dr Arnold Gesell, who founded the Gesell Institute for the study of the child in Yale University, New York. Beginning in the 1930s, Gesell studied chidren's development, using trained observers and two-way mirrors, so that they could watch children playing without being seen themselves. Each stage of development, from early infancy onwards, was carefully noted and compared.

One of the findings that Gesell noted was the way that development of physical co-ordination always seemed to follow the same orderly sequence. He found that an infant's ability to co-ordinate parts of its body always began with its head – the very first thing an infant learned to control was its mouth – and gradually moved down its body. An infant would learn to control its arms before it could control its legs, for example.

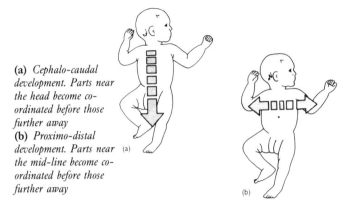

(a) *Cephalo-caudal development. Parts near the head become co-ordinated before those further away*
(b) *Proximo-distal development. Parts near the mid-line become co-ordinated before those further away*

Fig 2.8 Gesell's directions of development

Gesell called this the '*cephalo-caudal*' direction of development, meaning 'from head to tail'.

In addition to the cephalo-caudal direction, Gesell also found that an infant's physical development seemed to go from 'near to far'; in other words, from the centre of the body outwards. An infant learns to control its neck or its shoulders, for instance, before it can learn to reach out and take hold of things with its hands. Gesell called this the '*proximo-distal*' direction of development.

Gesell regarded these sequences of development as being fixed, and genetically determined. In his theories about the development of older children, too, he regarded development as being mostly controlled by genetics, and not particularly affected by the environment. A handbook on child behaviour from the Gesell Institute says: 'First of all, recognise your child's individuality for what it is and give up the notion that you either produce it (except through inheritance) or that you can basically change it.'

Gesell performed several experiments which supported his idea that child development was genetically determined. A famous study was one by Gesell and Thompson, in which they took a pair of identical twins (so that they could be sure that genetic influences were the same). One of the twins was given practice in stair-climbing, by being lifted up and down them by the researchers. The length of time that it took her to learn to manage stairs was measured.

During this time, the other twin was not allowed to climb stairs at all, but in other ways her movements were not restricted. So, as she played, she probably used all the actions that a child might use in stair-climbing, but just not arranged in that particular way. When she was finally allowed to climb stairs, she learned to do it very much faster than her twin had, and she didn't need anything like as much practice. Gesell said that this was evidence of *maturation*: the reason why the second twin didn't need as much practice was that she was older, and so had developed more. When a child reached the right age, it would be able to do things more-or-less automatically.

Fig 2.9 A Hopi Indian cradle board

A study by Dennis and Dennis, in 1940, looked at the development of walking in infants. They studied Hopi Indian children, some of whom were being brought up in the familiar 'modern' way, with nappies and cots; while others were being brought up in their traditional manner. These traditional child-rearing practices involved keeping the child strapped to a cradle-board for the first six months of its life. Except when the infant is cleaned, it doesn't have the opportunity to kick its arms and legs about as a 'modern' infant can. While they are on the cradle-board, they are either carried around on their mothers backs, or they can be propped up against a support, so that they can see what is going on around them.

Since the children did not get the practice with their limbs that a Western child might have, it was expected that these children would probably start to walk a bit later than ordinary children. But Dennis and Dennis found that there was no difference between the two groups; both sets of children walked at fourteen months. Nativists argued that this showed that walking must be purely maturational, not affected by the environment. However, empiricists have criticised this explanation, by pointing out that the child is not kept on the cradle-board after six months old, and so it has a good eight months' practice crawling and moving around before it starts to walk. Thus this study cannot be taken as very convincing evidence of a purely genetic factor.

Another cross-cultural study seemed to show that the environment does have an effect on development. A study by Ainsworth (1967) on Ugandan children observed that these children seemed to go through each stage of development earlier than Western children do: for instance, the average age for walking was thirteen months, rather than fourteen. Ainsworth thought that this was probably due to the extra stimulation which the children received in Uganda; instead of spending a large part of their time alone in a cot, they were always in the middle of things, and receiving a lot of attention from everyone. In a sense, this finding is similar to Levine's experience with the rats – if they received extra stimulation as infants, they developed earlier than normal rats! So it would seem that the environment can have some kind of effect, even if physical development is mostly genetic.

The last study I want to look at provides evidence for the way that genetic influences might work *with* environmental ones to achieve their effects. In 1971 J. M. Tanner studied growth rates, and the way that they progress steadily – although they can be faster or slower at different stages of development. Tanner found regular patterns of growth at different ages. What he also found, though, was what happened if a child had had a long illness, which had slowed down its normal growth rate. If this was the case, then when the child recovered from the illness, its growth rate was much faster than normal. It was as if the body was trying to 'catch up' with what it had missed. So even if you had an environmental factor like illness interrupting the genetic development, that genetic potential would still be fulfilled in some way.

This chapter has been mainly concerned with the development of behaviour, and fairly simple kinds of behaviour for the most part, like walking. In the next chapter, I want to look at the development of something much more complicated – the way that attachments develop between parents and their offspring.

Summary 1 Each cell of the body has the 'blueprint' for the whole development of the individual, stored in the genes, which are found on chromosomes.

2 Genes may be dominant or recessive. The sex of an individual is determined by the X and Y chromosomes – women are XX while men are XY.

3 Twin studies are useful in studying heredity, since identical (MZ) twins have exactly the same genotype.

4 Behaviour may be inherited too. Inherited behaviour is

usually stereotyped, and may be organised into quite complicated patterns. Lorenz called these 'fixed action patterns'.

5 Studies of animal behaviour show that both genetic and environmental influences may be important.

6 Evolution shows how genetic changes have allowed whole new species to develop. By using the phylogenetic scale we can assess which animals are closest to humans, and which ones are probably not very similar to us at all.

7 Studies of human development show that genetic maturation may be important in the development of basic skills.

Chapter 3 **Attachment**

Now and then, in the springtime, you may have seen a mother duck, with half-a-dozen young ducklings trailing along after her, following her everywhere she goes. But you're not very likely to have seen a mother cat with a trail of young kittens like that; very young kittens tend to stay in one place, and explore their surroundings gradually, from their 'base'. And human infants, as you know, can't move around on their own for a very long time after they've been born. Each of these species, though, needs to be looked after while it is young. Even though a duckling may be able to swim and walk around, that doesn't mean that it is completely able to look after itself; there are still dangers around, and things that it needs to learn from its parent. Young kittens need even more care when newly born, and human infants are almost completely helpless while they are very young. Without a parent nearby, none of them would survive for very long.

In this chapter, I want to look at the way that young creatures develop a *relationship* with a parent, or parents – the way that they will develop an *attachment* to one or two particular adults of their species, and not to others. We can see that these attachments are necessary because they help to protect the young one until it is old enough to look after itself. But this doesn't explain how they happen, and what influences their development.

Imprinting One of the first theories about how attachments happen was put forward by Konrad Lorenz, as a result of his observations of animal behaviour. (I mentioned some of Lorenz's work on inherited behaviour in the second chapter.) Lorenz adopted a method of study known as *ethology* which is the study of behaviour in its natural environment. Ethological studies are special ways of carrying out observations of behaviour. What it means is that, instead of taking your subjects into a laboratory and observing them there, you do your observations 'in the field', so that you can be sure that the subjects are behaving naturally (or at least, more naturally than they would in the laboratory!). The problem with an approach like this is that you can't really find out what is causing the behaviour – in a natural setting there are usually so many different things going on at once, that almost anything could be influencing what is happening. So Lorenz and his colleagues did some experiments as well, after their observations had shown them what sort of things to look for.

Lorenz was particularly interested in the way that young ducks and geese will follow their parents around, from very soon after they have hatched. He observed that a young duck, or goose, begins to follow its parent around within a day of its being hatched, and that they seem to avoid any other creature which comes near them – even other ducks and geese. While he was quite young, Lorenz had had some young geese 'adopt' him as a 'mother', and they would follow him around all the time, until they grew up. He even had to go swimming with them, so that they would learn to swim! Naturally, he was interested in why they developed this attachment, and how it came about.

Fig. 3.1 Ducklings imprinted on a human being
Lorenz found that ducklings would 'adopt' him if he was the first moving thing they saw

By experimenting in the laboratory, Lorenz found that young geese had an innate tendency to follow a large, moving object if they encountered it soon after hatching. If the object was removed before they had been following it for ten minutes, then the geese would just follow the next large, moving object that they came across. But after ten minutes things seemed to change. If the geese were allowed to follow a particular large, moving object for more than ten minutes, then they seemed to become attached to it and they wouldn't follow anything else. In fact, they seemed to avoid all other large, moving objects that they saw. So it seemed that after the goslings had been following a particular object for a while, that they suddenly developed a relationship with that object, and nothing else would do.

Lorenz called this process *imprinting*. It is a rapid attachment which is formed as a result of following. Imprinting seems to be a special kind of learning; although the following seems to be innate, the bird *learns* the attachment to this particular object. This makes sense, in evolutionary terms – after all, in the natural environment the only large creature that is likely to stay around for a whole ten minutes is most likely to be the mother – anything else would wander off before the ten minutes was up! So this time-gap would be a good way of making sure that the young bird forms its attachment to the right target.

Lorenz found that it was quite easy to tell whether geese or ducklings had imprinted or not. In one experiment he did, he mixed up some goslings that had imprinted on him, and some that had imprinted on a mother goose. The goslings were all put together under a box, and Lorenz and the goose stood in opposite corners of the room. When Lorenz's assistant lifted the box, each gosling made straight for its 'parent': those imprinted on the goose went straight for her, and those imprinted on Lorenz went straight to him. If he did this test with those which hadn't imprinted at all, he found that they would just wander aimlessly around the room.

By experimenting with different things, Lorenz found that the object for the goslings to imprint on didn't have to be moving. He managed to get some goslings to imprint on a stationary box. But the box had to be very brightly lit, and it had to stand out very clearly from its background. And also, it was important that the goslings didn't see any moving things during that period. So although Lorenz showed that it was *possible* to imprint on something that didn't move, he also showed that it was quite difficult to arrange. After all, in the natural environment, no mother goose or duck would remain perfectly still *all* the time.

Another researcher in this area, E. Hess, did an experiment in 1958 getting ducklings to imprint on remote-controlled duck models. The young duckling would follow the model around a circular track, and after ten minutes it would have imprinted on it. Hess found that, if the duckling came across obstacles in its path, so that it had to struggle to follow the decoy, then the attachment that it developed to the model seemed to be very much stronger than if it had just had a very easy path to follow with no obstacles. The more effort the duckling had to put into following the model, then the stronger the imprinted bond became.

Another study by Hess was reported in 1972. Up until then, most researchers had assumed that imprinting took place entirely after the young bird was hatched, and that it mainly

(a)

(b)

Fig. 3.2 The Law of Effort, as shown by Hess
(a) *The duckling follows the duck model and imprints on it*
(b) *When the duckling has to struggle to follow the duck while imprinting, the attachment it develops is stronger*

depended on visual stimulation – in other words, what the young bird saw. But Hess put hidden microphones into nesting boxes, and he found that *auditory* stimulation is important too, in other words, what the chick *hears*.

About a week before they hatch, young ducklings start to make small 'cheeping' noises in their shells. When the mother duck hears this, she starts clucking to the eggs, and she clucks more and more as the hatching time gets closer. When the chicks hatch, they are most likely to imprint on the object that they see that makes the same kind of 'clucking' noise as the one that they've been hearing through their shells. Hess found that by sitting next to a clutch of eggs and calling 'come, come' to them, the ducklings would imprint on him really easily when they hatched. (As long as he called 'come, come' to them, of course!) So it seems that it isn't just a large, moving object that a duckling will imprint to – it's a large, moving object that makes a familiar noise. Nature doesn't take any chances on the duckling choosing the wrong 'mother'.

These findings about imprinting were fairly clear, and didn't produce much disagreement between psychologists. But there were three main things arising from Lorenz's work that people did disagree about. The first disagreement concerned *when* imprinting had to take place; the second disagreement concerned whether imprinting had permanent effects or not; and the third one was exactly how far imprinting could be applied to other species, apart from ducks, geese, and farmyard hens. We will look at these arguments in turn.

Critical and sensitive periods

Lorenz performed an experiment with a set of ducklings, in which he kept them together and didn't let them see any large moving objects at all. After they had been kept like this for about 25 hours after hatching, he found that they seemed to have lost the ability to imprint – instead of following suitable objects, they would avoid them. He came to the conclusion that there was a *critical period* during a young bird's development, when it had to imprint. If this period went past without the bird imprinting on anything, then it never would. This critical period, Lorenz said, was within 4 and 25 hours after hatching. Before 4 hours old the ducklings would not imprint, and after 25 hours they wouldn't either.

This idea of a critical period for development is one that is used quite often, for different kinds of development. The idea is, that while a creature – human or animal – is developing, there are certain times of its life when it needs particular experiences from the environment. If it doesn't have those particular experiences at that particular time, then it won't develop normally. Some psychologists, for example, have said that there is a critical period for language development in children, and that if they haven't learned to talk by the end of that period, then they never will. (We'll be looking at this theory in the 'Language' chapter.) But a critical period is exactly that: *critical*. Whatever the learning is, it *must* happen during that time.

Lorenz's idea that there was a critical period for imprinting was questioned by W. Sluckin, in 1964. He tried exactly the same experiment as Lorenz had done, but this time instead of keeping all the young ducklings together, he kept each one isolated. When he did this, he found that the ducklings could still be imprinted on a parent figure (or any large, moving object), as late as four or five days after they had hatched. So evidently this 4–25 hours after hatching wasn't as critical as Lorenz had thought. Sluckin explained this by saying that Lorenz's ducklings had imprinted on each other, which was why they had avoided other objects. Because his own ducklings had been kept isolated, they hadn't been able to imprint on each other, and so their period of 'imprintability' had lasted for four or five times as long. But it was still true that the period described by Lorenz – 4 to 25 hours after hatching – was the most *likely* time for imprinting to take place, even though it wasn't critical. So Sluckin suggested that it should be regarded as a *sensitive period*, not a critical one. Although it wasn't the *only* time that imprinting could happen, it was still the best time for it, and the most likely.

Imprinting and its permanent effects

Another disagreement which psychologists had was whether imprinting had permanent effects or not. Imprinted birds will follow their parent around, and will learn all sorts of things from her: what sorts of things to eat, when to hide, how to behave towards other members of their species, and so on. Lorenz regarded this learning that young birds do from their imprinted mother as being vital to their development. It was only through the imprinted bond, he said, that young chicks and goslings would learn the correct social and sexual behaviour for their species. If they didn't have the right kind of imprinted parent when they were young, then they would never learn these things.

According to Lorenz, if a young duck was brought up by a farmyard hen – if it was imprinted on the hen and followed her around – then it would never learn to act like a proper duck, but would act like a hen, and when it grew older it would try to mate with hens, instead of showing proper interest in other ducks. This effect, Lorenz said, was permanent, and could not be reversed by later experience.

Other researchers, though, disagreed with Lorenz. P. Guiton performed a study on the effects of 'wrong' imprinting in 1966. He reared some male chicks in isolation for 47 days. During this time, they were always fed by an assistant who wore yellow rubber gloves, and in fact they imprinted on the rubber gloves. When they were released after the 47 days, they attempted to mate with the rubber gloves! This was exactly the kind of disturbance that Lorenz had talked about; the chicks had developed behaviour which was inappropriate, socially and sexually.

After this, though, Guiton kept the young cocks in a pen with several female hens of the same age. Although they were past imprinting age, the change in company had an effect. When the chicks were adult, they would mate only with hens, and wouldn't look twice at a yellow rubber glove. So it was clear from Guiton's experiment that this disturbed behaviour which might happen if a young bird imprinted on the wrong model, would only last if it never mixed with others of its own species. If the bird mixed with others of its own species later on, then the effects of imprinting weren't permanent and irreversible, as Lorenz had said.

Attachment in other species

The third argument – whether imprinting happens in other species too, and if so, in which other species – is one which we'll be looking at throughout the rest of this chapter.

For a long time, people have been interested in the way that a young animal develops an attachment to its parent, or parents. With human infants in particular, but also with some other species, it used to be thought that this feeling of love or attachment arose because it was usually the parents who fed the animal (or baby). Because it had been fed, the baby would feel comfortable and happy, and it would come to associate this pleasant feeling with the person who fed it – usually the mother. And, over time, this pleasant feeling would develop into an attachment towards the mother, and become more permanent.

Lorenz's work on imprinting showed people that attachment might develop from something quite different. Although it was true that the mother normally showed the infant bird how to find food, the attachment – the imprinting – had already occurred. So it was clear that imprinting was a completely different kind of method for an attachment to develop. As a result of this, other researchers began to investigate the ways that attachment develops in other species.

Harlow's monkeys　　One study of attachment in monkeys was performed by H. F. Harlow, in 1959. He took eight infant monkeys, and brought each one up separately in its own cage. In each cage there were two models, each large enough for a monkey to climb onto. One of the models was made from wire mesh, but covered with terry-towelling, and it had a round artificial 'head', with large 'eyes'. The other model was the same size, but it was just the bare wire mesh, and the 'head' was a crude, rectangular one.

Harlow wanted to investigate whether the infant would develop an attachment to these 'surrogate mothers', and, if they did, whether it would happen because of food being provided. He arranged feeding bottles so that the teat of the bottle stuck out from the model's 'chest'. With four of the monkeys, it was the cloth-covered 'mother' which fed them, and with the other four it was the bare wire 'mother'. If the old idea of attachments developing as a result of feeding was correct, then the first four should become attached to their cloth mother, while the second four should become attached to their wire mother.

Harlow's results were quite surprising to many people. Instead of the result he had expected, *all* the monkeys developed an attachment for their cloth mother, even if they were fed by the other one! As soon as they were old enough, the infants would climb up onto the towelling mother, and cling to it. When they were hungry, they would go across to the wire mother to feed, but they wouldn't stay there – they'd come straight back to the cloth mother.

Harlow also pointed out that the infants couldn't be going

Fig. 3.3 Harlow's study of monkey attachment

to the cloth mother for warmth. Each cage had a heating pad on the floor, which the infant monkeys were lying on originally. But as soon as they were old enough to get there, they left the heating pad and climbed up onto the unheated cloth model.

Harlow investigated the monkeys' reactions, to find out if they really *had* developed an attachment for the model, or if it was just something like a favourite chair where you sit when you're at home, but if it wasn't there it wouldn't bother you. To test this, he observed the ways that the infants reacted when the model was removed from the cage, and how they responded when they were faced with something new and perhaps a bit frightening.

When the model was removed from their cages, the infant monkeys appeared to become very distressed, but if Harlow removed the bare wire model, then they didn't seem to mind at all. When they saw something new and alarming, they seemed to use the cloth mother for reassurance. Harlow used a wind-up teddy-bear which marched along, beating on a toy drum. When the young monkeys saw this, they seemed to be very alarmed, and they would rush to the cloth model and hide their faces from the teddy-bear. After a while, though, they seemed to become a bit braver, and they would turn round and watch the teddy – but still holding on to the cloth model!

Harlow also tried a kind of 'open field' test with the monkeys. He would put them in a strange room, with some odd items that they hadn't seen before, like a crumpled up sheet of paper, a wooden block, a doorknob and a few other things. If they were put into a room on their own, the infants would be very distressed, and would tend to huddle in a corner, and not explore at all. But if the cloth mother was in the room as well, the infant would climb up on it straight away, and then gradually explore the room, returning to the cloth mother from time to time. Harlow described this as being very similar to the way that a human child will happily explore new places, but keep coming back to its mother, whereas if its mother goes away, or out of sight, the child will get very distressed, and may start crying. So he seemed to be showing that the infants really had developed an attachment for their cloth mother, and it wasn't just a nice place to cling. Incidentally, if the wire mother was in the strange room, and not the cloth mother, the infants were just as alarmed as if there was nothing at all, even if they'd been fed from a wire mother.

What Harlow's results showed, then, was the way that attachment could develop, not from the mother providing food or warmth, but from an entirely different process. He believed that the infants were showing a need for 'tactile comfort', a need for the reassuring 'feel' of a mother-figure. When he first reported on this experiment, his monkeys were very healthy, and seemed to be normal apart from being a bit timid, and easily frightened. So Harlow came to the conclusion that this attachment through contact was all that a young monkey needed – as long as it had something cuddly to cling to, it would be all right.

One problem with this conclusion, though, is the great difference in the heads of the two models. It could be that the models were preferred, not because of the terry-towelling covering, but because the cloth one had a more realistic 'face' than the wire one. So this would mean that it was *visual* stimulation which was important, what the monkey *saw*, as well as *tactile* stimulation, what the monkey *felt*.

Three years later, in 1962, Harlow produced another report on attachment in infant monkeys. During those three years, the monkeys raised with the 'surrogate mothers' had grown up, and it had become obvious that they weren't normal, healthy monkeys at all. Although they were fine physically – they were good weights, and had thick coats – they were not properly developed emotionally. For one thing, they were much more timid than other monkeys were. Although this had shown a bit when they were younger, it became even more obvious as they grew older. They were frightened by the slightest new thing. Also, they didn't know how to act with other monkeys. When they were put into a pen with monkeys that had been brought up by their own mothers, they were easily bullied, and wouldn't stand up for themselves. If they were attacked, they would either submit immediately, or they would run away.

When they were adult, they had difficulty with mating. Although they were obviously interested in having sexual relationships with other monkeys, the females had difficulty getting into the right positions, and the males did not succeed in successful copulation. Very few of the females ever mated successfully: only a couple of them gave birth to infants, and then it was found that they were inadequate mothers, who were unable to care for their own offspring. So it appeared that the early deprivation they had suffered – in not being brought up with other monkeys – had caused lasting damage to their social and emotional development.

Harlow concluded that these young monkeys were suffering from maternal deprivation, being deprived of a mother's care. But by experimenting by bringing up young monkeys in different ways, he found that it wasn't necessarily *maternal* deprivation that the young monkeys were suffering, but *social* deprivation – being deprived of *any* members of their own species. When he brought some other infant monkeys up on their own, but with 20 minutes a day in a playroom with three other monkeys, he found that they grew up to be quite normal. The other monkeys were the same age, and none of them was with their mothers, but it seemed that just having the company of other members of their species was enough to make sure that they developed normally, emotionally and socially. So it was social deprivation that these infant monkeys were suffering, not maternal deprivation.

Strictly speaking, too, it isn't right to say that the young monkeys had suffered deprivation. Being *deprived* of something, means that you have had it, and that then it was taken away from you. But these monkeys in Harlow's study had never had the company of other monkeys in the first place. So to be truly accurate we should say that the monkeys were suffering from social *privation*, not social deprivation.

By experimenting with infants being deprived, or suffering privation at different ages, Harlow concluded that there was a *critical period* in a monkey's life, during which it needed to form attachments with other monkeys. If it didn't, Harlow said, it would then suffer permanent damage to its social and emotional development, and it would never become truly normal. With some of these emotionally disturbed monkeys, he tried giving them a kind of 'group therapy' period, to see if they would recover. They were put on a 'monkey island' in a local zoo, where they were fed in different ways and they had to learn to live together. He also put with them one of the better-adjusted breeding male monkeys that they had, so that they would learn the right kinds of sexual behaviour for monkeys. But although they seemed to improve slightly while they were on the island, none of the disturbed monkeys mated successfully, and when Harlow brought them back to the laboratory, they were just as disturbed as ever. Because of this experiment Harlow thought that in rhesus monkeys the effects of social privation were permanent.

   This critical period that Harlow described was the first six months of life. If during this time the monkey had no chance to form an attachment to another monkey – not necessarily the mother – then it would suffer permanent social impairment, and would never form any attachment later in its life either. But if there was contact with other monkeys during this period, then the monkey would not suffer. Harlow thought that his findings could probably be applied to human infants too, except that, because rhesus monkeys develop faster, the critical period for humans would be about two years – the first two years of life. If a human infant was not able to form an attachment in that time, Harlow said, then it would probably grow up emotionally damaged.

Harlow felt that these monkeys had shown a kind of 'imprinting' in the way that they developed their attachments. Because it was clearly not food or warmth that the infants had responded to, he adopted the idea of 'imprinting' as a possible explanation of how it had happened. The problem is, that when we use 'imprinting' in this kind of way, we aren't meaning quite the same thing as the 'imprinting' which we looked at earlier on in this chapter. For one thing, Lorenz's studies with ducklings and goslings showed a rapid attachment to *one* other figure – but Harlow was talking about a more gradual attachment, and in some of his studies there were several monkeys together, not just two – and their attachments seemed to be to all of them. So we have to be careful that we don't use the same word to mean two different things, here.

Attachment in humans

Bowlby's theory of attachment

Another researcher, who thought that the idea of 'imprinting' might also apply to human infants, was J. Bowlby. In 1958 he wrote that an infant had to form an attachment to its mother during the first two years of life: that was a critical period, and if this bond were not developed during this time, then the infant would suffer both emotionally and socially. In the next chapter, we'll be looking more closely at Bowlby's ideas on maternal deprivation, but just now we are only concerned with his ideas on how attachments develop. The bond which the infant developed with its mother, Bowlby said, arose through an imprinting-type process, and was a very special one, quite different from any other bonds which the child might develop with other people.

This type of attachment, Bowlby called '*monotropy*'. What he was saying was not that the child would *only* like its mother, and no-one else, but that the child would develop a relationship with its mother that was different from all its other relationships. So the mother would become someone really special for the child, who couldn't easily be replaced. When Bowlby wrote about the 'mother', incidentally, he also included someone who wasn't the infant's natural mother, but who was a *permanent* mother-substitute for the child, an adoptive mother, for example.

Other researchers, though, didn't agree with Bowlby's idea of monotropy. In 1964, Schaffer and Emerson performed an ethological study of the attachments which babies make to other people. They observed such things as who the infant smiled at, and who it seemed to respond to most, and so they were able to build up a picture of the attachments which each infant had made, within its family. Some of the findings provided evidence that directly contradicted Bowlby's ideas about the ways that infants form attachments.

One of the first ideas that they contradicted, was Bowlby's theory that an infant forms only one main relationship (to its mother). In situations where there was more than one adult around quite a lot, they found that several infants formed *multiple attachments*; that is, they had more than one attachment to more than one person. And Schaffer and Emerson found that these attachments were *not* different in kind; there didn't seem to be one special relationship and one that wasn't as important, but the infants seemed to form them equally. Of course, in most families in England nowadays there aren't very many adults around for infants to develop attachments to – but in families where the fathers took a share in the child-rearing, then the infants quite often seemed to develop multiple attachments.

Another idea criticised by Schaffer and Emerson, was that an infant's main relationship will be formed with its *mother* – the 'primary caretaker' who looks after the child all day, and has most to do with it. In quite a few of the families they looked at – about one-third of their sample – they found that the infant's main attachment was to someone who was *not* the child's primary caretaker. It might be to the father, or to an older brother or sister, or perhaps another relative who lived with the family and had close contact with them, but it wasn't *necessarily* the mother (although for most families, of course, it was the mother). This finding challenged Bowlby's idea of an 'imprinted' bond developing. If it wasn't to the person who was with the infant for most of the day, then there must be more complicated reasons behind the development of attachment.

The answer, Schaffer and Emerson found, lay in the way that people *interacted* with the baby. The infant seemed to develop its attachments to those people who were most sensitive to what it wanted, and to its expressions and messages. The people who didn't take much notice of what the baby was doing – as long as it wasn't crying! – didn't seem to be the ones to whom the baby formed attachments. Of course, in most families the babies would form main attachments to their mothers, or primary caretakers, because they were the people who were with them all day, and so they had most opportunity to interact and play with the baby. But the attachment wasn't automatic; if the primary caretaker didn't respond to the baby much, while its father played with it responsively for an hour each night, then it would be the father that the baby would become attached to, not the mother. But of course, as we've already seen, the baby could quite well develop attachments to both of them.

Schaffer and Emerson coined the term 'sensitive responsiveness' to describe what the baby seemed to look for in its adults. It was the ability to respond and react to the little signals that the baby was putting out, as 'messages' to the other person. Although babies may seem to be pretty helpless, they have lots of small ways in which they can signal what they want – as long as the person they are with is sensitive enough to recognise them.

Parent–infant *interaction* What comes out of this work, and other similar studies, is that a baby isn't nearly as passive and helpless as it might appear. When a baby is born, it seems to arrive with a certain number of inherited abilities, which will not only help it to develop physically, but will also help it socially. For example, a study by Ahrens, in 1954, showed that baby humans will smile at a human face from a very tiny age – even at only a month old. And, of course, smiling is just the kind of thing which will encourage adults to have more to do with the baby – it's as if the baby is innately programmed to make itself attractive to other people.

If smiling in infants is inherited, then what is it that triggers it off? After all, infants don't smile at everything, and human faces come in all sorts of sizes and colours! Ahrens looked at just what *particular* thing it was about the face that would make infants smile.

At the earliest stage, she found that the thing which caused an infant to smile was the eyes in the face. Showing infants different cards, with drawings on them, she could find what

Fig. 3.4 Ahrens' faces
(a) *At one month. Only the eyes are necessary to elicit smiling in the infant*
(b) *At two to three months. A bit more detail in the face is required before the infant will smile*
(c) *At four months. All the usual features of the face must be present before the infant will smile*
(d) *At five months. Not only must all the usual features be present, but the face must be shaded to look three-dimensional, as well*

the *least* thing was, that the infant would smile at, and this was the result: if an infant was shown a white oval with two dots in it, then it would smile at it.

When it grew a bit older, though, it needed a bit more detail before it would smile. At two months it would only respond to a proper face shape, with eyes and the outline of a nose. At three months, it needed even more detail; all the features had to be drawn in – eyes, nose, mouth – before the infant would smile at it, and when the infant was four months old it would only smile at a drawing that was fully shaded in, so that it looked three-dimensional.

We can see from this study that the infant needs to have a more realistic picture as it grows older, but that throughout, the infant is responding to a social stimulus. In any human face, it is the eyes which stand out most – after all they're movable and shiny. And this is the first thing that the infant responds to.

Schaffer found that a baby doesn't develop its full attachment to another person until it is six or seven months old. Before that time, it will not be distressed if its mother leaves it, and it is handled by a stranger (unless the stranger handles it very differently, of course!), but at about six months it begins to recognise its 'own' people, and to prefer them. But Ahrens' study shows that, even before that time, the infant is equipped to interact with other people, and to set the basis for its later attachments.

Another study, by Wolff in 1969, looked at the crying behaviour of infants. By recording their crying, and the kinds of situations in which it happened, Wolff found that there were three different kinds of crying that infants could manage, and each of them had different meanings. Also, it was found that most mothers 'instinctively' recognise what each of their own particular baby's cries means. The three cries Wolff described were:

the hunger cry: this starts off unevenly, and not very loud, but it gradually becomes louder and more regular in rhythm.
the pain cry: this starts as a loud, long cry, followed by a long silence, and then a set of short, gasping breaths.
the anger cry: this is like the hunger cry, but it has different lengths in each part of the cry (cry-pause-breathe in-pause-cry).

So what Wolff was finding was that even from a very early age, infants have quite a good communication system, which their mothers can understand, and which may form the basis for later, more complicated communication systems.

Other studies have shown the way that the mother (or another person) and an infant engage in *interaction* with each other, even from quite an early age. A study by Stern, in 1977, showed that even at the age of three months, an infant will make head-movements in time with its mother, and will respond to baby-talk. If the adult is sensitive to these small actions which the child is making, then they can develop an interaction together, which helps the child's (and the parent's) attachment to develop. In a sense, the parent and the baby are having the beginnings of a conversation together!

Actually, this idea may not be as silly as it sounds. A study by Jaffe, in 1973, showed that the sort of interactions which parents and small babies have, use exactly the same time-gaps in their turn-taking as adults do in conversations. Jaffe suggested that this kind of interaction is what first introduces the child to the idea of social interactions, and taking turns to speak. And lots of baby 'games' which people play with them involve repetitive taking turns too – like the 'peek-a-boo' game. It's quite apparent that babies really enjoy these games, and it seems that this is even more evidence of the way that babies seem to be 'pre-programmed' to be sociable, even from their earliest months.

In view of all these findings on the way that mothers (or other adults – it sometimes seems shorter to say just 'mothers') and babies interact, we are starting to get a clearer idea of how human attachments develop. In a sense, the idea of 'imprinting' just isn't necessary any more – we are beginning to know more about *how* it happens than the idea of 'imprinting' would tell us. But anyway, we can be fairly clear that the most important thing in the way that human babies develop attachments is *parent–infant interaction* in the first few months of life.

Summary

1 The idea of *imprinting* was put forward by Konrad Lorenz. Imprinting is a rapid attachment formed as a result of following a large, moving object soon after birth.

2 Lorenz's work arose from *ethological* observations of goslings. Ethology is the study of behaviour in its natural environment.

3 Various experiments showed that young ducklings or goslings will imprint on a large, moving object; that the more effort they put into following the object, the stronger the bond becomes, and that they imprint most readily if the object makes a noise that they have heard before hatching.

4 Two major disagreements about imprinting were: (a) whether it took place in a critical or sensitive period, and (b) whether it had permanent effects or not.

5 Harlow studied attachments in monkeys, and found that infant monkeys would develop an attachment to a cloth model, even if they were fed by another wire model.

6 The monkeys studied by Harlow were socially and emotionally impaired when they grew up. Harlow thought that there was a critical period, in monkeys and humans, for attachments to develop.

7 Bowlby put forward the idea of 'monotropy', but evidence from Schaffer and Emerson seemed to contradict it.

8 Mother–infant interaction, in smiling, games, etc., seems to be the most important factor in how human attachments develop. Infants seem to be 'pre-programmed' to be sociable.

Chapter 4

Maternal deprivation

In the last chapter, I mentioned the way that the monkeys Harlow had used in his 'surrogate mother' study of attachment had grown up to be emotionally and socially disturbed. This finding had produced some extra evidence for debates already going on, about how children should be brought up. The debates mostly originated with the views of Dr J. Bowlby on attachment and what would happen if the child didn't have a strong, permanent attachment to its mother.

Bowlby's theory of maternal deprivation

In 1949, the World Health Organisation became concerned about the number of homeless children, or children who were growing up in institutions as a result of the war years. They commissioned Bowlby to look into this matter, and to report to them whether these children were likely to be suffering from their experiences, and what the best kind of upbringing for such children was.

Bowlby reported back to the WHO in 1951, and he also published a paperback 'popular' version of his report, so that it would be possible for everyone to look at his findings. His report was a long and detailed one, which had a great deal of influence among health care officials, social workers, and parents. But the conclusions that he came to were very controversial, and caused arguments right from the very beginning.

Bowlby's evidence

Bowlby's report included findings from some studies that he had made himself, but also from studies performed by other people. One of the studies that he included in his report was done by W. Goldfarb, in 1943. He looked at the effects on children of growing up in institutions. He compared two groups of children: one group which lived in a particular institution until they were three years old, and were then fostered, and another group of children who were fostered as soon as they left their mothers, and did not live in an institution at all.

Goldfarb found extreme differences between these two groups of children. The ones who had spent their first three years in the institution scored well below the fostered group, in terms of their ability to keep rules, their ability to make friends and to socialise easily with other people, and in their scores on intelligence tests. (The children were tested when they were about nine years old.)

Another study that Bowlby included in his report was by R. A. Spitz, made in 1945. Spitz had studied children who had lost a parent, and had shown that they often suffered from deep depression and slow development. Spitz also said that these effects could last in some children until adulthood.

Bowlby's main evidence was his own study on juvenile delinquency. He had a clinic in London for disturbed teenagers, and his subjects were selected from the people attending the clinic. He compared a group of forty-four juvenile thieves, with another group of juveniles who did not steal, but who were emotionally disturbed, which was why they were attending the clinic. By looking into their past histories, he found that seventeen of the 'thieves' had experienced a period of separation from their mothers at a very early age. But only two of the group who didn't steal had had that kind of separation. From this, Bowlby concluded that separation from one's mother in early infancy could lead to juvenile delinquency.

Another finding arose from this study too. Bowlby found that, among his seventeen maternally-deprived thieves, there were a couple who were even more delinquent than the others. These teenagers, he said, had no capacity for personal relationships – they were not fond of anyone, and they didn't particularly dislike anyone. But, perhaps because they didn't have any attachments to anyone else, they were very casual about crime, and didn't much care if other people came to harm through it. Bowlby called this characteristic 'affectionless psychopathy' and he found that these particular children had a history of being separated from their mothers in their early years. So this appeared to be an even more dramatic effect of maternal deprivation.

From these, and some other similar studies, Bowlby concluded that it was maternal deprivation which was causing all the damage. If children were separated from their mothers during the first few years of life, then lasting damage could result. A famous quotation from the 1951 report runs: ' . . . mother love in infancy and childhood is as important for mental health as are vitamins and proteins for physical health.'

In particular, the debates arose because Bowlby produced a list of the kinds of circumstances in which children were likely to suffer this kind of damage. Among more dramatic circumstances, like 'imprisonment of a parent' or 'social calamity – war, famine' he also included 'full-time employment of mother'. In other words, he was saying that these sorts of bad effects on children could arise if the mother in the family had a full-time job, and wasn't at home with the children all day. There were three main ways in which this damage could manifest itself, according to Bowlby: children deprived of their mothers could become juvenile delinquents; in extreme cases they might become 'affectionless psychopaths'; and their intelligence could be affected. These conclusions caused a great deal of debate and discussion throughout the country.

This was a particularly controversial thing to say at the time, because there was a political argument going on about a related question. During the war, it had been necessary for the Government to provide full-time day nurseries for working mothers, as they were needed to work for the war effort. By the early 1950s, there was pressure from the Government for these nurseries to be closed down, as there were not so many jobs available, and there were many returned servicemen seeking work. When Bowlby said, in effect, that it was damaging (or could be damaging) for mothers to work full-time, this was seized on by those who wanted to close down the day nurseries as extra evidence in their arguments. So the question very quickly became a political one rather than a psychological one.

Other evidence was brought forward which supported Bowlby's theory of maternal deprivation. A study by Patton, in 1963, showed that children who had suffered maternal deprivation could be undersized by comparison with other children of their age group – and that sometimes it could lead to dwarfism. Another study, by Douglas and Turner, linked the stress of going into hospital, and therefore being separated from the mother, to persistent bed-wetting in young children, which could last for several years.

Bowlby performed another study on children in 1956, this time on a group of children who had to go to a sanatorium for a while. He studied 60 children, who had been separated from their families from between five months and two years. All these separations had happened before the children were four years old. The children were compared with a control group of children who were in the same class at school. Bowlby took intelligence test scores for the children, and also asked for teachers' assessments of the children. He said that the children who had been separated from their homes scored less well in all the tests used, and these children also were said to get easily over-excited, and to daydream more than other children, according to their teachers.

Criticisms of Bowlby's evidence

Unfortunately, although all this evidence sounds very convincing at first, if we look at it closely it isn't as impressive as it sounds. None of the studies can really be taken as convincing evidence of maternal deprivation, either because they were badly controlled, and the results might have come from something else (as we discussed in Chapter 1), or because they aren't really about *maternal* deprivation, but about some other kind of deprivation. We will look at each study and see how these criticisms can be made.

Used as evidence for maternal deprivation, Goldfarb's 1943 study has two weaknesses. The first is that Goldfarb didn't find out *why* some children were considered suitable for immediate fostering, while others had to wait in the institution until they were three years old. There might have been some differences between the children in the first place – perhaps they seemed more disturbed, or perhaps they were slower to learn. And differences like these could have led to the different results for the two groups, not the effects of the institution.

The other criticism of Goldfarb's work as evidence for maternal deprivation, is the fact that children in institutions are deprived of a lot more than just their mothers. They are deprived of a normal family life, of their fathers, of other brothers and sisters, and all sorts of things. So if children suffer damaging effects from being in institutions (and we'll be looking at this again when we look at the development of intelligence), then you cannot simply conclude that it is the absence of the mother that is the cause.

Spitz's study cannot really be used as evidence for maternal deprivation for the same sort of reason. Spitz was talking about children who had lost either parent – mother or father – and not simply the mother. So here we're really talking about *parental*, not maternal, deprivation.

Bowlby's own study of juvenile thieves can be criticised in many different ways, and we will look at a few of these criticisms. The first is the way that the study was performed. Bowlby took current-day teenagers, and looked back at their past; this is called a *retrospective* study. This runs the risk of receiving distorted accounts of events that happened when the subjects were very young, or of there being incomplete records. How many of us have *all* the important things in our childhood written down? And it is very difficult for someone to remember their own childhood accurately – there could have been lots of other things that happened to those children in those years, which they didn't remember.

Another problem with a retrospective study is the way that it 'pre-selects' the sample of people. Bowlby chose delinquents and, looking back, he found separation. But the study cannot tell us how many children were separated from their parents and didn't suffer those effects. We could only find that out by taking a group of children at birth, and doing a *longitudinal* study. We might find, for instance, that only one child in ten thousand who is separated from its mother in the early years becomes delinquent. Or we might find that it's one in ten. But from Bowlby's study, we cannot make such conclusions.

Another criticism of Bowlby's study is that it ignores the twenty-seven juvenile thieves who were not separated from their mothers in their early years – clearly, with them, something else caused the problem.

Another problem arises from Bowlby's own approach to psychiatry. Bowlby was a psychoanalyst, and we will be looking more closely at that approach to development later on. But the psychoanalytic approach to child development is one which places a lot of importance on the first five years of life. Psychoanalysts (or most of them) believe that a child's personality is 'laid down' during those first five years, and that what happens during later childhood isn't so important. That means that Bowlby was only concerned with finding out about the first few years of life, and he didn't think that their later life was important. But most psychologists would say that the experiences that a child has when it is ten, or twelve, can have an important effect on the child too. If the child had a neglectful home when it was three years old, then there's a good chance that its home might have been neglectful when the child was eight as well – and this could have influenced it too. Or, the home life might have improved during those years. If we are trying to find out what might cause something like juvenile delinquency, it's important that we collect information about the child's *whole* life, not just a small part of it. As Bowlby only asked his subjects about their early childhood we do not know what influence their later family life could have had.

As regards the other studies: Patton does not seem to have taken into account the fact that children who are under stress often lose their appetites, and don't eat properly. Also, if a child's parents are often away, then it's possible that the child may be suffering from other kinds of neglect too – lack of the right kinds of food, or perhaps just simple poverty. All kinds of things apart from maternal deprivation could have led to the same result. After all, Patton found that children who were admitted to hospital often gained weight quickly – although, on the face of it, if maternal deprivation were the cause of their being underweight, then there wouldn't be any change – the children were still deprived of their mothers while they were in hospital!

Douglas and Turner's findings applied to any kind of serious stress which young people suffered, and not just to the lack of the mother. Bowlby's sanatorium study appears to have been much better performed than the 'juvenile delinquency' one, but it didn't come out with very clear results at all. Although, as a group, the sanatorium children scored lower on tests than the others, the differences were not very large – not statistically significant. By that, we mean that these differences could easily have happened just by chance; if you took *any* two groups of children, and tested them, you'd probably find small differences between the two groups. But they would just have happened by chance, they wouldn't necessarily have been caused by anything in particular. The differences that Bowlby found were so small that they could easily have happened by chance, and they don't really tell us much at all. Quite a few of the sanatorium children scored more highly than the 'home' children – it was only when the group's average scores were compared that they seemed to be lower.

There is one other, general criticism of Bowlby's theory of maternal deprivation. By saying that a child should have the constant care of its mother all the time, throughout its first five years, he was ignoring the way that many children throughout the world, and in our society too, are brought up. It has been quite normal in the more well-off sections of our society for children to be brought up by a nanny. She has most care of them, and the children only see their mother 'socially'. Bowlby was saying that it was important that the mother was the primary care-taker for the child, otherwise the child would suffer serious emotional consequences, and might well become juvenile delinquent. But many children from the affluent sections of our society have suffered Bowlby's 'maternal deprivation' for generations, and don't seem to become delinquents, or suffer particular damage!

The theory ignores cultural differences too. In many societies, the child is looked after by someone who isn't the real mother, or permanent mother-substitute that Bowlby talks about. In Israeli kibbutzim, the children are looked after by a professional child-nurse, called a metapelet, and only visit their parents in the evening after the day's work is over. In many places, grandparents or aunts look after the children during the day, while their mother is working. This used to be particularly common in England before the Industrial Revolution, and yet we don't hear of all the serfs and craftsmen being particularly delinquent! Nor do we find this in modern societies which work like this. So it seems that, just from looking around the world, we can find evidence against Bowlby's theory of maternal deprivation.

Recent findings on maternal deprivation

Although we may come to the conclusion that Bowlby was going a bit beyond the evidence, in saying that all these harmful effects came from children being deprived of their mothers, we still have to look at why these harmful effects happened in the first place. One of the most important writers in this area is M. Rutter, who published a report on maternal deprivation and the more recent research findings in 1972, and again in 1979.

Juvenile delinquency

One of the first things that Rutter looked at was the question of juvenile delinquency. He conducted several studies of his own on what seemed to be the causes of juvenile delinquency, and, in particular, concentrated on theft. He came to the conclusion that the main factor in the home, which seemed to be connected with young people stealing, was whether their home life was stressful or whether it was relatively calm. Teenagers from unhappy home backgrounds, where there was a lot of argument and quarrelling, and a lot of bad feeling, were much more likely to become delinquent than those whose homes were more stable.

This idea was supported by another study by Powers, Ash, Schoenberg and Sorey, in 1974. (You can shorten that to Powers et al. 1974) They looked at why some children only seemed to appear in court for theft or other such crimes once, and then did not get into any more trouble, while other children seemed to be in trouble again and again (this is known as 'recidivism'). They found that it supported Rutter's view about stress in the family home. The children who were only in court once, seemed to get into trouble at a time when there were serious problems at home; when it was all sorted out and things had calmed down, they didn't get into trouble again. But the children who were persistent offenders came from home backgrounds where there was permanent stress and lasting problems.

Affectionless psychopathy

Another thing that Rutter pointed out, was that it was important not to muddle up 'privation' with 'deprivation'. (We came across this in the last chapter, with Harlow's monkeys.) Deprivation, as we saw before, is when something is taken away from you, whereas privation is when you have never had

that something in the first place. For many of the institution
children that Bowlby was talking about, it was really privation
that they were suffering, as they had never been looked after
by their families in the first place. If a child had never had the
opportunity to form an attachment to anyone, then it wasn't
deprived, it was suffering from *privation*.

A study by Pringle and Bossio, in 1960, looked at what
happens when children suffer this kind of privation. They
studied children in institutional care who had been classed as
'maladjusted', and compared them with children, also in
institutional care, who were regarded as 'normal'. The main
difference between these two groups of children was the age
at which they had been brought into the institution. The
'maladjusted' ones had all been brought into the institution
during their first year of life, while the 'normal' children had
had at least a year at home before they were taken into care.

One of the symptoms which the maladjusted children
showed was that they did not seem to care about anybody else
very much. They hadn't got any loving relationships with
anyone, and they didn't hate anyone either; they had no real
relationships at all. And this is very similar to Bowlby's idea of
'affectionless psychopathy' – the 'maladjusted' children were
also very much more badly behaved than the 'normal' children.
So it would seem that the two studies are talking about the
same thing, and that it is closely connected with privation –
not having a chance to form any close relationships during the
first couple of years of life.

A study by Freud and Dann, in 1951, also supports this idea.
They studied a group of six children who had lived in a Nazi
concentration camp from a very early age. These children had
not made any relationships with adults, and according to
Bowlby they should have been suffering from 'affectionless
psychopathy', as they had all suffered maternal deprivation.
But while they were in the camp, these children had managed
to stick together, and had developed very close attachments to
each other. Although they were very suspicious of other people,
they showed no signs at all of being 'affectionless' or
'maladjusted'. So it seems that it is the inability to form *any*
attachments at all that leads to problems, not just the lack of
an attachment to the mother.

The other question, of course, is: is this effect permanent?
If a child has never been able to form an attachment to anyone,
and has grown up in an institution, does that mean that it will
be isolated from other people for the rest of its life? A study
by Tizard and Hodges, in 1978, looked into this question.
They looked at children who had spent their whole lives in
institutional care, and who weren't adopted until quite late on
in their childhoods. They found that, given time, even children

who had seemed 'affectionless' could develop a deep and loving relationship with the right adoptive parents. The problem seemed to be that the early stages in the relationship were difficult, while the child was settling down, and trying to believe that these new people really *did* care. But if the adoptive parents received support and help from the social worker involved, and if they were patient with the child, then they could overcome this problem, and the child would eventually learn to trust, and then to love them. But since it was so hard at the beginning, a lot of people gave up. It does seem from this, though, that even early privation can be successfully overcome in the right kind of environment. The attachments that these children developed with their adopted parents were very deep, and very close.

Low intelligence   Goldfarb's study, in particular, seemed to show that children who had suffered from maternal deprivation could end up less intelligent than those who had had a normal family life. As we have seen, though, it need not be the *maternal* deprivation which is having this effect, but it could be a more general effect of living in an institution. Several psychologists have studied the ways in which institutions may affect the intellectual development of children.

A study by Dennis, in 1960, looked at institutions which seemed to produce children who were very much lower than average, intellectually. He found that, although children were *physically* cared for, in the sense that they were given adequate food and clothing, they did not receive much *intellectual* stimulation. The children were very rarely played with, or talked to, by the staff in the institutions, and they were not particularly encouraged to develop imaginative play with toys either. Dennis concluded that this was what was limiting their intellectual development – not just being deprived of their mothers, but being deprived of other kinds of stimulation as well.

A study by Skeels, in 1966, supported this idea. This study started off almost by accident – Skeels had observed two very young children in an orphanage. The children were very intellectually retarded by comparison with others of their own age. Because of this, they were transferred to a home for people who were mentally subnormal. When Skeels visited the home a few months later, the change in the two children was tremendous; they seemed more alert, and intelligent, and in fact their IQ measurement had gone up considerably. Skeels discovered that, because the children were so young, they had been 'adopted' by the other people in the home, and had been petted, talked to, and played with a great deal. This had led to a change in their intelligence.

Skeels performed a larger, and more careful study of the same thing. He took some young mentally subnormal children, and put them in an institution where they would be looked after and played with by the older people there. The children all improved significantly, and in fact these improvements lasted until they were adult – those in Skeels' study eventually grew up, often married, and were able to work and become normal members of society. Those in a control group, who had just had the normal life in the first institution, were not able to look after themselves as adults, and their IQs remained in the 'subnormal' level. So, from these (and other) studies, it seems that low IQ doesn't arise simply from maternal deprivation, but from growing up in a poor, unstimulating environment. (Skeels' study is reported in more detail in Chapter 8.)

Rutter summed up the recent work on what children need with two main points:

1 that the child has the opportunities to form attachments with adults; and
2 that the child's home is relatively stress-free, and that relationships in it are 'warm' and friendly.

If these requirements are met, it doesn't really seem to matter whether the child spends all day with a father, a mother, or a number of different people. As Rutter points out, if a child's mother would become tense and irritable by staying at home to look after the child, then it is undoubtedly better that she goes out to work. Then, when she is with the child they will be able to enjoy each other's company. In the same way, the work on stress and delinquency may suggest that it is better to have a brief period of upset, than a continuing stressful one. If two parents can't live happily together, then it could perhaps be less damaging for the child if they lived apart, than if they tried to stay together for 'the children's sake', and simply ended up arguing and quarrelling. But it would depend on the individual family.

Attachments in institutions

But what about children who aren't able to live at home, who live in institutional care? According to Bowlby's theory, it would be better for a child to be with its mother – no matter how bad the home – than to be in an institution. Bowlby later changed his mind, pointing out that some institutions weren't all that bad, and some homes could be awful.

Social workers are often faced with the difficult decision of whether they should leave a child in its own home, where it may be suffering from neglect – or even in some cases from the risk of physical violence – or whether they should bring the child into care, and risk it suffering from the possible consequences of growing up in an institution.

With some children, of course, there isn't much of a choice; perhaps the parents have died, or for other reasons there isn't anyone who can look after them. But in other cases, it is much more tricky. A social worker has the legal power to 'break up' a family, and take children away from their parents if it is felt that the children are at risk – but how do you find out without waiting until a child actually suffers damage? And nobody wants to risk yet another case like the Maria Caldwell affair, where a child died because the social worker was reluctant to take action. At the same time, nobody would wish to remove a child from its home if it would be perfectly safe there.

Many children's homes are run by Local Authority Social Services departments. Usually, they are looking after children who are 'in care' because of a social worker's decision of this kind, and many of these children will go home at weekends to their parents. But other children in these homes are living there permanently and have no other home to go to. Unless they are fostered or adopted, then they will stay in the institution until they are sixteen. Most authorities try to make sure that no child stays in their homes for more than about two years – clearly, it's much better for the child to have a foster home if at all possible. Some Social Services departments also run 'Aunt and Uncle' schemes, where people can become 'Aunt' or 'Uncle' to a child in care. Although they won't be fostering them, they may visit the child, and perhaps have it to visit them in the holidays and at weekends. For some children, this can be the only contact that they get with the 'outside' world.

Other children's homes are run by various charities: Dr Barnardo's run many homes around the country, and so do the National Children's Homes. Mostly, these homes will have children who aren't 'in care' in the same way as those in Local Authority homes, but who are there as a result of the death of their parents or some other reason. They often run their own adoption and fostering schemes, too.

Something that needs to be looked at closely, then, is the sort of care children receive in institutions, and how it is different from the sort of care they receive in the home. Of course, when we consider this, we aren't talking about aspects of care like food and clothing – but of personal care, like whether the child feels secure, and receives affection and attention. In many children's homes, the staff are very warm, loving people, and it is a very far cry from the old Victorian style homes which we sometimes imagine. Nonetheless, there are often many more children than there would be in an ordinary family, and consequently there are many more pressures, and more competition for attention. Some institutions – although happily not so many nowadays – frown on the staff developing attachments to particular children. In some cases that particular member of staff is removed from the child's area, so that there is no contact between them. The reason for this is usually given as being the way that both will be upset when the child (or the member of staff) moves somewhere else, and that 'favouritism' affects the other children in the home, and leads to trouble.

Although on the face of it, this appears to be a perfectly sensible approach, it can have serious consequences for the emotional development of the children. Forming a close relationship with another person is an important part of our development, although, as we have seen, it doesn't matter if the relationship is formed with more than one person (as it might be in a normal family, with father, mother, and older brother or sister). It certainly matters if the child isn't allowed to form any close relationships at all, or to feel that its closeness is reciprocated.

In fact, one of the other aspects of institutional life, which is often quoted as deprivation, is also one of the things which protects the institution from the dire consequences of the staff and children becoming too close. The fact that the care staff in a children's home work set hours, and go off duty at the end of those hours, means that the child who has formed an attachment to a particular member of staff, will have interactions with other members of staff, and is more likely to maintain a balanced, sociable relationship with others in the long run. In a well-run home, with sensible management, the question of favouritism is easily resolved, too. A close relationship does not necessarily mean an exclusive relationship, or preferential treatment – something which most care staff will quickly recognise, when it is pointed out to them, even if they didn't realise it already.

Nonetheless, institutional life does present some problems; staff leave the home, for instance, either to obtain promotion elsewhere, or to vary their experience. So, unlike in a family, the child is faced with strong changes in the people around it, and this can be very disruptive. But, again, the disruption can be intensified by those running the home; I once worked in a children's home, for instance, where the children were not told when a member of staff was going to leave, because it was felt that they would become upset and disturbed. So they would have done, for a short while – but the disturbance was much greater when the children were suddenly told 'Oh, you won't

see so-and-so again – they've left!' Other homes I have worked
in adopted the policy of telling the children well in advance,
so that they could organise a farewell party, and so on, and
the children who had built up a special relationship with that
member of staff had time to come to terms with their
departure, and to cope with it constructively. If they had been
suddenly faced with a *fait accompli* – by being told that 'their'
member of staff had already left – they would have found it
very much more difficult to cope with, and they would also
have become much less likely to risk another close relationship
with another of the care staff.

One alternative to institutional care which many local
authorities are exploring is that of foster-homes. When a child
is placed in a foster home, it is on the understanding that the
placement is temporary; it might be removed to go back to its
real home, or to a special school, or whatever is deemed suitable
for it in the future. The family who are fostering the child are
aware of this, and in a lot of ways their job is much more
difficult than the job of parents who adopt their children.
Adoptive parents know that it is now *their* child – whatever it
may have suffered in the past – but foster parents don't have
that security. Often they are expected to provide a warm and
loving home for a child for a period of only a year, or even
less, and the child is also often encouraged to maintain links
with its 'real' parents and home. As can be expected this can
often lead to tensions in the foster-home; the foster-parents
may find it difficult to 'let go' of the child, once a bond has
been formed, or the child might become resentful and
suspicious. In particular, foster-parents often have problems
with children who have been in institutional care for a long
time, before being placed in the foster-home. A study by
Trasler, in 1960, found that this was the single factor, above
all else, that was likely to lead to a 'breakdown' in the foster-
home of a child.
   The reasons for this would appear to lie in the question of
forming attachments, and personal closeness. Perhaps owing
to the competition for attention in many homes, many children
aren't really offered much opportunity for developing close
relationships which others and, as has been said, in a few
homes it is actually frowned on. After several years of this,
when these children suddenly find themselves in a small home,
with only two adults, and few (if any) other children, they are
unable to cope with the closeness. Where previously they could
easily avoid adult attention, and anyway only received what
others in the home got too, now they find that they are the
focus of attention; many children find this a heavy pressure.
Many of them find it strange that the foster-parents aren't

going 'off duty', or, by behaving badly, will try to push their new foster-parents into rejecting them. If the social worker, who knows the child, is available for the parents to talk to – calling in frequently for a chat – then this sort of problem can be overcome; but sometimes the overworked social workers are not able to do this as often as is necessary. Instead, all they can say is 'ring me up if you have any problems', but many new foster-parents are not prepared to do that for what they consider 'trivial' problems. Because of this, the trouble escalates, and by the time the foster-parents actually do telephone the social worker, they are often at their wits' end, and the fostering breaks down.

In some local authorities, they have adopted a strong policy of fostering children whenever it is possible, and not having many children's homes at all. By paying foster-parents a professional wage (still cheaper than keeping up an institution), many more people are able to stay at home and foster difficult children, and by concentrating on the homes, the social workers can find time to give them the support that they need in the early stages of the fostering. These authorities are having much greater success with their fosterings, and the children benefit in consequence.

There are some children, though, who because of their earlier experiences are not ready for the closeness of foster-homes. After a period – sometimes as long as a year – they may be ready to try a foster-home, but if they were placed in one immediately on being brought into care, they would find it more than they could cope with. So although an authority that concentrates on fostering has fewer children's homes, it still tends to have some. It used to be said that: 'better a bad home than a good institution', but nowadays people realise that just because a home provides family, it isn't necessarily the best environment for children to grow up in; if it's a neglectful or cruel home the children will suffer far more than if they were to grow up in an institution, or fostered.

A study by Tizard and Rees, in 1974, looked into the question of whether children should always be returned to their natural homes whenever possible. The children they studied were a group of children who had been placed in a residential nursery at or before the age of four months. Round about the age of two years old, some of the children were placed for adoption, some were returned to their natural mothers (who were mostly single mothers, or who had been unable to cope for similar reasons, while the children were younger), while the rest of the children remained in the institution (because their mothers couldn't be traced, and so could not give permission for the child to be adopted). All the children in the study had originally come from similar backgrounds: from seriously disadvantaged homes, such that the children had been considered likely to suffer if they remained in them while infants; or such that the parents had been unable to cope with the child, and had asked the authorities to take it into care. Tizard and Rees also had a control group of children who were the same ages as the ones in the nursery, but lived in their parents' homes, in London.

They tested the children on such things as the way they were developing intellectually, and the range and 'breadth' of experiences they had had, so they were able to get a kind of 'development score' for each of the children, at the age of two. All of them scored similarly, not surprisingly, as at that point they were still in the nursery. Immediately afterwards, though, the children were separated as described above. When the children were re-tested at the age of four, some strong differences had started to show up between the groups.

The group that was most advanced intellectually turned out to be the children who had been adopted at the age of two, with the control group from ordinary London homes a close second. Surprisingly, the children who had returned to their natural mothers scored lower than those who had remained in the institution – despite the fact that they had been in a family setting, while the others had had the sort of 'multiple caretaking', and official disapproval of close relationships that we talked of before. So it seemed that, in some ways, the children had been put at a *disadvantage* by being returned home. On the other hand, it was the children who had been adopted or returned to their natural homes, who were the most friendly and co-operative when they were being re-tested, and who could chat most freely with the experimenters. So although they hadn't particularly benefited intellectually, the social development which they showed was promising. The institutional children and the control group tended to be very reticent and unwilling to chat to the experimenters during the re-testing. Overall, though, these results are very far from supporting the 'better a bad home than a good institution' idea.

One of the things that emerged quite clearly from that study was that the children who had been placed in adoptive homes had done generally better all round. When the same study was followed up later on – when the children were seven years old – the adopted children were found to be doing better than the restored children on all counts. They had developed close relationships with their adopted parents, and usually had far better relationships with the fathers, as well as the mothers, than the restored children did (Tizard, 1977).

It has often been said that children only benefit from adoption if they are adopted in the early years of life, perhaps in the first two years. Tizard and Hodges' study, in 1978, showed that this wasn't necessarily the case; even children who had been adopted after the age of four developed close and affectionate relationships with their parents, even if they hadn't had much of a chance to form relationships with people before that. And some specialised adoption centres in London have successfully placed children who are anything up to 13 years old ('Community Care', 1980).

How did the idea arise that only early adoptions work? The reasons might lie in the kind of problems we discussed earlier in connection with fostering: that social workers weren't able to give the sort of help that was needed; because of lack of time; and because prospective parents were not well-enough informed about the sort of problems that they were likely to face, when first taking the children in. Since modern agencies can specialise, and have staff who are only concerned with this particular work, they are able to devote a lot of time to counselling and supporting adoptive parents, and also to give counsel and support to the children – who, after all, are the ones who have had to adjust to a completely new environment! Whatever the reason, adoption, even when the child is quite old, seems to present itself as a good alternative to institutional care. A child who has been deprived of a 'normal family life' can develop personal attachments at any age, in the right circumstances.

Summary

1 Bowlby put forward the theory that maternal deprivation in infancy could lead to serious problems later, including juvenile delinquency and affectionless psychopathy.

2 Other studies appeared to support Bowlby's ideas. The question became a very important one as to whether a mother should go out to work, or stay at home and look after her children.

3 If Bowlby's studies are examined carefully, it can be seen that they do not provide very convincing evidence for the theory. Either they are concerned with other kinds of deprivation, or they are going beyond the evidence available.

4 Cross-cultural studies would also appear to contradict the theory of maternal deprivation.

5 Rutter said that stress in the family home rather than maternal deprivation led to juvenile delinquency.

6 Privation – the lack of opportunity to form attachments –

seems to be the cause of 'affectionless' characters. But they
can develop attachments later in their lives.

7 Children do not necessarily suffer from institutional care if
they are allowed to develop attachments to the staff in the
home.

8 Some authorities are trying to foster almost all of their
children in care. This seems to work much better than the
traditional set-up with many children's homes.

9 Adoption also seems to be a good alternative for many
children. When tested, many adopted children scored higher
on sociability and intelligence than children either with their
natural parents or in institutional care.

Chapter 5 **Socialisation**

Throughout the world, children are brought up in very different kinds of ways. Throughout the world, also, we find many different kinds of human society. In this chapter, we will look at some of the different methods of child-rearing, and the effects which they seem to have on the eventual development of the children involved.

First of all, we'll look at some child-rearing practices very different from those used in our society.

Cross-cultural studies of socialisation

The anthropologist Margaret Mead spent considerable time living with different tribes in the Pacific, observing the way that they organised their society and their lives. She found immense differences between tribes, in their habits and traditions, and also strong differences in the characters of the members of those tribes. We will look at three of the tribes that she wrote about, and their child-rearing habits.

The Arapesh tribe live in the mountains of New Guinea. They are a very poor people, often struggling to get enough to eat. Their society is very much concerned with co-operation and gentleness, and they are intensely interested in growing things – plants, animals, and children. Their babies, when they are born, are regarded as soft, vulnerable, and precious; they are fed, gently, whenever they show the least sign of hunger, and are protected and nurtured by both parents, equally, for an extended infancy period. Throughout childhood, the children are protected, and temper-tantrums, when they happen (usually because there isn't enough food), are appeased, and not regarded as something to be 'dealt with'. Their marriage system reflects the passive dependency of childhood. The husband takes a child-bride, and feeds and protects her, re-playing the role that his parents played for him, when he was a child. In this way, there is no strong break between the support and cherishing that they receive in infancy, and their adult life. The whole society is based around co-operation and gentle interest in others, rather than the self. Aggression and arguments are rare, although adults will sometimes break out in temper-tantrums. But the emphasis in adult life, as in childhood, is on co-operation and mutual dependency.

By contrast, the Mundugumor tribe are fierce, aggressive, and quarrelsome. The women are as intolerant as the men, and dislike rearing children. Children of the Mundugumor tribe have to struggle for the mother's breast, and she is likely to stop feeding them as soon as they appear the least bit satisfied – they are fed while the mother is standing up, and are never cuddled. Unlike the Arapesh, whose children are carried in soft bags, Mundugumor children have to travel in hard, scratchy baskets, and are always forced to assert themselves, and to fight. At the age of five, when Arapesh children are trailing around the village and playing, Mundugumor children may be sent as hostages to other tribes, knowing that if the war-plans change, their lives will be forfeit. They grow up there, and are expected to learn the language and roadways, in case a future war breaks out with the neighbouring tribe, and they have to be scouts. Because of their upbringing, they are well able to act independently, and to store up hostility against their host-tribe. As adults, although the Mundugumor are arrogant and warlike, they are also full of laughter and energy.

The third tribe which we will look at are the Samoans. They are a society of stable, balanced adults, who all work, and enjoy music, art, and dancing. They do not go in for excesses of emotion, or for laziness and apathy, but lead a life based around work and relaxation. Their children are nursed generously in infancy, and are given food and carried about by all the women in the large household – not just the mother. Later, they are looked after by a child-nurse, a girl of about six years old, whose job it is to look after the baby, and to get it out of the way if it shows anti-social behaviour, like throwing a temper-tantrum within earshot of the head of the household. Throughout this time, the emphasis is on the natural, gradual development of the child: 'While you may do inappropriate things just now, this is because you are young . . . you'll grow out of it.' The child is never punished – it is the child-nurse's responsibility to make sure that it doesn't annoy others, by taking it out of the way. It is fed when hungry, carried when tired, and allowed to sleep when it feels like it. At the age of five or six, this changes, and the children adopt their roles: little girls become child-nurses (a responsible and tough job) while little boys join the other boys, and learn to fish, canoe, climb trees, swim, and all the other skills which the men of the society are required to possess.

When they are adult, Samoan people are gentle, balanced, and serene – with a very stable family structure, and very little mental disturbance in the society.

Freeman, in 1983, suggested that Mead had exaggerated the influence of culture in the development of human personality – particularly in her description of Samoan life. He argued that she had been misled, mainly because she had only been able to stay in Samoa for a relatively short period of time, and also because many of her informants had been adolescent girls, whose information might not have been strictly accurate. Freeman saw the personal etiquette which makes Samoan culture appear so relaxed, as being necessary as a social control over aggressive impulses. He also argued that the society was not as sexually relaxed and open as Mead had suggested.

However, Strathern (1983) has pointed out that Freeman's judgement could also have been influenced by his social contacts – in this case, high-ranking males. As they were strongly involved with political issues, and as virginity is important for girls of high rank, they too may simply have been presenting their side of the case. Although Freeman did spend more time in Samoa than Mead, it is very difficult to obtain a purely unbiased view of any society. Other anthropologists (people who study human societies) have concluded that, although Margaret Mead's evidence may not have been very good, overall her conclusions were probably accurate (R. Ballard 1983).

In 1973, U. Bronfenbrenner published the results of a different cross-cultural study. Instead of looking at people in tribal societies, he looked at the way that children are brought up in modern, industrial societies. His study was a comparison of child-rearing in the United States of America, and the United Soviet Socialist Republic. He found enormous differences between the way that children were brought up in each society. For one thing, the Russians had a much more *planned* approach to the way that children should be brought up – they were very conscious of the fact that their children were going to be the adults of the future, and so the whole society was concerned with bringing them up in the 'right' kind of way.

As with most children, Bronfenbrenner found that the peer group – the other children of the same age which the child associated with – was important in moulding children's behaviour. In America, Bronfenbrenner found, the peer group would often influence the child *against* the society's values: it was considered 'creeping' to work hard in school, or to try to be good. But in Russia, the peer group worked very strongly *with* society's values, and this was deliberately encouraged from an early age. Children worked in 'teams', and were responsible for keeping their own discipline and making sure that each member of their team worked hard in school. If a child was lazy, or dishonest, then it would be the other children in the team who would deal with it, not the adults. Children were very conscious that they would grow up to play a full part in their society, and that their school-days were preparing for that time. It was everyone's *duty* to work hard!

Bronfenbrenner also pointed out that children in Russia aren't as 'cut-off' from the adult world as they are in America. Often, the workers in a local factory would 'adopt' a class at school, and the children would visit the factory, and be taken on educational visits by the workers. And *everyone* seemed to be interested in children. Bronfenbrenner was very surprised one day when he was going down the street with his small child. The child ran on ahead, and coming towards them was a 'gang' of teenage boys. Instead of ignoring the child, as American teenagers would have done, he was picked up, and petted by the lads, before being handed back to his parents.

But in America, Bronfenbrenner said, children aren't regarded as being so valuable; instead, they often have to take 'second place' to their parents' other interests, and are often left either alone, or with just the company of other children. He said that the average American child watches 22 hours of television a week – as much time as they spend in school! While Bronfenbrenner didn't like everything about the Russian system – the way that children were encouraged to 'tell tales' on each other, for example – he did think that perhaps having children a bit more involved in their society would be a good idea. He thought it likely that insufficient involvement by children in American society was a cause of vandalism and violence among young people.

The problem is, of course, that by taking such a deliberate approach to how children should be brought up, and by making sure that all the influences on the child work in the way that society wants them to, we are getting very close to the idea of children being 'brainwashed' into being just the 'right kind' of people. But Bronfenbrenner was saying that *every* society influences its children so that they grow up to fit into it, and perhaps people in the Western world should be a bit more aware of just how they want their children to grow up.

Child-rearing styles

In British society, parents use a variety of different methods for bringing up their children. Some children never receive any physical punishment at all, while others are slapped or spanked for misbehaving. Some children are sent to a playgroup at the age of two or three, others stay at home. Some children are sent to boarding school, some are taught at home, and most go to day schools. All-in-all, it's no wonder that people grow up so widely different, and with such different interests.

Independence   Several studies have been done with the intention of examining different ways that parents deal with their children. Several different *styles* have been found, which represent the different ways that parents would tend to handle their child overall – although, of course, there will be differences for individual events. But, roughly speaking, parents' styles can be sorted into four groups: authoritarian, democratic, permissive, or laissez-faire.

> *Authoritarian* parents are those who do not consult their children when decisions are to be made, but go ahead and order their children to do things. All decisions are made by the parent and the child does not have any say in the matter at all.
>
> *Democratic* parents are those parents who consult their children before they make decisions, but who still make the final decision themselves. However, they try to take what the child wants to do into account.
>
> *Permissive* parents are parents who allow the child to make its own decisions. Instead of telling the child what to do, they will ask it to decide, and abide by what the child has said. So, with permissive parents, the child has a great deal of freedom of action, but not a great deal of guidance from the parents except through discussion.
>
> *Laissez-faire* parents are those who leave the child to go its own way, entirely. They are not involved in any decisions which the child might make, and do not guide that child at all, either by praise or by blame.

It can be seen that these different styles have a lot to do with the amount of independence which the parents allow their child: the authoritarian parents do not allow the child any independence, while the laissez-faire parents allow their child complete independence, and responsibility for its own decisions. Several studies have investigated the effects of these kinds of styles on children, although, unfortunately, they have tended to investigate teachers and youth leaders rather than parents. There is a good reason for this: it might well be that some parents have adopted a particular style of child-rearing *because of their child*. For instance, if their child was continually disobedient, they might have started to use an authoritarian approach, because that was the way that they could keep the child under control, even though they may have wanted to use a more democratic approach. So when we are looking at parents' behaviour, we can't really be sure just which is the cause of a certain kind of behaviour and which is the effect. In the above example, the disobedience might have arisen from the authoritarian approach, or the authoritarian approach might have arisen from the disobedience.

In 1938, Lewin, Lippitt and White studied the effects of different styles of leadership on ten-year-old schoolboys. The boys all attended a club which was held after school, and which was concerned with model-making. The boys were divided into three groups, and each group had a leader who followed a different style – authoritarian, democratic, or laissez-faire. The boys who were in the group with the authoritarian leader were told what models they were going to make, and who they would be working with. If their work was particularly good, the team leader would praise them, but wouldn't explain his praise. Or, if their work was not so good, the leader would say so, but not explain in detail just why, or how it could be improved. The boys in the group with the democratic leader, on the other hand, were encouraged to discuss what model they were going to make, and who they would work with. If they did well, they were praised, and the leader took pains to point out just what was good about their work; if they did badly, then the leader would try to show them how they could improve it, and discuss it with them. The leader joined in with all the group activities, and was particularly friendly. The group with the laissez-faire leader was not directed at all: the boys chose what they wanted to do with no guidance from the leader who neither praised nor criticised their work. They had to work with no adult support or guidance.

The three groups provided very different results. Of the three, the boys in the group with the autocratic leader worked hardest, but when he left the room they would stop working, and they often quarrelled among themselves. Very often, they tried to get the leader's attention, but they were always very polite and respectful to him.

The boys in the democratic leader's group were far more cheerful, and didn't quarrel so much. They were interested in their work, and when they spoke to the leader, it was usually to ask questions about it. If the leader went out of the room, they still carried on working; and if they came across a problem, they would all try to find the answer to it.

The boys in the group with the laissez-faire leader were very disorganised, and didn't do very much work. If they came across any difficulties, they just gave up, and they very rarely asked the leader for help. The group itself was noisy and quarrelsome.

In a second part of the experiment Lewin, Lippitt and White changed the boys around, to see if, perhaps, it had just been that some boys were more interested than others. But, after they had sorted them into entirely different groups, they still got the same results, so they could say definitely that it was the style of leadership which was causing them. Unfortunately, there is always the problem with studies like this, that the children are already used to one particular style – the one their parents use – and so they may be reacting to a *change* in style, rather than to the style itself. (Most of the boys had parents who used a democratic approach.) But the study still shows us something about leadership styles, and their effects on children.

Baumrind, in 1967, performed a study which was an attempt to find out if child-rearing styles in the family went along with greater independence, as they had apparently done in the study by Lewin et al., where the boys in the 'democratic' group had worked more independently than the others. By looking at different kinds of approaches from the parents, Baumrind found three categories, which she called authoritarian, authoritative, and permissive. These turn out to be roughly the same as the authoritarian, democratic (authoritative) and permissive styles mentioned before. She found that children of authoritarian parents were fairly self-reliant, but tended also to be withdrawn and mistrustful; while the children of authoritative parents were mature and competent, and particularly independent. Children from permissive parents appeared to be immature and lacked independence and self-discipline. The study was done using interviews with parents, and observations at home and in the school.

The way that parents bring up their children seems to have quite a lot to do with the independence that they develop. It seems that children become independent as a result of having a mixture of responsibility and guidance; left with no guidance at all, as in the laissez-faire approach, they do not become independent; and if left with no responsibility, as in the authoritarian style, then they also don't become very independent (although they do become more independent than the laissez-faire parents' children).

Unfortunately, there are problems with these studies, and with other studies which have been conducted by interviewing parents about their child-rearing methods. One of the main problems is that there could be all sorts of things which are influencing the child, apart from the thing that we're interested in. Without getting a full picture of everything that's happened to the child, we can't be sure that our particular variable – for instance the amount of independence a parent allows a child – is exactly the one that's causing the effect. Most of these kinds of studies have only investigated one or two things, and not a very wide range.

Another problem is that parents don't necessarily behave in exactly the same way all the time. A parent might be authoritarian about table manners, but democratic about the way that pocket money is spent, for instance. When we ask for a single rating of each parent, it could be that we are being much too general; parents act in all sorts of different ways all the time, and this might make our study inaccurate.

A third problem with this kind of approach is the way that information is gathered. Most parents have a good idea of what the 'socially-acceptable' methods of child-rearing are, and what people expect other parents to behave like. So if parents are being asked about how they treat their child, they may be tempted to tell the interviewer how they would *like* to treat their child, or not to mention the bits that they think people won't approve of. So the interviewer may not get the true picture of how that parent treats that child at all.

Yet another problem is the way that people can jump to conclusions about what *causes* what. If I were to tell you that a good year for strawberries is also a good year for apples, you wouldn't think that the strawberries had caused the apples to grow well, would you? But you might think that perhaps both of them had been caused by something entirely different – for example, by a certain kind of weather. In this case, we'd say that the amount of stawberries *correlates* to the amount of apples, but doesn't *cause* it. In the same way, it could be that an authoritarian style *correlates* to boys working hard, but doesn't *cause* it; they might, for instance, be working hard because they have a clear knowledge of what they're doing, and they don't have to stop and think about it much. In most of these studies, it *seems* as if the parents' behaviour causes the child's behaviour, but we don't know that for certain. It might even be the other way round, or it might come from something totally different!

Achievement motivation

A feature of personality which is similar to independence in some respects, but in other ways quite different from it, is known as *achievement motivation*. This is the way that some children show a strong 'need to achieve' things – they become upset if they can't solve a puzzle, or do well in school, and they will work hard to manage it. Other children, though, don't seem to be that bothered. Although they will do the puzzles that are given to them, and will work in school, they aren't as 'keen' as the children with high achievement motivation, and success isn't as important to them.

Achievement motivation also seems to be affected by the way that parents bring up their children. A study by M. Winterbottom, in 1953, looked at achievement motivation in children, and at their parents. The children were given a sentence as an outline, and were asked to tell a story around it. A typical sentence was: 'Two children were running a race when one fell over'. The children who had high achievement motivation were expected to tell a story which showed the child being very concerned with winning the race; the children with low achievement motivation were expected to tell a story which wasn't so concerned with the result of the race, but which might, for instance, stress one child helping another. From the stories that the children told, Winterbottom obtained a score of achievement motivation level for each child.

When the mothers of these children were interviewed, it was found that the children with high achievement motivation had parents who expected them to manage things earlier (like going to school alone) than mothers of low scorers. They also tended to reward their children with hugs and kisses more; while the mothers whose children showed low achievement motivation didn't reward their children very often, but did tend to give them a lot of negative orders ('Don't do that'; 'You can't play with her').

Another study by Rosen and D'Andrade, in 1959, showed that the achievement motivation of children was connected with what their parents expected of them. If their parents expected a great deal, then the children, also, wanted to achieve very strongly. If the parents didn't expect very much of their children, then the children would have low achievement motivation.

Rosen and D'Andrade asked a blindfolded child to build a tower from building bricks with one hand. The child's parents were watching the child do this, and they were asked how well they thought the child would do. They found that those children with high achievement motivation had parents who expected more from their child; they set high standards of achievement. But they also praised and rewarded their child a lot more, and encouraged it while it was trying to build the tower. Parents of children with low achievement motivation didn't encourage their child much at all, they just watched. So it seems that high expectations from parents aren't the only things which lead to high achievement motivation in children, but praise and encouragement are important too.

Conscience We have just looked at the effects of parents praising and encouraging their children, but what about punishment? Many people have very strong views about punishment – that you should *never* hit a child, for example, or that some children need a good spanking now and again. But whatever kind of punishment people use, they all seem to agree that it should need to be used less and less as the child grows older. As the child grows, it's expected to develop a *conscience* that will tell

right from wrong, and direct the child's behaviour. There have
been several studies that have looked at the connection
between punishment, and the development of conscience.

A study by Mackinnon, in 1938, investigated this question. He
used college students, and put them in a room with a book of
problems which they were asked to solve. The students were
told that the answers were in the back of the book, but they
were asked not to look at them, but to try to do the problems
on their own. By using a two-way mirror, Mackinnon could
find if any of them did cheat when he was out of the room.
Out of 93 subjects, 43 of them cheated! When Mackinnon
asked the subjects later if they had cheated, about half of these
43 confessed, but half didn't. He found that the students with
strong consciences – those who had not cheated – were the
ones who had parents who relied on *psychological* rather than
physical punishments. Psychological punishments are the sort
where the parent expresses displeasure or hurt feelings at
something the child has done, while physical punishments are
ones which directly and materially affect the child – like losing
pocket money, or being slapped or spanked.

Psychological punishments rely much more on the *relationship*
which the child has with the parent or the adult who is doing
the punishing. Almost always, the child is expected to perform
some kind of action which shows remorse, by saying 'I'm
sorry', or by trying to make it up in some way. On the other
hand, physical punishment is much more direct and
automatic; the child suffers briefly and then the punishment is
over. The child isn't expected to do anything special, like
apologise, but is expected to avoid doing the offending thing
again.
    W. Hill said, in 1963, that it is probably the act of remorse
which makes the difference between psychological
punishment and physical punishment in the building up of
conscience. Since the child itself actually has to do something
to express repentance, it is more likely to 'internalise' – to
include in its own self-concept – the lesson. As a result of
this, the child learns more effectively to avoid doing the
'naughty' act. Since physical punishment can be avoided simply
by not being found out, and it makes little difference to any
other person, the lesson the child learns doesn't last as long.
Once the child is in a position where it won't be punished –
when it grows older – then there is no need for it to avoid the
'naughty' behaviour.
    If this were true, and it is really the act of remorse which is
important, then it wouldn't really matter *which* kind of
punishment the parent used, as long as the child also had to

apologise, or make recompense somehow. But it seems that parents who use psychological punishments also expect different kinds of behaviour from their children, when they are found out.

Sears, Maccoby, and Levin, in 1957, asked mothers about their children's behaviour, and whether they showed strong consciences; and also about the type of punishment which the children received.
They showed that children with strong consciences had parents who not only used psychological punishments, but also tended to make firm demands on their children, expecting them to show a high standard of moral behaviour. They also explained much more than the other parents why they demanded things of their children. Parents who had children with weak consciences tended to be very much more aggressive with their children, and as well as using physical punishments tended not to explain things to them.
It seems fairly clear that the way in which children are brought up can have considerable effect on this aspect at least of their later personalities. So what about other characteristics? How far can the way that children are brought up influence other sides of their adult natures?

Aggression   One characteristic which psychologists are interested in is *aggression*. We know that some people behave very much more aggressively than others, and that people show aggression in different ways – some people seem to 'channel' their aggressive energies into sport, or a competitive job, for instance, while others get involved in fights easily, or hit out at people when they are angry and frustrated. In fact, a very large part of aggressive behaviour seems to arise from frustration, rather than anything else. When playing in nursery school, children become very much more aggressive when they have only a small space to play in, and so are continually interfered with. Also, children behave more aggressively when they have just had a frustrating experience, for instance when they haven't been able to solve a puzzle. In adulthood, some people continue to react aggressively to frustrating events, while others don't. Why is this?

Newson and Newson, in a large study of child-rearing practices in Nottingham in 1968, found that there were strong class differences in the amount of aggression which children showed. They found that middle-class parents tended to object to their children showing aggressive behaviour, while working-class parents tended to encourage their children to 'stand up for themselves', and to fight back if they were pushed around by other children. When they looked at mothers and infants, they found that, even in the first year of life, infants from working-class homes received more physical punishment than did middle-class infants, and showed more temper tantrums already.

Boys tend to show more aggressive behaviour than girls, and it is sometimes thought that this, too, is a result of parental treatment. A study by Rothbart and Maccoby, in 1966, used tape-recordings of family behaviour. When they analysed the tapes, they found that mothers were far more tolerant of aggressive acts committed by sons, than of aggressive acts committed by daughters. Young boys, it seems, are expected to be aggressive, whereas girls are not.

Another study, by Sears, Maccoby, and Levin, showed that, if children are punished by the parents for being aggressive – and particularly if it is physical punishment – aggressive acts can actually *increase*! It seems possible that this comes about as a result of 'modelling' – the parents, by their own behaviour, show the child that aggression can be used – because they, themselves, are using it when they punish the child. Since the children see punishment, and aggression, as being adult-type actions, the children increase their own aggressive behaviour.

Imitation and identification

Imitation

Another study of 'modelling', or *observational learning*, was done by Bandura and Walters, in 1963. The children who they were testing observed a real-life, or a filmed, model which was either a child or an adult, performing aggressive actions towards a doll. Later on, the child's own behaviour with the doll was observed, and a note was taken of how much aggressive behaviour the child showed, in its own play with the doll. They found that children were very likely to imitate the behaviour of the 'model' whom they had watched, especially if the model was another child.

In one of these experiments they divided the children into three groups. One group was shown the model being rewarded (by approval from an adult, or by sweets) for showing aggressive behaviour; another group saw the model being punished; and the third group didn't see the model receive any consequences at all. The children's subsequent play reflected what they had seen. Those children who had seen the model being rewarded for aggressive acts themselves showed a high level of aggression in their play. The ones who had seen the model punished showed a low level of aggressive acts, while the no-reward, no-punishment group were in-between.

At this point, Bandura and Walters changed things a bit. They began to reward the children for copying the model, and

Fig. 5.1 Aggressive behaviour towards a bobo doll
After seeing adults act aggressively towards an inflated doll, children were more likely to behave aggressively towards it

very soon *all* the children were behaving aggressively with the doll, exactly as the model had done. So, although most of them hadn't imitated the model straight away, when they were in a position where they were rewarded for doing so, they did so easily. All the children were as good as one another in copying the model, and there were no group differences according to whether they had seen the model being punished or rewarded. So the actual *learning* involved must have been the same for all the children, even though their *performance* was different at first.

Bandura connected these findings to the way that children may learn violence from TV programmes. In this study, effectively, he was showing that children can still learn aggressive behaviour, even if they see that behaviour being punished. So perhaps it isn't enough that the 'baddy' should be punished in the end – children could still have learned to imitate the 'baddy' behaviour and if they were in a position where they might benefit from it, then they could imitate that behaviour again.

Imitation, like this, is an important way that children learn. It seems to be very much involved in sex-role learning: children learn what kind of behaviour is appropriate for girls or women, and what is appropriate for boys or men, by watching adults (particularly their parents) and how they behave. Later on, they come to *identify* themselves as male or female, and so no longer need to imitate others, but the seeds of this identification are laid down by the first imitative stage.

Margaret Mead described several different tribes, and their ways of socialising the children. Many of these were completely different, and show, perhaps, just how much sex-roles *are* learned, and may produce completely different societies.

Perhaps the most extreme example of this is among the Tchambuli tribe of New Guinea, in whom the sex-roles which we are used to are completely changed around. The women do the work, make all the major decisions, and control the households, while the men are not regarded as sensible enough to do any practical work, and busy themselves painting, shopping, carving, and dancing. Women are regarded as being strong and capable, involved in serious work. Men are regarded as being fretful, and irresponsible – they wear jewellery and ornaments, and they spend much time gossiping and quarrelling.

From the beginning this difference is expected of the children – in much the same way as the opposite differences are expected in our society – and, by the age of ten or eleven, the little girls are very different from the boys. They are more enterprising and alert, while the boys are timid and unable to concentrate on things.

In the Arapesh tribe, which I mentioned at the beginning of this chapter, the sex-roles are also different from the ones we find in our society, although they aren't as extreme as the Tchambuli. In the Arapesh, *both* sexes are gentle and co-operative, the males taking as much share in child-raising as the females. The kind of differences which we expect between men and women do not show up – the differences appear to lie only in the state of child-birth – and even here the father is considered as involved as the mother.

Among the Iatmul tribe, children of both sexes are brought up together and no differences are drawn until the early teens. Boys will look after children, play with the cooking pots, and go to mourning ceremonies (reserved for women only) with the women and girl children. When they reach their early teens, however, they are withdrawn from women's society, and are ceremonially initiated into manhood, after which they must associate with the men until they marry. So it is the ceremony of initiation which sets the boys apart, not the earlier upbringing.

As we can see from these studies, human beings are capable of a wide variety of different sex-role behaviour. In our own society, children learn the sex-roles expected of them in many different ways – through their parents' behaviour, through television, through the different toys which boys and girls have to play with (for example, boys' dolls tend to have uniforms and military equipment, while girls' dolls have fashions, and occasionally sports clothes or nursing outfits), through children's books, and many more. From the moment a girl baby is dressed in pink, while a boy baby is dressed in blue, our society says to the child 'you are a girl' (or a boy).

A study by Lloyd et al (1981) involved asking mothers to look after a one-month-old baby for a period of ten minutes. The infant was dressed either as a baby boy or as a baby girl – although the same infant was used on each occasion. Lloyd et al found that mothers treated the infant quite differently, depending on which sex they thought it was. If they thought it was a boy, they would play very actively with it, bouncing it up and down and handing it 'active' toys, like a rubber hammer. If they thought it was a girl, they would encourage it to be passive and inactive, talking soothingly to it, telling it how pretty it was and handing it soft, furry toys.

Identification As it grows up, then, the child is continually presented with models which it can imitate, and which provide information about the sex-role appropriate for it to play. Gradually, it comes to *identify* with its own sex, and to adopt that kind of behaviour. Also, of course, if a child shows the 'right' kind of behaviour, it is often rewarded by approval from its parents, or by getting an appropriate kind of response from another person. So gradually, more and more of the 'right' kind of behaviour is shown by the child, and in this way, too, it learns to behave in the way considered appropriate for its sex. By this process, known as 'operant conditioning' (we'll be discussing this more in Chapter 18), a child may learn the 'right' sex-role behaviour, even if it doesn't have a model present, as might be the case of a boy in a household without a father. In our society, through television and other media (books, films), there are plenty of 'models' from which a child may learn, as they learned in the Bandura and Walters experiments (p. 81).

This isn't to say that there are *no* differences between the sexes in their childhood behaviour. Young boys do tend to engage in more physical, rough-and-tumble play than girls, while young girls tend to be more advanced in learning and using language. Perhaps as a result of this, in our society young girls tend to do better at junior school than boys. But, for each kind of sex-typed behaviour like this, there will always be exceptions. There will be girls who enjoy rough-and-tumble play, and there will be boys who enjoy and are good at language. When we talk about these kind of differences, we are talking in *general* terms, not laying down hard and fast rules which all children will obey.

In the last century, Sigmund Freud developed a completely

different theory of how children come to identify with the appropriate sex-role. We will be looking at Freud's theory more closely in Chapter 7.

Status envy   Some psychologists have said that sex-role learning can be connected with 'status envy'. Status envy is when someone is envied – and therefore imitated – as a result of the things that they own or control. An experiment by Bandura, Ross and Ross in 1963 was set up to demonstrate that status envy may result in children imitating the person who had control over the things which were wanted. The children watched a film which showed two adults together. One of these adults had a large number of expensive and complicated toys, which the other adult seemed to want. The one who had the toys gave some of them to the other adult. After this, both adults played with the toys, but behaved quite differently.

The children who saw the film were observed, to see which adult they copied. If they were only interested in who had the toys, then, Bandura and the others thought, they would copy both adults equally, since, in the end, both adults had the toys. However, the children copied far more of the behaviour shown by the adult who 'owned' the toys, than the behaviour shown by the other adult. So the experimenters argued, from this, that it was the *control* over the resources which was important to the children – they were demonstrating how *status envy* may lead to imitation.

J. Whiting has suggested that it is the same process which leads to sex-role learning in children. He suggests that, as the child grows up, it sees its father having control over a valuable resource – the mother. As a consequence of this, the young boy imitates the father more, and so learns eventually to *identify* with the father. The child learns its sex-role as a result of status envy.

There are several problems with this argument. The first one, and perhaps the most obvious one, is that it doesn't explain why little girls, too, don't grow up to identify with their fathers; after all, they grow up in the same family, and see the same things happening. Another problem is that this kind of argument implies that, in a family where the father *doesn't* have control over the mother – where she is more independent, for instance, or where there isn't a father – then the little boys would not grow up identifying with the male sex. Although this is a popular myth (that homosexuals have domineering mothers, for instance), it has repeatedly been shown to *be* a myth. Children from homes where the mother is independent, or where the father is gentle and sensitive rather than domineering, are just as likely to grow up secure in their sexual identity as children from homes with more 'dominant' fathers.

The third argument against this theory is that it doesn't explain Margaret Mead's findings in New Guinea. In many of the tribes she studied, it was the *women* who were envied, for their control of a vital resource – child-bearing. Little girls grew up secure in the knowledge that they, too, would one day have a baby; while the little boys were much more uncertain about their place in the whole scheme of things. And yet most of these tribes (the Tchambuli being the exception) had the kind of sex-role behaviour where the women were responsible for child-rearing and preparing food, and the men were responsible for hunting and fishing. So, in these cases, it certainly can't be status envy on the part of the boys that leads them to identify themselves as male, since child-birth is the envied thing! Rather, it seems to arise from their imitating other males in their society, and being *rewarded* (by praise, or smiles), for doing so.

In this last section, I have talked quite a lot about *social learning* – the way that children gradually learn behaviour appropriate for their society. This is a dual process, which begins with *imitation*, and then, gradually, (perhaps as a result of approval) becomes more deeply engrained, and turns into *identification*. The differences between these two are important ones. When a child imitates another, it is copying an *act* – something that another person has done. But when it comes to *identify* with another, then the process is deeper and more personal. It is saying to itself: '*I* am like that person', so instead of simply copying what that person does, it feels itself to *be* like that person – the similarities have become a part of the child's own *self-image*.

There is another, extremely important way that children (and young animals) learn, while they are growing up. It's called *play*. We will look more closely at this in the next chapter.

Summary

1 All over the world, children are brought up very differently. These differences seem to lead to strong differences in the adults of a society, too.

2 In our society, we can identify four main *styles* of child-rearing and discipline: Authoritarian, Democratic, Permissive, and Laissez-faire. Each approach seems to produce different results in children.

3 Independence and achievement motivation have much to do with parents' expectations, and the rewards which parents give children.

4 Punishment may be physical or psychological. Psychological punishment seems to produce children with stronger consciences than physical punishment does.

5 Aggression seems to result from the use of physical punishment by parents, by providing a model for aggressive behaviour.

6 Sex-roles are not always the same in different societies, and seem to be learned by *modelling*, and later, by *identification* with others of the same sex.

7 Imitation and identification form the basis of the social-learning approach to child development.

Chapter 6

Play

What is play? Although many psychologists have tried to define play, it isn't an easy thing to define. Like so many other things which we study in psychology, we all know quite well what we mean by 'play', yet if we try to produce a definition of it, we get tangled up because the definition doesn't include everything that should be included, or because it includes things which we don't normally see as 'playing'. We tend to think of play as being an activity which happens simply because it's enjoyable, and for no particular purpose; but at the same time play represents an important method by which a young child learns skills and abilities which will be needed for later life.

Playing is a kind of activity which seems to occur only in mammals. While we can often see young mammals playing – kittens, lambs, young monkeys, dolphins etc – we don't tend to see it in young lizards or young fish. Part of the reason for this lies in the evolution of the nervous system, which we'll be looking at more closely in Chapter 15. Essentially, there is a particular part of the brain – the limbic system – which seems to control play, and those animals which evolved earlier don't seem to have a limbic system. Both the limbic system and play itself appear to be later evolutionary developments, which is why only mammals seem to play.

What is it, then, about play which makes it special? Well, for one thing, play seems to allow young mammals to practise actions and skills that they will need in adult life, but in such a way that they don't come to any harm if things go wrong and they haven't mastered the skill properly. If we take this view of play, we can see why it would evolve in creatures higher up the phylogenetic scale – if you're going to rely more on learning than on innate behaviour patterns, then you also need a way in which you can *practise* that learning safely. If the young cat first tries to pounce on something only when it is actually needing food, then it will get very hungry in the first few weeks! But if, while it's still a kitten being fed by its mother, it practises pouncing and other related skills, then by the time it's older and needs to fend for itself it will be able to manage relatively easily.

In many ways, children's play serves the same kind of

purpose. By practising and acting out features of its world, the young child gradually develops its abilities and its understanding of the world around it. This might be an understanding of the social world, by exploring possibilities through imagination, acting out social roles or taking turns with other children; of the physical world by playing with toys or developing physical skills; or of the cognitive world, by playing word-games or knowledge quizzes. Many children's games are very old: children played marbles in ancient Egypt, and 'hide and seek' in ancient Greece, while 'Tug of war' and 'hopscotch' were popular games with Roman children 2000 years ago. More adult-centred games, like tennis and hockey, were beginning to emerge in a basic form from the seventeenth century onwards, so were playing cards and dominoes, and it seems likely that these simply replaced older, similar games rather than forming a new kind of activity.

In 1969, I. and P. Opie investigated children's playground games by going round the country visiting children and asking them about the games that they played. They were particularly interested in playground games because these tend to be passed on from child to child, without adult intervention, and often such games are very old indeed. The Opies concluded that the playing of games was an important way in which children learn about the outside world and experience many of life's emotions. They also benefit the child socially, because games bring children together in an organised way, and help them to see the value of rules and structure in social interaction.

The development of play

Piaget (1952) saw play as falling into three main categories, each of which was more common during a particular stage of development. (We will be looking at Piaget's stages of development in more detail in Chapter 8.) Broadly speaking, these stages represented steps in the development of the child's thinking, and each step reflects the growing sophistication of the child as it develops its experience of the world. But these stages are also reflected in Piaget's ideas about the child's ideas of right and wrong, which we will be looking at in the section on moral development; and in the type of play in which the child engages.

This first of Piaget's stages is the sensori-motor period, from birth to two years, in which the child is mainly concerned with physical development and learning to make sense of the information it is receiving through its senses. So the kind of play in which the child engages during this time reflects this: it is play in which the child is practising skills. These are mainly physical skills, such as manipulating objects, or climbing on furniture; but the child will also be practising and exploring sounds, tastes and other features of the environment. Piaget referred to this as *mastery play*, because he saw the overall purpose of such play as the child learning to 'master' its environment, so that it could control its actions and operate effectively within its world.

The second of Piaget's stages is the pre-operational period, from two to seven years (approximately), in which the child is learning basic information about the world and how it works. During this time, Piaget said, the child mainly engages in *symbolic*, or *make-believe play*. This type of play involves children acting out imaginary situations, like playing at being different people that they have encountered, or making up stories and acting them out. Objects are sometimes used to represent something else – so for instance, a hairbrush might be used to represent a pet hedgehog, or something else that the child has encountered.

The third stage, the concrete operational period (from about seven to eleven years), involves the child developing *rule-bound play*. This is play in which there are definite rules, some of which are learned from other children, as in playground games like marbles or hopscotch; and some of which are learned from adults or older children, like card games or organised sports. According to Piaget, this form of play marks the development of full social participation on the part of the child. The previous forms of play were all fairly individualistic, involving only a slight amount of co-operation on the part of the child, but rule-bound play involves the recognition of general social concepts like 'fairness' and taking turns.

When the child first begins to learn this kind of play, it sees rules as being absolute and strict; but as it develops, it gradually realises that rules don't necessarily have to be rigid as long as they are fair to everybody. Piaget's view of how the child develops this kind of approach is closely tied in with his idea of the child's moral development, which progresses from a simplistic, 'black and white' view of right and wrong, to one which can take into account different factors and people's intentions.

One of the ways that Piaget studied children's ideas on play with rules was through the game of marbles. Piaget considered marbles to be a bit special, because it's a game that children learn from each other, and which they are very rarely taught by adults. By asking children of different ages to play marbles with him, and seeing how they explained the rules of the game, Piaget was able to get an insight into the child's ideas about games with rules; and by looking at how strictly they put the rules into practice, and how they reacted to cheating, he could get an idea of how their views changed with time.

Other researchers also investigated children's play, and many of them developed their own sets of categories of different types of playing. Sylva *et al* (1980) performed a series of naturalistic observations of 120 children in an Oxfordshire playgroup. Each child was observed for two 20 minute sessions, and the activities of each child were recorded. She made a broad distinction between *challenging play* and *simple play* (or *passive play*). Challenging play was play in which the child had to try to do something – to achieve some kind of new goal. Simple play, on the other hand, was play in which the child was simply engaging in actions or tasks which were well-known and easy, and which didn't present any particular kind of challenge. From her observations, Sylva developed four categories of play:

1 **Simple play**

   This was defined as play for its own sake, play which passed the time away, and which was undertaken in a passive, rather than an active, manner (e.g. building a tower unselectively, just using the first lego bricks which came to hand; or just riding a bike round and round with no particular goal.)

2 **Complex play**

   This was constructive, active play which had a well-defined target, e.g. selecting appropriately coloured lego bricks, or building a specifically shaped tower or building. Problem-solving play, like solving unfamiliar jigsaw puzzles or matching shapes, would also fit into this category.

3 **Practice play**

   Sylva defined this as being play which was preparation for adulthood, involving such things as the perfection of small or gross motor skills, from pulling faces to clambering on trees, playground apparatus or furniture. This type of play could be seen as being comparable with the 'playfighting' of kittens or other hunting animals, or the way in which the young of many species practise running fast or climbing. It provides them with skills which they will need as they grow older, because they are important for the survival of the species.

4 **Symbolic or make-believe play**

   This is play in which anything can be taken as symbolic of something else: a cardboard box becomes a house or a boat, or a corner of the room becomes a monster's lair. This type of play, Syvla thought, is strongly connected with a belief in magic, and the child's growing awareness of real and imaginary ways to deal with the world. Make-believe play also provides the child with scope for the development of social skills, because it leads to improvement in the child's vocalisation as it explains things to the others playing the game; and it includes a high level of social interaction if more than one child is playing.

Sylva saw these types of play as following a definite sequence in terms of the child's development. The main function of simple play, she argued, was for the child to release energies and tensions, and for sheer pleasure, whereas the more challenging forms of play served valuable developmental functions by allowing the child to practise skills and abilities. Sylva concluded that play needed to be directed towards more complex forms by others, in order for the child to learn most effectively. Just allowing the child to learn on its own through experimentation wasn't enough, because the child wouldn't be able to set itself the right kind of challenges.

With this idea, Sylva was challenging the orthodox Piagetian approach, which took the view that children would progress naturally through the different forms of play, and learn all that was necessary through their interaction with the environment. Piaget hadn't really thought that social influence was all that important, but Sylva argued that some type of social influence, and in particular guidance and the provision of challenges from adults, was necessary if the child was to develop its potential as fully as possible.

There have been many other systems for categorising the different types of play in which children engage. They have mainly been developed from observational studies in playgroups and nurseries, of groups of children of the same age, playing with or without toys. But for many children, most of their play is with siblings (brother or sisters) who may be much older or younger, and with their parents in the family home. It is only recently that researchers have started to investigate how families play together.

Cohen (1987) published a study of family play, which showed how one important milestone in family play was the point where the children could recognise the signal that what was about to follow was 'play', and therefore 'not for real'. One important sign for this is the *play face* – a special set of facial expressions which adults and children adopt when they are about to start playing. In fact, Bateson (1956) found that young monkeys and chimpanzees do this too; and argued that it was a crucial element for family play; and Bruner (1975) found that children can learn to recognise the signal even when they are very young, playing 'peekaboo' with their mothers.

Cohen found that from about a year old, his children were able to give their own 'play' signals, and he saw this as the beginning of conscious playing on the part of the child. But there can be many factors which affect the age at which this happens for any individual – for instance, older children will often encourage their younger siblings to begin playing, which could mean that they learn to initiate play earlier than single children do.

Types of play   There are many different activities which can come into the general category of 'play'. Among these are: physical play, play with objects, pretending, playing with others, and playing with words. We will look at each of these in turn, and at some of the main findings which researchers on play have come up with.

Physical play   This is the type of play which involves motion and action, and which is concerned with developing and perfecting physical skills. Physical play can happen at all sorts of levels – an adult who plays darts or pool in the local pub is engaging in physical play just as much as a toddler who is clambering on the furniture in the family living-room. The type of play concerned with developing motor skills is very similar to that shown by other mammals: the child practises things – like jumping, skipping, swinging on a bar, standing very still – until it is good at them. As it gets better at managing the games, the games themselves become more complex: simple chasing games become converted into games where you are only 'safe' if you are off the ground; learning to skip a rope becomes converted into an elaborate team game, with chanted songs and special steps. In this way, there is continual challenge and interest for the child, and the level of the game reflects the child's own stage of development of motor skills.

Even infants seem to derive a great deal of enjoyment from physical actions: Piaget (1952) described a baby which seemed to obtain enormous enjoyment simply from repeatedly throwing its head back, and then bringing it forward again, laughing as it did so. Babies often enjoy exploring the sensations of movement, and Piaget tied this in with his category of mastery play which we looked at earlier: they were enjoying the experience, and at the same time learning physical control.

As we get older, our physical skills become more sophisticated with practice. Among other skills, most children learn to do hand-stands and somersaults; to bounce and balance effectively, and sometimes to perform quite complicated sequences of action on climbing-frames and other apparatus. These are sometimes developed further through physical education in school; but many of them seem to be learned just for the fun of it – it seems to be personally satisfying to learn a new physical skill. Many children's toys encourage the development of physical skills, such as tricycles, bikes, and even musical instruments which require the co-ordination of different actions to produce a tune. In the later years of childhood, of course, this type of play often becomes structured into organised sports with definite rules, like tennis or football.

The development of physical skills and competences is important, both for the child's general health (the young of all species seem to need far more exercise than adults, probably to encourage muscle development and overall fitness); and also, according to some researchers, for its value in extending the child's experience and so encouraging *cognitive development*. Indeed, Piaget (1952) argued that it is only through performing operations on its environment – doing things with it – that the child obtains the basis for all its thinking, so without physical experience cognitive development couldn't happen at all!

Play with objects Exploring and playing with everyday objects or toys is something which begins very early in the child's life. Lowe (1975) performed a series of observations of children playing with objects at different ages, and found that there was a gradual progression in the way that the child dealt with them. The table summarises some of the main points of Lowe's findings:

Age of child	Activity
9 months	The child grasps objects and brings them to the mouth. Also waves things, inspects them and bangs them about.
12 months	The child looks carefully at things before mouthing, waving or banging them about; may 'practise' with familiar objects, e.g. putting a spoon in its mouth.
15 months	Objects are carefully inspected and familiar ones are put to their everyday, conventional use, e.g. 'pretend' drinking from a cup, or pushing a truck backwards and forwards.
21 months	The child now uses objects together, e.g. 'feeding' a doll from a toy bowl, or looking for a small toy to act as a passenger in a toy train.
24 months	The child's play with objects is becoming increasingly realistic, mirroring everyday life, like changing a doll's nappy, or driving toy cars along marked-out 'roads'.
30–36 months	The child begins to get toys to 'act' for themselves: a doll may drive a train, or put the other toys to bed; a toy car may be driven with realistic noises and other effects.

We can see from this table that as the child grows older it becomes more sophisticated in how it deals with its toys. One reason for this is physical: the development of *motor skills*. As the child grows, it comes to have better co-ordination and can grasp objects and manipulate them less clumsily. Each new type of object presents a new physical challenge for the child: for instance, putting a toy train set together involves being able to tackle quite an elaborate series of actions.

Exploration is another important aspect of playing with objects: children learn about things in their world, and what they can and can't do. Most importantly, perhaps, children learn how they themselves can produce effects by doing things to or with objects: the most popular toys tend to be those which respond or are changed when the child does something, and young children take great delight in making things spin round, move or make noises.

Hutt (1966) conducted a series of studies involving a 'supertoy', which was a wooden box with wheels, buzzers, bells, counters, pedals, and levers. Playing with the levers and pedals would produce one of several outcomes: either the bell or buzzer, or both, could sound; and the counters might be covered up or visible. In a study of three to five year olds playing with the box, Hutt found that if the 'supertoy' was set up to produce the maximum effect from the child's actions, so that the counters, bells and buzzers all went off at once, then children would play with it for much longer than if it only had one or two of these happening at a time.

Hutt also observed a number of two to three year old children playing individually with the box, and compared how much exploratory play and passive (non-exploratory) play they engaged in. Four years later, the same children were seen again, and it emerged that those who had been more concerned with exploring the 'supertoy' were generally more confident and more social than those children who didn't explore it. The exploratory children also had higher IQ levels overall. Hutt concluded that exploratory play was strongly linked with both mental and emotional development in children.

Exploring objects and becoming familiar with them seems to be an important aspect of play, as many parents have found when their toddler seems to be unable to keep its hands off everything in the kitchen! But through playing with things the child learns about the different properties of things and what they can and can't do. From a set of observations of children's play reported in 1977, Garvey described what happened when a three year old boy noticed a large wooden car for the first time:

1 The boy stopped, looked at the car and touched it.

2 He turned the steering wheel, felt the licence plate, looked for a horn, and climbed on it.

3 He then played with the car by putting things on it, such as plates or telephones, and taking them off again.

4 He then climbed into the car and drove it round and round, making engine and horn noises.

Garvey saw this sequence as illustrating four different stages in playing with objects. The first stage involved the *exploration* of the new toy. The child then moved on to *manipulation* of the object, seeing what it could do. From there, the third stage was of *practice* – trying out ideas to see what would happen. And the final stage was of *repetition* – driving the car round and round, but also developing the experience by adding elements from the imagination, such as the car noises. By the time a child reaches the fourth stage, the object has become known, and its possibilities can be drawn on later if necessary.

Another thing that happens is that the child is developing *cognitively*, by thinking about and planning the play. Rehearsing events that happen in real life, like nappy-changing, allows the child to develop its own understanding of what exactly is going on, which can be important for the child's developing sense of control over its environment. The forms of playing with objects which appear often show quite a sophisticated understanding of the requirements of everyday activities.

Pretend play Playing with objects can also be stimulating to a child's *imagination* – missing items from an action are often supplied by imaginary ones, like brushing a doll's hair with an imaginary brush, or 'pretending' that a particular corner of a room is a garage for the toy cars. As the child plays with different objects it comes to understand their possibilities better, and can explore alternative possibilities in how different toys can be used together. So, for instance, a child's handkerchief may at various times become a blanket, a tent for a small toy, a tarpaulin for a truck, or a nappy. Being able to use imagination in how objects are used could provide a foundation for the development of creative thinking in later life.

Fein, in 1975, studied how children use their imagination to 'transform' one object into another for the purposes of play. She tested 48 children, all about two years old, and asked them to perform specific play tasks using the toys provided. The toys were a toy stuffed horse, a plastic egg-cup, a flat metal horse-shape, and a shell. Fein considered that the metal shape and the shell, being more abstract, would require the children to use more imagination, or more 'transformational steps' if it was to be treated as if it were the 'real thing'.

The children were asked to 'feed' the stuffed horse or the horse-shape, using either the egg-cup or the shell. She found that the children could do this with the stuffed horse and the egg-cup quite easily. Most of the children could also do it using either the horse-shape or the shell. But very few of the children were able to 'feed' the horse-shape using the shell – it seemed that when both the toys involved were unrealistic, two-year olds were not able to perform the necessary transformations.

Cohen (1987) criticised these studies, arguing that the tasks involved were not like normal play, because it was the psychologist who was telling the child what to do, whereas normal play is invented and developed by the child. He also argued that it was unrealistic to judge a child's 'performance' on whether it could perform a feat of 'pretence' which didn't make much sense anyway. Often, such studies seemed to imply that the child was in some way inadequate, when really it was only being sensible and applying its knowledge of the world to the situation.

Golomb (1977) performed a set of similar studies to those in Fein's experiments, asking children to perform 'pretend' actions with 'right' and 'wrong' toys. Unlike most other experimenters, though, Golomb noted what the children said about the tasks as they were doing them. These comments often showed that the children were deeply concerned about what they were being asked to do, because the task didn't fit in with what they knew was right – like the little girl who objected on being asked to 'feed' a baby doll with a pencil, because she knew that pencils were poisonous. Golomb showed that children who had seemed to be making 'wrong' choices according to the standard psychological view of imaginary play were not incapable or being silly, but feeling unhappy about what they were being asked to do.

From Golomb's study and other evidence, Cohen argued that much of the experimental work on children's play simply doesn't take enough account of how the child understands the situation. (We will see in Chapter 8 that this has also been a problem for studies of children's *cognitive development*). Cohen pointed out that in these cases it is often the psychologists who seem to be using rather peculiar standards: 'Can you pretend an apple is a car? Top marks. Do you refuse to feed your teddy detergent? You must be backward.' (*The Development of Play*, D. Cohen 1987)

Playing with others Social play can take a number of different forms, but in general, it tends to be of three main types: free play, which is worked out by the participating children themselves as they go along; formal play, which has rules or clearly-defined patterns of behaviour, such as skipping games or card games; and creative play, which involves inventing new circumstances (like imaginary companions or environments) using known rules and symbols.

A study by Garvey, in 1977, showed that when pre-school children were left to play with a playmate of the same age, they would frequently engage in some kind of *dramatic play*, which involved familiar scenes and stories. Often, these games involved playing out family roles: younger children (about three years of age) tended to play games which involved mothers taking care of babies; while older children (four and five years old) were more likely to play games which reflected their growing awareness of the wider world, like husband-wife or doctor-nurse games. Sometimes, too, the children would act out fairy stories or fantasy roles, and Garvey noticed that in these, the older children were likely to take on the role of 'hero' or 'defender', whereas the younger children often adopted the role of 'victim'. Again, this might be connected with the child's growing knowledge and confidence in dealing with its world.

Parten (1933) performed a series of observations of pre-school children playing, which involved 42 nursery school children between two and four-and-a-half years, each observed for 60 one-minute sessions. In general, she found that the older the child, the more complex the play. Altogether, Parten identified five stages, or types of play which pre-school children showed:

1 *Solitary play*, in which the child seems to be completely unaware of other children, and plays entirely alone.

2 *Onlooker play*, in which the child doesn't actually play with other children, but watches what they are doing, and may sometimes react to their actions in some way.

3 *Parallel play*, in which two children may perform the same kind of actions with similar toys, often side-by-side; but they don't actually interact directly with one another.

4 *Associative play*, which occurs when two or more children do interact with one another, either by speaking or by sharing

toys and materials; but they don't share the play itself – each of them will be playing a different game.

5 *Co-operative play*, which involves playing directly with other children at the same game or task – possibly helping one another or taking it in turns.

Parten found that onlooker play seemed to be the usual form of play for two year olds, while five year olds mainly engaged in associative and co-operative play. It seems that this can have something to do with the child's previous experiences as well – Rubin, Maioni and Hornung (1976) found that the amount of experience that a child has had with other children in the early years would affect whether they engaged in associative and co-operative play at ages three and four – those who had more contact with others were more likely to adopt more social forms of playing.

More recently, some researchers have begun to question how far this type of approach to social play really takes into account what children are like. Their concerns centre round two closely-linked areas: firstly, just how far studies of playgroups and nursery groups do actually show what kind of play a child is capable of; and whether social play in fact takes place much earlier – possibly even from a few months old.

Many researchers who have looked at children playing in playgroups have found that social play seems to develop quite late: a study by Ross and Goldman (1977) found that only a third of two year olds could play 'turn-taking' games properly. But Bronson (1972) argued that the reason for this type of finding could easily be because most children engage in social play with older people, who they knew well because they were members of the same family, but the children that they met in the playgroup were relative strangers, so perhaps it wasn't surprising that young children didn't interact much with them.

The model of social play developing later in childhood is based around Piaget's idea that infants are completely *egocentric*, and that egocentricity gradually becomes less and less as the child grows older. (This idea is explained in rather more detail in Chapter 8). As a result, the young child is seen to be incapable of recognising other children as independent people with their own viewpoints, and it is thought that this means that they are not able to engage in truly social play until their egocentricity has reduced enough for this to happen.

However, there is a considerable amount of research which has been performed on sociability in infants, some of which we looked at in Chapter 3, when we saw how mother–infant interaction is important in the development of attachment.

Bruner (1983) discussed the role of the game of 'peek-a-boo', which mothers (and other people) play with quite young infants, to the child's evident delight. Bruner sees this game as forming an important basis for social interaction, with its structured form and scope for questions and responses. Bruner also showed how mothers adjust the game so that the child can grasp it more easily, and encourage a *handover* of the game at round about nine months of age, when the child tends to take over the game instead of simply responding when the mother plays it. If the child was egocentric, in the way that Piaget thought, then this type of social play between parents and children, or between children and their older brothers and sisters, wouldn't be possible – yet it happens.

Children in playgroups, really, are in quite an artificial situation: instead of playing with older, well-known people, as happens in the home, the children are placed with a number of other children of a similar age, whom they may or may not know but in any case don't live with. Consequently, they are less inclined to engage in social interaction, and it is only when they become older and more socially confident that social play begins. A young child who never engages in social play in the playgroup, though, may be a sociable and dynamic participant in social play in its own home with members of its own family.

In fact, there is surprisingly little psychological research on social play in the family, although this does seem to be the place where most social play goes on. Valentine (1942) described the play which went on in his own family, with their five children, using a 'diary method' of recording incidents day-by-day as they happened. On one occasion, he reported how a child of five months was fascinated by a game which involved Valentine lightly covering the infant with an eiderdown which the infant would then knock away. Valentine reports that this carried on for 100 turns, until he himself became tired of the game. He also noted that the enjoyable feature for the child in this type of elementary social play was the way that the adult and child were interacting, and that the child will carry it on for as long as possible – it's almost always the adult who becomes tired of this type of game first, as many parents will know!

Piaget also described many instances of interaction and social play with his own children, but seemed to ignore the social aspect of what was going on, largely focusing on the way that the child was developing its own understanding and skills instead. However, some modern psychologists are beginning to look at this area too: Cohen (1987) also used a diary method for recording the play that went on in his own family, and pointed out that playful episodes were equally likely to be

initiated by the child, either parent, or another child in the
family, from the time that the child was about two years old.
It does seem as though the emphasis on Piagetian ideas of
egocentricity has meant that we have ignored a very interesting
and important part of children's play – social play in the family.

Playing with words   Another kind of play which children use is language play.
Infants babble in the cot, practising sounds. As they make a
single noise over and over again, they are exploring that sound;
and as they do this they are becoming more and more skilled
at making it. As the child gradually acquires language it uses
this knowledge of the different sounds it has built up, and the
child starts to play with words.

Children who have just learned to talk tend to talk a great
deal to themselves, while they are playing and as part of their
play. Because this doesn't seem to have anything to do with
other people, it has become known as *egocentric speech*. By using
egocentric speech to plan what they are doing and express
themselves, children can practise their language use – if you
listen to a child playing like this you will often find that it is
using quite sophisticated expressions and tones of voice as it
talks, and often 'acts out' in speech the different ideas that it
is expressing.

Although this does serve partly as a rehearsal for
communication with others later on, Vygotsky (1962) saw this
as being much more to do with the child's internal cognitive
processes. Egocentric speech eventually becomes the personal
'inner speech' that we each use to ourselves in our thoughts,
in which ideas are highly condensed, and words are used as
symbols for our thinking in such a way that one word may
contain a great deal of meaning and associations. Many adults
revert to thinking 'out loud' when they have a lot on their
minds, and Vygotsky thought that expressing ideas out loud
was one way for the child to understand them more clearly.

Children often spend a considerable amount of time playing
word-games and exploring the other characteristics of
language, such as rhymes and odd sounds. We will be looking
at this in more detail in Chapter 11; but it seems clear that
by doing this they are extending and developing their skills
with language, just as much as physical play helps them to
develop strong muscles and healthy bodies. Playing with words
can take many forms, ranging from simply exploring the sounds
of words by repeating them over and over again, to chanting
rhymes, to producing highly sophisticated jokes and puns
based on double meanings, but many children seem to become
fascinated by language and the way that it can be used in so
many ways.

Play therapy   As a child engages in make-believe or 'pretend' play, it will often be acting out those problems and ideas that are concerning it most deeply at the time. Sometimes, as many parents know, the child's understanding of social roles and what is going on comes out very clearly in their play: many parents and teachers of small children get quite a shock when they hear their children acting the roles of 'mother' or 'teacher', and recognise their own mannerisms or expressions! By doing this, children practise and test out their knowledge of everyday events and other people's behaviour. Make-believe play is an important way for the child to develop its understanding of the world.

Very often in make-believe play the child will also express its own real-life worries or problems; and sometimes by doing this it can work out solutions, or help them a bit. The way that children do this is what lies behind the technique known as *play therapy*, because when children are disturbed or distressed by something going on around them, they often don't talk to adults about it – possibly because the problem has been caused by another adult, or because they feel that they wouldn't be able to explain it properly anyway. But if a trained psychologist or psychotherapist allows the child to play freely, while observing the play carefully, they can often become aware of what the problem is.

For instance, many child psychologists and psychotherapists have to deal with children who may have been sexually abused. By allowing them free play with dolls, they can often get a clear idea as to whether the child has had such experiences or not, because the kinds of play that a sexually abused child acts out with a set of dolls is very different from that of a child which has never been sexually abused. Also, by observing the play, a trained therapist can get an idea of what kind of emotional damage the child has suffered, which will show what kinds of therapy are likely to help the child most.

Play therapy is useful in other kinds of child disturbance too. In 1971, Axline reported on the way that play therapy had helped a small boy, known as Dibs, who was very unco-operative and a problem at school. During the play therapy sessions with Axline, the child repeatedly buried a male doll from the doll's house head-down in a sandbox. By doing this, Dibs was expressing the hostility he felt towards his father, who was very intolerant of the child. As Dibs managed to express his feelings like this, he gradually became able to overcome his mixed-up emotions about his family, and learned to relate to them more positively. (Of course, we all affect other people by our behaviour, and as Dibs changed, his parents did as well, and became more caring towards him. This was an important part of the therapy too – but an indirect result of it.) Eventually, the problems in the family were resolved, and from being a highly disturbed, disruptive child, Dibs became much more relaxed, and his whole home set-up became easier.

Playing, then, is a vital form of learning for the developing child. It doesn't really matter whether the child plays with specially-designed toys, or with small copies of the tools used by adults, as happens in many other cultures of the world. What matters is that the child is able to imitate and to practise skills and the social roles which it encounters in its society, so that it will be able to develop proficiency in them for when it grows up; and so that it can develop a store of useful skills (in actions or in words) which it can draw on if it needs to. In the next chapter we will look at some other approaches to understanding child development which have been put forward by psychologists.

Summary

1 Piaget classified play into three main types: mastery play, symbolic play and rule-bound play.

2 Sylva saw social influences as being very important in play, particularly if it provided challenges for the child.

3 From infancy through to adulthood people engage in physical play, which becomes more complex as basic skills are mastered.

4 Exploring and playing with objects is also important in the child's developing understanding of the world.

5 Pretending allows the child to develop its world-knowledge, while playing with others encourages social skills, and may occur from very early on within the family.

6 Many children enjoy playing with words and sounds, and language games help the child to develop its communicative skills, which egocentric speech may help it in planning and thinking.

7 Play therapy is often used to help disturbed children, because play can provide an insight into a child's problems even if it is reluctant to talk to others about them.

Chapter 7 **Some theories of child development**

In Chapter 5 we looked at the ways in which parents can influence their children's development, by encouraging some kinds of behaviour and by punishing others. Also, the way that parents can provide a _model_ for children to imitate was included. This kind of approach to child development is known as the _social-learning_ approach – it tries to explain the way that children develop through the kind of society that they grow up in, and the way that some types of behaviour are influenced by social interaction.

There are other ways of looking at child development. Some of them will be dealt with in this chapter, while others won't be looked at until later on in the book; for instance we will look at the stimulus-response approach to development after we've looked at stimulus-response theories of learning, in Chapter 18. Here, I want to examine an approach to child development that has been mentioned before, but not in much detail – the _psychoanalytic_ approach.

The psychoanalytic approach

This approach is quite an old one. It was first started by Sigmund Freud towards the end of the last century. Freud was mainly interested in mental illness, the kinds of disorders that we would call 'neurotic' nowadays. He had developed a technique of 'free-association': he would ask his patients simply to describe whatever came into their heads at the time that they were talking, no matter how silly it might seem. By doing this, many of his patients revealed memories from their childhood, which had disturbed them a great deal at the time, and which had resulted, in the end, in their neurotic adult behaviour. (For example, someone who was afraid of mice might have been very frightened by one as a child. Although they did not remember the childhood event, the fear would have stayed with them, even when they were adults. Freud's 'free-association' method would encourage them to remember this frightening event in their past, and so they would 'come to terms' with their fear, and not be so frightened of mice any more.)

By working in this way with his patients, Freud found that many of them had similar kinds of memories of their childhoods. From these memories, he developed a theory of child development, in which he described three main stages in a child's development.

Psycho-sexual
stages of
development
Freud considered that the first five years of a child's life was all-important in the way that its personality would develop later on. Unpleasant childhood experiences could leave lasting scars, which would affect how that person would react to new situations and events. He did not think that the later stages of childhood were particularly important in forming personality – by that time, he said, the foundations had already been laid by the child's experiences.

Freud called the first stage of development the *oral stage*. This is when the child's main interest, and its focus for all pleasurable experiences, is its mouth. From birth, Freud said, all satisfaction that an infant receives is through its mouth – it finds sucking and biting intensely pleasant experiences. What is important for child care at this stage, Freud said, is that the child should have plenty of opportunity to suck and to obtain pleasure from oral contacts. If it is deprived of its mother's nipple, or of something else to suck, then later on as an adult it could become orally fixated, always needing to put something in its mouth, fingers, for example, or a cigarette. The way that the child obtained satisfaction from its oral activities could also influence its personality in other ways, Freud said. If it mainly obtained pleasure from nibbling and biting, it could grow up to become a highly aggressive person; while if its main pleasure came from sucking and swallowing, it could become a very gullible kind of person in later life.

Freud developed the concept of *libido*. This is a kind of free-floating sexual energy, which is the source of all pleasure, and even of friendship with other people. During the first stage of development, the child's libido is all focused on its mouth, but as the child grows older, then it gradually shifts to another part of the body. When this happens, the child enters the second of Freud's psycho-sexual stages of development.

The second stage is called the *anal stage*. The child enters this stage from when he is about two years old, and at this point he begins to become very interested in defecation. The child is usually just becoming toilet-trained at this time, and is getting a great deal of pleasure from excreting. Pleasure is now centred around this part of the body. Because of this, Freud said that it was particularly important how parents handled the process of toilet-training their children. If they were too strict, the child might become very frightened of 'letting go' of its faeces, and in later life it would become a mean and grasping person. Freud called this an 'anal retentive' personality. But if they were too tolerant about it, then the child might end up the kind of person who gives away everything that they have, and doesn't keep anything for themselves, which Freud called an 'anal-expulsive' personality.

When the child is about three and a half or four years old, the libido gradually shifts again. From all pleasure being focused on the anal region, the child now starts to derive pleasure from its genitals. During the *phallic stage* pleasure is centred around the genitals. During this stage, the child begins to identify with its parent of the same sex – it adopts its sex role. Freud had very definite ideas about the way that this happened in children, and he said that the development of sex-role identification always had to follow the same course, or the child would grow up 'wrongly'.

The way that the appropriate sex-role was adopted, according to Freud, was through the Oedipus complex. Oedipus was a Greek king of legend, who killed his father and married his mother. (He didn't realise either was his parent at the time, though.) According to Freud, when a small boy enters the genital stage, he becomes very possessive of his mother, and jealous of her affection. He sees his father as being a serious rival for his mother's love. Because the child sees himself as being in competition with his father in this way, he also comes to feel that his father is a threat to him. It is apparent to the boy that his father is very powerful, and has the power to make important decisions for the child. So the child feels himself to be trapped in a dangerous situation. His main rival – his father – is also the powerful man who can control his life.

Because this situation isn't bearable for the child, he copes with it by coming to *identify* with his father. By emphasising the ways that he is *like* his father, the child hopes to make his father friendly towards him, and not hostile. So, in this way, the threat is prevented, and the child develops sex-role identity, by identifying with his father.

Other Freudian theorists saw a similar process happening with girls. When a young girl enters the phallic stage, they said, she becomes aware of the fact that she is lacking a penis. She interprets this as meaning that she has at some point been castrated, and blames her mother for this, when she discovers that her mother, too, doesn't have a penis. But this blame and hostility to her mother is not bearable, because for the four-year-old child the mother is too powerful. So the girl, according to Freud, comes to identify with her mother as a way of successfully coping with the hostility she feels towards her.

Some modern psychoanalysts have said that the concept of

'penis envy' shouldn't be taken literally. They say that it was used as a symbol for the way that women in nineteenth century Vienna led very restricted lives, and had very little power over what they could and couldn't do. According to these theorists, the child's 'penis envy' wasn't real, but was her discovery that she had been born a girl, and so she would have to live a very restricted life. The girl would resent this, and come to blame her mother for it. But other writers think that the Freudians actually meant the idea to be taken literally, as with the Oedipus complex.

Adult personality　Freud also developed a theory about adult personality. Throughout the stages of childhood, he said, the adult personality was gradually developing. The first part of personality, which we are all born with, Freud called the *id*. This was the part, he said, where all the primeval instincts and impulses were; the part concerned with sexual energies, basic desires and needs. He said that adults never lost this part of their personality as they grew older, they just developed ways of coping with it a bit better than they could when they were younger. The id, he said, was totally selfish. It worked on the *pleasure principle* – insisting that any need or desire should be instantly fulfilled.

As the child grew older, Freud said, it became apparent that it couldn't just satisfy any of its needs or desires whenever it wanted to. Reality meant that sometimes the id would have to wait, or even to do without. So a second part of the personality developed, which was more in touch with outside reality. This he called the *ego*. The ego's job was to keep the demands of the id in check, gradually satisfying them whenever possible, but only in a realistic kind of way. If you got very angry with someone, then the demand from your id might be to attack them – but that isn't very realistic, or socially acceptable. So the ego would take over, and find a way that the id's demands could be satisfied, but in a better sort of way – perhaps by making a very sarcastic remark, or something similar. In the same way as the id works on the pleasure principle, the ego works on the *reality principle*.

For the small child, Freud said, the parents are the representations of absolute authority. They represent society and society's demands on the child. They tell it what it ought to be doing, and how it should behave. But, as the child grows older, another part of its personality develops which takes over this function. Freud called this the *super-ego*. In a way, the super-ego is a kind of internal 'parent' – but a very authoritarian one! It's the part of personality which makes demands of duty, and of what society expects, on the person.

In its own way, the super-ego is as unrealistic as the id, and the ego has to make sure that the super-ego's demands are coped with realistically as well. The ego ensures that the individual takes care of herself: the super-ego might, for instance, regard enjoying food as being too greedy, and demand that the person didn't do it at all! So the ego needs to keep unrealistic demands in control, and to maintain a balance between the demands of the id and the demands of the super-ego.

Because Freud saw personality in adults as being about a dynamic balance between these three aspects of personality, his theory is often called a *psycho-dynamic theory*. There would be continual give and take between the id and the super-ego, with the ego acting as a go-between. A psychologist who didn't think much of psychoanalysis once described it as: 'A battle between a sex-crazed monkey and a maiden aunt, being refereed by a rather nervous bank clerk'.

'Little Hans' Most of Freud's work was done with adults, as I mentioned before. But there was one important study that he conducted on a four-year-old boy, known as 'little Hans'. Freud only actually spoke to little Hans once, after the problem had been solved, but Hans' parents were close friends of Freud's and they wrote to him often, describing what Hans had done or said recently. Freud would write back, giving his interpretation of what these things meant. When Hans was four, he developed a phobia: he became frightened of going outdoors because he was frightened of horses, of which the streets were full in those days. Freud became very interested in this, because it gave him a chance to investigate whether his theories about how phobias develop were true.

Hans became afraid that the horses he saw in the street would fall over and make a lot of noise, or that they would bite him. Since the family lived just opposite a large coaching inn, where there were many horses, he refused to go out of the house. This fear developed quite suddenly, and his parents were unable to see what had brought it on. His father talked about it a lot with him, practising the psychoanalytic 'talking cure' method with him, by suggesting possible reasons for things, and seeing if Hans agreed with him.

Gradually, Hans' father and Freud came to some conclusions about the phobia. They thought that Hans was really expressing the conflict brought on by the Oedipus complex, and that he could only really express this through his fear of horses. It was quite clear that Hans was very fond of his mother, and enjoyed being with her. His father and Freud thought his fear of horses represented his fear of his father, and his worry that they would bite him was an expression of the fear that his father would punish him for being a rival for his mother's affection by castrating him. Gradually, Hans' phobia disappeared, until eventually it was completely gone, as he came to accept this interpretation presented by his father. Freud interpreted this as a sign that the boy had successfully resolved his Oedipus complex by identifying with the father, as he had been encouraged to do.

Another interpretation of a part of Hans' phobia was made: during the period when the phobia was going (in that Hans would leave the house but was still frightened), they became aware of the fact that he was very much more frightened of horses drawing large loads – furniture vans or buses (yes, they did have horse-drawn buses!) – than he was of horses that only pulled small carts. Shortly before the phobia started, in fact, Hans had seen a horse drawing a bus fall down and die, which had frightened him considerably.

Hans had a young sister, called Hanna, who had been born when he was about three. Like most children of the time, he had been told that the stork brought her, but he was uncertain about this. Freud interpreted his fear of heavily-loaded carts as an expression of sibling rivalry – the jealousy that a child feels when a younger one comes along and takes up the mother's attention. He equated the heavily-loaded carts with his mother when she was pregnant, Freud said, and that was one reason why they frightened him. He was worried that yet another child would appear, which would be even more competition for him.

Many objections have been made to the Freudian approach to phobias. One of the main ones is the accusation that it is 'taking a sledge-hammer to crack a nut'; that, for instance, Hans' phobia could well have been caused simply by his being so frightened the day he saw the bus-horse fall down; and that it died away as a result of his seeing more and more horses (even though he tried to avoid it), and realising that they weren't so likely to fall over. Also, Hans' father repeatedly assured him that his 'nonsense', as they called the phobia, would soon be gone, and it might well have disappeared because Hans believed him.

Other faults can be found with the way that the study was conducted in the first place. Hans' father obviously couldn't have included everything the boy did in his letters to Freud; Hans was a lively and enquiring child, and his father wasn't at home all the time. So when he was writing to Freud, Hans' father is very likely to have *selected* those things which seemed to him to be most important. As Hans' father was well aware of Freud's ideas, and completely agreed with them, it is also likely that he would have left out the bits that didn't fit with the theory (thinking they weren't important) and included the bits that seemed relevant. It is almost certain that the reports that Freud received were already biased in this way.

Another criticism is the way that his parents said that they were completely baffled by how Hans' phobia had developed, and yet his mother had been with him on the day that he saw the horse fall down (and make a lot of noise). Hans' phobia, it turned out, developed almost immediately after this experience, and yet his parents didn't think that it was important. In a way, though, that wasn't their fault; in Chapter 18 we will be looking at Pavlov's theory of classical conditioning, which can explain how a shock like that can have such a dramatic effect, but Pavlov didn't publish his theory until much later on. So the idea that one major shock could cause a phobia had not been suggested, and we can't really blame Freud for not thinking of it.

General criticisms of Freud's theory

Many other criticisms have been put forward about Freud's theory in general. One of them has been the way that Freud insisted that it is the first five years of life which are all-important for development, and yet there seems to be very little evidence to prove this. In fact, in the next chapter we will look at some cases of children who suffered serious deprivation in the first five years, and yet recovered later on and became normal teenagers. And, although many people have tried to show such influences by careful studies, none of them has succeeded.

This emphasis on the first five years, though, has caused some problems for the study of child development. One of the reasons why Bowlby (Chapter 4) was so ready to jump to the conclusions that he did was because he accepted this idea of the early years being crucial. But other studies seem to show that it is not that simple. A. Clarke concluded in 1968 that *all* the years of childhood are important in the development of personality – someone can be damaged by an unhappy or stressful later childhood, as well as by an early one, while another child may completely recover from a damaging first few years if put in a better environment later.

Another criticism of psychoanalysis has been the way that, although it has been practised as a treatment for neurotics all through this century, psychoanalysts have been very reluctant to investigate whether, in fact, they really *did* help people with their treatment. It wasn't until Eysenck published a study in 1965 that anyone began to look into this at all. Eysenck's study compared people who were receiving psychoanalysis with people who were suffering from the same kinds of problems, but not receiving treatment. He found that about two-thirds of those receiving treatment recovered from their problems but also that two-thirds of those without any treatment recovered in the same length of time! So this study suggested that, in fact, psychoanalysis wasn't doing that much good at all.

Some cross-cultural studies have also provided criticisms of Freud's theory. A study of the Trobriand Islanders, by Malinowski in 1927, showed that the successful resolution of the Oedipus complex wasn't necessarily as important as psychoanalysts had thought.

Among the Trobriand islanders, it is the mother's brother who is the child's guardian, not the child's father. According to Freud, a child feels the need to resolve its Oedipus conflict mainly because the father has so much power over the child. In a society where the father is not the child's guardian – and so does not have this power – the child is not so worried by the father's competition for the mother's affection. On the basis of this theory, Freud would have expected the Trobriand Islanders to grow up uncertain about what sex they are – or, at the very least, Freud would expect a high level of homosexuality. However, the Islanders don't show such tendencies and appear to be well-adjusted to their appropriate male and female sex roles.

Yet another criticism is the way that Freud developed his theory using relatively few subjects, at a time when life was very different from today. With only one child subject, but more adults, some psychologists have asked whether his theory can really be considered to apply to everyone. It is thought that Freud's emphasis on sexuality arose from the atmosphere of sexual repression that was common all over Europe in the Victorian era. It may easily be that, with people today growing up in a less inhibited atmosphere, they just aren't the 'reservoir' of seething desires and impulses that Freud implied in his descriptions of the id and its working.

Many psychologists nowadays would be more interested in describing how people are different from each other in so many ways. In general, though, psychoanalysts have been more interested in describing the *mechanisms* that people use to cope with disturbing memories or irrational behaviour, and not with analysing individual differences.

Anna Freud's theories   Freud's daughter, Anna Freud, developed his theory a bit further. In particular, she was interested in how it worked with children, and how a child's ego would manage to cope with the conflicts and challenges that it got from the id and the super-ego.

She looked particularly at what Freud called 'ego-defence mechanisms'. These were ways that the ego would protect itself if the impulsive demands from the id became too strong, or if the authoritarian super-ego was asking too much. Sometimes, also, the person might feel 'threatened' by something that was happening in the real world, and the ego would develop defences to protect against that as well.

In addition to defending the person against the various threats that might occur, the ego's job was to keep things balanced and harmonious. So when it was using these 'defence mechanisms', it was cutting out things which might destroy the dynamic balance between the three parts of the mind by allowing one side to get too strong.

For example, if a male child is going through the Oedipus complex stage, he may well become unconsciously frightened of his father, because he sees his father as a rival for his mother's love, and the father is much bigger and more powerful than the child. But consciously, the child knows that the father is fond of him, and that he should be fond of his father. So his ego is unable to admit that he is frightened – that would spoil the balance between the child and reality. Instead, the child may cope by what Anna Freud called 'denial in phantasy'. He may invent, for instance, an imaginary lion, which will be his friend and will go everywhere with him. The lion represents his father – big and powerful (in the same way that Freud thought that horses probably represented little Hans' father). By making the lion into an imaginary friend, the child is able to cope with his unconscious fear of his father. So the ego has successfully 'defended' itself against this problem.

Other defences which children develop, according to Anna Freud, are things like 'identifying with the aggressor'. If a child feels someone to be very frightening, it may cope with this fear by identifying with that person; like the child who comes home and plays at being 'dentists', after a particularly unpleasant visit.

The idea of 'play therapy', described in the last chapter, is based on the way that a child may have developed these kind of 'defence mechanisms'. Because of these, the child would be unlikely to be able to explain directly what is wrong; nonetheless the problems may appear in a disguised form in the child's playing. By allowing the child to play freely, and observing the way that it plays, the therapist may be able to identify what is bothering the child, and so be able to help it.

Moral development   The psychoanalytic idea of the super-ego is the way that Freud and others thought that the child would develop ideas about what is moral and socially acceptable. They saw the super-ego as being an internal 'parent' figure – the strict figure of authority from childhood being internalised and becoming a conscience for the child, within its own personality.

Other psychologists have put forward different ideas as to how moral development happens. In the last chapter, we looked at some studies which showed how physical or psychological punishment might connect with how strong the child's conscience becomes. The social-learning approach sees moral development in children arising from the interactions of the child with its parents and other people in the society.

Piaget's theory of moral development

Another theory of moral development was put forward by Piaget, whose theory of cognitive development we'll be examining in the next chapter. Piaget developed a complete theory of cognitive development in children which was based on *observations* of children at play, and the *clinical interview* method, in which he would discuss things with children or set problems for them and deduce how they were reasoning from the things that they said.

When he was studying moral development, Piaget used the game of marbles to find out how children understood ideas like 'fairness' and how rules should operate. He chose marbles because it's a game that children play, which has definite rules but which isn't taught by adults. He would ask each child to explain the rules to him; and would play marbles with them, seeing how they dealt with problems (like cheating) which arose during the course of the game.

Piaget also developed problem stories which he would tell the children, which would allow him to see how they made judgements about right or wrong. One of the stories, for instance, described a child who was playing with her mother's scissors and accidentally cut a hole in her dress. Sometimes Piaget would describe it as a big hole, and sometimes as a small hole; and in some stories the child was shown as being disobedient while in other stories it wasn't. He found that younger children would often tend to judge how serious the case was by the amount of damage that was done, which he described as the *external responsibility* of the character in the story. But older children would look at the intentions behind the action, judging disobedient acts as being more serious. This is the *internal responsibility* of the character in the story.

Piaget said that the child's moral development passed through three main stages. The first stage lasted until the child was about seven or eight years old, and during this stage, the child's idea of what was 'right' or 'wrong' depended on what was allowed by adults in the child's world. If something wasn't allowed, then it was wrong, and it was as simple as that. One story which Piaget told to illustrate this described a child having to choose between getting a 'fair', equal solution to a problem, or obeying its parents. When Piaget asked small children what the child in the story should do, they all said that it should obey its parents. If it didn't, the children said, then it would be 'wrong'. Piaget named this approach *moral realism*.

Gradually, Piaget said, children progressed from this stage into the second one, where they were more concerned with justice, and with 'fair' decisions. If they were told the same kind of story when they had reached this stage of moral development, then the children would say that the child in the story should do what would get the most equal, 'fair' solution, even if it did mean being disobedient. During this stage, Piaget said, children were very concerned that sweets and things should be divided equally, and that everyone should be equal. This stage usually lasted from the ages of about eight to eleven years.

The third stage, after eleven, was a time when the child gradually came to see that simple 'fairness' or 'equality' wasn't always enough. Piaget described that as the idea of *egalitarianism* (that everyone should be treated equally) giving way to the idea of *equity* (some people might start off with less in the first place, so that they might need *more* than their 'fair share' to bring them up with other people). The idea is that justice is not always achieved through simple equality, but that sometimes you have to compensate for circumstances, too. Piaget named this approach *moral relativism*.

Throughout these three stages, Piaget identified a gradual shift from what he called *heteronomous morality* – morality which is seen as depending on external rules or laws, to *autonomous morality* – morality which is decided by the individual in accordance with their own principles of justice and honesty.

Other researchers agreed with Piaget's ideas as to how moral development happened. A study by Durkin, in 1959, asked children what the right thing to do was, if one child hit another child. He found that older children were much more likely to ask for more information before they made a judgement about what was right or wrong in the case. Younger children tended to make very clear, sweeping decisions, like that it was always wrong, no matter what had happened beforehand.

Tapp and Levine, in 1972, asked children whether they agreed with the statement 'a rule should never be broken'. Most of the six-year-olds that they asked agreed with the rule, but when they asked older children, they said that it would depend whether the rule was a sensible one or not. This is just

the kind of difference in making moral judgements that Piaget
would expect from his theory.

Kohlberg's theory of
moral development
In the late 1950s another theory of moral development was put
forward, by L. Kohlberg. Kohlberg did not completely disagree
with Piaget's theory, but he felt that it did not go far enough.
Like Piaget's, Kohlberg's theory has three main stages but
Kohlberg divided each of these stages into two parts: an early
and a later part.

The first part of this first stage, which Kohlberg called *the pre-*
moral stage, is where a child obeys rules, not because it believes
in the rules, but purely in order to avoid punishment. If a child
was asked 'why should you always be on time for school?', for
example, it would say that the reason was because you would
be in trouble if you were late. The important thing, then, is
that 'good' behaviour is 'good' because it saves trouble.
As the child progresses through this stage, though, it moves
on to the second part, where it comes to see the reasons for
keeping rules, not in terms of avoiding trouble, but in terms of
good things that happen if you do keep them. So at this stage
then a child might say that it was a good idea to be on time
for school because 'then the teacher will be pleased with you'.

The stage of conventional morality is the next stage which
Kohlberg described. During this stage, the child mainly judges
actions by what the *intention* was of the person doing them. So
they would be more likely to consider *why* someone had done
something, before they said it was 'good' or 'bad'. If the person
had done whatever it was in order to help someone else, then
the child would come to the conclusion that the act was 'good'.
In the second part of the stage, the person has become more
concerned with keeping society running smoothly, and
maintaining law and order. They would now say that it is
everyone's duty to keep things going well, and an act would
be judged according to how well or badly it helps people to do
this.

In the third stage of moral development – *the stage of autonomous*
morality – the person has developed the idea that things can
be more valid than simply the rules or laws of that particular
society or social group. In this stage, the person will tend to
be interested in the ways that laws and rules are changed, and
the ways that different societies have different ideas about
what is 'right'. If a particular rule or law appears to be wrong,
then the most important thing would appear to be to change
that law, in accordance with legal principles and procedures.

In the second part of this stage, the individual has developed an abstract 'rule' of justice, or philosophy, which can be applied to different sets of laws in different societies. An idea like: 'goodness is the greatest possible freedom which is compatible with equal freedom for other people', might be an example of this kind of principle. The person has adopted a kind of 'universal' ethical idea, and this, in Kohlberg's theory, is the highest kind of moral reasoning.

Kohlberg investigated moral reasoning, by asking people what was the right thing to do in a given situation. Unlike Piaget, though, he didn't just ask children, he asked adults as well. He might describe, for example, a man who broke into a chemist's shop, to get a drug which would cure his dying wife. By asking people to judge the rights and wrongs of the case, Kohlberg was able to divide their responses into his three (main) stages. People at different stages would give different kinds of answers, and they would be concerned with different aspects of the problem.

These theories of moral development have been put forward to try to describe some of the ways that children's thinking changes as they get older. In the next chapter, we will look at some other theories which have examined changes in the ways that people think as they develop, and some of the evidence that has been put forward to explain this.

Summary

1 The idea of psychoanalysis was developed by Freud, at the end of the last century. By the technique of 'free-association' Freud was able to uncover memories of his patients' childhoods. He used these as a basis for his theory of development.

2 Freud said that children went through three stages in the first five years: the oral stage, the anal stage, and the phallic stage. Each stage could have lasting effects on adult personality.

3 A study of a small child called 'little Hans' showed how Freud's theory could be applied to child problems.

4 Freud described adult personality as having three parts: the id, the ego, and the super-ego. The ego had to keep the balance between the two other parts.

5 Anna Freud described some of the ways that children could develop defence mechanisms against unpleasant ideas or threats. The technique of play therapy is often useful in studying children's problems, as their defences may show more clearly in their play.

6 Piaget put forward a three-stage theory of moral development. At first the child kept rules because adults told it to, later on the child became more concerned with the idea that rules kept equality, and later still it developed the idea of equity – compensation for those who had less to start with.

7 Kohlberg thought that Piaget's theory didn't go far enough. He put forward a more complicated theory of moral development, which had six parts to it, and ended with the highest development of all – adopting an abstract principle of social justice.

Chapter 8

Intellectual development

In the section on child development, we looked at some of the theories that have been put forward about the way that children develop moral judgements and ideas. In this section, I want to look a bit more generally at the ways that children's thinking develops as they grow older – what psychologists call *cognitive development*.

As children grow, and get more and more experience of the world, and of how things work in it, they also start to develop their own ideas about things. Play, as I mentioned before, is one of the ways that they develop intellectually, but all the time a child is building up a store of information and experience which will be used to develop understanding of the world.

Piaget's theory of intellectual development

One of the most famous theories about how a child's mind develops was put forward by the Swiss psychologist, Jean Piaget. Piaget thought that intellectual development happened in stages, and that a child would only go on to the next stage once it had completely mastered the first one. In this way, each stage formed a kind of 'building block' for the next stage to rest on. In each stage, Piaget said, the child would develop new ways of thinking which had developed out of what went before, but which were different from previous ways.

The central concept of Piaget's theory is the *schema*. A schema is a kind of cognitive, or 'mental' structure, which the child uses as it interacts with the outside world. A schema contains *all* the ideas, memories and information about a particular object that a child associates with that object. It is *hypothetical* – that is, Piaget deduced that schemata (schemata is the plural of schema) must exist, but we can't actually see or observe them.

Schemata develop as a result of our interaction with the environment. For example: for a young child, the way that a TV set comes to be 'on' would gradually develop as an idea perhaps from the notion that 'the picture just happens', to 'mummy does something, and then the picture happens', and gradually to 'you press this button and the picture happens'. The child has developed a schema about the TV set.

As it grows older, and its experience widens, the schema may also grow to include other machines – radios, record players, washing machines. But it all started with the child getting a set of ideas about how to operate machines – how they are turned on – which could then be applied to other machines. This schema needn't just involve the machine itself; the child may include the twisting motion you must make with your fingers to turn some knobs, or the way that you feel a slight 'click' through your fingers when you press the knob. The schema will include the *whole* of the experiences connected with turning on the TV. It may also include, for example, the visual experience of the brightening screen, and (for some children) the high-pitched whine which the TV makes, which some people can hear and others can't.

Once the schema is developed, it will be applied to other situations if at all possible. After all, the schema contains all the experiences that were used to deal successfully with something before; so when faced with a new thing, it is sensible to see if that same experience will work again. So, if you know how to turn on a TV set, and you want to turn on a radio but don't know how, then the first thing you are likely to try is the behaviour that was successful in turning on the TV. You'll tend to look for a knob or switch similar to the TV one, and turn it or press it as you would for the TV. In other words, you are applying your *schema of TV operation* to a new object – the radio.

When you do that, you may find one of three possible results. Firstly, you may be completely successful, and turn on the radio at first go. Secondly, you may be partially successful, but instead of turning a knob, you must press a button; or instead of the left-hand knob, it's the right-hand one which matters. Or thirdly, you may fail completely, in which case you would abandon that schema, and possibly try another one from your store of experiences – or maybe just give up! (In the latter case, you would probably form a new schema about things which can't be operated in that way, but look as though they can.)

If the first possibility happens, and you are completely successful in your attempt to apply one schema to a new situation, then this new information is said to have been *assimilated* into the schema. The schema now applies not simply to TVs, but can also be applied, just as it stands, to radios as well. So the operation of radios has been assimilated into the schema, which previously was only applied to TVs. Assimilation is an important part of the development of schema; by this process, they come to include new information, and so are applicable in wider circumstances.

Usually, though, you get the second result. You're unlikely, in practice, to find a radio with controls that are *exactly* the same as those on a TV. Probably there will be some similarities but also some differences. So when you try to apply your TV schema to the radio, you will only be *partially* successful: you're on the right track, but you have to do something a little differently to what you did before. When this happens, the schema you are using needs to be adjusted a bit before it can be applied to both situations – it must stretch to accommodate both the turning on of the radio, and the turning on of the TV. This process of stretching is called *accommodation*, and it means that the new information coming in actually alters the schema a little. It is not simply assimilated.

Together, these two processes of assimilation and accommodation – assimilation being the way that new information is fitted into the schema, and accommodation being the way that the schema itself is altered to fit the new information which is coming in – form the basis of cognitive development. They work together. It would be almost impossible to find assimilation happening without accommodation, and it would also be almost impossible to find accommodation happening without assimilation. But, as they work, they extend and develop the schemata, and so our ways and strategies for understanding the world are extended and developed.

However, assimilation and accommodation don't just happen! They occur because of the *interaction* of the individual with the environment. If you never come into contact with a radio, or anything similar, then there is no way that your TV operating schema will be developed so that it applies to other things – it needs the *action*, and the *effects* of that action, for the new information to be gained, and for the processes of assimilation and accommodation to occur at all. (You remember that they were only happening in the context of how we make sense of a *new* event, i.e. the radio.) Without such interaction with our environment – without coming into contact with new events, and new information – we would continue to use the schemata we already have, and there would be no need for them to change! So the development of schemata rests on *operations*, those actions and interactions which the child performs with the environment. Operations in this sense may be purely 'mental' – only in the mind – but they are nonetheless concerned with manipulating a piece of the environment, 'experimenting' with it, and looking at the results.

For example: if you add three and two, you are performing an *operation*, as Piaget would mean it, regardless of whether you added it on paper or in your head. Furthermore, you are using your schema of *adding* to perform that operation, and your schema of adding can equally well be used to perform other operations – five and seven, for instance, or ninety-three and seventy-two. So an operation is a kind of *action*, but it can be in your head as well as with your body.

This is where the stages part of the theory comes in. Piaget says that children perform different *kinds* of operations at different *stages* in their cognitive development, and that a child who hasn't reached the appropriate stage can't perform that particular kind of operation. It wouldn't be possible, for instance, for an infant in the first stage to perform an operation belonging to the third stage.

Piaget outlined four main stages of cognitive development, and gave approximate ages at which children reached those stages. He stressed, though, that these ages are only averages; individual children might go through the stages at a different speed (but they would always go through the stages in the same order). These stages he called the sensori-motor stage; the pre-operational stage; the concrete operational stage; and the formal operational stage. In each of the stages, the child is able to tackle different kinds of problems successfully.

The sensori-motor stage – from birth to about eighteen months

This is the period when the child is gradually learning to interpret the information coming in through its senses, and is also learning motor co-ordination – the control of its body, grasping things, walking, and so on – hence the name: the sensori-motor stage. At first, according to Piaget, the child has only a limited number of reflexes, which form the basis of the first schemata. As the child develops its body schemata, the range of activities is increased. At the beginning of the sensori-motor period, soon after birth, the child has absolutely no awareness of anything outside itself – anything it comes into contact with, Piaget says, is regarded as a part of the child itself. This is known as *egocentricity*. The self (ego) is the centre of everything. Gradually, over the sensori-motor period, the child learns to realise that there *is* an outside world, and that it exists even when the child isn't paying attention to it.

One of the experiments which Piaget performed to illustrate egocentricity in this period, was to show infants a toy, and then to hide it, by putting a cloth or something similar over it. Although the infants had been very interested in the toy, and although they had seen it being hidden, they didn't make any attempt to get the toy out from under the cloth. Piaget says that this is because they don't have an *object concept*: when the toy is out of sight, then, as far as they're concerned, it doesn't exist any more. Only gradually does the child come to realise that things *do* exist independently.

There are criticisms of Piaget's experiments and his conclusions, and we will look at them at the end of this section. Meanwhile I will continue describing the stages and the experiments which Piaget used to demonstrate them.

The pre-operational period – from about eighteen months to about seven years

In the *pre-operational* period, the child is preparing for the next stage, the concrete operational period. It is gradually discovering and establishing rules about things, which it will apply to different situations, and, as with the sensori-motor period, the schemata it uses are becoming more complex and wider in scope. At the beginning of the pre-operational period, the child may learn that its daddy is a man; it may then over-generalise that 'rule', and may call all men 'daddy'. Quickly it learns that this isn't right, but throughout this period, it will tend to over-generalise the new 'rules' it comes across in this way. It develops these rules and schemata through its interaction with its environment, until by the end of this period, it has a good 'store' from which it can draw in new situations, and it is ready to enter the concrete operational period.

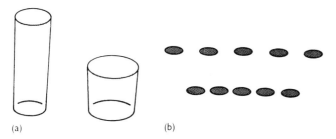

Fig. 8.1 Conservation of volume (a) and number (b)

One of the experiments Piaget used to show the limitations of the child at this point – it can interpret some things successfully, but not others – was to do with *conservation*. He said that if you show a child two beakers of water, one of which is tall and thin, the other short and fat, and ask the child which beaker contains more water, the child will say 'the tall one', even though they both contain the same amount. Piaget said that that is because the child hasn't learnt to *conserve* volume, to realise that something may have the same volume, even though it is a different shape. Similarly, Piaget said that if you roll a piece of clay into a sausage-shape, show it to the child, and then roll it into a ball, the child will say that there is more clay in the sausage-shape.

Piaget said that the child's difficulty with conservation comes from the way that it has to take two features of the thing into account at the same time. So if it is trying to conserve number, for instance, with a row of five buttons spread out and a row of five buttons close together, the child will say that the spread-out row contains more buttons. This is because it can see that that row is *longer*, but it couldn't also take into account the fact that the space between each button is larger.

At this stage, too, Piaget said that the child is still *egocentric*, but that this egocentricity will gradually lessen throughout the stage, and will be almost gone by the next stage of development. What is striking about the child in the pre-operational stage, Piaget said, is the way that it is unable to 'decentre'; that is, to see things from someone else's point of view. He set up an experiment to demonstrate this: he made a model of three mountains – one with a cross on the top, one with a cabin on, and one with snow. The child sat at the table where these model mountains were, and the experimenter put a small doll at another place. Using a set of pictures, the child was then asked to say what the doll could see. The children almost always chose the picture which showed what they, themselves, could see, and not the picture which showed what the doll would be able to see. Piaget says that this is evidence that the child isn't yet able to 'decentre' (to put itself in someone else's place) as it is still too egocentric.

Fig. 8.2 Piaget's 'Mountains' study
A doll is placed in front of three model mountains, and the child is asked to describe what the doll can see

*The concrete'
operational stage –
from seven to about
eleven years*

In this stage, the child is able to work things out 'mentally'. It can use the schemata and the 'rules' that it has developed, to interpret and to make sense of its world, and it can solve problems by thinking about them, rather than by having to play with models. But, Piaget says, the problems which it can solve must always deal with real-life objects – the child isn't yet able to deal with abstract concepts, or symbols. For example: a child in the concrete operational stage wouldn't be able to solve the problem 'X is greater than Y; T is greater than X; which is the smallest?', but it would probably be able to solve the problem: 'John is older than Billy; Fred is older than John; who is the youngest?' Although it's the same problem, the first one is expressed symbolically, while the second one talks in *concrete* terms, about people and their ages. So the child who is in the concrete operational period is still limited in the kinds of problems which it can solve, although, of course, it can handle far more than the child who is still in the pre-operational period. And it can, now, 'decentre': it can imagine itself in someone else's place and understand what they can probably see.

The formal operational stage – from eleven years to adulthood

The child in the *formal operational stage* is now able to use scientific reasoning, and to operate using symbols as well as real-life examples. It can deal with abstract concepts, and can reason logically. This period, once it has settled and become consolidated, forms the basis of the kind of 'mental' activity which the child will use throughout its adult life: it is able to form hypotheses, and to test them out, as a scientist would, and as adults do on day-to-day matters.

Piaget stresses that these stages are not fixed and definite. The child moves *gradually* from one stage to the next, and, within each stage, the child develops its ability to form and modify schemata, through the processes of assimilation and accommodation.

Piaget's theory has been called a maturational one, because the child progresses through the stages in the same order as other children and it wouldn't be possible to 'skip' a stage, or to go through them in the wrong order. But it isn't purely maturational, in the sense of being completely genetically determined, because each stage depends on what the child has done previously. Only by its interaction with the environment – by performing operations, and by forming schemata – does the child progress through the stages; it doesn't just happen automatically. The child needs the experience in order to build up schemata in the first place. So in that respect, it is not correct to call it a maturational development in the same way that walking is. On the other hand, in normal children (that is, in children who have the opportunity to interact with their environment), it does progress alongside the child's physical maturing, and Piaget certainly thought that there was a strong genetic influence in cognitive development.

Criticisms of
Piaget's
experiments

Piaget said that young children were essentially *egocentric* – that is, they were unaware of a world which was separate from themselves, and which continued to exist even if it was out of sight. He said that his experiments with infants, where he covered up an object in which they were interested and the babies did not try to reach it, demonstrated this egocentricity, as the children seemed not to know that the object continued to exist while it was out of sight.

This seems on the surface to be a reasonable explanation for why the child doesn't try to get the object. But M. Donaldson showed, in 1978, that Piaget's idea of egocentricity isn't quite that simple. For a start, if the child has no knowledge of the object once it's out of sight, then *how* the object disappears shouldn't make any difference to the result. But it does matter. If the object is made to disappear by switching off all the lights in the room, the child will still reach for the object as if it could see it. And yet the object is just as much out of sight, as if it were covered by a cloth (Bower and Wishart, 1972). Bower suggests that the reason for this is not that the child has no object concept, but that it hasn't yet learned that objects can be moved in that way. So it is confused by a cloth covering the toy.

Another of Piaget's experiments was to do with the way that egocentricity gradually gives way to the ability to *decentre* – to put yourself in someone else's place, and say what they might see, or feel. His 'mountains' experiment seemed to show that children in the pre-operational stage could not do this. But Hughes, in 1975, devised a similar problem for children, but one which would draw more on the child's previous experience. He set up four walls in a sort of cross-shape, and used two dolls, a policeman doll and a boy doll. The policeman was placed at the end of a wall, so that it could 'see' into two of the four sections made by the walls, and the child was asked to put the boy doll somewhere where the policeman wouldn't be able to see it – to 'hide' the boy from the policeman. Hughes thought that that would make more sense to the child doing the test, since almost every child has had experience of hiding from someone, in play. (And most children aren't very interested in mountains.) But the problem is still the same as in Piaget's experiment: if the child was unable to 'decentre', it wouldn't be able to put itself in the place of the 'policeman' doll, and work out what he could see, and what he couldn't.

Hughes found that, not only could the children manage this task perfectly well, but they were also able to 'hide the boy' from *two* policemen, when another doll was used, and that involved taking two different points of view into account.

Fig. 8.3 Hughes' 'Policeman doll' study
First, the boy doll was put into each of the numbered areas and the child was asked whether the policeman could 'see' it. Then the child was asked to 'hide' the boy doll from the policeman

Donaldson argued that the reason why children could manage Hughes' task, but not Piaget's, must be because they did not fully understand with the mountain task what they were supposed to do. She says that Hughes' task *made sense* to the children – they knew what they were trying to do, and they knew (or could imagine) why. The important thing then is that the experiment should make sense to the child, otherwise it will just be confused, and will guess rather than say that it doesn't know.

Similar sorts of criticisms have been made of Piaget's conservation experiments. He performed many of them, about conservation of weight, length, volume, and number, but all the experiments took the same form. For conservation of volume, the experimenter would show the child two containers of coloured liquid, which were the same size, and contained the same amount of liquid. He would ask the child whether the two amounts were the same, to which the child would answer yes. Then he would say 'now watch what I do', and pour the liquid into two different containers, as described before; he would then ask the child, again, whether the two amounts of liquid were the same. Typically, the child would give a different answer, and Piaget interpreted this to mean that they were incapable of 'conserving' volume. He thought that they only looked at one part of the problem – the way that the water came up higher in the tall jar – and didn't take other things into account (like the shorter jar being wider).

S. Rose and M. Blank suggested in 1974 that one of the reasons for this result might be the way that the children were asked *twice*, as if the experimenter expected them to give a different answer. They tried the same tests, but only asked children at the end whether the water in the two jars was the same. They found that they got far more correct replies. So they argued that it was likely that the child was taking the way that the question was repeated in the standard Piaget experiment, as a hint from the experimenter that they should say something *different* in their second answer. (After all, why else would they be asked twice?) Again, it's a question of the way the child *makes sense* of the experiment.

Another criticism of Piaget's approach was the way that the experimenter drew attention to what was going on when he changed things: 'Now, watch what I do'. J. McGarrigle (1974) thought that too would influence the child's final decision. Since the experimenter had drawn attention to what he was doing, then the child thought that something special must have been done, even if it didn't see it. So McGarrigle used a character called 'naughty teddy', a small teddy bear who would 'swoop' out of a box, and mess up experiments. By using 'naughty teddy', he could change the things around in exactly the same way that they had been changed in Piaget's experiments, but without making a big fuss about it. (Or rather, making a different kind of fuss – 'naughty teddy's done it again!') He found a considerable difference: far more children between the ages of four and six 'conserved' successfully than had done with Piaget's experiments. They had still been paying attention, but they were aware that nothing particularly special had been changed.

These findings, and several others, seem to show that the results which Piaget found were more a result of *the way the question was asked*, than what the children were actually capable of. In many of Piaget's tests, the questions were asked in a manner unusual to the children; while in others, the experimenter set up *expectations* in the child giving an answer different to the one that it would normally have given. So it seems that if we want to find out about the ways that children think it is quite important to ask questions that make sense to *them*, and not just questions which make sense to the person doing the experiment.

Another criticism of Piaget's theory has been of the way that he only used a very small number of children for his observations – about half-a-dozen, including his own children.

Because of this small number, it could be said that his results probably weren't typical at all – we need to have a large sample of subjects if we want to be able to generalise our findings.

A further criticism was made by J. Bruner, who pointed out that Piaget didn't think that language was particularly important in intellectual development. Obviously, Piaget thought that it was important that the child did acquire language, but he believed that the most important thing was the child's interaction with its environment, whereas Bruner, as we will see in the next section, considered that being able to categorise and to organise concepts in hierarchies was an essential tool for thinking, and that language was necessary for this.

Bruner's theory of representation

J. Bruner put forward his own theory of intellectual development. It does not contradict Piaget's theory, but instead runs side-by-side with it. Bruner was interested in the ways that children come to *remember* things in different ways. He'd observed, for instance, the way that, if an infant is hitting a string of rattling beads across its cot, and you take the beads away, it will often carry on making the same actions, even though it isn't hearing the noise any more. Bruner thought that it was probably *remembering* the sound of the beads and the actions, by the activity itself. There are lots of different ways of 'coding' memories for storing – we might remember sound patterns, or pictures, or other kinds of images. Bruner thought that this mental representation happened in different *modes*, as the child developed.

The first mode – enactive representation

One of the best ways of finding out what this is, is to try the old party game of trying to describe a helter-skelter without moving your hands or your body! Because you're not allowed to move, you become much more aware of the moves that you *want* to make – your memory of the helter-skelter has been stored as a kind of 'muscle memory' – the feel of it is what you remember. Since the very first kind of learning which a baby engages in is control over its body (how to control its arms, to reach for things, etc.) then, Bruner says, this is also the first method of *representation* that the baby learns. Its first memories are stored as *enactive* representation, because they are concerned with *actions*.

Adults, too, can use enactive representation (as in the helter-skelter game), but, unlike the infant, they also have the opportunity to use other kinds.

The second mode – iconic representation

This comes from the word '*icon*', which means an image, like a statue or a painting. Iconic representation is 'picture imagery', storing information in the form of 'mental' pictures, or images. (This can also include sound images, or smell images.) By developing iconic representation, the child extends the range of things which can be stored in the memory, as some information clearly isn't suitable for enactive representation – for instance, remembering a photograph, or what someone looks like.

There are advantages and disadvantages to iconic representation. An experiment by Kuhlman, in 1960, showed this: he compared children who used iconic imagery a great deal with children who used symbolic representation (the third mode), on two different tasks. The first task was to remember an unfamiliar (fairly complicated) shape, with an equally unfamiliar nonsense syllable as a name. As he expected, children who used iconic representation were better at this than those using symbols. They could remember the shapes better, as they could 'picture' them in their minds.

The second task, though, was to look at a set of pictures, which had one thing in common – for example, they might see a picture of a duck swimming, an ostrich, a seagull flying, and a penguin. Then they were asked what it was that the pictures had in common. The children who used symbolic representation found this much easier than the ones who used iconic representation, because the iconic imagers only

Fig. 8.4 (a) Kuhlman's shapes (b) Kuhlman's pictures
Iconic imagers could remember unfamiliar shapes and names, but were unable to classify sets of objects or animals which look dissimilar

remembered the pictures. They found it difficult to see the *similarities* between them, as the pictures were deliberately different from each other.

As we can see from this, there are times when iconic representation is useful, and times when it isn't. In order to cope with the kind of information which can't be stored as iconic images, Bruner says, we develop a third kind of representation – symbolic representation.

The third mode – symbolic representation

This is the ability to represent and store information by using *symbols* instead of images. Since symbols are not restricted by what things look like, or sound like, a great many more things can be stored in the memory by using them. For example: it would be very difficult to picture a vacuum – an emptiness that doesn't even contain air – in our minds. But, by using the word, which is a symbol, we can store information about a vacuum – like the phrase 'nature abhors a vacuum', for instance – with an idea of what we mean. Without the symbol we would find that information very difficult to represent in our minds.

Bruner showed how symbolic representation allows the child to be much more flexible in its use of memories. Bruner and Kenney (1966) performed a study in which they used children with iconic memory and children who used symbolic representation. They arranged different glasses in order of size, on a grid. After the children had looked at them, they were asked to replace the glasses on the grid in exactly the same way, from memory. All the children could do this successfully. But when they were asked to replace the glasses in reverse order – the experimenters placed the smallest glass on a different corner and asked the children to complete the pattern – only the children with symbolic representation could manage it. They could adapt their memory to a new situation, whereas

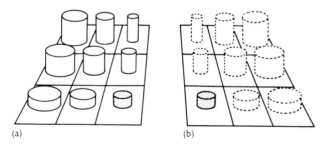

(a) (b)

Fig. 8.5 Bruner and Kenney's study
Children from five to seven were shown the arrangement of glasses in (a), and, when it was dismantled, were able to reconstruct it. However, when the shaded glass was placed as in (b), and the children were asked to complete the pattern, only the older ones could do it

those with iconic representation could only remember what the original pattern had looked like, and they couldn't adapt that memory.

Symbolic representation also allows us to arrange information in certain kinds of ways; this can mean that we remember it much more effectively. One possibility which it allows was demonstrated by Kuhlman's study: the children with symbolic representation could use *categories*, and see relationships between things, much more clearly than the ones who used iconic representation. Once we can group information into different categories, and types, then we can remember how things connect together more readily.

This leads us to the second thing which becomes possible when the child develops symbolic representation: the development of *hierarchies*. We can group things into different *levels*, as well as different types of things. This way of arranging information can make it much easier to remember quite a lot of facts.

A study by Bower in 1969, showed just how effective hierarchies could be. He asked subjects to memorise a list of 112 different words – quite a lot to learn all at once! All the words had something to do with places where people live: like flat, town, street, bedsit, and so on. One group of subjects was given the list in a random order, but the second group was given a list which was arranged hierarchically: starting with the largest, like country and county, and ending with the smallest, like bedsit. From the 112, the first group remembered, on average, 21 words. But the second group remembered an average of 73 words – more than three times as many! So this shows how the ability to organise information into hierarchies can help us to remember much more; and this wouldn't be possible without symbolic representation.

I have said that words are symbols. So in one sense, symbolic representation is available to us from the moment we start using language; equally, iconic representation is available to us from the moment we start to see. However, Bruner says that these forms of representation tend to emerge gradually as the child deals with more and more complex material. For most young children, iconic representation is enough for their daily needs, but as they get older and start to deal with more abstract concepts, then they need another method for representation. It's easy enough to picture 'Susan went to school', but it's not so easy to picture 'The essence of the controversy was elusive'. But, through language and the use of symbols, we can store the second sentence as well as the first.

Environment and intellectual development

Piaget's and Bruner's ideas are two of the theories about cognitive development in children. Other ideas have been mentioned, and we will deal with them in the appropriate sections. For instance, Lenneberg puts forward the idea that there is a critical period for language development in children, which lasts from about eighteen months to twelve years of age, and we will look at this theory in more detail in the chapter on language development. But what sort of things influence children's intellectual development? We have talked about stages the child might go through, as it develops, but we haven't talked of what *affects* those stages, and if we can find any reasons why children grow up with different cognitive functioning – for instance why some do well at school, and some do well at practical work, but not at school.

Stimulating environments

When we start to look at this question, we find ourselves going back to some of the work on maternal deprivation which I talked about in Chapter 5, and in particular to Goldfarb's study of mental retardation.

If you remember, Goldfarb published a study in 1943, which compared two groups of children. The children in one group were brought up in an institution – an orphanage – until they were about three years old, and those in the second group were put into foster homes as soon as they left their mothers (soon after birth). The children in the first group were fostered when they were three, but they showed noticeable differences in sociability and by comparison with the others were slightly mentally retarded.

This idea that the environment could affect intelligence was carefully investigated by many researchers, both with humans, and with animals. An experiment by Rosenzweig and Bennet, in 1968, compared gerbils which were brought up alone in bare cages, with gerbils which grew up in groups, and had many different playthings in their cages. They found that the second group was much better than the first at learning to solve problems, and also had larger, heavier brains – their experience had influenced the *physical* growth of the brain.

A similar study was done by White in 1971. He was concerned with the development of visually directed reaching, which infants usually develop at about five months of age – the ability to reach out and successfully grasp something which has been seen. By comparing one group of infants in a state hospital, with another, similar group, who were also in the hospital, but who were given special treatment, he found that this ability – which is normally considered to be *purely* maturational, like walking – could be induced to develop earlier.

An experimental group of one-month-old infants was given more handling by the nursing staff than the others, and was

Fig. 8.6 White's enriched environment for infants

also given patterned sheets, rather than white ones, and brightly coloured mobiles over the crib. In addition, these infants were frequently placed so that they could see what was going on around them (normally, the crib was surrounded by a lining so that they couldn't). He found that they managed successful visually directed reaching at three and a half months, instead of the normal five, because of the extra stimulation.

This sort of improvement has shown up in intelligence test results, too. One of the first studies that found this effect was performed by Skeels and Dye, in 1939. It all started accidentally; two children at a state orphanage were given intelligence tests at thirteen and sixteen months of age, which showed them to be seriously retarded. Since it was regarded as unlikely that they would ever improve, they were placed in an institution for the mentally retarded. A few months later, the psychologist visiting this institution was amazed to see that the children appeared to have improved dramatically; when they were re-tested, they proved to have gone up considerably in IQ score. One had gone from an IQ of 46 to an IQ of 77, while the other had gone from an IQ of 35 to an IQ of 87. (We'll be looking at IQ measurement in the next chapter – for now, it's sufficient to say that the average IQ is 100, and 95 per cent of the population have IQs between 68 and 132). So the increase had been quite striking.

On examining this result further, the reasons seemed to lie in the attention which the children had been receiving in the institution. Since they were so young, the other girls had made 'pets' of them, as had the staff, and so they were played with, and talked to, and received a great deal of attention. To continue this improvement, the two children were fostered at three and a half, by which time their IQs had risen to 95 and 93.

Skeels and Dye set up a more 'controlled' study, in which the same thing happened, but with a larger group of children. By comparison with a group which remained in the orphanage, the children who went to the institution for the mentally retarded increased in IQ steadily from an average IQ of 64, to an average of 86. Many years later, in 1966, Skeels did a follow-up study, and found that these differences still showed: the children who had been moved to the mentally retarded institution, and had been fostered later, had all finished high school. About a third of them had gone to college, had married, had children of normal intelligence, and had been self-supporting through their adult lives. The people in the group which had stayed in the orphanage, on the other hand, had mostly remained institutionalised, and were not able to earn enough to be self-supporting. They were still mentally retarded, while the experimental group showed no signs of being so.

So we can see that early experience can have a considerable effect on development in later life. But the central fact seems to be that the same kind of experience *continues*; when it is changed, as in Skeels and Dye's experiment, then the damage can be repaired.

Severely deprived children

But how early does the change have to be? Skeels and Dye's infants were all less than two years old. What would have happened if they had been older? Many people believe, or used to believe, that there were 'critical periods' for this kind of cognitive development, and that if the child was deprived of the stimulation which it needed during that particular time, then it would never be able to 'catch up', and the effects of the deprivation would always show.

Examples of this were pointed to in the cases of the 'wolf children', who were sometimes found in remote areas. While legends often said that they had been brought up by animals, many psychologists consider that they were in fact mentally retarded children who had been abandoned in these remote areas by parents who were no longer prepared to feed them. They were claimed to be 'unteachable' – they couldn't speak, never acquired language, and couldn't be trained to live 'normally'.

There is much recent evidence, though, to show that that isn't necessarily true, and that, given the right kind of treatment, children who suffer this kind of deprivation in their early years can recover from it quite well. In 1976, Koluchova reported on a pair of twin boys who had been brought up in appalling circumstances, and who were seven before they were discovered. Their mother had died when they were born, and their father married a woman who disliked them intensely. They lived in a small closet – with straw instead of a bed – and, although they were fed, they received virtually no other care. They were often beaten, and had no toys or other playthings, except a few building bricks, which they would play with sitting at a bare table. Often they were kept locked in the cellar. This lasted for five and a half years, and when they were discovered, they couldn't talk, and showed much fear and suspicion of others. They couldn't recognise pictures – never having seen any – they had rickets, and their IQs were in the 40 range. After spending a period in a children's home after discovery, they were fostered with a particularly warm and intelligent foster mother, who lived with her sister. They improved rapidly, and by the age of fourteen they had IQs of 100 and 101, and were intending to do technical training after leaving school.

However, this improvement didn't come from nowhere. The twins received intensive treatment and support all round – from their foster mother and her sister, from their school and teachers, and from the psychologist who was appointed responsible for their development. Another girl, later, was adopted by the same family. She, too, had suffered serious neglect and deprivation from a very early age. From birth she had been hated by her mother and been grudgingly fed, and hadn't even been able to develop bodily hygiene habits. She was removed from her home at four years old, and fostered with the twins – who by then were much older – and she also improved rapidly. Several other studies have shown the same result – that even seriously damaging early experiences can be recovered from, if the child is placed in the right kind of environment later. So on the whole, there doesn't seem to be much evidence to support ideas of a 'critical period' in intellectual development, although there may be a 'sensitive period'.

These cases, though, are very unusual ones. For most children, their environment is much more stimulating than it was for the Koluchova twins. As more research came through about the ways that 'enriched' environments could help children intellectually, people became more and more interested in the question of pre-school provision for children, nursery schools and the like. In America, a whole programme was set up to try to improve the pre-school experiences of poor children, and to 'compensate' for home environments where the children weren't getting much intellectual encouragement or stimulation.

Project Headstart   This project, called 'Project Headstart', provided children from deprived areas with extra classes and tuition, playgroups and visits, while they were in their pre-school years. The children involved all showed noticeable improvements in their IQ scores, and in their achievements in school. But as the children outgrew the Headstart years, and went through normal schooling, the improvements seemed to vanish. They became very much more slow at school learning, and their IQ improvements disappeared.

For several years, psychologists thought that improved nursery school education without a continued improved out-of-school support system wouldn't make that much difference to the children. The scheme, which was set up in the 1960s didn't really seem to have an effect. But when the first Headstart children grew up to be teenagers, some recent research supported the scheme. I. Lazar, (1982) showed that there did seem to be improvements in the achievements of these children; at the age of 14, children from Project Headstart were scoring consistently more highly on school tests than those of the same age who hadn't had nursery education. Lazar considered that this was probably due to the way that many parents became much more interested in their child's education as a result of Project Headstart, and so they may have encouraged their child more.

Headstart was an American project – what about pre-school provision for children in Britain?

Pre-school   In Britain, children often need to be looked after away from
experience in   their natural family. In many families it is necessary for both
Britain   parents to work, in order to keep up financial security. In other families, both husband and wife may work because of careers, or because of the social relief from the pressures of being housebound. And, of course, in many families, there *is* only one parent, who, as the sole provider, is obliged to work in order to support his or her family. So, clearly, it is necessary for there to be some kind of set-up where the children can be looked after, during the day, until they are old enough to go to school. In previous ages, of course, this wasn't usually a problem. Parents were free to go to work, since the family unit was much larger, comprising uncles, aunts, and grandparents, as well as husband, wife, and their children. But since the development of the industrial society, families have become very much smaller, and the care of infants and toddlers has largely become the responsibility of two people, sometimes only one.

So what is available for people, if they are to work, and need somewhere for their child to be looked after during the day? There are four main types of pre-school provision for child-care, each of which works differently, and may have different effects for the children who experience them. The four types are: playgroups, nursery schools, child-minders, and day nurseries.

Playgroups are relatively informal. They usually have about six to twenty children, and are often run by some of the mothers of the children. They usually last for about three hours in the day – often the morning – and are held in a specific place, which must have been approved by the Social Services Department of that area. The people who run the playgroup, too, must have received Social Services approval.

Nursery schools are the traditional 'kindergartens'. The staff tend to consist of a couple of trained teachers, and a nursery nurse, with qualifications. They are particularly concerned with developing 'creativity and expression' in children, and the actual working day runs from 9 to about 3.30, although they will take children before these hours if necessary, and keep them later too. They are run by the state, and so don't charge fees for attendance, but they don't really cover a whole working day, for a parent who must work full hours.

Child-minders are usually other mothers who look after children during the day, at their own homes. Usually they, too, have children at home, and the minded children are looked after together with the minder's own. Because each child-minder is different, the children receive very varied kinds of care – some are taken on trips and visits, and others stay at home. Child-minding has several advantages for a parent, for instance, the child can be left as the parent goes to work, and picked up on the way home. Child-minders are paid by the parents, and should be registered by the Social Services Department, although some are not. Because it usually just involves an agreement between the parents and the minder, it is almost impossible to *enforce* registration.

Day nurseries are professionally staffed, and maintained by the local Social Services Department. The children may be left for the whole working day, and an attempt is made to provide a 'home from home' for the children who go there. Some day nurseries are also maintained by charitable organisations, or employers, such as large factories or universities. They include the usual types of playgroup activities, painting, modelling and so on, but there are also cots, where the children can rest in the afternoons. Day nurseries vary considerably in atmosphere and the organisation of activities, and may range in size from below 20 to above 40 children, although most are within these sizes. They take children of quite a wide age-range.

These different types of pre-school day care are by no means the same in their effects on the children who use them. I shall discuss each of them, briefly, and attempt to show what some of the main research has found for each.

Playgroups were found, in a study by Sylva, Roy and Painter, in 1980, to provide children with quite a lot of different activities, which were very often led by one of the adults who ran the centre. Children were sociable and friendly with one another, and, because of the way that the playgroups tended to be arranged, were certainly developing the social skills which the parents had hoped they would, when they sent them to the playgroup in the first place. Because of the kinds of places where they were often held – which were frequently also used for other purposes at other times of the week – the playgroup leaders were a bit limited in the kinds of activities they could start, as everything had to be put away at the end of the session which meant that less time was available for play. Interestingly, playgroups seemed to provide children with a lot of story-telling and nursery-rhyme singing – far more than the other kinds of pre-school provision did.

Nursery schools were also the subject of the study by Sylva, Roy and Painter in 1980. It was found that the children who attended nursery schools and nursery classes spent much of their time engaged in 'creative' activities such as painting and modelling, and pretend play was very much encouraged. The main emphasis of nursery school, and nursery classes (which are often attached to an older-age school) was on the development of the 'natural child', rather than more traditional things like story-telling or school-preparation games (like number or spelling games). But, in terms of the children's social development, there was much activity and social play by the children, and they did appear to benefit more than children who stay at home, in this respect.

A study of *child-minders* was carried out by Bryant, Harris and Newton, in 1980. Since individual homes are so different, there were many difficulties in drawing hard-and-fast conclusions. However, their report wasn't as optimistic as the one by Sylva, Roy and Painter had been. (These reports were all part of a major study, called the 'Oxford Pre-school Research Project'.) Many of the children they studied, who were left with minders during the day, spent much of their time being quiet and listless. The researchers found this worrying, since children of that age are very often extremely noisy and bouncy. In some cases, they found, this could be attributed to the character of the child-minder herself, as not being particularly 'motherly' towards the child, but in some cases this clearly wasn't the reason. They thought that it could be the fact that the child is away from its *own* home and its own family, and in the home of another child, where none of the toys or people were its own. Most children would find this difficult to come to terms with, and the researchers felt that this might explain the listlessness. Incidentally, it didn't apply to *all* the children who were placed with child-minders, but it did apply to a good number – about seven out of ten. By comparison with other forms of day care for pre-school children, minding came off very poorly.

As another part of the Oxford Pre-school Research Project, a study was done on *day nurseries* by Garland and White, in 1980. Day nurseries have a very much longer day than other forms of day-care, and, as a result of this, must provide a wide variety of activities for the children. Very often day nurseries would have some of the day given over to free play, some to school-preparation type activities, some to rest, and so on. The children received good, interested care, and tended to be sociable, and boisterous – they didn't find the same sort of quiet, listless behaviour that had been found in 'minded' children. Unfortunately, day nurseries are also the most expensive form of day care, because they use professionally trained staff, and because of the long working day that they cover. Because of this, they are also the least common; it is very much easier to get a place for a child with a child-minder than in a day nursery. Because they are trying to give the children a 'home from home', day nurseries are often organised in family-type groups, where one special adult has care of a few children. Not all nurseries work this way, though; others are more general. Day nurseries largely seem to have a relaxed, happy atmosphere, in which the children thrive.

This, then, is a general picture of the day care available for young children throughout the country. Most studies seem to suggest that children benefit socially from having extra stimulation – in the way that playgroups and nursery schools provide – and from mixing with other children of their own age. As regards their intellectual development, as well, the children who are in some kind of organised daytime activities seem to benefit. But, as with so many of these kinds of things, there are never enough to go round! Places in day nurseries, as I said before, are hard to get hold of, and some children can be on the waiting list for years. Playgroups, too, tend to 'fill up' very quickly once they start, and often have to turn children away.

In this chapter, I've talked generally about intellectual development, and I've often mentioned the results of IQ tests. In the next chapter, we'll have a closer look at the way that intelligence tests have developed, and perhaps some of the problems that can be involved with intelligence testing.

Summary

1 J. Piaget, a Swiss psychologist, said that intellectual development happened in stages. The four main stages are: sensori-motor; pre-operational; concrete operational; and formal operational.

2 During each stage, cognitive development depends on the formation of schemata, by the twin processes of assimilation and accommodation.

3 Donaldson et al. showed that Piaget's findings may have arisen from the way that the studies were done in the first place. Other criticisms have also been made.

4 J. Bruner put forward a theory about the way that memories are stored. He said that it developed through three modes: enactive, iconic and symbolic representation.

5 Early experience has been shown to be important in cognitive development. Studies showed that the environment could have a dramatic effect in this.

6 Project Headstart was set up in America to provide pre-school experience for young children in deprived areas. Some improvements were noticed from it.

7 Pre-school provision in Britain is of four main kinds: playgroups, nursery schools, child-minders, and day nurseries. Each provides different kinds of care and experiences for the child.

Towards the end of the last century, scientists began to become
very interested in the way that people could be obviously
similar – in belonging to the same species – and yet, at the
same time, every individual was different. People were
different shapes and sizes, and some people were obviously
better at certain skills than others. In particular, they became
interested in the way that some people were, or appeared to
be, more _intelligent_ than others. Was it inherited? Certainly,
the noted academics of the time often came from families which
had produced other academics: one of the most famous
investigators of individual differences was Frances Galton, who
was a cousin of Charles Darwin, the man who developed the
theory of evolution which we looked at in Chapter 2. So
perhaps, people thought, intelligence was inherited, producing
families of high intelligence, and families of low intelligence,
with most families being somewhere in the middle.

One of the first attempts to _test_ intelligence systematically, took
place in France at the end of the last century. The reasons
for this lay in the way that those children who were not good
learners were educated. Previously, they had been kept at
home, because they didn't benefit from school education; but
in 1881, the French Government passed a law making school
education compulsory for all children. Because these children
now had to attend school, special schools were set up, much
like the ones that we have today. But they needed to have some
way of sorting out the children who were to attend these
special schools, to make sure that they would really get the
children who wouldn't manage in ordinary schools.
Accordingly, Alfred Binet was commissioned to develop some
means for doing this.
    Binet was particularly concerned that the children's grading
should not just depend on what they had already learned.
Since some children had had opportunities to learn, while
others hadn't, he wanted to develop a test which would enable
him to measure their _potential_, not what they had already
managed. He was also concerned that people should have a
means of assessing the child that did not depend on the parent's

report. He felt this was necessary because parents who wanted their children to go to ordinary schools would overstate their child's intelligence, while those who wanted the free board and lodging that the special schools provided for the children, would imply that their children were less capable than they in fact were. So an objective test which didn't depend on parents' reports or previous learning was necessary.

Together with a colleague, Theodore Simon, Binet developed a test for children which was based on the idea of *mental age*. By collecting data from vast numbers of children, they gradually worked out a range of different things that an average child could do when it had reached a certain age. The test that they developed was based on this range, and children were asked different questions, and their answers compared with the results obtained by other children of the same age. According to the questions which the child was able to answer, they could get an idea of the mental age of the child, or of how it compared with *average* children.

This test enabled Binet and Simon to sort out children who were mentally retarded, and needed to go to a special school. It was possible to detect these children because they were not able to manage the same problems as normal children of their age, but instead could only do much simpler problems. The questions themselves were, as I mentioned before, carefully chosen so that they didn't give an advantage to a child who had learned more, for instance in reading and writing. Instead, they involved problems like pointing out what was missing from a picture of a familiar object, or (for very young children) pointing to the nose, eyes, and mouth on a picture of a face.

A variation of the original Binet test is still used today, although it has been frequently revised and modernised. Since Binet's time, too, many other intelligence tests have been devised, but all of them make an attempt to conform to Binet's idea, that what the child has actually *learned* isn't important. It is the child's *potential* that the test should be examining.

Gradually, as intelligence tests became popular, so also did the *Intelligence Quotient* (IQ). This is a sort of score, based on Binet's idea of mental age, and which shows how much someone's intelligence (as measured by an intelligence test) compares with that of other people of the same age. A person's IQ is calculated by this formula:

$$\frac{\text{mental age}}{\text{chronological age}} \times 100$$

Chronological age is the person's real age – that is, the number of years that person has been alive. As you can see from this formula, if a child had a mental age of 9, and had been alive for 9 years, its IQ would come out as exactly 100. On the other hand, if it had a mental age of 12, but its real age was 10, then it would have an IQ of 120. If its mental age was 9, and it had a chronological age of 10, then its IQ would work out as 90.

We can see from this, that the 'normal' IQ is 100, since that is the time when your mental age and your physical age are the same. But it is quite common for people to have IQs anywhere between 68 and 132. The standard deviation of IQ scores is 16, which means that *most* people – 68 per cent in fact – get an IQ score between 84 and 116. Almost all the rest of the population come within the next 16 points, so that 95 per cent of the population have IQs between 68 and 132. So we wouldn't consider an IQ of 80 particularly low, but we would consider an IQ of 50 low – and also very uncommon!

Defining intelligence

But what *is* intelligence anyway? It's all very well to develop tests which measure intelligence, or which are supposed to measure intelligence, but that's not really any good if you can't say what intelligence is in the first place!

Most of us have a rough idea of what we mean when we say that someone is 'intelligent'. But when we try to pin it down, and to develop a *general* rule that would apply to *all* the people whom we think of as being 'intelligent', then it's not so easy. We might consider someone intelligent, for instance, because they had been to university and had a degree; and yet, we might also think, if we knew that person fairly well, that sometimes they seemed to be quite stupid. Or we might think someone was intelligent because of the way they talked, and the way that they approached problems – and yet that person might have left school without any qualifications. 'Yes, but that's a different *kind* of intelligence', you might say. True – that's the problem! There are so many different ways that people can act intelligently – what about a football player who plays a quick and thoughtful game? Or the person who can't spell at all, and doesn't like reading, and yet can usually come out of a game of poker or three-card brag in profit? Actually *defining* what we mean by intelligence can be one of the hardest problems of all, and yet we all use the word, and we know what we mean when we use it.

Over the years, psychologists, too, have had the same problem. One of the first attempts at defining intelligence was put forward by Spearman, in 1904. He thought that intelligence could be divided into two kinds: a *general* factor, which applied in all instances of 'intelligent behaviour'; and lots of *specific* factors, which belonged to the particular tasks that someone might attempt. So, for a particular problem – like solving a maths equation – both the 'g' factor *and* an 's' factor would be working together; but the 's' factor would be the set of abilities concerned with maths problems. For another kind of problem, like a jigsaw puzzle, the 'g' factor would remain the same, and would affect the way that people tried to solve the puzzle, but the 's' factor would be different from the one they had used for the maths problem. This is known as the two-factor theory of intelligence.

Some psychologists disagreed with Spearman's idea of a 'general' intelligence. Thurstone, in 1938, published his own definition of intelligence: he thought that it consisted of lots of *different* abilities, all working together when the problems required it, or working separately if they didn't. The sorts of abilities which he meant were the ability to visualise ('picture') shapes and distances accurately; the ability to comprehend words easily; the ability to use words fluently; mathematical ability; numerical ability (not the same thing!); logical reasoning, and so on. But all these abilities were *separate* – people might possess them in different amounts, but together they added up to a person's intelligence.

Guilford, in 1967, went even further. He proposed that intelligence is actually made up of 120 different factors, which all worked together to produce 'intelligent behaviour' of all the different kinds which could be observed in people. His model for this was something like a cube, which is made up of several smaller cubes, each small cube representing a different ability.

Arguments like this can go on forever, as it's almost impossible to come to any real agreement about *exactly* what is involved in intelligence. In the end, we have to settle on some sort of vague definition, like the one which was put forward by A. Heim, in 1970: 'Intelligent activity consists of grasping the essentials in a situation and responding appropriately to them'. Although this definition doesn't actually tell us very much, it does seem to sum up what most of us mean when we talk of intelligence.

Hebb's theory of intelligence

In 1949, D. O. Hebb argued that much of the disagreement about intelligence came about because people were very often talking about two different things when they talked of intelligence. The first, according to Hebb, was the *potential* intelligence encoded in the genetic 'blueprint' for the developing person – in other words, how the actual nerve cells (neurones) in the brain would develop, and the possible amount of intelligence which that could provide, *if it had an ideal environment to develop in*. But the second was how much intelligence actually *did* develop, as a result of the experiences of the individual.

As you can see, this is the familiar issue of how the genetic programme is affected by the environment, which we looked at in Chapter 3. And Rosenzweig and Bennet's experiment with gerbils, which I mentioned in the last chapter, would seem to support this view. If you remember, the gerbils which were brought up in the 'enriched' environment, with toys and playmates, actually developed larger brains than the ones which were brought up alone. While both sets of gerbils had had the genetic potential, not all of them had been able to realise that potential to the same extent.

Hebb called this potential intelligence *Intelligence A*. The other intelligence, the one which we actually develop, he called *Intelligence B*. So intelligence A is the genetically coded, potential intelligence, while intelligence B is the part of intelligence A which has developed, as a result of the interaction of the individual and the environment.

If we accept Hebb's view, we can see that the kind of argument in the nature/nurture debate on intelligence, which tries to say how much of intelligence is genetic, and how much is environmental, isn't a very sensible kind of approach. According to Hebb's view, in a sense all intelligence is genetic, but in another sense all intelligence is environmental. The two factors – genetics and environment – work together to form the individual's intelligence.

With most things, it isn't really practical to ask how much is environment, and how much heredity. A bird's egg, for instance, goes through a sequence of development after being laid, until it is ready to hatch. That sequence of development, where the new chick is formed, comes about as a result of the 'genetic blueprint', so in a sense, it's purely hereditary. But take away the environment which the egg is in, and what happens? The egg gets cold, and the embryo dies. On the other hand, if there wasn't any hereditary component, there wouldn't be any egg at all! *Both* the environment and the genetic blueprint are necessary for survival – you couldn't have one without the other.

Another psychologist, P. Vernon, proposed an addition, in 1950, to Hebb's intelligence types A and B. He said that within type B was a section which he called type C. And type C was that part of an individual's intelligence which an intelligence test actually measures.

An intelligence test cannot really measure every kind of intelligent behaviour that an individual might show, it can only take a selection – a *sample* – of different kinds of intelligent behaviour. For example we would probably agree that a person who was involved in a train crash, and stayed calm and helped to get other people out of the carriage, was showing intelligent behaviour. But, short of setting up a train crash ourselves, we couldn't *test* that. We might try, for instance, by asking a person what they would do in that situation. But there is always the possibility that they would say something different – people often surprise themselves in an emergency, and are far more capable than they ever thought they would be. So asking the question wouldn't truly sample the behaviour.

Other kinds of behaviour, though, we can sample. We can ask someone to solve an arithmetic problem, or memorise and repeat a string of letters. Or we could ask them to work out connections between different items – like kayak, yacht, liner, canoe, and catamaran.

Of course, there are problems with this approach too. That last question would be very easy for someone who knew that they were all types of boats. But what about someone who's never heard of a kayak, or a catamaran? How would they answer it? It seems that, very often, a test gives an advantage to people who have had a certain type of upbringing, or who have come from a certain cultural background. Although people who design intelligence tests try to keep them 'culture-fair', so that they don't give an advantage to one person over another in this way, it is very difficult to manage. Most intelligence tests suffer from *some* problems in terms of cultural bias, but writers of intelligence tests try to keep this as small as they can.

The nature/nurture debate on intelligence	Although Hebb tried to point out that intelligence is *both* genetic *and* environmental, some psychologists have still become involved in the argument as to which is the more important factor. This started at the very beginning of this century, when Sir Francis Galton was investigating intelligence in different families.
Galton's family studies of intelligence	Galton was interested in the way that intelligent parents tend to have intelligent children, while parents who are only average often seem to have average children too. He proposed that a new science should start up, called *eugenics*, by which intelligent individuals would have children together and less intelligent people would be prevented from having children, through compulsory sterilisation in an attempt to improve the quality of the human race. But Galton may not necessarily have been correct in thinking that family intelligence was inherited. For one thing, parents who have had a good education and are generally considered 'intelligent' may provide different environments for their children to grow up in. Their children may have a lot more books, or educational toys, and their

parents may encourage them to ask certain kinds of questions more. So it may not necessarily be inherited intelligence that is being passed on in families, it may just as well be environmental.

Twin studies of intelligence   A different way of looking at the nature-nurture debate on intelligence has been by making identical twin studies. Identical (MZ) twins, as we saw in Chapter 2, have exactly the same heredity, because they've come from the same zygote and have the same genes and chromosomes. If you had a pair of identical twins, then, and they were brought up separately, and ended up with different IQs, you would know that this difference couldn't have come from heredity. It must have come from the environments that the twins have lived in.

Studies like this that have been performed with identical twins, have sometimes used fraternal (DZ) twins as well. The idea is, that since DZ twins are different genetically – in the same way that brothers or sisters are different – then, if they are brought up in the same home, and in the same way, any differences in the IQs must come from heredity factors as their environment has been the same.

The most famous and influential twin study of all was performed by Cyril Burt (1955). Burt claimed to have investigated 53 pairs of identical twins who had been brought up in entirely separate environments, and to have found such high correlations between their IQs as to provide clear proof that intelligence must be inherited.

Burt's findings had a massive influence on the English education system. Burt argued that a child's ability to learn was innate, and that was why some children were successful in education and others weren't – the environment was pretty well unimportant. Those who didn't have the innate ability, Burt argued, should have a different kind of education, more geared towards practical or manual work. Even nowadays, many teachers still hold this idea, although there isn't really much psychological evidence for it.

In 1976, Oliver Gillie published a front-page article in the *Sunday Times*, in which he argued that Burt's research was faked: he had invented his data, and published papers from two research assistants who didn't really exist. Later investigations showed that Gillie's assertions were true: despite their being so widely accepted and so influential, Burt's findings were fraudulent.

This is an important case, because it shows how ready people were to believe that IQ was inherited, and how they overlooked many quite obvious inaccuracies in his data – some of which were pointed out by Kamin (1974) but ignored until Gillie's article. Not only that, but Burt's figures formed the basis for many other pieces of research which rested on the idea that IQ was inherited, such as the work by Jensen (1969) which we'll be looking at in the section on race and IQ.

There have been other twin studies, but they too have had serious weaknesses – although the researchers in these cases do at least seem to have been honest! In 1928, Newman, Freeman and Holzinger published the results of a study of separated identical twins; and another study, by Shields, was published in 1962. Their major findings are given below.

Study	MZ apart	MZ together
Newman et al	.67	.91
Shields	.51	.83

The figures in this table are known as *correlation coefficients*. They are ways of saying how far one thing varies if another thing varies. For instance, if you had a perfect correlation between twins' IQ scores, you'd be saying that if one twin from a pair had a high IQ, then the other from that pair would always have an equally high IQ, whereas if a twin from another pair had a low IQ, then the other twin from that pair would always have an equally low IQ. In other words, you'd be saying that the twins' scores varied together, according to the pairs. Here, we haven't got a *perfect* correlation like that – a perfect correlation would be 1. (Or +1, if we want to be very accurate). But the closer the figure gets to 1, the closer the correlation is between the pairs of twins, the more they vary together. So a correlation of 0.9 is a closer correlation than one of 0.6, because it's closer to 1.

As you can see from the table, both these studies imply that it is growing up in the same environment which produces the similarity – when the twins are brought up separately there is some correlation, but not a very strong one.

Newman et al found that the correlation between the IQs of ordinary siblings (brothers and sisters) was about .64 if they were brought up together, so their results implied that the inherited similarities did make some kind of difference.

There are problems with these studies, though. One is that correlations can only show how two measurements vary together – whether one gets bigger when the other gets bigger, and vice versa. They can't tell us what *causes* the variation, which might be all sorts of different things. So just because two things correlate highly, we can't jump to conclusions about *why* they do.

Another criticism has been made of the studies themselves.

Newman et al selected their subjects for the experiment by asking for volunteers by post. Because they didn't interview their subjects until after they'd selected them, they may have rejected some pairs of identical twins because they didn't sound similar enough. It's only recently that scientists have been able to test people to find out if they really are MZ twins or not – some twins are very similar, but then so are some brothers and sisters. Newman et al wanted to avoid including twins who *seemed* identical but weren't really, but they may have gone too far the other way.

Shields' study, too, has been criticised; mainly because of what counted as a 'separated' pair of twins. The normal situation for these twins was that one of them had been reared by the mother and the other one by a close family member, like an aunt or grandmother. Often the twins were frequently together and went to the same schools, so their environments couldn't really be considered to be all that different. In some cases, too, the children had only been separated for a relatively short period of time. Similar criticisms have been made of other twin studies, as well.

Adoption studies   We can see from these problems that twin studies aren't much use to us in finding out whether intelligence really is inherited. Another kind of study looks at children who have been adopted when they were young, and to see whether their IQs are closer to their *biological* parents, or to their *adopted* ones. If they are closer to the adopted ones, then we might think that the environment is more important, but if they are closer to their biological parents, then we may conclude that heredity matters most.

A famous study by Skodak and Skeels, in 1949, adopted this approach, and appeared to show that there is a very high heredity factor in intelligence – adopted children had IQs which were much closer to their natural parents. Another study, by Jensen in 1969, reported the same thing. However, other studies have not agreed.

One problem with the Skodak and Skeels study is that their data can be analysed in more than one way. When they published their results, they showed quite a high correlation between adopted children and their biological parents, about 0.44. But other psychologists have found that if their results are re-analysed, then they get totally different findings – a correlation of about -0.2. So it seems that we can't place very much reliability on the Skodak and Skeels findings of inherited intelligence.

Often this type of study is made on a very small sample, which means that it is difficult to generalise the results. Another problem is the tendency of adoption agencies to 'match' adoptive parents to natural parents, a process known as 'selective placement'. Because they make an effort to place the child in the same sort of background and home as it has come from, the differences between the natural parents and the adoptive parents in IQ may not be all that large – we may only be talking about very small differences in measurement.

The studies that we looked at in the last chapter put forward a different kind of picture – they showed how intelligence *could* be influenced by the environment – often dramatically. But it does seem as though Hebb's idea of intelligence A and intelligence B is a sensible one – that we have the genetic *potential*, but it's up to our environments how far we actually realise it!

The 'race and intelligence' debate

This debate was triggered mainly by an article by Jensen, in 1969, about American black populations. Jensen accepted Burt's findings, and concluded that differences in intelligence were 80% inherited and only 20% environmental. He also observed that in IQ tests black Americans scored consistently lower than white Americans. From these two things, he concluded that there must be a genetic, racial difference in intelligence between white and black people, and that therefore they should receive different types of education.

This argument caused a considerable amount of argument – in much the same way as Bowlby's pronouncements on maternal deprivation caused such a stir in this country. And, as with Bowlby, researchers quickly pointed out many of the fallacies in Jensen's reasonings.

We have already looked at one of these – whether, in view of the criticisms which have been made of Burt's studies, Burt's assessment of heritability can be accepted. But there was other evidence which showed that this difference between white and black Americans didn't come from genetic factors, but had more to do with the types of environments in which the two groups grew up.

One study demonstrating this was by Tyler, in 1965. Tyler showed that black people from northern USA scored more highly on IQ tests than those from southern USA. Since there are wide differences in the way the black people live in the north and the south of the United States, we would attribute this to environmental factors. If it were genetic, then you would expect the black population everywhere to score similarly. Tyler also showed that black people who moved from the South to the North gained in IQ points – even more evidence of an environmental influence.

A study by Labov, in 1972, pointed out that children from black families in the United States often suffered from poor schooling and bad housing, and that it wasn't correct to assume that environments were the same for both black and white Americans. And many people pointed out the way that IQ tests were biased in favour of children from white, middle-class American homes – those from other backgrounds suffered in the tests because they hadn't gathered the right kind of background knowledge in the first place.

To support this, a study by Scarr and Weinberg, in 1976, looked at the IQ scores of black children who had been adopted by white families. They found that these children scored just as well as white children in IQ tests. So where the environments were the same as white children, there wasn't any evidence of an IQ difference. It seems that Jensen was rather jumping to conclusions when he said that there was a genetic racial difference in IQ.

Many researchers see the work of Jensen and the others as revealing a basic racism on the part of the researchers. Brooks (1984) pointed out that ever since IQ tests were first developed, girls have scored more highly on the same tests than boys – if you take the test scores themselves, the difference is about the same as Jensen's observed differences between white and black populations. But from the beginning the 'norm' or standard for the girls was adjusted, so that when the basic scores were translated into IQ measurements the IQs for boys and girls came out the same. If these researchers were really so bothered about racial differences, Brooks argues, then what they should be doing is adjusting the 'norms' for people of different racial backgrounds, to allow for the general difference. The fact they they don't even consider this shows that, despite claims to the contrary, these researchers are being racist in their approach to the question.

Overall, there seems to be no valid evidence that black people are any less intelligent than white – and many studies which have controlled properly for background and cultural bias in the tests used come out with results that go in the opposite direction! A study by Tizard, in 1974, found that black and mixed-parent pre-school children in London did better than white children on tests of mental performance. What's most important in this question is the type of education and expectations which the child experiences throughout its schooling: not the colour of its skin.

There are many ways in which the environment can affect intelligence – over the last two chapters we have looked at some of them. But sometimes, an environmental effect may look like a genetic one. Cravioto, in a study of children in Mexico, showed how a good diet with plenty of protein was important for the development of intelligence and motor co-ordination. Even if people are well fed in later life, the damage done by an inadequate diet during childhood may still stay with them. And, through the process of 'transgenerational transmission', which I mentioned in Chapter 3, Rose has pointed out that this may carry on to the next generation too. A mother who was undernourished as a child may not have been able to develop properly, and so when pregnant may provide a damaging environment for a child. When the child is born, it may appear that its low IQ is genetic, but it could in fact be an *environmental* effect, from the previous generation. Rose has demonstrated that this can happen with rats, and he says that this could also account for some apparently genetic IQ differences in human beings, too.

Language is often considered to be an important part of intelligence – but how do children learn language? In the next chapter we'll be looking at some of the theories which have been put forward about this, and some of the evidence as well.

Summary   1 Binet developed the first intelligence tests at the end of the last century. Later on the idea of the IQ developed –

$$\frac{\text{mental age}}{\text{chronological age}} \times 100$$

2 Defining intelligence is very difficult. Hebb described Intelligence A and Intelligence B. Vernon later added the idea of Intelligence C.

3 IQ tests can give some people an advantage, if they come from a particular type of background.

4 Galton thought that intelligence was inherited because it was passed on in families, but this could be environmental too.

5 Twin studies have appeared to show that intelligence was inherited. But their results are open to criticism.

6 Studies of adopted children have shown that there may be a strong hereditary influence, but these too are not very conclusive.

7 Jensen suggested that black Americans scored lower than white Americans on IQ tests because of a genetic racial

difference, but other studies have shown that this difference is much more likely to have arisen through environmental influences.

8 Some environmental effects may be 'disguised' and appear as genetic effects, because of transgenerational transmission.

Chapter 10   **Measuring mental characteristics**

As we saw in the last chapter, intelligence testing developed through the twentieth century, in an attempt to produce a way of measuring a mental characteristic in an objective, scientific fashion. The branch of psychology which is concerned with mental measurement of this kind is known as *psychometrics*. In this chapter we will look at some of the issues which come up when we try to measure mental abilities objectively.

Problems of mental measurement

There are a number of problems which appear when we start to look carefully at what is involved when we are developing psychometric tests. One of the most obvious problems, of course, is that we can't actually observe mental characteristics. We can't see intelligence, or personality – all we can do is to infer that they exist, from what people do or say. So psychologists who are trying to produce objective measures of mental characteristics need to be very careful about making sure that they really are measuring what they are supposed to measure. In psychometric terms, this is known as ensuring that the test has *validity*.

Another problem with trying to produce objective ways of measuring mental characteristics is making sure that what we are assessing is something which is consistent – that it is truly a characteristic of the person, rather than just being the result of something temporary, like mood or the situation they happen to be in at the time that they take the test. In psychometric terms, this is known as making sure that the test has *reliability*.

And a third problem which comes up when we are trying to measure mental characteristics is to do with what we can reasonably expect. There's no point producing a measure of intelligence, say, or personality, if you have no idea what the final scores mean when you have got them. You need to know whether the person you have been testing is reasonably typical, or if they are exceptional by comparison with other people. So you also need to make sure that your test will reflect the general differences in the population, and you can only do that by testing a large number of people and finding out what the normal results of the test would be. In psychometric terms, this is known as *standardisation*.

Validity, reliability and standardisation are the three most important concepts in mental testing. Because of this, it is worth taking a deeper look at how they are applied to psychometric tests.

Assessing the validity of a test

On the surface, it might seem an easy thing to make sure that a test is really measuring what it is supposed to measure. But it isn't really as easy as all that. For a start, we can't just make judgements about what seems right, because it's too easy to be taken in by fashionable ideas or false beliefs. Two centuries ago, for instance, it was a common belief that you could tell people's characters by the bumps on their skulls. People at that time believed that mental faculties, such as reverence, compassion, or sensuality would show up as enlargements in the brain, and that these in turn would enlarge the skull above it. Evidence from a *phrenologist* (the expert who did the bump-reading) was even accepted by courts of law as evidence of that person's character, and court judgements were sometimes based on it. Since it was such a commonly-held belief at the time, if someone in those days had attempted to produce a psychometric test, they would have thought it absolutely necessary that such a test should include measurements of skull shapes. Although we like to believe that we, in our day, are more enlightened than that, the truth is that every age has its fashionable beliefs, and so just looking at a test and judging that it probably measures what it is supposed to measure just isn't enough.

Face validity

We do still expect a psychometric test to look roughly as though it measures what it is supposed to measure, though. This is a form of validity known as *face validity*, or sometimes *surface validity*; and although nobody would be happy with it as the only form of validation, at the same time, it's unlikely that we would really be happy with a test that didn't look as though it had any connection with the thing it was supposed to be measuring. We are happier with, say, an intelligence test which consists of mental problems than we would be with an intelligence test which consisted of shoe sizes and knowledge of golf courses. But on its own, face validity is never enough.

Criterion validity

So if we can't use face validity to assess the validity of a test, what can we use? One option is to match it up with some other measurement, and see how it compares. This is known as *criterion validity*. There are two kinds of criterion validity: *concurrent validity* and *predictive validity*. Concurrent validity compares the results of the test with some other criterion which is in existence at the time. So, for example, the results of a personality test designed to measure levels of anxiety might be

compared with the same person's measurements of
physiological indicators of anxiety, like measures of GSR and
heart rate obtained using a polygraph (see Chapter 17).

Predictive validity, on the other hand, compares the results
of the test with some outcome which hasn't happened yet. So,
for example, we might test the predictive validity of a job
aptitude test by seeing how well people who scored in a certain
way in the test actually did when they were taken on for the
job in real life.

Of course, criterion measures of validity also depend on what
we believe, to some extent. If we believe, for instance, that
intelligence is what helps people to get on in school, then we
might try comparing the results of an intelligence test with
school success, on the grounds that the two should correlate
positively (we looked at correlation in the last chapter). But if
you believed that getting on in school really depends on other
things, like whether the teachers like you, or whether you have
the right kind of accent, then you wouldn't pick school success
as an appropriate criterion to assess the validity of an
intelligence test.

Construct validity   The third type of validity is known as *construct validity*. This is
all to do with the psychological theory which underlies the
test. For example, Sternberg's (1985) theory of intelligence
argues that the 'mental abilities' part of intelligence consists
of three different components: *metacomponents*, which come into
play when the person is taking a general overview of things,
such as when planning or making decisions; *performance
components*, which are the mental skills and abilities needed to
carry out specific tasks; and *knowledge-acquisition components*,
which are the mental skills and abilities involved in picking up
new information. According to Sternberg's theory, a test will
only be valid if it contains items which are designed to test
each of these three components of intelligence. If it doesn't,
then it couldn't be regarded as a true measure of intelligence.

So construct validity, too, depends on beliefs to some extent
– the beliefs we hold about what the thing that we are
measuring 'really' is. If we are to assess the construct validity
of a psychometric test, we first of all need to know what it is
that we believe the test is about – and that isn't as easy as it
sounds. Actually defining psychological characteristics can
sometimes be the hardest thing of all – and, as we saw in the
last chapter when we looked at theories of intelligence, each
definition contains a hidden theory about what the mental
characteristic in question is really like.

Ecological validity   A fourth type of validity has become increasingly important in
recent years. This is all to do with how much a psychological

test, or the measures used in a psychological study, actually reflect their equivalents in real life. It is known as *ecological validity*. Some psychologists, for example, have criticised intelligence tests because they tend to be concerned with pencil and paper problem-solving, and they consider that this is not a realistic description of what intelligence is like in real life, which might include, say, quick-thinking at times of emergency, rapid repartee in conversations, or all sorts of other skills.

Some new approaches to psychometric assessment have attempted to tackle the question of ecological validity by simulating real-life situations. For example, rather than asking people to complete a questionnaire, a test of a manager's decision-making ability to make appropriate decisions might involve giving each manager or potential manager a limited amount of time to make decisions about a number of problems which they might come across in a typical working day. In such situations, the testers hope that the test will be more useful because it is closer to the types of decisions which managers would normally face. In other words, it has higher ecological validity.

Response bias and validity

There are other problems to do with validity, as well. One of them is how we make sure that the test isn't producing what is known as a *response bias* – a tendency to answer the questions in one way rather than another. For example: if you ask someone a question like 'In general, would you describe yourself as a sensible person?', most people would answer 'yes' simply because almost everyone thinks of themselves as sensible. Also, people generally tend to say 'yes' rather than 'no' – perhaps because we generally prefer to conform to others rather than disagree with them (see Chapter 20). So the validity of such a test would be questionable, because the questions themselves would be producing the answers, rather than their really coming from the person's underlying personality.

The way that the question is phrased can also produce a response bias. If you ask a question like 'Which are you normally, generous or miserly?' people will always tend to answer 'generous', because the word 'miserly' tends to be associated with very unpleasant characters – it has negative connotations. But if you asked: 'Which are you normally, generous or prudent?' you would get a very different range of answers, because 'prudent' is a much more positive way of saying that someone is cautious in spending money. It's OK to be prudent, it's not OK to be miserly, in society's terms.

The third type of response bias comes about when people are trying to present themselves in the best possible light. If you were doing a psychometric test, you might try to answer the questions so that you would seem to be a really good person, or one who never does anything wrong. Some psychometric tests have special 'lie-detector' questions built into them, so that it is possible to tell if someone is doing that. For example, if there was a question like 'Have you ever told a lie in your life?' and someone answered 'no', it would be a reasonable guess that they were not being strictly truthful, since even the most honest people have usually told one lie sometime, even if it was only when they were a child. These lie-detector questions are scattered through the test, and if someone scores more than a set number of them (not just one – after all, there always *might* be someone who has never ever lied!) then the tester knows that they cannot take the test results as being an accurate reflection of that person.

A more general form of response bias, which affects whole groups of people rather than just one or two, concerns what happens when a test is biased towards members of a particular culture and not other people. In the early days of intelligence testing, for example, Goddard (1913) gave intelligence tests to people from Central Europe who wanted to enter America. The tests were very culture-specific, asking people for instance to give the nicknames of American baseball teams, or identify items from American daily life. Although his interpreters pointed out that they could never have done the tests when they first arrived, Goddard insisted that the tests were an accurate measure of intelligence, and that they showed that certain groups of central Europeans were below average in intelligence. As a result, American immigration laws were introduced which restricted entry for those groups, and resulted in large numbers of Poles and others being unable to escape to America during the Second World War. Instead they were sent to the concentration camps.

Assessing the reliability of a test

As we saw earlier, the reliability of a test is all about whether the test produces a consistent result, and doesn't change just because someone's in a bad mood, or because they happen to be in a difficult situation, or for other temporary reasons of that kind. In other words, we want to be sure that if the same people are tested, the test will still give the same results.

Test-retest reliability

So how do people go about making sure of that? One of the obvious ways, of course, is to give people the same test twice, leaving a space of time in between. Then the results would be correlated, to see if they were roughly the same. This is known as the *test-retest method*. Of course, you wouldn't expect the two sets of scores to be absolutely identical, but if the test is reliable, you would expect a very high correlation, say, at least 0.9 between the scores on the two occasions.

The problem with the test-retest method, though, is that the correlations might become artificially high because people taking the test for the second time might remember what they said the first time. So most of the time, we need to use measures of reliability which wouldn't allow that to happen.

Split-half reliability   A second method of testing for reliability which is sometimes used by people developing psychometric tests is the *split-half method*. In this technique, the items of the test are divided into two separate halves: for example, all of the even-numbered items might be put together as one half-test, and all the odd-numbered ones become another test. Then one of these half-tests would be given to a group of people on one occasion, while the other half-test would be given to the same people some time later. The results of the two halves would be correlated, and if they reached 0.8 or higher, the test would be judged to be reliable.

One of the problems with the split-half method, though, is that it can be quite difficult to balance the halves. It isn't often as simple as just taking odd and even numbers, because in most psychometric tests there are a number of different scales which are being assessed. One question might be giving answers which relate to one scale, like, say, openness to experience, while the next question might relate to something entirely different, like decision-making ability. So to use the split-half method, the two half-tests need to be very carefully matched, to make sure that the questions for each sub-scale are equally shared between each half-test. Also, of course, it's possible that having a shorter version of the test may itself affect the outcomes to some extent – subjects may have less time to get bored, and so answer each question more carefully. Although this would be the same for each half-test, it might mean that the correlation which they provide is higher than the correlation of two full-sized versions of the test would be.

Alternate-forms reliability   The third type of reliability is known as the *alternate-forms method*. In most cases, when psychometric tests are first developed, two equivalent versions of the test are produced, carefully matched for difficulty and for the type of test items which they contain. This makes it much easier to check the reliability of the test, because one version can be given to subjects on one occasion and the second to the same subjects later. Since the actual test items are different, the subjects won't be affected even if they do remember what they said before; and since they do a fully-fledged psychometric test on each occasion, they will be showing what the proper experience of the test would normally be.

Standardising a test

Developing a psychometric test doesn't just involve trying to develop measures which are reliable and valid. Even if we achieved this, the results of a test still wouldn't tell us anything much. To interpret test results, we need more information, and that information has to be about how most people would score on that test.

Population norms

Standardising a test involves giving it to large numbers of people, in order to develop what are known as *population norms*. Population norms describe the pattern of results which the test would give if enough people took it – in other words, they describe the results which are typical, or normal, for a given population. Obviously, when we are giving population norms, we couldn't describe the results that would be typical for a whole population by giving just a single score: there are too many differences between people for that. So instead, population norms tend to take the form of a set of tables, divided into different categories which tend to have different typical scores.

For example: in personality tests, it is more common for men to score highly on certain types of questions (like, for instance, those to do with assertiveness) than it is for women. On that sort of measure, a typical score for a man would be different from a typical score for a woman. It would also be different for different age-groups: people who were in their thirties or forties might score differently on assertiveness from those in their late teens. So the population norms would have separate tables for men and for women, and these tables in turn would be divided into ones for different age-groups.

One of the problems of this practice, of course, is that by having different tables for men and women, it is easy to end up reinforcing stereotypes. Intelligence tests, for example, have different norms for men and for women. This is because, ever since the first intelligence tests were developed, girls have scored more highly on specific test items than boys. So the 'average' score for girls on intelligence test items tends to be higher than the 'average' score for boys. Obviously, if they were regarded as representing the same population, this would mean that girls tended as a group to have higher IQs than boys. So they are regarded as coming from different populations, and the population norms are different for boys and girls: a girl has to score slightly higher than a boy in the same test to achieve the same final IQ .

When we are talking about aspects of personality testing, it is also important that population norm tables are really reflecting the current situation by being kept up to date. Population norm tables are developed when a test is first published, and are revised when the test is put out in a new edition. Maintaining population norms as a fully accurate picture of the population would involve re-testing large numbers of people on a frequent basis. In an area like personality testing, where social assumptions about personality and gender role have changed so much over time, such testing would be essential for the population norms of the test to reflect the population at large: as gender roles have become more flexible, what was considered a 'normal' personality for a woman in the 1950s would not necessarily be considered normal today.

Of course, this also links with the nature/nurture debate. Some of the older psychometricians, like H. J. Eysenck, believe that personality is innate, coming from inherited biological origins and not particularly influenced by the environment. If you take such a view, then naturally you would not see it as being so important that standardisation norms are re-calculated to keep them up to date, because if personality is genetic in origin it would be fixed and not changeable. But very few modern psychologists would take such an extreme view: most psychometricians recognise that a society or culture does have some kind of influence on the personalities which develop within it, if only because it sets standards and norms which people try to live up to, and which they bring their children up with.

The normal distribution

Population norms in psychometric testing are based around the idea that the results in the population as a whole will be distributed in a certain kind of way. Most people in the population will score in the middle, some will score high, and some will score low. But the number of people who score very high or very low on the test – if it accurately reflects the population – will become fewer and fewer towards the extreme ends of the scale. This is known as the *normal distribution curve*.

The idea that psychological characteristics will show a normal distribution curve in the population as a whole is a

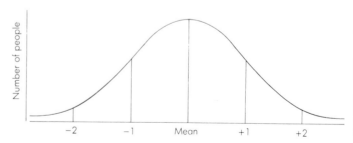

Fig. 10.1 The normal distribution curve

very fundamental assumption in psychometric testing. Psychometric tests of all kinds take it for granted that their particular mental characteristic will be normally distributed. So in creativity testing, for example, it is taken for granted that a few people will be very highly creative, most people will be only averagely so, while a few will be very uncreative indeed. Similarly, in personality testing, it is taken for granted that, say, some people will be extremely extravert, others will be extremely introverted, while most will be somewhere in between the two. Or in occupational testing, it is assumed that some people will be extremely decisive, others will be extremely indecisive, while most come somewhere in between.

As you can see, the idea has face validity – it seems very plausible. But the trouble is that we don't really know whether it is true or not. The way that human characteristics produce a normal distribution curve if enough people are measured was identified by Galton, in 1888. But Galton was describing the pattern of results from measures of physical characteristics, not mental ones. He had opened an 'anthropometric centre' in London, where people could pay 3d and be measured in all sorts of ways: height, breadth of upper arm, lung capacity, strength of grip, and so on. It was very popular with visitors, and as a result Galton obtained all sorts of physical measurements from several thousand people. When they were plotted on a graph, they showed normal distribution curves for each different physical characteristic.

Galton went on to argue that, since mental characteristics were presumably dependent on physical ones, they must show a normal distribution too. But that's actually a very questionable argument: nobody has yet managed to show that mental characteristics do really depend on physical ones, at least in any subtle sense (obviously, if you had most of your brain removed, you wouldn't think too well!). We don't really know if mental characteristics really are normally distributed, because psychometricians have always taken it for granted that they are. The results of psychometric tests are always normally distributed, but that's because they are designed that way. If a new test was designed which gave different results, people wouldn't accept it as being valid. So how would we ever know?

Standardising on other tests

Which brings us on to another aspect of standardisation. Standardising a test doesn't just involve giving it to large numbers of people and seeing what the results are. It also involves comparing these results with other, more established tests. So, for example, every intelligence test which is developed goes through a standardisation procedure which involves comparing its results with the *Stanford–Binet* – the first major intelligence test. And a test that gave very different results would be assumed to be worthless.

The population norms which are obtained from a test are, as I said, the pattern of results obtained from giving the test to large numbers of people. These are usually given in the form of a table, so that the tester can look up a particular score, see how typical it is, and how it should be interpreted – as typical, or as unusual, and if unusual by how much. We need to know, for instance, what a typical test result would be, so that we can see whether the result obtained by one person is reasonably typical or very uncommon. That means that we need to know what the *mean score* given by a test is – the average score. But we also need more information than that: it's all very well saying, for instance, that the mean score given by an intelligence test is 100, but supposing you got a test score of 120? Is that still average, or is it unusual? It's not possible to tell just from the mean. What we also need to know is how the scores are 'spread out' – how much they are likely to vary. The measure of spread is known as the *standard deviation*. We need both items of information to interpret the score. The tables of population norms which are developed as a result of standardising a test are based on the means and standard deviations of the test results for that section of the population.

Nomothetic and idiographic tests

The development of population norms also relates to whether a test is *nomothetic* or *idiographic*. Nomothetic tests are concerned with identifying characteristics of people in general, and measuring how a given individual measures up on a scale which represents the whole range of the population. Idiographic tests, on the other hand, are not concerned with making comparisons between one person and another. Instead, they are concerned with describing just one individual.

So, for example, Eysenck's personality test, which measures everyone on the extraversion and neuroticism scales, is a nomothetic test, and so is Cattell's 16PF, which identifies sixteen personality factors which apply to everyone. Since people have different personalities, according to this model, they score differently on each of the sixteen personality factors – but the factors are considered to represent the major aspects of human personality in general. And in order to make sense out of them, it is necessary to know how other people scored: it tells us nothing to say that someone scored 12 on the neuroticism scale, for instance, unless we know what the normal range is, and how extreme a score has to be before it counts as unusual.

The Q-sort and the repertory grid, on the other hand, which we will be looking at later in this chapter, are idiographic tests. The Q-sort indicates how a person sees themselves – their self-concept – and how that compares with their ideal self, while the repertory grid gives an insight into how a person sees and interprets their world. These tests are self-contained, in the sense that they provide a therapist with information about that person anyway – they don't need to be compared with other people's scores before they can make sense. So for idiographic tests, population norms are less important.

We can see, then, how validity, reliability and standardisation play a central part in the development of psychometric tests. When we are trying to measure mental characteristics or abilities, we have to make sure that the tests we produce are valid, and really measure what they are supposed to measure; that they are reliable, and give a consistent picture of that individual; and, usually, that they will let us know how that person compares with others in the population. But, as we've seen, actually achieving all of that isn't as easy as it sounds.

Tests and theories

As we saw when we looked at construct validity, there is some kind of theory about what is being tested underlying each psychometric test. People who develop tests ask certain questions rather than others, and they choose those questions because they feel that they will allow the tester to find out relevant information. Whether you judge that information is relevant depends on what you think it is relevant to – in other words, what you judge to be the important underlying features of what you are looking at. Perhaps the clearest way of seeing how underlying theories affect what is being tested is by looking at four different types of personality tests, and the theories which underlie them.

Projective tests

For example: Freud (1901) developed a theory about the human personality which saw the human mind as being like an iceberg, with ⅘ of it below the surface. Although the unconscious mind, according to Freud's theory, is the main factor in motivating human behaviour – the main influence in why people act as they do – it is not something that we can be directly aware of. It remains hidden, and can only be discovered indirectly, through symbols in dreams, slips of the tongue, or by the unconscious mind projecting its concerns or obsessions onto ambiguous or neutral stimuli.

Because the influence of the unconscious mind is so difficult to get at, it wouldn't have been possible to develop a psychometric test which asked people direct questions. So instead, those psychometric tests which are based on Freudian or other psychodynamic theories take a more indirect approach. They involve showing the subject some kind of ambiguous figure, or shape, and asking them to say what the image represents. The idea is that, since there is no obviously right

Fig. 10.2 What does this ink-blot remind you of?

answer in the material itself, the answer that they give will indicate the concerns of the unconscious mind. These are known as *projective tests*.

The most famous of these projective tests is the *Rorschach ink-blot test*, in which people are shown large shapes made from ink-blots, and asked to say what each shape reminds them of. Then their answers are checked in standardisation tables, which identify the most common responses and those which are less common. Another famous projective test is the *Thematic Apperception Test*, in which a subject is shown pictures which have scenes involving real people in them, but the pictures are ambiguous. For example: one picture shows men lying around in a field, but there is nothing in the picture to indicate whether the men are alive and just resting, sleeping, or dead. So when someone is asked to explain what is happening there, the interpretation which they give comes from their own minds and reveals their own unconscious impressions, rather than coming from the stimulus itself.

In both of these tests, the subject is asked to respond to a number of different pictures, not just one or two. By looking at the individual's total responses to the whole set, the idea is that a trained tester can build up a picture which will help them in psychoanalysis – a kind of therapy designed to explore the person's unconscious mind, based on Freudian ideas.

Tests of personality traits

Some psychologists have taken what they describe as a behaviourist view, which is that personality is only the sum of the ways that people act. Rather than resulting from unconscious motives and drives, as Freud argued, these psychologists consider that what we mean by personality, essentially, is the sum of different types of behaviour. So the tests which they develop ask about a range of different behaviours, and then look to see which of these behaviours link together.

The heart of this approach lies in the statistical technique known as *factor analysis*. This is a way of finding out which scores out of a large set seem to be grouped together. For example: when Cattell was developing his model of personality, he began by obtaining data from life-record information, including things like school grades or absence from work, self-ratings, and objective tests. From these he developed a large range of questions, and tested them on a large number of subjects. By applying factor analysis, he showed that the answers to these questions tended to cluster together, into sixteen major personality traits; and he used this as the basis of his model of personality.

Cattell argued that his sixteen personality factors would provide a 'picture' of someone, but only if it was taken along with an individual description of that person, because everybody has unique characteristics too. So when Cattell's 16PF test – the test which he developed – is used in personnel selection or in clinical assessments, it is always accompanied by an interview or some other way of assessing the person's own individual characteristics.

Eysenck (1947) also developed a trait theory of personality, using the behaviourist assumption that personality was simply the sum of behaviour. Also using factor analysis, he concluded that the essential features of personality could be expressed in terms of two major factors. One of these was concerned with how outgoing the person was: at one extreme were highly sociable extraverts, while at the other were the quiet, isolated people described as introverts. The second dimension was concerned with how anxious or calm the individual was: at one end was neuroticism, and at the other stability.

Although Eysenck argued that these two factors had a *biological basis* – the introversion/extraversion dimension relating to the levels of activity in the cerebral cortex, and the neuroticism dimension relating to the activity of the autonomic nervous system – his two dimensions were originally identified through factor analysis of responses to questions. It was only later that Eysenck correlated these dimensions with other behavioural measures, and argued that they probably had a biological origin.

Fig. 10.3 Eysenck's theory of personality

The Q-sort Some tests are based on different underlying theories. For example: the theory of personality developed by Carl Rogers (1961) argued that people have two very basic needs: one for positive regard from other people (love, affection, or even just respect), and the other to develop their own abilities and aptitudes (which Rogers referred to as *self-actualisation*). People who feel secure in their positive regard from others have a strong basis from which to explore their own self-actualisation. But people who feel less secure, and are constantly anxious that they will lose the affection or love which matters to them, find that harder to do, because they can't risk the disapproval which might come if they did something that the other person didn't like.

This means that, unless they find a relationship which will give them the secure affection that they need, these people are always trying to live up to other people's ideals. As a result, they tend to develop unrealistically high personal goals: they feel they always have to do things perfectly, and should never make mistakes; and if they fail in this they worry about it. The therapy that Rogers developed to help such people was aimed at helping them to feel secure in their personal regard from others, so that they could take risks and make mistakes without feeling so bad; and therefore they could also go on to develop their own interests and abilities more positively.

The psychometric test which was developed to help therapists who were applying Rogers' theory looked at the way that people who have this type of problem tend to have such unrealistically high personal goals. It's called the *Q-sort*, and it consists of a set of cards giving short personal descriptions, like 'Sometimes I get very impatient' or 'I am generally friendly'. The person is asked to sort out the statements into piles which express how accurate they are – whether they are very like them, for instance, or very unlike. They do this twice, once to describe their self-concept: 'Myself as I am'; and once to describe their ideal self: 'Myself as I would like to be'. Then the difference between the two sets is calculated as a correlation coefficient (see Chapter 9 for an explanation of correlations).

Most people have a reasonable agreement between the self-concept and their ideal-self, even though they are not exactly the same. Most of us would like to be a little bit better than we are. But people suffering from the problem which I described above often have very extreme differences between their self-concept and their ideal-self concept: their ideals are unrealistically high, and so they see themselves as continually failing to reach them. This shows up in the very low correlation coefficient given by the Q-sort.

The repertory grid Another theory of personality concentrates on the ways that people understand their world, and that too leads to a different type of psychometric test. The theory of personal constructs developed by Kelly in 1955 is almost exactly the opposite of the behaviourist approach, in that it argues that what is really important is what is going on in someone's mind. Rather than personality simply being the sum of people's actions, personal construct theorists see personality as reflecting the personal theories or ideas which each individual uses, privately in their own minds, to explain their experiences. Kelly believed that this takes the form of a number of personal constructs – dimensions which people use to construe, or make sense of, their experience – and that we have developed these out of our own personal experience. Since everybody's experience is different, that also means that we make sense out of the world in different ways.

So a test which is designed to reflect personal construct theory needs to identify the personal theories which an individual uses in understanding the world. This test is known as the *repertory grid*. It begins by taking a number of 'elements' – perhaps a set of significant people in the subject's life or perhaps something less personal, like animals or consumer objects. The person is then asked to take the elements in sets of three, and to say how any two of them are similar, and different from the third. The descriptions that they give are then noted down as being the constructs. For example: if someone is comparing the three elements of their tutor, their brother, and their best friend, they might say something like 'My tutor and brother are similar because they both enjoy playing sport, but my best friend doesn't'. That would give 'sporty/non-sporty' as a construct which that particular person used to describe people. Someone else might never use that one at all.

The person takes the elements in various sets of three, and compares each set. Each time they do so, another construct is added to the list – unless they use the same one again, of course! Then a grid is drawn up, with the elements across the top, and the constructs down the side. The person is asked to indicate how each of the elements fits with each of the constructs, using a tick or a zero. Then the therapist and the subject together can look at the grid and see what it tells them about how that person sees the other people in their world.

In a sense, we could describe Cattell's and Eysenck's theories of personality as 'bottom-up', in that the answers to the questions came first, and it was the pattern from the data which led Cattell to develop his sixteen-factor theory of personality. The projective tests, the Q-sort and the repertory grid were 'top-down', in the sense that the theory came first, and the tests were developed to reflect the theory. But we can see how the different theories produced very different kinds of psychometric tests. Both Rogers and Kelly were *phenomenological theorists*, emphasising how important it is to see things as the person sees them; and their tests reflect that. Eysenck and Cattell, on the other hand, were behaviourist in their approach to testing, and so their tests assume that the questions they are asking can be treated as 'objective' data.

Classifying psychometric tests

There are a number of different ways that we can classify tests. As we have already seen, psychometric tests can be very different in form. One way of classifying them is to look at their subject matter. For this purpose, we will look briefly at five types of psychometric test: intelligence tests, personality tests, creativity tests, diagnostic tests, and occupational tests.

Intelligence tests

In Chapter 9, we looked at some of the more contentious issues concerned with intelligence testing. Effectively, there are two kinds of modern intelligence test: individual and group tests, and this distinction to some extent – though not entirely – is connected with the idea that we looked at earlier in the chapter – how a test may be either idiographic or nomothetic.

Individual tests provide a detailed picture of one individual, and in that sense they are idiographic, whereas group tests provide general scores which allow several people at a time to be compared, which would make them nomothetic. But the individual tests aren't purely idiographic, since they can still only be interpreted fully by looking at how they compare with the population norms. Although they tend more towards the idiographic end of the distinction than group tests do, they are only about half-way along the scale, as it were.

Individual tests are those which are designed to be administered to one person at a time. Two of the most well-known individual intelligence tests are the Wechsler scales – the *Wechsler Adult Intelligence Scale* (also known as the *WAIS*) and the *Wechsler Intelligence Scale for Children* (*WISC*). These consist of a number of different sub-tests, divided into two sets. One set is to do with verbal, and the other with non-verbal abilities, and each of them provides its own scores, which are then combined to calculate the overall IQ. So, in addition to a general intelligence score, the Wechsler scales provide a measure of *verbal IQ* and *performance IQ*. This can be useful in clinical work, where someone may score very differently on the two scales, and this can give an insight into why they are having problems in life.

In addition, the Wechsler scales provide the tester with a test profile for each of the different measures used in the test, and this too can often highlight specific problems. The verbal IQ is calculated from six sub-tests: information, comprehension, arithmetic, similarities (saying what two things have in common), digit span, and vocabulary. The performance IQ is assessed from five sub-tests: digit symbol (in which a set of symbols has to be substituted for numbers), picture completion, block design (copying a pattern by combining special blocks), picture arrangement (combining a set of pictures so that they tell a story) and object assembly (putting pieces together to represent a complete object).

As you might imagine, administering all of the different tasks involved in the Wechsler scales takes some time, even though only a limited period of time is allowed for each task. And only one person can be tested at a time. Group intelligence tests are more 'economical', in that large numbers of people can be tested simultaneously, but they don't give such detailed information. For that reason, individual intelligence tests are mostly used in clinical work, while group intelligence tests tend to be used more for educational or personnel selection.

Because they are designed for large numbers, group intelligence tests consist of pencil and paper tasks. These usually take the form of multiple-choice items, which include such tasks as vocabulary tests, pattern matching, arithmetical sequencing, and 'odd-one-out' problems. Heim (1970) pointed out that in some of the less well-designed group tests, the questions can sometimes reflect the idiosyncracies of the tester, and may have more than one right answer. However, in this country at least, some of the most popular tests are the AH group tests, designed by Heim, so hopefully they do not suffer from this problem!

There are three levels of AH tests in popular use. The general one, for those of average or slightly above average intelligence, is the AH4. A much more difficult test, for those with above average intelligence, is the AH5. And then there is also the AH3, for those of average intelligence or slightly below, or for those who have had limited formal education and little exposure to intelligence testing. Heim (1970) pointed out that there is a large skill aspect to doing intelligence tests, so people who may do very badly the first time they ever take one may do much better as they get used to doing paper and pencil problems under time pressure. Also, the AH3 contains fewer verbal problems and more visual or performance ones, so that it is less likely to be affected by prior educational experience.

Personality tests   As we have already seen, personality tests can take a number of different forms. Since these were described in detail earlier in this chapter, there's no point describing them again here, so you will have to look back to the section on 'Tests and theories' if you have forgotten what they are like! The Q-sort and the repertory grid are both purely idiographic personality tests which give detailed information about one person, but can't really be used for comparing different people. The two psychodynamic tests, Rorschach and the Thematic Apperception Test, tend towards the idiographic end of the scale, although they are not purely idiographic because they still require the use of population norms before they can be interpreted fully.

As with the individual intelligence tests, these individualised personality tests tend to be used mostly for clinical work. For the most part, however, the personality tests which are used for personnel selection or career guidance tend to adopt the questionnaire-style approach typical of Cattell's 16PF test, in which people are asked to answer a set of pencil and paper questions about their usual behaviour.

Personality tests tend to result in personality profiles, rather than in single scores, although the simplest test – the Eysenck Personality Inventory (EPI) gives only two personality scores – one for introversion/extraversion, and one for neuroticism/ stability. Cattell's test gives a profile for all sixteen personality factors, and so it is often used in personnel selection, where managers may be looking for certain kinds of personality attributes among the applicants for a job.

reserved	outgoing
less intelligent	more intelligent
affected by feelings	emotionally stable
submissive	dominant
serious	happy-go-lucky
expedient	conscientious
timid	venturesome
tough-minded	sensitive
trusting	suspicious
practical	imaginative
forthright	shrewd
self-assured	apprehensive
conservative	experimenting
group-dependent	self-sufficient
uncontrolled	controlled
relaxed	tense

Fig. 10.4 Cattell's personality dimensions

There are more specific personality tests, too. For example, Adorno (1950) developed a test known as the F-test, to measure authoritarianism (F stood for Fascist). And Friedman and Rosenman (1974) developed a scale which was designed to identify whether someone was a Type A individual, and therefore liable to high stress levels and vulnerable to heart disease, or a more easy-going Type B (we will be looking at this in more detail in Chapter 23). These 'narrow-band' personality tests can be useful in identifying particular attributes, although there is always a danger that they will simply be used to label people, rather than to indicate how they might focus their energies on changing or developing.

Creativity tests   The problem of what creativity is is one which is very elusive indeed. Great artists, scholars and scientists are undoubtedly creative, and yet capturing what it is about them which produces this creativity seems to be almost impossible. And yet, trying to identify which people are more creative than others may be quite important, if society is trying to use their energies positively. Hudson (1966) showed how it was possible that people who were more creative in the way that they thought could be disadvantaged by the educational system, which tends to emphasise strictly conventional thinking.

Perhaps the biggest difference between creativity and intelligence tests is that they tend to be open-ended, and don't have 'right' and 'wrong' answers. There are a number of different types of problems that are used to test creativity, but in general they tend to emphasise either handling novelty or the ability to produce interesting and uncommon responses to problems.

Some creativity tests emphasise verbal skills quite strongly. One of the most well-known creativity tests is of 'uses for things', in which the person is asked to think of as many uses as they can for some object, like a brick or a paper-clip. A similar test, which relies much more on vocabulary, is 'word associations', in which the person is given a word with several possible meanings, like 'drive' or 'fair', and asked to give as many meanings as possible. 'Fables' is another test, in which the person is asked to make up different endings for stories or fables. Sometimes these are left open-ended, but sometimes the person is asked to provide three endings: a humorous one, a moral one, and a sad one.

Assessing non-verbal creativity is rather more difficult. One test of numerical creativity is 'Problem-devising', in which the person is given a long paragraph which has a number of numerical statements, and asked to make up mathematical problems based on the paragraph. Another test which has a visual bias involves asking people to produce a drawing of a scene, like 'playing tag in the playground'. But, as you can imagine, assessing creativity levels with tests like these is not an easy task.

There are other ways of assessing creativity too, and we will be looking at some of these when we look at problem-solving, in Chapter 13. These have tended to look at things like lateral thinking or divergent thinking by giving people puzzles to solve. But whether these tests are really measuring creativity is an open question.

Occupational tests Occupational psychology is concerned with all of the different aspects of working life, including the study of how organisations work, how people are selected for jobs, and how different working conditions (psychological as well as physical) affect people. Although occupational psychologists also use personality and intelligence tests, there are several tests which have been developed specially for the occupational sector. These include tests designed to help in personnel selection and recruitment such as achievement and ability tests and aptitude tests, which indicate whether a particular person is suitable for a particular job or not; vocational guidance tests, which are used to help people decide about their future careers, or in a career change of some kind; and even organisational questionnaires, designed to help people evaluate the type of organisation that they are in and to identify ways in which it might work better.

Tests which are used for personnel selection and recruitment are some of the most widely used. Some of these are personality tests which are more targeted towards the occupational context than the general ones. For example, two very popular personality tests used by occupational psychologists today are the Myers-Briggs Type Indicator, which identifies the basic personality types described originally by Jung; and the Occupational Personality Questionnaire (OPQ), which is actually a set of nine sub-tests which deal with three areas: ways of relating to others, styles of thinking, and dealing with feelings. The fact that these tests are designed specifically for occupational contexts means that their population norms, too, involve large samples from different occupational categories (managers, clerical workers, and so on), which makes them more useful to personnel officers than the ordinary, wide-ranging personality tests.

The Myers-Briggs and the OPQ are pencil and paper tests, but occupational tests can take other forms as well. There are a number of situational tests, which are designed to imitate the working situation, and show how someone would operate under pressure. Sometimes these are group tasks, in which a small group of applicants for a job might be asked to work as a team in building a bridge out of Lego, or a tower from newspapers. Observers watch the members of the team to see how they interact with one another, who takes the lead, who gets on with the job quietly, and so on. Another group exercise is the leaderless group discussion, where the group of interviewees is expected to discuss a topic while they are being observed. The idea is that aptitudes for different occupational tasks, like management or technical roles, will show up in how people go about these tasks.

Other situational tasks are more individual. One of the most popular is the in-basket exercise, in which people are given a limited span of time in which to deal with the simulated contents of a manager's in-basket. This test requires people to make decisions about appropriate actions quickly, and it tends to be quite good at showing, for instance, whether someone is able to delegate a task to someone else, and whether they can judge priorities sensibly. Another simulation involves drawing up a short-list for interview from a number of application forms of candidates for a hypothetical job.

Increasingly, some large firms have been turning to specialised occupational assessment centres for this type of evaluation: people who are being considered for promotion will visit the centre for two or three days – sometimes even a week – and will undergo a range of different types of tests provided by specialised occupational psychologists. This type of intensive experience allows the psychologists to draw up a very detailed profile of that individual, which they then provide to the employer who can use it as a basis for making decisions.

Some aptitude tests are tailor-made for particular jobs. Kellett and Morris (1992) reported on the development of an aptitude test for postal workers. The development of the aptitude test began with a thorough job analysis: what the workers concerned actually did was carefully examined, and test items which seemed to be equivalent to these tasks were developed. The test was initially tested on people who were actually doing the work, to make sure that it really did reflect the demands of the work properly, before it went through a series of assessments of reliability, validity, and the process of standardisation which we looked at earlier. When the researchers examined the *predictive validity* of the scale, by comparing new employees' scores on the test with supervisor's ratings of them at least six months later, they found that more of those who received a lower grade on the test were rated as working at 'below acceptable' standards by their supervisors than those who had scored highly.

However, this raises one of the most important points about the use of psychometric tests in job selection – and in other contexts as well. Although the predictive validity for this test was considered reasonably high, it didn't account for everyone. There were still those who scored well in the test who performed below standard in the real job, and – more importantly – there were those who performed badly in the test who performed well in the real job. All occupational psychologists insist that test scores should never be taken as being an absolute indicator of suitability – they are designed to help people to make decisions, by providing them with additional information. They are definitely not designed to make the decisions for those doing the selection!

There are also very stringent requirements about how tests have to be administered. Having an informal, friendly atmosphere can produce quite a different response from people than being in a cold, unfriendly formal situation, and even the use of slightly different words in the instructions has been shown to make a difference to how people perform. Since most tests are done under time-pressure, it is easy for people to lose concentration, or to be thrown off-balance or be upset. So test conditions have to be carefully standardised, and testers need to be carefully trained in how to conduct tests properly. The British Psychological Society offers a certificate of competence in occupational testing to personnel officers and others who find they need to use psychometric tests as part of their work, and this helps to make sure that the people who are administering these tests really know what they are doing.

As we've seen, then, psychometric tests can be very different and are used to serve many different purposes. All psychometric tests represent an attempt to measure some aspect of the human mind, and none of them can claim to be absolutely successful in that, although some seem to be a bit more successful than others. But people are also influenced by other factors, like the way that they understand what is going on around them, how they see the other people around them and how those other people behave, and by what is happening to them in their personal lives. No psychometric test can predict or assess those factors, and in the rest of this book we will go on to look at other factors which affect how people act.

Summary

1 Psychometric tests represent attempts to measure mental characteristics in some way.

2 It is important that a psychometric test should have validity – it should measure what it is supposed to measure. There are several ways of assessing validity, although not all of them are equally useful.

3 Psychometric tests also need to be reliable – giving consistent results. A psychometric test has to be carefully assessed for reliability before it is published.

4 Most psychometric tests are standardised to ensure that they are comparable to other tests of the same kind, and to establish what the normal test results would be in a general sample of the population.

5 Different types of psychological theories have produced some very different ways of assessing mental characteristics. Some of these are idiographic, and will just describe a single individual; others are nomothetic and concerned with general personality traits.

6 There are several types of tests. Some of the most well-known and frequently used ones are intelligence tests, personality tests, and creativity tests.

7 Tests used by occupational psychologists include specialised personality tests, situational tests which imitate the job situation, and specialised aptitude tests designed for particular jobs.

8 Psychometric tests can never be taken as providing absolutely definite knowledge. They should only be used as additional information, not as the sole basis for making decisions.

Chapter 11 **The development of language**

If we were asked to pick out one thing which, above all else, made us different from other animals, most of us would probably choose the same one – language. No other animal uses language as we do, or seems to be able to. Through language, we can widen our whole world. We can learn about other people's experiences, and so avoid having to learn purely by our own mistakes; we can express how we feel or how we have felt in the past; and, most important of all, we can *interact* with others, with some kind of assurance that we share the same meanings.

Of course, our social interaction is by no means confined to language. The next chapter will be looking at ways that we interact *without* language, by non-verbal communication. But through language, we can transmit more complicated messages, and deal with subjects that would be almost impossible to communicate without words. So how is it that we come to have this amazing gift? And why do we find it so easy?

Language acquisition

People who work with computers have found the job of teaching a machine to use language, in the same way that we speak it, to be one of the hardest tasks of all. Our languages are so complicated, and so full of rules, that computers can't handle them, they have to use a simplified version. And yet, a five-year-old child can use that same language that causes the computer so much difficulty!

So how *do* we learn to use this language so quickly? What are the actual processes that take place while a child is learning its first language, and are they the same as the processes of learning a second language?

Association theories of language development

Several theories have been put forward to explain the way that children acquire language. The oldest one was some kind of (rather vague) idea that language was learned by *association*: the child learned to associate a word with an object; a verb with an action, and so on. But clearly this isn't enough to explain everything about language acquisition – what about those words which don't have corresponding action – like 'curiosity', or 'idea'? And it also doesn't explain how we come to *use* language, to make up our own sentences, and to turn sentences round in such a way that they make questions, or commands. To say that we learn 'radio' by associating it with the object doesn't explain why we also learn to ask 'is this a radio?', 'where is the radio?', 'how does a radio work?' or even: 'the radio is on the desk'. The central question is how we learn to manipulate words – and a simple 'association' theory can't explain that.

The operant conditioning approach

In 1957, B. F. Skinner (who we will meet later, in connection with the 'operant conditioning' theory of learning) put forward a slightly more sophisticated version of the 'associationist' approach. From a very early age infants babble while they are in their cots, or playing, making different vowel and consonant sounds. According to Skinner, when this babbling produces something that resembles a word, the parent *rewards* the child by smiling, and by repeating the sound. By operant conditioning (Chapter 18), the child is then more likely to repeat that sound, and gradually it comes to 'shape' these sounds into actual words. Then the parents will start to reward the child when it produces *strings* of words, and so, gradually, it comes to produce more and more complex language. If it forms a sentence the wrong way round, like 'the television is under the flowers', instead of 'the flowers are on the television', then it doesn't get the reward of smiling and approval from its parents, so it learns not to do that, but to do it 'correctly'. Skinner talks of 'verbal behaviour', and regards language as being essentially similar to any other kind of behaviour – if we do it, and it has a pleasant consequence for us, then we are more likely to do it again; if it doesn't have a pleasant consequence, then we're not so likely to do it again.

While some part of Skinner's views are undoubtedly valid, it seems too simple to explain some of the more complicated forms of language. It also implies that each child must go through a gradual and lengthy process of trial-and-error learning, as it gradually learns the right and wrong ways of saying different things. But children learn language very much faster than that – to go through all the possible sentences which a child might say, and learn them all by trial-and-error would take much longer than the four or five years which children take.

Chomsky's theory of language acquisition

N. Chomsky, a linguist, objected strongly to Skinner's theory, and put forward an opposing one, in 1965. In this, he proposed that children have an *innate* 'language acquisition device' (LAD), which enables them to collect linguistic data from the world around them, and by a sort of 'decoding' process, to extract rules of grammar from them. He said that what the child acquired wasn't so much the language itself, as a 'deep and abstract theory' which lay behind the language. Children learned abstract ways of manipulating the language, regardless of what their natural language was, through the innate device; and it was just the vocabulary and the 'surface rules' of their own language which varied, according to the child's nationality and culture. All languages, Chomsky said, had the same kind of 'deep structure', and the general principles of language which the child learned could, therefore, be innate, and not too dependent on the experience which the child had.

The kind of evidence that Chomsky put forward for his theory was the way that children pick up rules about language so quickly. For instance, being able to reverse the pronouns in a sentence depending on who is speaking: a child refers to itself as 'I' and the person who's talking to it as 'you' very easily – yet the language that the child hears from the other person, has them the other way around. Also, children learn the rules about verbs and nouns going together very quickly indeed. Chomsky thought that this had to be innate, as it happened too rapidly to come from the child's experience, and it applied to children speaking all kinds of different languages.

A similar theory was put forward by Lenneberg, in 1967. He said that language development was maturational: although the child did progress through definite stages as it grew older, this was a more-or-less automatic progression. The child didn't need to be taught language; as long as it heard language being spoken around it, it would pick it up very easily.

Nativist approaches to language learning were very popular with psychologists for a while. Many people disagreed with Skinner's ideas, and Chomsky seemed to be providing a useful alternative. But it tends to present a rather mechanical picture of the child – you feed in spoken language to the ears, and a grammar and language use comes out of the innate language acquisition device – a bit like a computer. The child itself doesn't seem to be very active in the learning of language; it seems just to happen automatically, as long as people are using language in the child's environment.

Since Chomsky's theory was first published, there have been many studies of children just learning language, and of the kind of sentences they would manage and the mistakes they made. Often, a mistake will tell you quite a lot about what a child has learned, and the way that it is learning. For instance, if a child says 'foots' instead of 'feet', we can deduce that it has learned the rule for making plurals – add an 's' onto the

end of the word – but it hasn't yet learned that 'foot' is an
exception to the rule. But the picture which emerges from
these studies, is that the child seems to take a much more
active part in its learning process than Chomsky's idea of an
innate 'language acquisition device' would imply.

A study by Bard and Sachs, in 1977, looked at whether children
did simply pick up language from hearing it spoken around
them. They studied a child called 'Jim', who was born to two
deaf parents. Jim wasn't deaf at all, though, and so his parents
didn't teach him the sign language that they used with each
other, as they wanted him to grow up using normal language.
He only learned a few gestures of sign language – just enough
to communicate with his parents.

Jim watched TV and listened to the radio a great deal, so
he heard quite a lot of spoken language from a very early age.
But he didn't pick up rules of grammar, or go through the
language stages which Lenneberg had described. Instead, his
speech development was seriously retarded, and wasn't
corrected until he started sessions with a speech therapist. As
soon as he started these sessions, Jim's speech improved
dramatically. He started the sessions when he was three and
three quarters, and he could speak normally for his age by the
time he was four!

It was clear from this study that Jim was *ready* to learn to
speak, otherwise he wouldn't have learned it so quickly. But
despite all the spoken language he had heard from the TV, he
had not learned. He needed the *human contact* with the speech
therapist, before he could learn to speak.

It seems, then, that Chomsky's idea of an innate 'LAD' doesn't
really go far enough. Children may be predisposed to learn
language, but they certainly don't pick it up automatically. They
need contact with other people, who are using language *with*
them. Hearing it spoken around them without the human
contact, isn't enough.

Recent studies, in particular one by J. and P. de Villiers, in
1978, suggest that a child understands the language *in context*
first, and only later comes to understand what each individual
word means. In this, you would need the human interaction
to make the context clear. When a parent says 'Where's your
teddy? Ah, *here* it is!', they are saying the words in context. At
the same time as they are speaking, they are looking around,
and the speech ends with the teddy being picked up and
presented to the child. And while this is going on, the child is
understanding perfectly well what is being said, even if it hasn't
grasped each particular word. It is the human interaction

which matters most – without that, the child won't learn language at all.

Parent/child interaction

A study by Stern, in 1978, showed that the basic patterns for speech communication are actually set down long before the child actually starts to talk, in the interaction of a mother and an infant (or a father and an infant). In the course of baby games, like 'peek-a-boo' the child learns the give-and-take part of human interactions – that things happen in turns, and so on. As they learn to speak, this taking turns is also used; conversations tend to be ordered – mother says something, child says something, mother says something, and so on. Also, the child sees this pattern being repeated when adults talk to each other. Patterns like this are important for development of *social* speech.

The study by J. and P. de Villiers, in 1978, examined the ways that parents talked to their children. Adult speech tends to be quite complicated, and also to be full of half-finished sentences, and sentences which run into one another. But their study showed that, in fact, parents talk to their children quite differently. They use simpler sentences, and will repeat what they say a lot more. For example, a mother might say to a small toddler: 'Put the red truck in the box now.' As she talks, she is emphasising the important parts of her sentence, and repeating them, so that (eventually) the child understands clearly what it should do. By tailoring their speech to the simpler forms that the child will understand, they make it very much simpler for the child to comprehend, and to learn 'rules' for language.

Parents also often *expand* their children's speech. When a toddler points, and says 'more milk', the mother may well say 'you want more milk?': the same thing as the child was saying, but including more words, and closer to adult speech. Thus, the parent is providing a simple model for the child to copy. Later on, when the child says 'I want more milk', the parent may well say: 'Can you have some more milk please?'. Again, the speech used is tailored to be just a bit more than the child is already managing.

Very often, a parent talking to a child who is just learning to talk will use a familiar sentence 'frame', to introduce a new word. This might develop into a sort of a chant, or it might just be a well-known question. 'What's this? It's a *cow*. And what's this? It's a *duck*. And what's this? It's a *frog*.' and so on. Because the rest of the sentence is familiar, the child learns the new word, as its attention is drawn to it.

Stages in acquiring language

In 1973, R. Brown published the results of a longitudinal study on the way children acquire language in their pre-school years.

The study was a close look at three children (Adam, Eve, and Sarah) and their speech was recorded for four hours every month, throughout their first five years. By getting a set of recordings at regular intervals, in this way, Brown wanted to be able to see the way the children's speech *gradually* developed, and the stages that the children went through.

He found that children's language development could be roughly divided into five stages, and that at each stage the children would use different types of sentences, gradually increasing in difficulty. In the first stage, children tend to say only two-word sentences, which might involve possession: 'my ball'; absence: 'allgone ball'; or a simple description of an action: 'Adam hit ball'. The things that they say tend to relate simply to objects around them.

By the second stage, the language is beginning to get more complicated. They might say things like: 'that a book', or use a verb in the past tense: 'Adam walked'. Although the sentences are still simple two-word ones for the most part, they have started to use endings on words, instead of just saying the simple word on its own: 'I walking', or 'Adam's ball'.

At the third stage, they have begun to ask the 'why' questions; what, where, why, and so on. They have also started to ask other kinds of questions too, like: 'Does Eve like it?' and 'Where did Sarah hide?'.

The fourth stage is even more complicated: they will tend to use simple sentences involving more than one clause: 'Who is that playing the xylophone?'. Before this stage, if they wanted to ask the same question, they would have probably made two sentences: 'Who that?' 'Play xylophone'. But by this time they can join the two together into one sentence.

In the fifth stage, they have learned to use conjunctions as well, which means that they can join sentences together: 'I did this and I did that too', and they can have more than one subject in a sentence: 'You and I play over here', or 'John and Jay are Boy Scouts'. By this time, they are well on the way to being able to cope with school, with learning to read and the formal kind of language that they will meet there. In short, by this time they have developed the language skills which they will need; they can turn a sentence around if they want to, changing 'that's your cat' to 'is that your cat?', or mix together two sentences which deal with the same thing; 'Mary who lives over there goes to our school', instead of 'Mary lives over there' and 'Mary goes to our school'. They can *use* their language as they want to.

Language in an autistic child   In addition to Adam, Eve, and Sarah, R. Brown studied an autistic child called John. Autistic children tend to be withdrawn from other people, frequently from infancy; they dislike being cuddled, and don't smile at other people. This continues throughout their childhood, and they don't engage in normal social interactions like ordinary children.

Some autistic children hardly ever speak, but some do speak quite a lot and John was one of those. When his speech was looked at, Brown found that it contained quite a lot of differences from the speech of normal children. For one thing, when he wanted to say something John didn't seem to invent *new* sentences for himself, but repeated phrases and sentences that other people had said to him. Even the voice inflections and accents were repeated – he didn't change the way he said the words either.

One of the most striking aspects of this, was the way that John had never learned to change the pronouns of a sentence around, as ordinary children do. Since he repeated what he had heard from others, when he talked about himself he said 'you', which was, of course what he had heard, and when he talked of his mother, he said 'I', as she had done when she was talking to him. Changing things around so that they apply to the appropriate person is one of the first things which children learn, as they learn language – but John never had.

One way of interpreting the differences betwen John's speech and that of ordinary children, is to refer to what I said before about the need for *human interaction* when children are learning to talk. Since an autistic child is withdrawn from social interaction, and avoids human contact, then perhaps this explains why their speech patterns are disturbed. (John's errors of speech were typical of other autistic children who had been studied).

Critical periods in language development

In 1967, E. H. Lenneberg proposed that there was a critical period for language development and language learning. During this period, Lenneberg said, language learning took place quite easily – children didn't need special instruction, but would pick up language easily and readily. After this period, which was after puberty (about twelve years of age), learning languages became very much harder. He believed this was caused by physical changes which took place in the brain during puberty and, no matter how hard someone might try, he or she would never become fluent in another language, but would always sound like a foreigner. If no language at all had been learned by that time then the child wouldn't ever really learn it.

There are problems with this theory, though. One is that there doesn't seem to be much evidence of these physical changes in the brain. Another problem is that there have been many cases of adults moving to another country which uses a different language, and learning to speak it fluently.

Unfortunately, not many systematic studies have been made of these. A third problem is that it isn't really true to say that children learn language without being taught; we saw this when we looked at the way parents talk to their children. Their use of simplified speech is a teaching method, just as much as lessons in a classroom. It's true that children don't need *formal* teaching but it appears that adults don't either. Certainly, modern language schools teaching adults today seem to be using a method very similar to the one that parents use with children; that is, simplified sentences, from which the person can work out the rules that apply in that language.

Perhaps the most convincing evidence against Lenneberg's theory, though, is the case of Genie, a child who was found in Los Angeles in 1970. Like the twins whom I mentioned in Chapter 8, she had been seriously deprived, confined to a small curtained room, and strapped either to a cot or to a potty chair. If she made any noises, she would be beaten by her father, who used to bark at her like a dog sometimes, but didn't speak to her. A few minutes each day her mother would feed her with baby food, but not speak to her. By the time she was found, she was thirteen years and seven months old, and had been living like that for the whole of her life. According to Lenneberg, she would have been past the 'critical period' as she was well past puberty.

When she was found, Genie was unable to speak, and could only understand a few simple commands. Since then she has lived in a foster home, and has gradually learned to talk through hearing language spoken and having the same kind of interactions from her foster parents as a small child would have. She hasn't attended special speech therapy sessions. Gradually, she has progressed through the same stages that Brown's children did, and has achieved virtually normal speech.

There are some differences, though. She has some problems in actually pronouncing some speech sounds, though in some respects she seems more advanced than young children. For instance, she learned to use all the 'wh' questions at about the same time, while young children normally learn 'what' and 'where' first, and only learn 'why', 'when', and 'how' later on. She also doesn't often produce new questions, as children often do. Nonetheless, her case appears to give us clear evidence that it *is* possible to learn language after puberty, even though it may be harder. Perhaps Lenneberg should have called it a 'sensitive period' rather than a 'critical period' (see Chapter 2).

Language in schoolchildren   By the time a child goes to school, it is easily capable of expressing itself in language, and of experimenting and playing with words. When it arrives at school, it inherits straightaway a wealth of rhymes, jingles, and word-games which have been passed on from child to child, often for hundreds of years. Unlike nursery rhymes, which are passed from adult to child, these verses are passed on by other children, and don't belong to the adult world. Through these traditional games, rhymes, puns, and so on, the child continues to explore and experiment with its use of language, and to practise words and sets of words.

In 1959, Iona and Peter Opie published a study/collection of playground traditions. They collected many of their examples by travelling around the country and chatting to children; other examples came from teachers or parents who wrote to them from all over the world. Very often, they found that a rhyme which children used *was* world-wide, for instance the rhyme:

'Adam and Eve and pinch-me
Went down to the river to bathe
Adam and Eve were drowned
Who do you think was saved?'

is popular in the USA, France, Spain, Holland, and several other countries in versions appropriate to the local language. Similarly, riddles like 'Why did the jam roll? Because it saw the apple turnover', and 'What would Neptune say if the sea dried up? I haven't a notion (an ocean)' are ways that children explore, practise, and experiment with their language. This 'playground culture' is very rich in puns, and rhymes especially: children *enjoy* 'playing with words'.

Of course, playground rhyme isn't the only way that children continue to learn and practise language. In school they learn the more formal kinds of language that are used in their society; and as they learn more about each other, and about people, they develop tactful or friendly ways of addressing others, and so on. But always, language develops in a *social* context – through the child's interactions with others, and its exploration with different forms of communication.

Language is by no means the only form of communication that people use, though. In any face-to-face conversation, spoken language is backed up by a whole lot of visual signals. If we are saying something, which we think someone might 'take the wrong way', we smile as we say it, and that passes on the message that we aren't being critical, or hostile. If we want to show someone that they have our undivided attention, we sit facing them, and look at them as they talk. In the next chapter, we'll be looking at these non-verbal aspects of communication, and how they affect us in our day-to-day lives.

Animals and language

I began this chapter by saying that most of us would pick language as the one thing which makes us different from other animals. But is it such a clear difference as it appears? If we, too, have evolved, and progressed through the same sort of evolutionary stages as other apes, then surely we should be able to find some kind of language use in apes – or at least, an *ability* to use language? Somewhere, there must be a kind of half-way mark between a non-language using animal, and a language-using animal.

In the 1950s and 1960s this question was thought to be fairly clear. Since various attempts had been made to teach chimpanzees to talk, and they had all failed, people concluded that, if there had been a half-way point between language using and non-using, then it was back in the past, in a remote ancestor of humans, but not of chimpanzees. People, it was said, were *unique* in being able to use language – if a chimpanzee couldn't do it, then no other animal would be able to either.

Washoe

In 1966, A. and B. Gardner began to question these conclusions. Yes, it was true that no-one had managed to teach a chimpanzee to talk. But, even in the wild, chimpanzees don't use many vocal signals – less than some kinds of monkey, for instance. But they are very inclined to notice visual changes, have very good eyesight and are quite mobile with their arms and hands. So why not see if they were *really* unable to learn language, or if it was just that they couldn't *talk*. After all, many deaf children don't actually learn to talk, but they rapidly become fluent in sign language.

The Gardners started to train a young chimpanzee, named Washoe, in 1966. By 1969, they were able to report on her progress. Washoe had indeed learned the sign language that she had been taught, which was a language used by deaf people in North America, called Ameslan. She was repeatedly observed and tested, and proved to be unquestionably using the language to communicate with her keepers. One of the first things that had to be established was whether she was consciously grouping words' together, as we do when we make a sentence; and she turned out to be doing just that. In Ameslan, when a sentence is finished, you drop your hands down to the side for a few seconds, which Washoe was doing at the appropriate times. She was able to join words into combinations which she hadn't met before – on one occasion, when she saw an aeroplane flying low overhead, she turned to her keeper and signalled 'you, me ride plane' – although she hadn't met that particular combination before. Another time, she saw a duck, and didn't have a word for it, so she signalled two words – 'water bird'. Examples like this provide good evidence that she is actually *using* the language that she has learned, and not just parroting.

Of course, she isn't wonderfully fluent in it. When her speech is analysed, it turns out to be similar to that of a child in the first of R. Brown's stages, with simple sentences and negatives. But it was enough for her to be able to express herself, and to ask questions. Although she seemed to have a clear idea of word-order in simple examples, for instance, she knew the difference between 'Washoe tickle' and 'Tickle Washoe', there did seem to be confusion in some of the things she said. Eventually the Gardners found out that the fault wasn't Washoe's, but theirs! Because they didn't use Ameslan as a first language, but had learned it for this purpose, they were using word-order to express subject and object, as we do in English. But true Ameslan speakers don't do that, they express it by movements and not by word-order. Since Washoe had had teachers who were true Ameslan speakers as well as the Gardners, she had become confused about the rules in this case!

Several other chimpanzees followed Washoe and there are about a dozen chimpanzee Ameslan speakers in America now. Deaf humans who use Ameslan can understand what they say quite well, although they report that they tend to have what might be called a 'chimpanzee accent' – that is, characteristic ways of making the signs. Later on, when Washoe became too big to have around the house, the Gardners gave her to San Diego zoo. When she gave birth to a baby chimpanzee, it was observed that she seemed to be teaching Ameslan to the baby, as well! Whether this will continue, or whether it's just a one-off thing, we will be able to tell in time. Certainly, these chimpanzees have shown a far greater aptitude for sign language than people suspected possible, and the more the experiments progress, the more they seem to be able to develop it.

Koko the gorilla   Another American psychologist, Penny Patterson, conducted an experiment to see if gorillas, like chimpanzees, could learn sign language. She trained a young gorilla, Koko, to talk by means of signs, and this seems to have been fairly successful – though not, perhaps, as successful as Washoe. Koko did seem to pick up the idea of communication by signs, though, and also 'talked' with a younger gorilla that Penny trained later, called Michael.

Sarah   Another, entirely different, form of language training was used for a chimpanzee called Sarah. Sarah was taught by means of a set of symbols which represented items or verbs. The symbols themselves were magnetic-backed pieces of plastic, which she placed on a metal board. Using operant conditioning techniques (rewarding her with a piece of fruit if she did it right), Sarah was taught to associate the symbols with their meanings, and to form sentences with them. Some of the symbols couldn't be pictured, for example 'big' and 'little', or 'colour of', 'round', and so on. She learned to form sentences such as 'Mary give apple Sarah', and 'Sarah insert banana pail', and she also was able to use new words in sentences which she hadn't met when learning the word. So there was some element of learning to *use* the words there.

There is some doubt, though, as to whether Sarah is really using language in the same way as a child would. Although she can arrange things in order when asked, she doesn't use the words when left to herself – unlike Washoe, who 'talks' to herself often. And although she has a large vocabulary, she doesn't form new combinations of words, as Washoe has done. (On the other hand, Washoe only uses her hands, while Sarah has to use pieces of metal and plastic, and perhaps Sarah wouldn't see them as *flexible* for this reason.) But she has virtually never *started* a 'conversation', while Washoe does this all the time. (And, of course, humans do too.)

Even with Sarah, though, it's been shown that chimpanzees are far more capable than people thought they were in the 1960s. And Washoe, together with the other chimpanzees who have been taught in Ameslan, seem to show that language can, possibly, be shared among other animals too. At the moment, attempts are being made to find a similar sort of 'language' to suit dolphins, as Ameslan suits chimpanzees. Perhaps we will finally be able to discover what children's books have been writing about for so long – what it feels like to be an animal.

The evolution of language

There is just one more study to do with non-human animals and language that I would like to mention. A report from D. Cheney and E. Seyfarth, in 1980, is concerned with a study of vervet monkeys, in Kenya. Among other findings, they found that vervet monkeys have three *different* alarm calls, which serve to alert the rest of the monkey troop to the presence of a threat. And the thing which decided the difference is the actual *kind* of threat that is being presented. The monkeys have three main predators – leopards, martial eagles, and pythons – and each of these creatures causes a vervet monkey to utter the appropriate alarm cry.

In evolutionary terms, this makes a lot of sense. After all, if you are being threatened by an eagle, you need to get under cover; but if you're being threatened by a snake, then you need to get up a tree and away. But an interesting thing was the way that the young members of the troop learned the alarms.

While they often gave an alarm call when it wasn't quite necessary, it tended to be in response to a similar kind of threat. Thus they would give the leopard alarm for lions, cheetahs, hyenas, or warthogs; or the snake alarm to a variety of snakes. As they got older, though, these mistakes became less common, and they narrowed it down until they were only responding to one of the three actual predators. This is very similar to the way that human children tend to over-generalise words, when they are first learning them; for instance calling all animals 'doggy', or all bath toys 'duck'.

Perhaps, then, these vervet monkeys are giving us an example of the very first stages in language development – the use of specific 'words' for a specific purpose. It may well have happened similarly with the ancestors of humans, until, gradually, a fuller and richer language developed, growing into the kind of languages we have today.

Summary

1 Language is an essential part of human society, through which we can express ideas which are far more complicated than signs could be.

2 An old theory held that children learn language by association. This turns out to be a bit too simple to explain some of the more complex kinds of language.

3 B. F. Skinner suggested that children learn language by operant conditioning – parents reward the child (with praise) for getting it right. This also seems to be a bit too simple.

4 N. Chomsky said that children have an innate data-processor which enables them to extract rules of grammar.

5 Recent studies show that human interaction is central in language learning.

6 R. Brown conducted longitudinal studies of children's language development and found five definite stages that the child goes through.

7 Autistic children develop peculiar speech patterns – only copying speech from others, and not composing it themselves.

8 Parents help their children develop speech in a number of ways: by simplifying what they say, by expanding what the child says, etc.

9 Lenneberg suggested that there was a critical period for language learning. Studies of Genie, an abandoned child, dispute this idea.

10 Children continue to develop their language through traditional games as well as schooling.

11 Some chimpanzees have been taught sign language, and appear to use it as a two-year-old uses spoken language. A study of vervet monkeys in the wild suggests that they have the very beginnings of a 'language', using different cries for different kinds of threat.

Chapter 12

Non-verbal communication

Spoken or written language provides us with a method of communication that no other animal has developed – the ability to use symbols and to combine those symbols in elaborate ways, in order to represent events which can be, at times, very distant or abstract. But, in many ways, language alone is not enough for us to communicate all that we want to. Usually, we need to add things to what we say, or write, to make sure that we aren't going to be misunderstood by the person to whom we're talking or writing. If we write to a friend, for instance, we may use an exclamation mark after we've said something surprising; or we might underline a word to give it more emphasis.

When we do this, we are trying to use these punctuation marks to copy something we do easily and naturally in everyday conversation. Whenever we talk, we stress some words and not others, we raise the pitch of our voice slightly at the end of a question, or we pause very slightly before saying a particular word – all of which serve to make the meaning of what we are saying clearer. But most of all, in ordinary conversation we have *feedback*, from the other person. By all sorts of small cues, we can tell if they have understood what we have said to them, or if we need to elaborate it a bit. If they haven't understood us, they might say so, and so ask us for more information – or they might simply look puzzled, or blank, and we would realise from their expression that we needed to say more.

Feedback – knowing what the results of our actions have been – is crucial to many forms of human behaviour. When we first learn a new skill, like a baby learning to grasp a rattle, or an older person learning to play darts, we need to know the results of our actions in order to improve our performance. If we didn't know whereabouts on the board the darts had landed, we wouldn't know how to correct our actions and get nearer the number we're aiming at. It's the same with conversation: if we don't know how the other person has taken what we say, then we don't know what we should do to correct the misunderstanding, or wrong impressions.

There are some kinds of communication, though, which don't involve feedback in that way. These are *involuntary communications*, where we accidentally give someone information about ourselves, without realising it. The old saying about 'animals can sense fear' is the sort of thing I mean. When we are afraid, we give off signals, like trembling, or being white-faced, which tell others about our personal state. Although we don't mean to, we are communicating our fear to others – passing on that particular message.

Non-verbal communication, or NVC as it is often called, refers to all these kinds of communication. Essentially, it includes any kind of communication that doesn't use words. Verbal communication is what we actually say – the language that we use – while non-verbal communication can include any other way that we transmit information, voluntarily or not, to other people. There are several different ways that NVC can be used, and we will be looking at four of them: NVC used to assist speech; NVC used instead of speech; NVC used to signal attitudes; and NVC used to signal emotional states.

NVC as an aid to speech   In any ordinary conversation, non-verbal communication is as important as the actual words which are being said. This becomes most apparent when we think about talking to others on the telephone. Some people find this extremely difficult, and tend not to have long conversations at all. Others don't find it so hard, but even then, we notice differences in how we put things over. We tend to use stronger changes in our tone of voice – we laugh aloud where normally we would smile, and so on. By doing this, we *compensate* for the fact that we can't see the other person, and we provide the feedback which they need.

Posture   In normal, face-to-face conversation, this feedback is provided by several different signals. One of the ones which we unconsciously take a lot of notice of is the way that people sit when they talk to us. If someone is sitting upright, in an 'alert' posture, we take that as a sign that they are interested in what we are saying to them. Because of this, we are likely to talk more, and to find that we enjoy talking to them – we like to feel that others find us interesting. On the other hand, if someone is slouching in their chair as we talk, or facing in another direction, we take it as a sign that they are bored, and that works the other way. Only very close friends, or people in a group where such behaviour is considered normal, can get away with giving those kinds of non-verbal signals without

Fig. 12.1
Matchstick men
Although we only have a few lines to go by, we can recognise different attitudes in these matchstick men. Posture is an important non-verbal cue, which we use a great deal in day-to-day life

transmitting the message that they are bored; most people will take it as a 'negative' sign.

Eye contact   Another conversational signal is *eye contact*. If we look at someone while they are talking to us, they take it, again, as a sign that we are interested in what they are saying, and so they will talk more. If our gaze wanders around the room, then they take it as a sign that we're not interested. We have quite complex (and unconscious) rituals about eye contact and speech. When a conversation first starts, both people look at each other, then, as one speaks, the listener looks at the speaker. When the speaker has finished talking, he or she looks at the listener, who takes this as a cue to talk in turn. While someone is actually speaking, though, they tend only to look at the other in order to emphasise a particular point, not all the time.

Of course, this example refers to an 'ideal' conversation – where each party has something to say, and each is very interested in what the other is saying. But we do expect a similar sort of thing to happen when we are in a conversation with others. If we are talking to someone who *doesn't* give the right signals – for instance, someone who never meets our eyes, or who gazes at us all the time, and never looks away – we feel uncomfortable, and we aren't very likely to want to be in conversation with that person again. Because our use of non-verbal signals is so familiar, we don't tend to notice it until it isn't used in the ways that we expect.

Gestures   While we are talking, too, we look at the other person for confirmation that they have understood us. They provide this, by using gestures like nodding, or smiling, and by making small sounds, to show that they understand what we are saying. (On the telephone, these small sounds are used much more, as they have to take the place of nodding and smiling.) A study by A. Kendon, in 1967, showed that people also tend to 'mirror' the facial expressions of the other person – if they look worried, the listener will adopt a worried expression too; while if they look pleased, then the listener will too. In this way, we reassure the speaker that they are being attended to, and that we comprehend what they are saying.

Paralanguage   Tones of voice, too, are an important part of non-verbal communication in conversation. Verbal communication, remember, is strictly to do with the words we use – but we don't just speak those words flatly. In fact, if we did meet someone who spoke in a flat tone, and never varied the pitch of their words, we would probably think that they were suffering from a mental illness, rather than anything else. And we can use our tone of voice to convey all sorts of messages – warmth and friendliness, anger, cheerfulness, sadness, and so on. In 1959 Davitz and Davitz analysed vocal expressions and tones, and found that there were eight clearly distinguishable patterns of voice, which correspond to different moods: affection, anger, boredom, cheerfulness, impatience, joy, sadness, and satisfaction. One of the things which a successful stage actor or actress must do, is to master all these tones and patterns of speech, so that these states can be easily portrayed from the stage to people sitting quite far away, in the balcony of the theatre.

NVC used   Very often we find ourselves in a situation where we can
instead of   dispense with speech altogether! For example: suppose that
speech   you're at a coffee bar with a friend, and you're talking to some other friends. Someone suggests that you all go to their house for the afternoon. You look at your friend and raise your eyebrows slightly. She nods – and so you both go along with the others when they leave. Clearly you and your friend have communicated with each other. You've asked her 'Do you feel like going along?', and she's answered 'Yes'. But not a word was spoken, you did it all by sign language. Furthermore, she might have given a more complicated reply; supposing she'd shrugged her shoulders? You'd have taken that to mean something like 'why not – there doesn't seem to be much else to do'; or if she'd made a face, you'd have taken that to mean that she didn't think much of the idea. At no point, though, would you need to use words in this communication.

From this example, you can see that we can use NVC to get over quite complicated messages. In addition, we have a range of signs which are generally accepted to mean a certain thing, at least in our society. If someone nods, we take it to mean yes, or agreement; if they shake their head, we take it to mean no. A wink, or a 'thumbs up' sign, have a definite meaning, which depends on the context in which they are made, but we have no difficulty interpreting them.

These non-verbal signs are by no means the same as some of the codes that are used for transmitting messages. Semaphore, for instance, is *not* a non-verbal means of communication because it uses letters of the alphabet to form words. So although it is a kind of sign language, it is *verbal* communication, rather than non-verbal. A language like Ameslan, too (see previous chapter) would be considered to be verbal communication, as there are definite words that are used, and combined together in different ways. The gestures which most of us make in ordinary circumstances, though, are non-verbal, and can often, as we have seen, replace speech completely.

NVC used to signal attitudes In addition to specific messages that we transmit by using gestures, we also transmit information about attitudes to others – often quite unconsciously. If we like them, we'll tend to stand closer to them, to smile more often, and to make more eye contact with them, than we would to someone we disliked.

Pupil size Quite often, we interpret attitude signals completely unconsciously. For example: if we look at a person we like, our pupils get larger (dilate), without our having any control over it at all. In 1963, E. Hess did an experiment to see if people reacted to this. He took the same two photographs of a girl, and re-touched one of them so that the pupils of her eyes became larger. When asked which photograph they preferred, almost all of his subjects said that they preferred the one with the re-touched pupils, even though they couldn't say what the difference was! Although they were using this non-verbal cue – pupil dilation – they were doing so completely unconsciously.

Proximity and eye contact In the same way, we will tend to react more favourably to someone who makes eye contact with us a lot; as I said before, they are signalling that we are interesting, and we find this very reassuring. Another important non-verbal cue for attitudes is one that I touched on at the beginning of this section – proximity. We all have a very definite idea about 'personal space', and we feel threatened if someone invades our personal space by standing too close to us. If we do find ourselves in a situation where we have to stand closer to people than we would like, then we tend to cope with it by avoiding all eye contact with those people. Usually we do this by looking upwards, which is why advertisements in lifts and tube trains, for instance, are placed above eye-level – so that they catch the attention of rush-hour commuters. An experiment by

Argyle and Dean, in 1965, was set up to test the way that people avoid eye contact if they are too close to another person. They found that when people were standing ten feet apart, they made a great deal of eye contact – about sixty five per cent of the time was spent either in eye contact, or by one person looking at the other. When they were six feet apart, it was still high – about sixty three per cent, but when the subjects were only two feet apart, looking and eye contact dropped to only forty five per cent of the time. (The subjects were engaged in a three-minute conversation during this time.)

If we feel close to someone – a good friend, or a lover – then we are prepared to allow them very much closer to us than we would an unknown person. Physical proximity seems to link very closely with feelings of security and safety in this way. We tend to feel disturbed if someone breaks these 'unwritten rules' and if they approach us too closely, we will lean away from them, or back away. People who break these 'rules' can often find themselves very isolated and find it difficult to make friends, though they don't understand why. Recently, much work has been done training psychiatric patients in non-verbal communication, in the hope that, as they develop more appropriate social skills, so they will be able to develop a more satisfying social life, and thus become more able to handle their day-to-day problems.

Posture   Another way we have of signalling attitudes is body posture. We can read a whole set of attitudes from seeing someone in a particular position. If, for instance, we saw a person sitting on a park bench with their head in their hands, without needing to talk to the person to find out, we would translate that as a message of depression or despair. If we saw someone walking along the street in a very upright and bouncy fashion, we'd assume that they were feeling cheerful, and we'd probably expect them to be smiling too. We often have more knowledge of these signals than we think – but, as with so many other aspects of NVC we only become aware of them when someone is giving the 'wrong' signals. Suppose we saw that person walking jauntily down the street, but when we got close, we saw that they were crying? We would find it very difficult to know how to interpret these two signals, as we would be getting two conflicting messages. We'd probably decide that they were trying to cover up their misery, by pretending that there was nothing wrong.

Incidentally, in general women tend to be much more sensitive to these kinds of signals than are men. But men who are involved in work dealing with other people – doctors, social workers, counsellors and so on – can be just as sensitive as women –

it is men who work in 'thing-orientated' jobs (i.e. jobs which
are concerned with things, and not people) who are least
sensitive. This suggests that there is some kind of learning
involved here, particularly as men who change from a thing-
orientated job to a people-orientated job become much more
sensitive to these signals. So it's unlikely to be an innate
difference – it probably ties in with the learning of sex-roles
in our society.

NVC used to signal emotional states

The fourth use of NVC that we will examine is the way in
which it is used to transmit messages about emotional states.
Many of our extreme facial expressions seem to be innate –
they are the same in other human societies, and similar
expressions are used by other primates. These are expressions
like anger, fear, happiness, or sadness. Another indication that
they are likely to be innate is the way that children who are
blind and deaf still show the same patterns, although they
could not have observed them in others.

Interestingly, if we simply look at a photograph of someone
in an extreme emotional state, we find it very difficult to guess
exactly which emotion they are showing – we may well mistake
someone who is shrieking with laughter, for someone who is
terrified. But in real life, of course, we don't just see a one-off
shot, such as a photograph gives – we see the way that the
expression develops, and the expressions which follow it, and
are connected with it. So there isn't any confusion, as long as
we see the expression in context.

Facial expressions

In 1966, Osgood carried out a study of facial expressions, and
found that they could be sorted into seven main groups:
happiness; surprise; fear; sadness; anger; disgust or contempt;
and interest. Each emotion is expressed by a characteristic
pattern involving the whole face – human beings have more
facial muscles than any other primates – as we use our faces
to communicate so much. We can tell how used we are to
using information about faces, simply by looking at cartoon
faces. They very often aren't detailed at all, but with a few dots
and lines, the cartoonist can give us a complete message about
the emotional state of that person.

Speech errors

Emotions can also be signalled by errors in speech. An increase
in the number of 'um' and 'ah' errors was shown by Mahl, in
1965, to happen when someone was uncertain of what they
wanted to say; while increases in errors like stuttering, slips of
the tongue or repetition were signs of anxiety. Very often, we
can give away our emotional state by such small signs, which
others may often interpret unconsciously. Other small signs
can be associated with rage or fear; both of these, for instance,

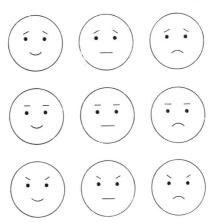

Fig 12.2 Cartoon faces
Although only the eyebrows and the mouth have been varied, each face seems to have a different expression. Imagine how much more information we get from human faces, where many more muscles can be changed

involve a tensing of the muscles as the body gets ready for action (see Chapter 17), and very often this shows as trembling, or twitching hands. We also still have what is called the *pilomotor response*. When an animal with fur is alarmed, its fur bristles, and stands on end. We do this too, but because our hairs are so small, it only shows up as bumps in the skin – 'goose-pimples' – which we get when we are afraid; or the 'prickling at the back of the neck' that some people talk about! Also, as I mentioned in an earlier section, our tone of voice can convey information about our emotional state, and often gives it away.

The importance of NVC

We attach a great deal of importance to non-verbal messages. A study by Argyle, Alkema, and Gilmour, in 1971, looked at what happens when people are given a verbal message in a non-verbal style that contradicts the message. They used three styles of non-verbal communication to deliver the verbal messages: a friendly style, which used a warm, soft tone of voice, a relaxed posture, and an open smile; a neutral style, which used an expressionless voice and a blank expression; and a hostile style, which used a harsh voice, a frown, and a tense posture. They also used hostile, neutral, and friendly messages, and combined each style with each message – so you might get a hostile message delivered in a friendly way, or a friendly message delivered in a hostile way.

They found that the non-verbal cues were extremely important in how people interpreted the messages. When they analysed their results, they found that the non-verbal cues had

had about five times the effect of the verbal ones – if people were given a friendly message in a hostile manner, it wasn't the words that they took note of, but the non-verbal cues. A study by Mehrabian, in 1972, found that out of three types of message (facial expression, words, and tone of voice), the words were the *least* important. People attached more importance to tone of voice, and most importance of all to facial expression.

Cultural differences in NVC From these studies, we can see that non-verbal communication forms an important part of our social interactions. But not everyone agrees on the correct 'forms' of non-verbal communication; there can be strong cultural differences between different societies.

For example: we tend to take it for granted that if someone nods, they mean 'yes', and if someone shakes their head, they mean 'no'. But in Greece, when they want to say 'no', they *raise* the head slightly, which can lead to confusion with people from another country. People from Arab countries, too, tend to stand much closer to other people than we do, and we can often find this quite difficult to cope with. They, in their turn, do not understand why we are being so hostile, and backing away.

Though in some cultures there are well-developed NVC signals concerned with touching, or close contact, because of the physical distance that we tend to keep between us and others, there are far fewer 'touch' signs in our society. You might shake hands with someone when you first meet them, but the rest of the time it is quite uncommon for us to touch. In our society, only parents and lovers engage in much touching of each other.

Other signs that we are quite used to using can have an entirely different meaning in other societies. The 'thumbs up' sign, for instance, which is quite acceptable in England and America, is regarded as a serious insult in some Mediterranean countries. (This has caused quite a problem for some hitch-hikers!) Many other signs change their meaning in different countries, too, but there isn't space to go into them all.

One thing these differences do show, however, is that many non-verbal signals are learned rather than inherited. A study by Andrew, in 1965, showed that we share many basic emotional expressions with other animals – expressions of pain, or angry ones like snarling. But if all our non-verbal communication were inherited, then we would expect people to use much the same signals wherever they lived, and it's quite clear that they don't. It seems to be that emotional expressions are innate, while those used to signal more complicated messages are learned through experience and socialisation.

How NVC can be studied

Obviously, when we are doing studies of something which is largely unconscious, like NVC, it's difficult to observe it directly. It is very difficult for people to act naturally, when someone is sitting there with a notebook, and recording their actions. As a consequence of this, most NVC studies have taken place in a room with a two-way mirror, so that an observer can watch two or more people interacting without being seen by the people in that room.

A technique frequently used, often in conjunction with the two-way mirror observations, is that of making a video recording of the interaction that takes place. In this way, a movement can be replayed more slowly, and analysed; or expressions that only take a fraction of a second, and which an observer would miss if they were watching the individual 'live', can be detected.

Very often, NVC studies use 'stooges' – people who act in a certain way to get a reaction from the person being studied. In this way, things like the effect of nodding on another person's conversation can be discovered; or what sort of signals will encourage people to continue to talk, and what sort of signals will stop them. Stooges are usually actors, who have a good degree of control over their body-movements and facial expressions.

Although we do use auditory signals – like tone of voice – visual signals of NVC are by far the most important to us. The visual sense is the most highly developed of the human senses, and that possibly explains why we place so much more importance on visual NVC cues, than on the actual words that might be contained in a message. In chapter 14, we will look more closely at visual perception, and how it develops but in the next chapter we will look at the other cognitive processes of thinking and remembering.

Summary

1 Often language is not enough for us to express what we want to say clearly. We tend to use other forms of expression as well – non-verbal communication.

2 Successful communication depends on *feedback*, and this is a major use for NVC.

3 Communication may be intentional, or it may be non-intentional. Sometimes we transmit information accidentally, through non-verbal signals.

4 NVC may be used as an aid to speech: to signal when it is

someone's turn to speak; or to signal interest in a speaker's words. People who don't give the right non-verbal signals often find it difficult to converse with others, or to make friends.

5 NVC may replace speech altogether. People can communicate by signals, or a specific gesture may come to have a special meaning in a society.

6 NVC may transmit information about attitudes. Posture, pupil size, proximity and eye contact all tell us something about a person's attitude to another person.

7 NVC may also give information about emotional states – fear, anger, etc. Very often these signals 'leak' accidentally, and tell others about that person's emotions. Errors in speech, too, can give emotional information.

8 Argyle et al., in 1972, showed that when two messages conflict, people attach *more* importance to non-verbal cues.

9 Studies of NVC use two-way mirrors; video recordings; and 'stooges' – without these techniques, problems of self-consciousness would make it difficult to get information about this area of communication.

Chapter 13 **Thinking and remembering**

'Cognition' is the general term which we give to mental activities like remembering, forming concepts, using language, or attending to things. In its early days, psychology was considered to be entirely the study of mental life, and early psychologists such as Wilhelm Wundt (1905) studied such mental characteristics as memory, attention, and the process of thinking. Many of these researchers, including Wundt himself, developed extremely rigorous methods of investigating mental processes, and in so doing set the foundations for much of modern experimental psychology. But overall, as we saw in Chapter 1, the main method which they used was *introspection*, with trained subjects reporting on the thoughts or mental experiences which they had while they were performing mental tasks.

Unfortunately, human mental processes aren't easily examined by *introspection*: we can be fooled too easily by our own unconscious biases and ideas. So although the early psychologists did gain a certain amount of insight into mental processes this way, others objected to the method as unscientific and lacking objectivity. The rise of behaviourism in American and British psychology meant that psychology largely stopped studying mental processes: Watson (1913), argued that mental processes could only be inferred through behaviour of one kind or another, and not observed directly, and that psychologists should restrict their interest to what could be observed and measured. Moreover, Watson also believed that all human behaviour would eventually be explained in terms of learned associations between stimuli and responses, without any need for thinking about the mind. This approach left little room for mental processes: even thinking was considered to be simply sub-vocal speech.

Although behaviourism dominated psychology for some time, there was always a certain amount of opposition to its mechanical views of human mental processes. In Europe, a school of thought known as *Gestalt psychology* emerged, which emphasised a more holistic approach to the understanding of human beings. The *Gestalt psychologists* saw the whole of an experience as more than just the sum of its parts, and argued

201

that looking at small elements, like stimuli and responses, couldn't tell you what the whole experience was like.

In the late 1950s and early 1960s, psychologists were increasingly seeing the behaviourist approach as useful but limited. Taking the new work on computers and communications technology for their inspiration, they became interested in how human beings process the information which they receive through their senses. The rapid growth of defence technology during the war had meant that psychologists had needed to investigate cognitive activities like sustained attention, because lives could depend on knowing, for example, how long an operator can remain staring at a radar screen without making serious mistakes.

The information processing approach became very popular, and cognitive psychology rapidly became a central part of psychological knowledge. Cognitive research includes several different facets of mental life, such as the use of imagery in representation, processes of decision-making and problem-solving, and reasoning. In this book, we will look at three main areas of cognitive psychology: perception, which we will look at in the next chapter, and thinking, reasoning and memory, which we will look at here.

Thinking
: There are all sorts of different kinds of thinking, ranging from simply trying to work out how to solve a puzzle, to pondering on deep and abstract issues. Although psychology hasn't begun to investigate all of these, there has been quite a lot of reseach how we go about solving problems.

Learning sets
: As we will see in Chapter 18, quite a lot of research on animal learning was concerned with looking at how animals solve problems using trial and error – trying out different actions until they hit on one which produced the result they want. Further research into this area also showed that animals can develop *learning sets*, which means they can learn to solve whole types of problems, rather than just the individual problems themselves.

Human beings can develop learning sets, too. Luchins, in 1942, presented subjects with a series of puzzles in which they had to calculate how a certain amount of water could be obtained by using different-sized water jars and pouring water from one to another. Since all of the problems had the same type of solution, the subjects rapidly became very good at solving them. But then they were given a different problem, which could either be solved in the same way, or by a different but much quicker method. None of the subjects who had done the previous puzzles saw the quicker method, although those who hadn't had that previous experience saw it straight away.

What had happened was that the previous experience had given the first set of subjects a learning set – they were 'set', or ready, to solve problems in that particular way, and so didn't notice other possibilities. Learning sets can be helpful at times, because they allow us to solve some problems more quickly by applying our past experience, but there are some situations when they can become a hindrance.

Insight learning A different type of thinking was identified by Köhler, in 1925, as a result of research with chimpanzees. Köhler set mature chimpanzees a number of different problems to solve. Typically, these involved trying to obtain a banana or some other piece of fruit, which was placed just out of reach. Sometimes it might be suspended from the ceiling, sometimes it would be placed outside the bars of the cage. Each time, there would be items provided which could be used to reach the fruit – maybe some boxes scattered around the cage which could be piled up, or some sticks which would fit together to make a long one which could reach outside the bars. In one case, the fruit was outside the bars, and only a short stick was in the cage, which was too short to reach the fruit. But it was long enough to reach a longer stick, also outside the bars. To solve the problem, the chimpanzee would have to use the short stick to pull the longer one inside, and then use the longer stick to pull the fruit in.

Köhler found that the behaviour shown by the chimpanzees suggested that they were solving this problem purely cognitively – by thinking about it. Typically, he found, the chimpanzee would make a few unsuccessful efforts to reach the fruit – perhaps jumping up and down, or reaching through the bars – and then appear to give up. But then it would suddenly jump up and begin to pile the boxes on top of one another, or to pull the sticks in, as if it had gained a sudden insight into the nature of the problem and how it could be solved. Köhler called this *insight learning*.

Human beings, too, show insight learning at times. Have you ever been just thinking over something, when suddenly the answer comes to you in a flash? We call this the Aha! experience, and it seems to happen purely because we are mentally putting the pieces of the puzzle together. In other words, it seems to be a purely cognitive type of learning.

Latent learning and cognitive maps Another cognitive type of learning was demonstrated by Tolman in 1932. Tolman performed a series of studies with rats, in which he showed that if they had been given a chance to explore a complicated maze, they would store that knowledge, and apply it later if it became advantageous for them to do so – in other words, if they were then rewarded for reaching the end of the maze quickly. Tolman's work on *latent learning* was important, because he showed that, even in animals, not all learning is immediately shown in behaviour, at a time when many psychologists insisted that behaviour was the only thing which psychology should be interested in.

But Tolman also went on from there to develop the idea of *cognitive maps*. He argued that what had happened in the animal studies was that the rats had developed a mental map of the maze, which they could then apply when they needed to. Tolman argued that human beings do the same kind of thing: we develop cognitive maps, which we use when we are going from one place to another.

Other researchers have also investigated cognitive maps, and have found that, rather than being an accurate picture of what is there, they tend to reflect our own experiences. Saarinen (1973) asked college students to draw maps of their university campuses. The students tended to enlarge the buildings which were important to them, and to shrink the ones which they didn't know. They were also often completely wrong when trying to describe unfamiliar areas. And Briggs (1971) found that when people were trying to estimate how far it was from one landmark to another, they would tend to underestimate the length of a familiar journey, but exaggerate distances which were unfamiliar. This might explain why a new place, like a school or a college, can seem very big when we visit it for the first time, but 'shrink' when we have been attending it for long enough to get used to it.

Concepts   Another type of research into thinking has looked at how we classify information into concepts. When we're developing concepts, we tend to use a set of defining *features*, like, say, 'Horses have hooves'; 'Horses neigh'; 'Horses eat grass' etc. But we also use a set of rules which say how these features go together, like: 'If it has hooves and neighs, but isn't eating grass, it is probably still a horse'. Collins and Quillian (1969) asked subjects to identify whether different features belonged to a concept or not, like 'Is a robin a bird?', or 'Does a shark have fins?'. By making minutely accurate measures of the time that it took people to answer the problem, they suggested that we store concepts in a hierarchical way, with more general concepts being subdivided into more specific ones, like in a tree diagram.

Rosch (1973) argued that when we are making a judgement about whether something belongs to a concept or not, we don't just match it up against a list of features. Instead, we have an idea of what a typical member of that concept would be like – a *prototype* – and we match the object up against that. In a study which asked subjects to say as quickly as possible

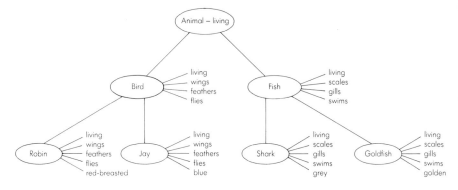

Fig. 13.1 Hierarchical storage of concepts

whether something belonged to a concept or not, Rosch found that they took longer to judge the ones which were different from the prototype than they did ones which were similar to it. So, for instance, it would take less time to judge the statement 'An apple is a fruit' Than it would to judge 'A tram is a vehicle'.

In a later study, Rosch et al. (1976) showed that all concepts are not equally significant. When subjects were asked to list all of the features which they associated with different concepts, it emerged that there seem to be three different levels, which Rosch called superordinate, basic, and subordinate. For example: 'animals' might be an example of a *superordinate concept*; 'dog' would be a *basic concept* within that, and 'poodle' would be a subordinate concept within that. According to Rosch, it is the basic level concepts that we use most of the time in everyday life.

When subjects were to list all of the features associated with different concepts, they managed far more for basic level concepts than for the others, suggesting that these were more important. Also, it became apparent that basic level concepts all had actions associated with them: we act differently with something belonging to the concept 'dog' than we do with something belonging to the concept 'chair', but by and large we act similarly towards all examples of chairs. Rosch et al. suggested that this is how we form prototypes. If we act in the same way with a number of items, we tend to put them into the same category.

Schemas   In Rosch's model, concepts become very similar to schemas, the cognitive structures proposed by Piaget and Bartlett because schemas are also ways of representing past experience in such a way as to guide our actions. In Piaget's theory of cognitive development, which we looked at in Chapter 8, we saw that Piaget considered the development of schemata to be the basis for all cognitive development, as it is in this way that we build up our understanding of the world and how we should act in it.

Some cognitive psychologists, too, have seen schemata as the centre for all cognition. Neisser (1976) proposed that cognitive processes in general are based on a *perceptual cycle*, in which we form anticipatory schemata which tell us what to expect, and which channel that we will then notice, guiding our actions accordingly. So this model could explain what is happening in the studies of learning sets which we looked at earlier in this chapter. The experience of the previous problems set up an anticipatory schema, which channelled the person's perception, so that they only noticed those bits of the problem that they were expecting. This guided their behaviour, so that they went on and solved it in the way that was familiar to them; and didn't even spot that there was a simpler way of going about it.

Reasoning   Reasoning is the process of working things out: working out why things happen, or what the solution to a problem is. A number of studies have investigated how human beings go about reasoning. One of the first findings which emerged from this research is that human beings don't seem to think in a straightforward, logical manner, like computers do. Instead, they apply a much broader and more sophisticated world-knowledge to problems, which means that, although in strictly logical terms they may make 'errors', when it comes to predicting what real human beings are actually likely to do, they tend to be pretty accurate.

For example: Wason (1968) showed that one of the tendencies of human reasoning is that we tend to look for confirming instances, when often the logical way to proceed is to look for disconfirming ones. Wason set up a card puzzle, in which subjects were showed four cards, each showing a letter or a number on the side that was visible. Then they were given a rule, such as: 'if a card has a 7 on one side, it will have a C on the other', and asked to find out whether the rule was true or not. Wason found that subjects tended to turn over those cards which would confirm the rule, rather than the ones which would prove it wrong. When we're looking at this problem in the form of cards, we can see that the logical answer isn't the one that people normally go for.

But what happens when we look at problems like this in real life, for example, if I said to you 'If it rains, I shall go to the cinema'. If you then met me later on, at the cinema, you'd probably conclude that it was raining. But that isn't strictly logical – I didn't say that I wouldn't go to the cinema at any other time, only that I would go if it was raining. In reality, though, if you saw me at the cinema, it would almost certainly have been raining. The logical interpretation of what I have said leaves it wide open – but as human beings, we apply a wider world-knowledge: we know what people normally do, and what they mean when they say things like that. We don't use formal logic, because we apply our social knowledge instead.

If you found a few problems reading through that last paragraph, don't worry: it isn't your fault. Another finding, from Wason and Johnson-Laird (1970), is that human beings find it harder to interpret a negative sentence like, 'I didn't say that I wouldn't go to the cinema' than to interpret a positive one like 'I said I would go to the cinema'. Wason and Johnson-Laird found that it takes us longer to work out the meanings of negative statements, and that we're more likely to get it wrong when we do finally work out what they mean.

Cognitive style   People also differ in how they go about reasoning. Hudson (1966) identified two major differences in cognitive styles, among a large sample of schoolboys. Some of the boys – generally the ones who were good at the sciences – showed *convergent thinking*: they approached problems in a strictly logical manner, and tried to work things out and to analyse problems in such a way as to find the 'right' answer. The second group – generally the ones who were good at 'arts' subjects – showed what Hudson called *divergent thinking*. They tended to approach things in a less logical way, but were much better at finding novel solutions to problems, or at thinking up unconventional uses for objects like a brick or a paper-clip. Hudson argued that this second style of thinking was just as useful as the first, because it was through divergent thinkers that new approaches were developed; but that the educational system tends only to value the first type of thinking.

Other investigations of *cognitive style* were concerned with how people go about forming or learning new concepts. Bruner, Goodnow and Austin (1956) asked people to work out the rules of a concept by selecting instances from a range of 81 cards varying in number and type of symbol, and type of margin. Each time the subject chose a card, they were simply told whether it was, or wasn't, an example of the concept. The experimenters then looked to see how long it would take e.g. to discover what the concept actually was (people 'red circles' or 'three symbols and one border').

Bruner, Goodnow and Austin found that there seemed to be two major strategies which people adopted in searching to identify concepts. They described these *wholist* and *partist*.

Wholist approaches involved taking the first correct card as being typical of the whole concept, and then modifying their ideas as further information came to hand. People who adopted partist strategies, on the other hand, would take just one feature of the card (like, say, circles) and look to see whether other correct instances would share that feature. Bruner, Goodnow and Austin felt that this approach to concept formation could also be generalised to strategies in learning. Some people, they argued, like to see the whole pattern first, and then fit the smaller bits into it, whereas others like to get to grips with things just one piece at a time, and fit everything together at the end. So teaching would be most effective if it was fitted to the cognitive style which the individual preferred.

Features of problem-solving

We have already seen how the development of learning sets can sometimes inhibit problem-solving, although usually it will help it. There are other ways that problem-solving can be inhibited, too. These are like mental 'traps' which people seem to fall into very easily, but which can limit how well we can tackle problems.

Functional fixedness

One of these is known as *functional fixedness*, and it is concerned with the way that we often think about objects purely in terms of how they are normally used. While this is usually OK, it can sometimes blind us to the idea that they can be used in a different way.

Glucksberg (1962) studied functional fixedness by providing subjects with a box of matches, a small candle, and some drawing pins, and asking them to mount the candle against a wall. Most of the subjects found this impossible: they would try to use the drawing-pins to pin the candle to the wall, and when that was unsuccessful, would not be able to think of anything else to try. But the few who could go beyond their functional fixedness would take out the tray of the matchbox, pin that to the wall, and then mount the candle on it. By thinking of the properties of the matchbox itself, instead of just thinking about its function they were able to solve the problem.

Einstellung

Another limitation in human problem-solving is known as *Einstellung* – a name that was given by the Gestalt psychologists, who saw it as closely linked with the perceptual principle of closure, which we will be looking at in the next chapter. Einstellung refers to the way that our thinking seems to become very easily limited by the boundaries of the problem that we are dealing with, so that we don't think of solutions which go beyond those boundaries. Perhaps the clearest example of Einstellung is found in the nine-dot problem, in

Join all the dots with four straight lines, without taking your pen off the paper or going over the same line twice

Fig. 13.2 The nine-dot problem

which nine dots are set out in a square shape, and the person is asked to join all the dots with four straight lines, without lifting the pen from the paper. Try it, before you read the next paragraph. Try it on some friends, too.

As you'll probably have found, this problem can only be solved by going outside of the boundaries of the square. But most people, when they're trying to solve it, look for solutions which will stay within those boundaries – and so they can't do it. That's an example of Einstellung – although there is no need to, we limit our thinking by trying to keep it within existing boundaries.

Lateral thinking

In 1977, de Bono described a technique for overcoming Einstellung and similar limitations to problem-solving, which he called *lateral thinking*. Lateral thinking was a deliberate attempt to go beyond the boundaries of a problem – to step sideways, as it were, and look at things from a different angle. Instead of approaching problems from the usual angles, de Bono would recommend people to think about the fundamentals of the problem, and to see whether the basic assumptions they were making about it really were necessary. For example, if a business woman or man were faced with difficulties in working out how to travel from one place to get to a meeting somewhere else, the conventional way would be to look for ways to get there in time. But the lateral thinking approach might be to ask whether it was possible to avoid making the journey at all: perhaps the purpose of the meeting could be achieved just as well by using telephones and faxes, or teleconferencing. By looking at the assumptions in the problem, and stepping sideways to avoid them, lateral thinking can help to overcome many of the problems of Einstellung and functional fixedness which inhibit problem-solving so much.

Groupthink

In 1972, Janis described a group decision-making phenomenon which can also seriously limit effective problem-solving. *Groupthink* happens when a particular group, organisation or committee defines what it regards as important so strongly that it makes it almost impossible for anyone to give a different view. In such cases, anyone who disagrees openly with the views expressed by the majority is seen as being 'disloyal', or as letting the side down in some way. What happens then is that the pressure on everybody to conform means that the group becomes unable to receive unwelcome information, and it can often end up making disastrous decisions because it has become so out of touch with reality.

One example of groupthink described by Janis was the American decision to invade the Bay of Pigs, in Cuba. This turned out to be a military disaster which could easily have been avoided if those making the decisions had been a little more in touch with reality. As a result of that experience, the American President of the time, Kennedy, took steps to make sure that it wouldn't occur again, by deliberately encouraging disagreement and debate, and by making sure that even unwelcome information was properly considered. Janis argued that groups with very strong leaders were particularly vulnerable to groupthink, and that only conscious efforts to overcome it were likely to be effective.

Brainstorming   A group technique which has been developed for improving problem-solving is known as *brainstorming*. Although it doesn't tackle the problems presented by groupthink, it can be of value when a group is trying to think of a new approach to something, like a name or marketing idea, so brainstorming is used quite a lot in organisations and training companies. The idea behind brainstorming is to encourage people to think freely and let their imaginations wander. Most of the time, we don't let ourselves do that too easily – if our thoughts do wander, we keep our ideas to ourselves because we don't want to look stupid. So brainstorming techniques are designed to make sure that people can feel free to say whatever comes into their minds, without feeling embarrassed.

The way that they do this is by separating out the idea-producing stage from the evaluation stage. In the first stage of the brainstorming process, any idea at all is suggested: the idea is that people can say anything at all which occurs to them, no matter how silly it seems. Nobody is allowed to talk about whether an idea would be practical, or realistic, or anything like that. The ideas which are produced during this stage are all noted down. Later, in the second stage, they are looked at and evaluated to see which ones are practical. By separating evaluation from idea-producing, people feel much less inhibited in saying things which occur to them: they know that nobody is going to laugh at them or think they are stupid if they say something silly. So brainstorming can produce much better results when there is a particular thing to think of in the usual way.

Creativity   Strategies like lateral thinking and brainstorming help people to develop new, rather more creative, approaches to problem-solving. But it's not clear just how closely this type of strategy links with real *creativity*, of the kind that we recognise in writers and artists. Ghiselin (1952) performed a series of biographical studies of highly creative people, and found that there seemed to be three distinct phases in the creative process.

The first phase is that of *familiarisation*. During this time, the artists, writers, or scientists spend a great deal of time becoming familiar with the tools and techniques of their specialism. This process can take many years, and often there is very little to show for it during that time. Einstein is reputed to have once said 'Genius is 1% inspiration, 99% perspiration' – implying that inspiration is only likely to come after considerable amounts of dogged hard work. For an artist, that can mean learning different painting techniques and handling different media; for a writer, learning to write for different types of audience or in different types of ways; for a scientist, becoming familiar with research techniques and discoveries in their field; for the musician, practising until they can produce any sound they want out of their instrument. In all of these cases, the person becomes so familiar with the tools of their trade that they know exactly how to produce the result that they want.

The second phase is *incubation*. A person who is about to produce a highly creative piece of work often reports a kind of 'latency period', when nothing much seems to be happening. The ideas that they had seem to have shifted into the unconscious regions of their mind, and they are not consciously aware of them. But it is clear that something is happening, because at the end of the incubation period the person often gets a sudden burst of inspiration: a scientist may suddenly perceive the theoretical links which will account for her experimental results; an artist may suddenly develop a clear impression of the image that they want to paint, or a musician may almost 'hear' the piece of music which they want to produce. This is the third phase of the creative process, that of *activity*. The individual suddenly has an insight or revelation about what they are doing, which tends to be accompanied by a burst of activity, as they work to capture the ideas which have emerged from their unconscious mind.

In many ways, then, 'real' creativity seems to be different from the sort of problem-solving which is being addressed by lateral thinking or brainstorming techniques. As a different aspect of human thinking, creativity is an intriguing process, and one which we are as yet very far from understanding fully. The message, though, seems to be clear: it doesn't happen without a lot of hard work and preparation beforehand!

Remembering   Ever since psychology first began, psychologists have been interested in how we remember things. One of the very first systematic studies of memorising was reported by Ebbinghaus, in 1885. Ebbinghaus and his research assistant painstakingly memorised hundreds of lists of nonsense syllables, and then tried to reproduce them. Ebbinghaus used nonsense syllables so that they would be coming to each one 'fresh', and not be trying to learn words that they already knew, but of course the problem with that is that most of the time, everyday memory does concern things that we already know something about. So even from the beginning, the experimental study of memory processes had some weaknesses.

Forms of remembering

However, that doesn't mean that this work was totally useless. There were a number of different effects which Ebbinghaus found as a result of these studies: like, that it was easier to remember the first and last items in a set, and that learning sessions seem to be more effective if they were short, rather than prolonged. In particular, Ebbinghaus was able to identify several different forms of remembering. The first of these, and the one which people mostly think of when they think of memory, is *recall*: simply being able to bring the information to mind. But *recognition* is also a way of remembering: we may not be able to recall something, but if it is presented to us we may know that it is what we were trying to remember.

In addition, Ebbinghaus found that there were two further ways in which traces of something that had been learned could still remain, even if the lists themselves could not be recalled or recognised. One of these is known as *redintegration*: even if a list had been apparently forgotten, the person could often put it together in the same order that it had originally. Similarly, you may think that you have forgotten something, but by carefully recalling everything that is associated with it, you may sometimes find that you can reconstruct that memory. And finally, even if all other traces had been lost, Ebbinghaus found that there were *re-learning savings* on a list which had been learned before. In other words, if you've learned something once, it won't take you as long to learn it second time.

Imagery in memory

Memories can be stored in different forms. In Chapter 8, we looked at Bruner's theory of representation, which showed how children develop and use different modes of representation – *enactive, iconic* and *symbolic* – as they grow older. But although we use the different types of representation as we get older, we still retain the ability to use the others. Adults use iconic and enactive representation too – it's just that they use a higher proportion of symbolic representation than small children do.

Using imagery can help us to remember. In 1975, Atkinson asked students to learn the meanings of lists of Spanish words. One group was not asked to use any technique to learn the words: they mostly tried to learn them by heart using repetition. But the second group was explicitly instructed in the 'key-word' visualising technique, in which you form a visual image which looks like the sound of the foreign word. So, for example, the Spanish word for 'horse' is 'caballo', which has a sound in the middle which sounds like the English word 'eye'. In this example, the students would be asked to form a visual image which would link the meaning of the word – a horse – with the sound of the word – an eye – perhaps producing something like a visual image of a horse's eye. When the two groups were compared, those who had used the key-word technique remembered 88% of the words that they had been given, whereas those who had not used any particular technique remembered only 28% of the words.

Strategies which help us to remember are known as *mnemonics*. There are other types of mnemonics, apart from visual imagery, like the sentences which can be made from first letters. Many people remember the order of the colours of the rainbow by remembering the sentence 'Richard Of York Gave Battle In Vain'. The first letter of each word in the sentence is the first letter of each of the colours of the rainbow: red, orange, yellow, green, blue, indigo, violet. Mnemonics like this can provide you with useful help, if you have a list or a sequence that you need to learn.

The two-process theory of memory

One of the early introspectionists, William James, proposed that we have two entirely different ways of storing memories. One of these is a short-term memory store, which contains just the information that we are using at that particular moment; and the other is a long-term memory store, which keeps information in memory for later recall. The two kinds of memory – *short-term memory* (STM) and *long-term memory* (LTM) were, James proposed, quite different in their ways of working, as well as in the amount of information that they could hold.

Short-term memory

One of the most well-known characteristics of short-term memory, is that it only seems to hold a limited number of items. Miller (1956) proposed that this limited number was in fact seven, plus or minus two. In other words, most people can recall about seven items from a list which is read out to them; but some will be able to remember more – generally eight or nine – while others will typically only remember five or six. The amount of information which could be held in memory could only be increased if it was put into larger 'chunks' – so we might only be able to remember seven isolated letters if they were read out; but we might remember seven words instead, which would contain a lot more than seven letters.

Other researchers investigated other characteristics of short-term memory. For instance, Conrad (1964) showed that we tend to code short-term memory using *acoustic coding* – forming a sound image of the information – whereas we are more likely to store long-term information in terms of what it actually

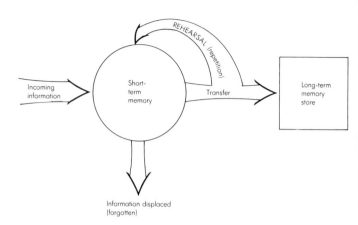

Fig. 13.3 The two-process theory of memory

means. The acoustic coding could be identified by looking at the mistakes which people made when they were trying to remember a string of letters or numbers. If someone said 'five' instead of 'nine' in a list, then that would be a signal that they were going by the sound of the word, because the sounds are quite similar. But if they said 'three' instead of 'eight', it would imply that they were using visual coding.

Long-term memory   Researchers investigating long-term memory also found that it had distinctive characteristics. For example: Tulving (1972) made a distinction between episodic and semantic memory. *Episodic memory* is the type of memory that we normally think of when we think about memory – our memory for facts, events, and episodes. But this isn't all that memory is about. We also know a lot of 'how to' information – we know how to catch a bus, or how to understand what someone is saying to us, or how to make a cup of tea. This isn't memory for specific things, but memory for how to go about just everyday living, which Tulving referred to as *semantic* memory. (Semantic means to do with meaning.)

Atkinson and   In 1977, Atkinson and Shiffrin produced a formal version of
Shiffrin's model of   the two-process theory of memory, in which they proposed that
memory   all information which is entering the memory passes into short-term memory first. Most of it is then lost from short-term memory – it decays quickly, or is displaced by other information coming in. But some information does transfer to long-term memory, and the way that it does that is through rehearsal. If we rehearse information, going over it again and again, we can keep it in short-term memory for longer; and it becomes

strengthened enough to be transferred to the long-term memory store.

There are a number of problems with this theory. One of the main ones is that, if it was true, then rehearsal would be a good way of learning things. But, in fact, rehearsal has actually been shown to be quite a bad way of memorising information. Bekerian and Baddeley (1980) conducted a study of the effectiveness of rehearsal by looking at how much people remembered of new BBC radio frequencies when they changed. The new frequencies were broadcast several times a day for months, and most radio listeners heard them well over a thousand times. But Bekerian and Baddeley found that very few people could actually remember what those frequencies were, even for their favourite channels. Clearly rehearsal in itself just isn't enough.

Levels of processing

In 1972, Craik and Lockhart produced an alternative to the two-process model of memory. Rather than suggesting that there were two entirely separate memory stores, with one serving as the entry point for information, they suggested that, in reality, there was only one store. What determined whether it would be retained or forgotten wasn't which store it had entered, but how deeply the information had been processed when it was first learned. So material which has only been superficially processed, like the telephone number that you look up, is quickly forgotten. Information which is processed more thoroughly because it means something to you, or because you have deliberately tried to make sure that you understand it, doesn't get forgotten as easily.

To illustrate this, Craik and Lockhart performed a study in which subjects were asked to look at words and answer questions about them. They weren't asked to remember the words, but the questions meant that the subjects had to process them to different degrees. One group was only asked to process the information superficially – they were already looking at the words, and they were asked questions about what they looked like – whether they were written in capital letters, for instance. A second group was asked to say what the words sounded like, by answering questions like 'Does it rhyme with . . . ?'. So this group had to process the information a bit more deeply, by changing its form. A third group was asked questions which meant that they had to think about the meaning of the word, like 'Would it fit in the sentence "He wore the . . . "?'.

When, later, Craik and Lockhart tested subjects to see how many of the words they remembered, they found big differences between the groups. Those who had only processed the information superficially remembered only about 15% of the list, those who had converted them to auditory images remembered about 35%, whereas those who had processed them semantically (for meaning) remembered roughly 70% of the total number of words on the list.

In another study, Bower and Karlin (1974) showed subjects pictures of faces, and asked them about what they could see. Some of the questions were straightforward visual ones, like asking whether it was a male or female face. Other questions asked the subjects to react to the faces they were looking at, like saying whether they thought it was a likeable sort of person or not, and a third set of questions asked subjects to make deeper judgements, like whether they thought that person was honest. As Craik and Lockhart had done, Bower and Karlin found that the more deeply the person processed the information, the more likely they were to remember the face afterwards.

Duration of memory   Craik and Lockhart used the concept of *levels of processing* to explain why it is that we remember information for so many different periods of time. There are some things which we never forget, and some which we remember for a good few years. But other items of information may stay with us only for a few months, or even weeks. Still more information remains accessible to memory for just a few days: 'What did you have for breakfast a week ago last Tuesday?'. If we think of memory as having two stores — a short-term and a long-term store — then we need to explain how the long-term store doesn't always retain information for the same length of time. But if we look

Fig. 13.4 Effects of different levels of processing (Craik and Lockhart 1972)

at information in terms of how deeply we process it, then we can see why some information is remembered for longer. If it means a lot to us, we will process it – we'll think about it, and what its implications are – and by doing so we'll be processing the information.

Memory as an active process   Most of the work on models of memory tends to assume that all we are doing when we remember something is simply recalling what happened. But it isn't really like that – memory isn't just factual. Instead, we change our memories, adjusting them to fit our expectations and assumptions, even though we believe that we are remembering exactly what happened. You may have experienced this if you've ever been to see a film which you saw a long time ago and really liked. Often, you can remember scenes from the film clearly, and yet when you see them again they seem quite different. It isn't the film that's changed – it's your memory, which has become adapted and adjusted to fit your other impressions and expectations.

One of the first of the studies showing this was conducted by Bartlett, in 1932. Bartlett asked subjects to read a long passage, and then to write down what they remembered of it. Then, later, they were asked to read what they had written down, and again to write down what they could remember. As this process, known as *serial reproduction*, continued, Bartlett found that the story which he had given them to read changed, according to the cultural group that the person was from.

The story itself was an American Indian legend, called 'The War of the Ghosts'. Since it was a traditional legend, it dealt with the spirit world as well as including accounts of what the living characters had done. Bartlett found that his Western subjects found it more difficult to remember the aspects of the story which were concerned with spirits, and they tended to leave those bits out when remembering the story, and to change the story so that it became more like the kind of adventure story that they were used to. By the time the story had been through four or five stages of serial reproduction, it was often nothing like the original. People's memories of what they had read had changed, until it was more in line with their cultural and personal beliefs.

A study by Loftus and Loftus (1975) showed how easily our memories for events can become distorted by what happens later. They showed subjects a film of a car accident, and then asked them questions about the scene. Both groups were asked the same questions, except that one group was asked 'How fast were the cars going when they hit one another?', while the other group was asked: 'How fast were the cars going when they smashed into one another?'. A week later, they were asked about the film again, and particularly whether there had been any broken glass around after the accident. There hadn't, and the first group remembered that accurately. But the people in the second group were quite positive that they distinctly remembered broken glass lying around. It seemed that the use of the more dramatic words in the question had meant that their memories, too, had become dramatised.

Bower (1981) asked subjects to note down everything pleasant or unpleasant that happened to them during one week in a diary. Then they were put into a pleasant or unpleasant mood using hypnosis, and asked to remember what had happened. Bower found that subjects remembered the events which fitted with the emotion they were feeling at the time – if they were in a bad mood, they remembered more unpleasant things, and if they were in a good mood, they remembered pleasant ones.

We can see, then, that as human beings we are *actively* involved in thinking, reasoning and remembering. Our memories don't act like an accurate tape-recording, even though we feel as though they do. Instead, they reflect our expectations, emotions and impressions as well.

Forgetting

What many people seem to want to know when they are studying memory, isn't so much how to remember, as how to avoid forgetting! That's particularly true if you have exams coming up – and as we have already seen, psychological theory can suggest a number of ways that memory can be improved. Understanding why we forget things may show us how we can avoid forgetting them, too, so we will look at some of the explanations which have been put forward, and see which of them can be of value to us.

Decay of the memory trace

One of the earliest ideas about memory was that each item left a kind of 'memory trace', or engram, in the brain. This gradually weakened if it was not used, but was strengthened each time the item was recalled. Although this does seem to be a plausible theory, I'm sure you will realise that it's one which is almost impossible to test – how do you tell that an engram is there if you don't recall it? So how would you know that one had gradually weakened and died away? If you wanted to go by this theory, though, the message for your revision would be that you should make sure that you recall the information often in order to strengthen the engram.

Brain damage

Some types of forgetting happen because the brain has become damaged or diseased. If you have a head injury in an accident, that can sometimes mean that you don't remember the events which led up to the accident. Yarnell and Lynch (1973) interviewed American football players who had accidents while playing that caused concussion. They asked them about their team's play strategy as soon as they came round, and again some twenty minutes later. Interestingly, they could remember it straight away, but not later on – and the memory didn't seem to come back afterwards either. This implies that there is some kind of *consolidation period*, while memories become fixed in the brain, and that this can be disturbed if there is an injury. However, in terms of your revision, unless you tend to engage in serious head-banging while listening to heavy metal music and revising, this probably isn't going to be the main reason why you forget things.

Another kind of amnesia, known as *Korsakoff's syndrome*, can result from serious and prolonged heavy drinking. In this syndrome, people become unable to remember any new information, although they can still speak and carry on a reasonable conversation. Sacks (1985) described a patient with Korsakoff's syndrome who had been actively employed in the services until 1965, but whose memory had become so impaired with continual heavy drinking that he could only remember events up to 1945. He became very disturbed when he saw himself in the mirror, because he still imagined himself as the nineteen-year-old he had been in 1945, which was when he had started his heavy drinking. Seeing an old man instead was a nasty shock, and just as disturbing each time he saw it. Sometimes, if indirect methods are used, people with Korsakoff's syndrome can learn something, although it is difficult for them. Jaffe and Katz (1975) described a patient suffering from Korsakoff's syndrome who was unable to remember the nursing staff's names; but when the staff wore initials, which gave a cue as to what their names were, he managed to learn them.

Korsakoff's syndrome is an extreme one, which develops gradually over years. But it is important to remember that alcohol itself is an amnesiac drug – people drink to forget things, which is why it is popular. And that's exactly why it's not a good idea to drink if you are trying to revise for an exam. Since the whole point of revision is to remember things, taking a drug which encourages you to forget would be rather a stupid thing to do!

Ageing Many people believe that your memory automatically gets worse with increasing age but there is some evidence which suggests that this isn't really inevitable. Harris and Sunderland (1981) compared subjects aged between 20 and 36 with retired people aged between 69 and 80. They found that the younger subjects experienced much more memory failure than the older group; and this difference was even more extreme when they compared younger subjects with a pre-retirement group aged

between 50 and 60. But in both cases, the older subjects
believed they had more memory failure – they noticed their
lapses of memory and attributed it to ageing because they
expected their memories to get worse, whereas the younger
subjects didn't worry about theirs!

There are, of course, some types of ageing where memory
loss does happen, although, despite society's stereotypes, they
only affect a small minority of old people. In such cases it
usually occurs as a result of brain damage through *senile
dementia* or *Alzheimer's disease*. Such people often become quite
confused, but they also tend to make their memory worse by
trying to remember things. Kral (1978) showed that when
patients with senile dementia are asked to remember lists of
words, they don't pay attention to the meaning, and they tend
to just wait passively if they are given extra time, instead of
using the time to learn. Receiving information passively is a
very bad memorising technique at any age. And the memory
tasks themselves – usually lists of words to be memorised – are
meaningless and boring, so the subjects wouldn't have wanted
to try very hard. That makes it a bit difficult to find out just
how much old people really can remember – you'd have to
look at information that really mattered to them before you
could really test that.

*Motivated
forgetting*

Freud (1901) believed that we forget things because we don't
want to remember them. Things that we forget, he argued,
are either traumatic or unpleasant for us, or could be associated
with things that are traumatic or unpleasant. So we forget
them – we repress the memory – because in that way the
unconscious mind can protect itself from harm. Although
Freud was rather extreme in insisting that all forgetting arises
from *repression*, it certainly seems to be the case that we forget
things which we don't want to remember, or because they don't
fit with what we are currently experiencing. So next time you're
having difficulty getting something to 'stick', try asking yourself
do you really want to remember it? If you don't, then you'll
need to find some other type of motivation – like learning it
for a quiz with some friends – which will help you to remember
it.

Interference

Interference theory suggests that what you remember can be
interfered with by other information that you learn. *Proactive
interference* is when information that you have already learned
affects how well you remember the next topic; *retroactive
interference* is when learning new information affects how well
you can recall information that you learned earlier. Research
into interference suggests that it is mainly similar material

which interferes – so one of the ways of tackling it when you are revising is to make sure that you really understand the differences between the topics that you are covering. If you just treat them all superficially, as if they were all the same, then they will be more likely to interfere with one another in your memory than if you really understand what each topic is about.

Holmes (1974) argued that the reason why we don't learn so well when we are worried or anxious is because the anxieties keep bringing up extraneous thoughts, like 'I'm going to fail', or 'I'll never remember all this', which interfere with what we are trying to remember. In the end, all we remember are the anxious thoughts, rather than what we are studying! If you are the type of person who does get that anxious, then the way to improve your memory is to manage that stress – do things which are going to allow you to work off the anxiety, like taking strenuous exercise to burn off the adrenaline (see Chapter 17), and taking time off from study to do something which will give your brain a rest, like going to the pictures. You'll be likely to concentrate much better as a result!

Context   The context can be helpful when we are trying to remember information. Abernathy (1940) gave students class tests in their normal classrooms, and also in unfamiliar rooms. They remembered more when they were in their own rooms. Other researchers have found that context can be recreated mentally. Williams and Hollan (1981) asked subjects to recall the names of school-friends. Although the subjects thought they had completely forgotten those people's names, when they were asked to imagine themselves back in the room, and to think as much about the context as possible, Williams and Hollan found that they often managed to retrieve the names after all.

Flashbulb memories are ones when a particularly powerful event seems to have 'fixed' the context as part of the memory. Brown and Kulik (1977) asked subjects 'What were you doing when you heard that President Kennedy had been assassinated?'. Seventy-nine out of eighty subjects remembered exactly where they had been and what they had been doing. Researchers have found similar effects for the explosion of the space shuttle Challenger, and for memories of an assassination attempt on President Reagan in 1981. Interestingly, though, these flashbulb memories may not always be accurate. Linton (1982) reported a subject who had a vivid memory of being interrupted by a friend and told about Kennedy's death while she was studying in her school library, and yet that friend was not even attending the school at that time!

One of the most powerful mnemonics, the *method of loci*, uses context to help memory. This method involves mentally re-tracing a familiar walk or journey, and visualising each item on a list at a particular location. Then, to recall the list, the person goes back over the walk and can visualise the items one at a time, in their new contexts. In this way, what was previously a disconnected list acquires a context, and becomes much easier to remember. In revision, this is often useful if you have a long sequence of names to recall. If they are technical terms, you may find it useful to combine it with the 'key-word' technique which we looked at earlier in the section on memory.

Memory cues   *Cues* are items of information which help us to recall others: they seem to lead us, mentally, towards the thing that we want to remember, and they can make a great deal of difference to how much we recall. Tulving and Pearlstone (1966) asked subjects to remember groups of words, under headings: 'animals', 'rocks', 'trees', etc. When they were tested, one group of subjects was given category names, but the second was not, and both groups were asked to recall as many of the original words as possible. Those who had been given the cues recalled far more than those who were just asked to remember. The study of symbolic representation by Bower which we looked at in Chapter 8 also shows us how powerful cues can be, and suggests that one way of revising effectively might be to organise the information you have to learn into a set of tree diagrams or flowcharts, so that one idea can lead naturally on to the next.

Processing   As we saw earlier, the *levels of processing* theory suggests that the more deeply we process information, the more we are likely to remember it. Morris et al. (1981) asked football supporters and other subjects to come to the laboratory on a Saturday, and allowed them to hear the list of that day's results just once. When they asked them to remember, they found that the football enthusiasts were much better at remembering the scores than people who were not football supporters. When it was just made-up scores, though, there was no difference between the two groups. But the football supporters tended to think about the meaning of the real scores, making connections and drawing out implications. If you can manage to do that with your revision, too, you would be likely to do well in your exams.

The levels of processing approach to memory helps us to make sense of a number of different features of memory, like how emotions, motivation and ideas can affect it. We are likely to think more about something that we feel strongly about, so we are more likely to remember it. If we believe that something was more likely to happen, we are more likely to practise visualising it instead of what we really did see, so the accuracy of our memory can be affected. And, of course, if we don't care about something, then we are not likely to give it much mental processing and we are more likely to forget it. That's something worth remembering when it comes to exam time!

In the next chapter, we will go on to look at another aspect of cognitive psychology, that of *perception*, and how we interpret information which we receive through our senses.

Summary

1 Cognitive psychology is the study of mental activity such as thinking, reasoning, remembering and perception.

2 Studies of thinking have included learning sets, insight learning, cognitive maps and concept formation, and schemata.

3 Studies of human reasoning show that human beings often apply sophisticated social knowledge, and so may appear to be making 'errors' in logic. But problem-solving is also affected by mental set and cognitive styles.

4 Creativity seems to involve three stages: a period of familiarisation, then a period of unconscious incubation, followed by the creative period of activity, when the end result is produced.

5 Research into memory has explored different forms of remembering and the value of using imagery to improve memory.

6 Theories of memory include the two-process theory.

7 Memory is an active process which can be affected by moods, language, and expectations.

8 We may forget things for a variety of different reasons, including lack of cues or being in the wrong context.

Chapter 14

Perception

In the last chapter, I described some aspects of cognitive psychology – how people think and remember, and process information.

In this chapter, I want to look at perception. Perception is more than just receiving information with our senses; it is also *making sense* of that information, how incoming messages are organised and made sense of by the brain. If you see a picture of a simple shape – like a square – all you are actually seeing is a pattern of light waves. But your brain receives this information, and organises it so that it makes sense to you, and then you recognise it as a square. As your brain does this, it is using not just the messages coming into your eyes, but also your past experiences of similar shapes, and your understanding of what a square should be like. That involves applying your knowledge of the world, and other cognitive processes, as well as just receiving the information.

The effects of expectation on perception

We can see that perception is more than just seeing, when we look at how what we expect can affect what we perceive. Bruner and Minturn (1955) demonstrated this by showing groups of subjects either letters or numbers quickly, and asking them to write down what they had seen. Then they showed them an ambiguous figure, which could be seen as either a letter or a number. The subjects who had previously seen numbers interpreted the figure as a number, while those who had seen letters thought that it was a letter that they had seen. In other words, they had seen what they expected to see.

There have been other studies which have shown similar effects. Sometimes, the first thing that we see sets up an expectation about what we are likely to see next. This is known as a *primacy effect*. Jones (1968) asked subjects to watch someone solving multiple-choice questions, in such a way as to receive instant feedback about whether the answer was right or not. Each subject saw the person get 15 out of 30 questions right in total, but one group saw the person get most of the right answers first, while the second group saw the person get the early ones wrong, but then get more right towards the end. When they were asked to estimate how many the person had solved correctly, the average answer for those who had seen the more correct ones first was 18.6, while the average for the other group was only 12.5. The first few answers had set up expectations about that person, and this had influenced how successful they were perceived as being.

Other kinds of expectations can affect perception too. Solley and Haigh (1958) asked children to draw pictures of Father Christmas, at intervals through the month leading up to Christmas and the month after. As the children became more excited and their expectations grew, the pictures which they drew became larger and more detailed – Father Christmas would be shown surrounded by presents and toys. But afterwards, the pictures became smaller and the number of pictures declined. It seems that the children's perception of the Father Christmas figure, at least as reflected in their drawings, was strongly affected by their expectations.

The perceptual cycle   Neisser (1976) proposed that perception isn't just a single process: we don't just look at someone once, judge them, and leave it at that. Instead, we are continually adjusting our perception: it is a continuous cycle, in which what we expect to see affects what we look for, and what we look for affects what we really do see, and what we really do see in turn affects what we expect to see. This *perceptual cycle* is going on all the time, and Neisser saw it as being at the heart of all cognition.

Neisser believes that, whenever we are active and not asleep,

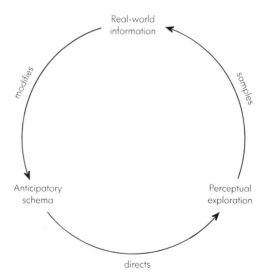

Fig. 14.1 Neisser's perceptual cycle

we are unconsciously anticipating what is going to happen next. We have a kind of mental schema, rather like the schemata we looked at in Chapter 8, called an *anticipatory schema*. This contains the memories, expectations and plans for action which are relevant to the situation that we are in. So we don't just approach things with a blank mind, ready to take in information; we anticipate what is likely to happen, unconsciously.

The anticipatory schema channels our attention towards the stimuli which we think are likely to be relevant. All the time, we are actually being flooded with sensory information: try stopping reading this book for a minute, and noticing what is about you. There is tactile information, from your clothes and wherever you are sitting or lying; visual information from the room around you (if you're indoors as you're reading this); you'll probably be able to hear some sounds, and so on. But most of the time, we don't take any notice of all of this extra information, because the anticipatory schema directs our perceptual exploration of the world.

This means that we only sample some of the information which is actually available to us from the outside world. We notice some things and not others, and, by and large, the information which we notice is the information which is relevant to the anticipatory schema. But that doesn't mean that it is always exactly as expected – quite often it isn't, and then the anticipatory schema will be adjusted, to cope with it. So the information which we actually receive in turn modifies the anticipatory schema.

This, then, is the perceptual cycle: the anticipatory schema directs our perceptual exploration of the world; the perceptual exploration takes a sample from the available information; and the sample of information, in turn, modifies the anticipatory schema.

Recognising shapes and patterns

Clearly, our previous experience and our existing knowledge play a great part in what we perceive. And, as Neisser showed, the information that we actually receive through our senses also plays some part in directing and channelling our perception. But our sense receptors are simply a large number of sensitive cells, as we shall see in the next chapter. For example, the way we receive visual information is as a set of minute dots on the retina, with each dot being one light-sensitive cell. So the next question we have to ask is: how is that information turned into meaningful information?

Figure-ground perception

One answer to this is that it seems to be very basic to our perceptual system to interpret what we see in terms of figures set against backgrounds. This becomes particularly clear when we look at ambiguous stimuli, like Rubin's vase. In this image, there are two possible figures: the vase or the silhouettes. But when we look at one of them, the other disappears – it becomes just the background. Although we can look at either one of them in turn, and can even flick quickly between them, we can't see them both simultaneously, because our perception is so strongly directed to see one figure against a background.

Fig. 14.2 Rubin's vase

So how does this happen? Partly, because our perception is organised according to a set of principles which encourage us to perceive a complete figure if there is even a suggestion of one in the information that we are receiving. These principles are known as the *Laws of Prägnanz*, or sometimes as the *Gestalt principles of perception* – because they were first identified by a group of psychologists in the 1930s who were known as the Gestalt psychologists.

These Gestalt principles are all about how we group different visual stimuli together into meaningful shapes – how we see things as 'belonging'. There are four of them: the principle of proximity, the principle of similarity, the principle of closure, and the principle of good Gestalt.

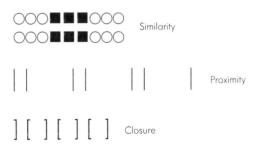

Fig. 14.3 Gestalt principles of perception

The principle of *proximity* is simply that we will tend to see things as belonging together if they are near to one another. If you were to look at a disorganised set of dots, with some of them closer to each other than others, you would tend to perceive the ones which are close together as a group. The principle of *similarity* is that we will group together things which are similar to one another. So if we have a group of, say, x's and o's arranged randomly, we will naturally tend to see all the o's as belonging together. As a general rule, the principle of similarity is stronger than the principle of proximity: we're more likely to see similar things as belonging unless the distances are very exaggerated.

The principle of *closure* is stronger still. If a stimulus seems to suggest a completed figure, the brain perceives it as whole even though it isn't. We can see this very clearly in the illusion known as the 'invisible triangle' – even though it is only suggested by the missing shapes, we still see the triangle very clearly – and even the page sometimes appears to be slightly whiter within the triangle than it is outside. The brain completes the lines to form a complete figure.

Fig. 14.4 The invisible triangle

The fourth Gestalt principle is the principle of *good Gestalt*. This is hard to describe, but we seem to have a perceptual preference for figures which involve clean, distinct shapes rather than ones which are 'bitty' or disorganised. So our perception will naturally tend to identify those kinds of shapes or figures more easily than others.

Perceiving distance   Another important part of perceptual organisation, and one which also contributes to how we see figures against backgrounds, is known as *depth perception*. This is all to do with how we can tell how far away things are. Since the retina itself, which receives the messages about the outside world, is like a curved screen, we have to use what are known as *depth cues* to show us where these are.

Having two eyes both looking in roughly the same direction gives us some important cues to depth, because the images that the two eyes receive are very slightly different, and things that are very close to us are more different than things which are further away. (Try holding a pencil at different distances from your nose, and lining it up with some distant object. Then open and shut each eye in turn, and see how far the pencil seems to move, relative to the background.) This is known as a *binocular depth cue*, because it takes two eyes for it to work.

We also use *monocular depth cues*, which work just as well with one eye as they do with two. These are the cues which you are using when you see depth in a picture or photograph – how we can tell how far away from us things are. Our eyes receive an image from the outside world which is picked up on the retina: a layer of nerve cells spread across the back of the eyeball. The image is spread out across the retina rather like a curved photograph, and this is the image which the brain has to decode into something which represents the outside world.

There are seven monocular depth cues: relative size, height in plane (how high up something seems to be), superposition (whether one object seems to be covering up another), shadow, motion parallax (the way things seem to move relative to one another when you, the observer, move), gradient of colour (things which are farther away seem greyer), and gradient of texture (things which are farther away seem smoother).

There are several visual illusions which seem to work by using depth cues. Gregory (1963) argued that the reason why one of the strongest visual illusions, the Müller-Lyer illusion (see figure 14.12), works is because it draws on the way that we use our knowledge of depth cues to interpret visual information. So we see the line with the outward-pointing 'fins' as being like an inner corner of a room, and we enlarge it mentally because it seems to be further away from us than the fins are. But we see the lines with the inward-pointing 'fins' as being like the outer corner of a building, and so mentally we 'shrink' the line to allow for the way that it would be closer to us, and therefore appear bigger.

Other visual illusions, too, seem to use depth cues like height in plane of relative size to have their effect. Researchers have also used some aspects of depth perception to explore whether visual perception is innate or learned. This concerns the nature/nurture debate in perception, and we will now go on to look at this in more detail.

Studies with infants (neonate studies)   One of the ways that people have tried to investigate the nature/nurture debate on perception has been to study babies and young animals, and to see whether they are able to perceive

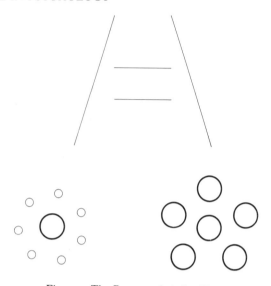

Fig. 14.5 The Ponzo and circles illusions

things when they are first born, when they haven't had time to learn from their visual experience.

A popular idea of what new-born babies actually experience was put forward by the introspectionist psychologist, William James. He considered the amount of visual stimulation (light waves) which surrounds us, and also the amount of sound stimulation, and he thought that it was unlikely that the new-born infant was able to make sense of all this as soon as it was born. Instead, the child must be almost overwhelmed by what James described as 'a blooming, buzzing, confusion' of sound and vision, as well as the information coming in through the other senses. As the child developed, James thought, it would gradually learn to sort out this confusion, and make sense out of the different sensory information that it was receiving.

Fantz's study   In 1961, Fantz set up an experiment that allowed him to see what babies preferred to look at. He devised a piece of machinery that allowed him to see what babies' eyes were focused on. Then he showed infants a choice of two pictures, or patterns. By seeing which one the infant looked at more, he was able to work out the sort of patterns they preferred. Since it wasn't likely that the infants would prefer something that didn't make sense to them, he was able from this study to deduce what they could see.

Fantz found that, in general, infants preferred complex patterns to plain ones. He was careful to match the amount of black-and-white in his patterns, so that it wasn't just that

Fig. 14.6 The equipment Fantz used for his study

infants preferred a light or a darker pattern. But if they had a choice between a plain half-black and half-white shape, and a chequerboard pattern, the infants would look at the chequerboard more. So Fantz concluded that at the very least, infants had an innate ability to distinguish patterns, and so they must be able to see figures against a background from the very beginning.

Fantz also discovered that infants preferred to look at pictures of faces. (This is similar to Ahren's study, which we looked at in Chapter 3). He showed infants three shapes. One was a drawing of a face, with eyes, nose, mouth etc, all in the right places. The second was the same shape, and with the same markings, but in this one the features were all scrambled up, for instance the mouth was at the top, and an eyebrow down the side of the face, and so on. The third shape was the same outline as the other two, but the top half was dark and the other half light. Fantz had made sure that this one contained exactly as much light and dark colour as the other two, but it was in two plain halves, and not in a pattern.

The infants looked at the 'face' shape most of all, then next at the 'scrambled' face, and not much at all at the plain shape.

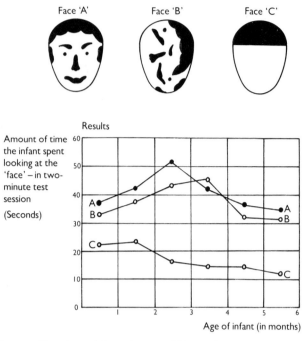

Fig. 14.7 Fantz's models, and some of his results

Fantz said that this showed how infants could perceive human-type faces from very early on in their lives, suggesting that it was probably innate.

Bower's study   Another study on what infants could and couldn't see was done by T. Bower, in 1966. Bower wanted to find out if infants could allow for the way that the image of an object changes, depending on how far away it is, or what direction it's facing. Objects that are a long way away look smaller than close-up objects. In everyday life, we allow for this – if we see someone down the street, we don't think that they are small and growing larger as they walk towards us! Instead, we assume that they are the same size all the time, even though the actual image that our eyes receive – the retinal image – is changing in size. This is known as *size constancy*. Similarly, a teacup at an angle looks different from a teacup seen from the side. But we have *shape constancy*, which means that although the image our eyes receives is different, we still perceive the teacup as being the same shape.

Bower was interested in the question of whether we develop size and shape constancy through our childhood, or whether

30cm³ cube   Experimenter ready to 'peek-a-boo'   Screen raised while cube is changed   Record attached to infant's left pillow

Fig. 14.8 Bower's 'peek-a-boo' experiment

infants have it from birth. To find out, he first of all took some young infants, and trained them to turn their heads when they saw a particular shape – a thirty-centimetre cube.

The infants learned this by a process known as *operant conditioning*, which we'll look at more closely in Chapter 18. Each time the infant turned its head to one side, when it saw the cube, it was rewarded by an experimenter jumping up and playing 'peek-a-boo' with it. The baby learned that if the cube was there, it should turn its head and it would get a game. (There were pressure-switches in the pillows on either side of the infant's head, so that the movement could be detected – young infants can't move very much, even though they can move a bit.)

When the baby had learned to respond when it saw the cube, Bower tried showing it different cubes, and seeing if it would respond when it saw those as well. He tried cubes at different angles, to see if the baby had shape constancy, and would respond to the original cube no matter what angle it was at. He also tried different sized cubes at different distances, arranged so that the retinal image in the eye would be exactly the same size, even though the cube was actually a different size. For instance, a larger cube would be further away than the original cube had been, and a smaller cube would be nearer.

Bower found that the infants had fairly good size and shape constancy. It wasn't as good as an adult's, but it was still much better than it would have been if the baby had had to learn from experience. So he concluded that, to some extent at least, shape and size constancy were innate.

Gibson and Walk's Another experiment with infants was performed by Gibson and
'visual cliff' Walk in 1960. They were interested in the way that infants
perceive depth – how far away something is. Mostly, we
perceive depth by *binocular disparity*: because we have two eyes
receiving similar information, we can compare the messages
from both eyes and see how far away things are. Each eye
gives a slightly different picture, and the nearer things are, the
more different their position seems to be. You can try this out
by holding out a pencil and, with one eye, lining it up against
something in the background. If you then close that eye and
open the other, the pencil seems to have jumped a bit. This is
because each of your eyes gives you a slightly different picture.

We can also see depth from other cues, though – *monocular
depth cues* (cues that can be seen with one eye). For instance, if
something seems to obscure our view of another thing, we
assume it is in front. Or if things seem to get smaller, we may
assume that they are getting further away. It isn't often that an
adult will make a mistake about how far away something is,
unless they are in a really unusual situation. But what about
babies?

Gibson and Walk developed a device called 'the visual cliff'.
This was a table topped with strong glass – strong enough to
support a child's weight. Beneath the glass, on one side of the
table, was a piece of checked material, right up against the
glass. On the other side of the table, there was also checked
cloth under the glass, but this time it fell away below it. There
was a board dividing the two halves of the table. It was called
a 'visual cliff' because it *looked* like a drop down, but it wasn't
really, as the glass was very strong.

Gibson and Walk tested the infants by placing them on the
centre board and asking their mothers to call them from one
side or the other. When the mothers called from the 'shallow'
side, the infants would crawl to them quite happily, but when
they called from the 'deep' side, most of the infants (92%)
refused to cross over it. They also tried the infants wearing a
patch over one eye, to see if it was binocular or monocular
cues that the infants were using. But the infants wouldn't cross
the 'deep' side at all, showing that they could use monocular
cues to depth.

Gibson and Walk also tried this with animals – day-old
chicks, new-born goat kids, and kittens. None of them would
go on the 'deep' side. Some rats that they tested would,
however. But if the rat's whiskers were removed, they wouldn't
go on the deep side either.

This experiment seemed to show that depth perception was
innate, at least for the day-old chicks, goat kids, and kittens

Fig. 14.9 The visual cliff

with their eyes newly open. But there are problems in saying that it showed that for the human babies. Since the infants were old enough to crawl, they would have had at least six months' visual experience. During that time, they could easily have learned about things that get nearer and further away; and have learned not to go near edges – perhaps by simple games like 'throw-your-teddy-out-of-the-cot'. So it doesn't really show that they had innate depth perception at all. So although Gibson and Walk's study does show that depth perception may be innate in animals, it doesn't really tell us much about human depth perception.

One of the problems with trying to study perception in infants, though, is that the ability could still be innate even if the infant hasn't developed it yet. It might be that certain types of ability develop as a result of *maturation*: they are inherited abilities, but they don't show until the child has reached a certain age. So just studying what infants can and can't perceive may not tell us much about the nature/nurture question.

Studies with blind people

One way of getting round the problem of maturation is to look at people who have been blind until they were adults, and have then regained their sight. Because they are adults, there is no question of their being too young to have developed a certain ability. In some ways, these people represent a kind of 'new-born adult', as far as vision is concerned.

von Senden's study

One such study was performed by von Senden, in 1932. He studied blind people who had had their sight restored by surgery, usually by a corneal graft. He found that from the beginning these subjects could distinguish figures against a background, and they could also distinguish colour (although they couldn't *name* the colours). But if they were shown lines of different lengths, they couldn't say what distinguished them, although they might say that they looked 'somehow different'. When they encountered familiar objects, they couldn't name them unless they were allowed to touch them first – then they recognised them. Over a period of time, though, von Senden's subjects did manage to achieve normal perception, thus showing at least, that perception *can* be learned.

Gregory's study

Another study of a blind person who had his sight restored was performed by R. L. Gregory in 1963. He studied one man in particular detail, and noted how his perception developed. Gregory's subject may have been different from those studied by von Senden, in that all his life he had had a very strong wish to see. Since he had dreamed of being able to see, he had often handled objects and tried to imagine what they must look like. When his sight was restored, unlike von Senden's subjects, Gregory's subject was able to name familiar objects by sight. He could also tell simple shapes quite easily – von Senden's subjects couldn't recognise a triangle without counting the corners first. Some things, though, he had to touch before he could name, like the others – it was only familiar objects which he could recognise. And he often made mistakes in judging distances: he thought that he would be able to reach the ground from his window, by hanging down from his hands, but in fact the window was about ten times higher up than that.

Unfortunately, all these studies suffer from serious problems. Although they do seem to imply that figure-background perception and colour perception are innate, they are inconclusive about the other aspects of perception, and this could well be because of these problems.

One of the first problems is that they deal with a very small number of people – they tend to be case studies rather than general studies. And the data are often collected in an unsystematic kind of way – by simply chatting with the subject, and perhaps testing them a little. Neither Gregory nor von Senden seem to have given their subjects the standard visual tests, which might make it easier to compare their results.

Another problem, which particularly applies to Gregory's subject, is the way that he had wanted to see so badly. Because of this, he had built up strong expectations of what seeing was like, and when he did finally regain his sight he found things very drab and disappointing. And it's possible that his emotional disturbance may have influenced the way he reacted to the different tests Gregory asked him to do. We can't assume that Gregory's results were typical of the normal development of vision.

The final problem I want to mention with these studies, is that the subjects were adults, who had already developed the use of their other senses. This meant that they were quite well able to perceive in some ways already (for instance, they knew things well by touch), and they were able to 'transfer' messages from one sense to their new sense of sight. This is known as *cross-modal transfer* – changing from one sensory mode (touch) to another (sight). For instance, they could recognise things by sight *after* they'd been allowed to touch them. By transferring the information from their touching, they were able to 'see' things clearly.

The point is, that if we want to find out whether a sense – vision – is innate or learned, then we have to study only that sense, and how it is used. Cross-modal transfer means that people are using other senses, which they have been developing for the whole of their lives – so we still wouldn't know whether their visual perception is learned or innate.

Studies using deprived environments

Some researchers have tried to find the answer to this question by bringing animals up in restricted or deprived environments. By doing this, they can see if the animal's perception develops normally, through maturation, or whether it depends on certain kinds of experience.

Riesen's studies

One of the first studies of this kind was performed by Riesen in 1950. He brought chimpanzees up in total darkness, and brought them into the light for the first time at the age of sixteen months. He found that their vision seemed to have suffered a great deal; they couldn't learn to tell the differences between simple patterns, and they couldn't learn to avoid things which would give them an electric shock. So it seemed as if Riesen had shown that they needed practice in order to see.

The problem with this study by Riesen was pointed out by L. Weiskrantz, who said that during the long period in darkness, the chimps' retinal cells and their optic nerves had degenerated. (We'll be looking more closely at the structure of the eye in the next chapter.) Nerve cells tend to waste away if they aren't used, in the same way that muscles wither if they aren't exercised. If this physical atrophy happens, then it wouldn't be the effects of not being able to *learn* at all.

Following this criticism, Riesen repeated his experiment in 1966, but this time he brought the chimps up with translucent goggles on. These goggles let the light through (but not the patterns), so the optic nerve and the retinal cells would receive some light and dark to stimulate them. The chimps' vision turned out to be a bit better than those from the first experiment, but much worse than normal chimpanzees. They were much slower at learning to grasp things, or discriminate between patterns to avoid an electric shock.

This experiment showed that if normal vision is to develop, it is quite important to have visual experience in the early months.

Blakemore and Cooper's study

In 1966 Blakemore and Cooper investigated whether visual experience would affect the type of perception that developed. They developed an environment with only vertical lines in it, and no horizontal lines at all. When they placed young kittens in this 'vertical world', from the moment their eyes were open, they found that the kittens' vision developed accordingly. Although the cats had had visual experience, so the optic nerve and visual equipment had been stimulated, when they were tested they were only able to see vertical things. They would avoid obstacles like table-legs quite easily, but they would trip over ropes stretched out horizontally in front of them. So it seemed that the time they spent in the drum – the vertical world – had been spent *learning* to see. If perception were innate, then they shouldn't have had any difficulty.

This study has been criticised over the development of particular retinal cells. As we will see in the next chapter, some cells in the visual system seem to be mainly concerned with particular kinds of lines. It is always possible that the kittens had the cells to receive horizontal lines in the first place, but that they had *atrophied* – wasted away – because they weren't

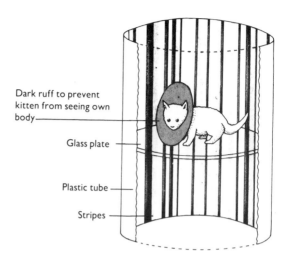

Dark ruff to prevent
kitten from seeing own
body

Glass plate

Plastic tube

Stripes

Fig. 14.10 A kitten in a 'vertical world'

being used. Or, instead of atrophy, those particular cells may
have been used for other purposes, like seeing vertical lines
instead of the horizontal lines that they would originally have
been sensitive to, if the cats had had normal experience. So
although this experiment does seem to show that perception is
learned, it still isn't totally convincing.

Held and Hein's   Another study of what happens when you restrict experience
'Kitten carousel'   was performed by Held and Hein in 1963. They developed
an apparatus which allowed two kittens to have exactly the same
visual experience, but only one of them could move about.
This apparatus – called a 'kitten carousel' – consisted of a
pivoted bar, which controlled two kitten harnesses. One
kitten's harness just went around its body, but it could still
walk around. Whenever this kitten walked, it also moved the
other kitten, which was suspended from the other end of the
bar, in a basket or 'gondola'. So when the first kitten walked
in one direction, it also swung the other kitten with it, thus
giving the two kittens identical visual experience.

When the kittens were tested, it was found that the 'active'
kitten could see perfectly well – it had no problems avoiding
obstacles or barriers. But the 'passive' kitten didn't seem to be
able to see at all; although there was nothing wrong with its
eyes or optic nerve, it didn't seem to be able to *use* the
information that was coming in. So this study seemed to show
quite clearly that it is necessary to have physical experience as
well as just visual experience, if normal perception is to
develop.

Pivot

'Active' kitten in harness

'Passive' kitten in basket

Fig. 14.11 Held and Hein's 'Kitten Carousel'
*Since the active kitten moves both itself and the passive kitten, as it moves
around they both receive the same visual stimulation*

**Cross-cultural
studies**

More evidence of the way that different experiences may affect
our perception can come from cross-cultural studies – studies
of people living in different types of societies. Because their
visual experience is concerned with different types of things,
then if perception is learned, we would expect them to perceive
differently. But if perception is inherited, we would expect
everyone to see things in much the same kind of way.

Turnbull's study

A study of pygmy perception was made by C. Turnbull in
1961. Because pygmies live in dense forest, they aren't used
to seeing things a long way away. Turnbull took a pygmy out
into the open plains, and showed him a herd of buffalo grazing
a long distance away. When he asked what they were, the
pygmy said that they were insects, and wouldn't believe that
they were buffalo because they looked so small. When he saw
a boat some distance away across a lake, he thought it was just
a scrap of wood floating. So this study would seem to show
that perception is quite strongly affected by the environment
that we grow up in. Because that pygmy had never seen things
from a great distance, he wasn't able to use the 'depth cues'
that we use all the time. But his perception was adapted well
to his environment in the forest, and he didn't make any
mistakes there.

Segall and Campbell's study

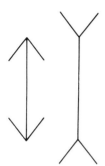

Fig. 14.12 The Muller-Lyer illusion

Another cross-cultural study was made by Segall Campbell and Herskowitz, in 1963. They looked at a particular visual illusion, which has quite a strong effect among Europeans. The illusion was the 'Müller-Lyer' illusion – two equal lines, with arrowheads at each end. The line with the arrowheads pointing outwards seems longer, to Europeans, than the line with the arrowheads pointing inwards, even though they are exactly equal.

Many people have explained the 'power' of this illusion in terms of the way that our environment is one containing many straight lines and right-angled corners. This 'carpentered' environment means that we are very much on the look-out for depth cues to do with straight lines, and the Muller-Lyer illusion may arise from that. Segall et al. tested the Muller-Lyer illusion on people who live in an environment where they don't have that many straight lines and right-angles – Zulus living in their tribal communities. They found that the Zulus weren't fooled by the Muller-Lyer illusion at all; they saw the two lines accurately, as being equal.

This seemed to show that Segall et al. were right in thinking that it was the 'carpentered' environment of Europeans that made them so readily fooled by this illusion. But later researchers suggested that it might not have been that at all – it could have been the way that Europeans are much more used to interpreting paper-and-pencil drawings than tribal Zulus are. Either way, it still shows that experience affects the way that we perceive things.

Witkin's study

In 1962 Witkin performed a study of African people. He was interested in the way that people keep their sense of balance. Most Europeans tend to rely on sight a great deal for their sense of balance – they are easily taken in by illusions where the wall appears to lean over, and they will often feel themselves to be falling even when they are not, if their eyes are telling them so.

Witkin wanted to know if this was the same for everyone, but when he compared Europeans to Africans, he found that the native African tribes-people didn't depend on their sight nearly as much; they used other senses, like hearing, and the kinaesthetic senses (which tell you what positions your muscles and joints are in). Witkin described the tribal Africans as being 'visual field independent' because they didn't rely on the sense of sight so much for this, while he described Europeans as being 'visual field dependent'. Again, his study seemed to show that experience makes a lot of difference to the ways that we perceive things – and to how much importance we place on each particular sense.

Annis and Frost's study

Annis and Frost, in 1973, performed a cross-cultural study of Canadian Cree Indians. Some of these people lead their traditional lives in Canada, leading a nomadic life in tepees. Some, though, have a 'western' style of life, living in houses and towns. Their environment is a 'carpentered' one, where all the lines (or most of them) are either vertical or horizontal (try looking around you), and the corners are right angles. But the traditional environment has lines at all angles, and not nearly so many right angles.

Annis and Frost tested their subjects on a task involving judging whether two lines were parallel or not. They used pairs of lines at all sorts of different orientations. The urban Canadians turned out to be very good at judging parallel lines when they were either horizontal or vertical, but they weren't very good at it when the lines were at an angle. The traditional Cree Indians, though, were good at judging lines no matter at what angle they were presented. Again, the environment seemed to have an effect on our perception.

Cross-cultural studies seem to show the strongest effect of learning on our perceptual abilities. But some other studies, too, show that perception is quite flexible, and we can learn to adjust to new types of perception.

Distortion and readjustment studies

Stratton's study

One of the first studies of this kind was performed by Stratton, in 1897. He wanted to see if he would be able to adjust to upside-down vision, given enough time. Stratton used a lens that inverted the image going into one of his eyes, so that everything was upside-down. He kept the other eye covered all the rest of the time. After a few days, Stratton found that he was adjusting more and more to his upside-down vision – he stopped bumping into things so often, and gradually he didn't even notice that things were upside-down.

Hess's study

Fig. 14.13 Prism lenses on a cockerel

Stratton's study showed that people could learn to adjust if their vision was distorted, but when this was tried on birds, it didn't produce the same result. Hess, in a study in 1956, put prism lenses on the eyes of some chickens. This had the effect of distorting their vision, so that things appeared about ten degrees to one side of where they really were. The hens didn't learn to adjust at all – when they pecked at corn, they always pecked to the side and couldn't allow for the distortion.

We can explain the two different findings by looking at the *phylogenetic scale*, which I mentioned in Chapter 2. As we saw then, animals which are higher up the phylogenetic scale rely much more on learning, and less on inherited behaviour. Since birds are much lower on the phylogenetic scale than humans, they may not be able to manage this kind of learning, while humans can. This difference can also explain, perhaps, why the animals Gibson and Walk tested were so reluctant to walk on the 'visual cliff' even when they were new-born.

Kohler's study   Another more recent readjustment study was performed by Kohler, in 1962. He wore goggles with the left half of each lens coloured green, and the right half coloured red. After a few hours, Kohler found that he didn't notice these colours any more, he had adjusted to them. But when he took the goggles off, he found that he now saw the *opposite* colours, for a while. These 'after images' show that his brain was coping with the goggles by 'cancelling out' the colours, and when he took the goggles off it took some time for the 'cancelling' process to stop. But it did show, again, that the human visual system is quite flexible and adaptable. Before he tried the experiment, Kohler had thought that he wouldn't be able to adapt. He had thought that perception was innate, but his study showed that it could be learned. However, we can't necessarily take this to mean that *all* perception is learned – it could be that an adult's perceptual system is different from a baby's, and that babies can't adapt so easily.

As you'll have noticed as we worked through this chapter, none of these experiments really provide *convincing* proof for either side of the nature/nurture debate on perception. The cross-cultural studies would seem to imply that there is some learning involved, while the neonate studies seem to show that some perception is innate. It's most likely that the answer is

(a)

(b)   (c)

Fig. 14.14 Red-green goggles, as used by Kohler
(a) *Goggles* (b) *At first, a white object to the left appears green, but after a while returns to its original colour* (c) *After removing the goggles, the same object appears red, but after a while returns to white*

somewhere between the two. There are many different aspects of perception, some of which may be inherited, while others may come from different experiences within the environment. Since perception consists of many different abilities, not just one, then we are not likely to find one single answer to this question. But we can come to some conclusions. Figure/ground perception does seem to be innate, for instance, while more complicated things like depth perception seem to require experience.

In the next chapter, we'll look more closely at the way that our senses work, and how we come to process the information that we receive through our eyes and ears, so that it reaches the brain and can be interpreted.

Summary   1 Perception is the process of receiving and interpreting information from our senses. It can be strongly influenced by our expectations.

2 Neisser's theory of the perceptual cycle proposed that we have an anticipatory schema which directs our perceptual exploration of the world, but this in turn is modified by the information which we receive.

3 We seem automatically to organise our visual perception into figures against backgrounds. The Gestalt principles of perception show how some of this organisation happens.

4 There are two kinds of visual cue that we use to judge how far away something is: binocular depth cues, which involve both eyes working together, and monocular depth cues, which work just as well if we only use one eye.

5 Various studies have investigated the nature/nurture debate on perception. Experiments with infants by Fantz and Bower show that there may be some innate abilities. Studies with animals by Gibson and Walk show that depth perception may be innate.

6 Studies of blind people who have had their sight restored show that figure/ground perception may be innate, but other abilities may be learned.

7 Deprivation studies by Riesen, Blakemore and Cooper, and Held and Hein show that experience – both visual and physical – is necessary for the development of normal vision.

8 Cross-cultural studies show that people develop perception appropriate to their environment. Readjustment studies by Stratton, Hess and Kohler show that people can adjust to distorted vision, but that birds cannot.

Chapter 15

Sensory information processing

In the last chapter, we looked at the process of perception, and how it develops. Throughout that chapter we were talking about *visual* perception – the way that we come to understand the information we receive from our eyes. In this chapter, I want to look more closely at how that information gets to the brain, in order for the process of perception to start to work.

The processes of vision

The process by which we receive light information and translate it into information for the brain can be divided into three parts. The first part is the way that the light information is collected, and organised as information that can go to the brain. The second part is the way that that information is transmitted to the appropriate parts of the brain, and the third part is what happens to the information when it reaches the brain and is analysed.

How the information is collected

The main function of the eyes is to pick up light information, so that it can be coded and sent to the brain. All the different parts of the eye have a role to play in the way that light information is collected.

When light first reaches the eye, it passes through two transparent membranes that cover the front of the eye. The first is a thin coating called the *conjunctiva*, which protects the eye from dust and grit, and which is 'washed' each time we blink. This keeps our vision clear all the time. Behind the conjunctiva is a transparent disc called the *cornea*. This is slightly curved, and begins a process of bending the light rays in towards the centre of the eye, so that they can be received more effectively. When they have passed through the cornea, the light rays pass across a space, which is filled with a clear fluid called *aqueous humour*. The fluid also helps to bend the light rays inwards, and also keeps the front of the eye properly in shape.

When they have got this far, the light rays pass through a small hole into the back part of the eye. This small hole is called the *pupil* – it's the dark spot in the middle of the eye. The pupil is surrounded by a band of muscle fibres, called the *iris*.

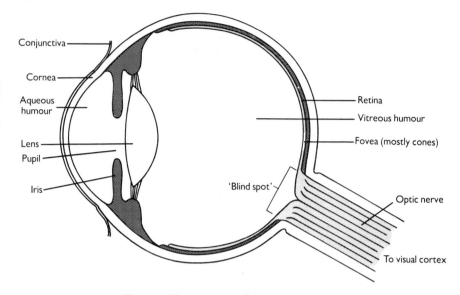

Fig. 15.1 The structure of the eye

This is the bit that can be different colours – blue or brown, or sometimes green. The iris provides a way for our eyes to adjust to different light levels. During the daytime, it is very bright, and so we only need a small-sized pupil to let enough light into the eye for us to see clearly. But at night, under artificial light there is much less light around. Our eye needs more light to be able to see, and so the iris contracts, making the pupil expand, or *dilate*. The larger hole lets in more light, and we can see just as clearly as we could during the day.

When the light has passed through the pupil, it immediately comes to an important part of the eye – the lens. This is a transparent oval just behind the pupil, which focuses the incoming light coming onto the retina at the back of the eye. It is the lens focusing which gives us such a clear image when we look at things, because it adjusts its shape to the thing we are looking at.

If we are looking at something a long way away, the lens is pulled out to be long and thin, by the suspensory ligaments which hold it. But if we are looking at something nearby, then the lens becomes thicker and shorter. In this way, it *accommodates* itself to the thing we are looking at, and by doing so it makes sure that the clearest image is focused on the retina.

From the lens, the light passes across the eyeball to the retina. Since the lens is focusing it onto the retina, it's important that the eye keeps its shape – if the retina was moved a bit, then the image wouldn't be focused. So the eyeball is filled with a clear fluid called *vitreous humour*, through which the light rays pass from the lens to the retina.

At the back of the eyeball, then, is the retina, and this is where the light rays are translated into the electrical messages which the brain will receive. The retina consists of three layers of cells, each layer being different. At the very *back* of the retina – furthest away from the pupil and the lens – are the cells that actually pick up the light information – the rod and cone cells. These cells contain a chemical which bleaches when it is hit by light, and so sets up a small electrical charge. This is then passed along to the next layer of cells – the bipolar neurones – and then on to the third layer of cells, called the ganglion cells.

I've mentioned that there are two different types of cells – rods and cones – that pick up the light information and change it

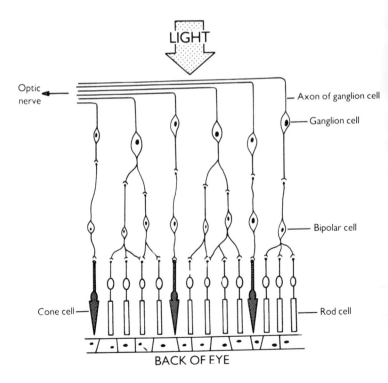

Fig. 15.2 The retina

into electrical messages. These two types of cells also have
different functions. Rod cells are used for seeing in dim light
conditions. They are very sensitive to slight changes in light
intensity. Most rod cells are found towards the edges of the
retina – the peripheral vision. It is because the rod cells are so
sensitive, that we can detect even very small movements out
of 'the corner of our eyes' – they attract our attention, and then
we will turn and focus our vision fully on the moving thing,
whatever it is. Rod cells also allow us to see in very dim light,
for instance, at night in the countryside. It may take a bit of
time for our eyes to adapt to the dark, so that the rod cells get
working fully, but when they do we can see in what might have
seemed like pitch blackness.

Cone cells are better for clearer vision, in bright lighting.
Most cone cells are near the centre of the retina. The *fovea*,
which is the spot that we focus most clearly on, is made up
entirely of cone cells. Cone cells are the cells which see colour
– rod cells can only see black and white. (That's why things
look so different in moonlight – because you're only seeing
them in black and white!)

Colour vision

Two different theories have been put forward as to exactly *how*
we see colour. The first theory is known as the *Young-
Helmholtz* theory, as it was developed by the psychologists
Young and Helmholtz. This theory says that there are three
different types of cone cells, each of which responds to a
different primary colour. One type of cone cell responds to
red light, one to blue, and one to green. Because all coloured
light consists of mixtures of these three, then we would see
colours by the different cone cells being stimulated. (A colour
TV works like this – it has small dots on the screen which are
the three primary colours (for light) of red, blue and green; by
different mixtures of the dots being lit, you see lots of different
colours.) When all three types of cone cell were being
stimulated we would see white. (The primary colours for
mixing light are not the same as the primary colours involved
in the mixing of paints or other pigments.)

The other theory of colour vision is known as Hering's
opponent-process theory. This still involves three types of cone
cells, but each would have two different ways of working. One
type of cell would pick up red when it was working one way,
and green when it was working the other way; another type of
cone cell would pick up blue and yellow, and the third type
would respond to brightness and darkness. Hering thought that
the two ways of working were because a substance would build
up in the cell when it was working one way, and then it would

break down and disappear when the cell was working the other way.

Hering put forward this theory to explain negative after-effects. Negative after-effects can be seen if you look at a red object for a long time. When you look away from it, you get an after-effect of an image of the object in your eyes – but it is green, not red. This is like the effect that Kohler had with his red-green goggles, that I mentioned in the last chapter. Negative after-effects are difficult to explain, but they do happen, and need to be explained somehow! This theory also explains why colour-blind people are usually only blind to certain types of red and green, but not to blues or yellows.

It seems from recent research that *both* theories may be partly right. Cone cells do seem to contain different kinds of chemical, which each respond best to different colours of light. But some of the ganglion cells seem to work in different ways according to different colours – some, for instance, will give an 'on' response to red light, but an 'off' response to green light – much like the opponent-process theory. But it isn't caused by substances building up in the cell – rather, one colour makes the cell more likely to fire – *excites* it; while the other colour *inhibits* the cell, and makes it less likely to fire. And, of course, it's the ganglion cells rather than the cone cells that Hering predicted. But it does seem to be a kind of opponent-process, working alongside a type of Young-Helmholtz mechanism.

With any nerve cells, if they are stimulated all the time, they will gradually build up *inhibition*, and stop firing. Because of this, our eyes are continually making small movements – little tremors and jerks. These movements are too small for us to notice, but they make sure that the image of our retina isn't hitting the same cells all the time – if it did, after a while we wouldn't notice the thing we were looking at, but this way we can keep our eyes focused on something without it seeming to disappear.

In 1961, Pritchard performed a study which showed how this happens. He fixed a miniature projector and screen to a contact lens, so that it would project an image in front of the eye. Unlike most images, though, this one would move with the movements of the eyeball, so the image would always fall on the same nerve cells in the retina. Pritchard found that the image would fade very quickly – it usually lasted only for a couple of seconds and then the subject would become unable to see it.

How the Once the cone and rod cells have generated the electrical
information is message, that message is transmitted to the part of the brain
transmitted concerned with vision. It passes from the rod and cone cells
to the next layer in the retina, the bipolar neurones. From
them, it goes to the ganglion cells. These ganglion cells each
have a very long stem, called an axon, which passes the
electrical message right out of the eyeball and along to the
brain.

The axons of the ganglion cells all collect at a particular
point on the retina. Because they are all bunched together at
this point, obviously there isn't any room for rod and cone
cells, so this point is called the *blind spot*. We don't notice it
in everyday life, because our brain fills in the gap for us, but
you can find it with a special exercise. Make two dots on a
piece of paper, about six inches apart, and stare at one of them
with one eye; then, if you move the piece of paper backwards
and forward, the second dot will disappear. This is when its
image is falling on the blind spot. It disappears because your
brain is filling in background for you – and the background is
plain paper!

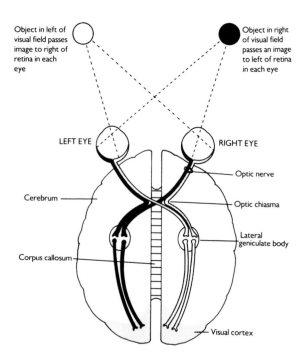

Fig. 15.3 The pathways of the optic nerve

From the blind spot, the axons of the ganglion cells form the *optic nerve*. A nerve is a collection of axons all bunched together, so that they appear like a thread. The optic nerve passes along to a place behind the eyes known as the *optic chiasma*.

At the optic chiasma, the two optic nerves, from the two eyes, join together. But almost immediately they separate again, into two separate nerves. But this time, the axons carrying the message from the left side of each eye have joined together, and the axons carrying messages from the right side of each eye have joined together. The reason for this is related to the question of *binocular vision*, which I mentioned in the last chapter. As one of our most important depth cues, we compare the images which we receive from each eye. Since the two images are slightly different, we can tell how far away something is. The cross-over at the optic chiasma means that the nerve fibres carrying the similar images will go to the same side of the brain, so that they can be compared together. The fibres for the left side of each retina go to the left side of the brain, while the fibres from the right side of each retina go to the right side of the brain. (The brain is divided into two, nearly identical halves – like a walnut, only much bigger.)

After the optic chiasma, the optic nerves continue on their way. They finally end in the part of the brain called the lateral geniculate body, in the thalamus, and new nerve cells pick up the message and take it on to the visual cortex, where the information is finally decoded. The visual cortex is found right at the very back of the brain, and this is where the electrical messages coming from the eyes are sorted out, and arranged into messages that make sense for us.

How the information is decoded Most of our knowledge of how the brain interprets information from the retina comes from the work of two researchers: D. Hubel and T. Wiesel. They experimented using *micro-electrode recording* techniques, and found out a great deal about how individual cells in the visual cortex work. Micro-electrode recording involves using a microscopic electrode, small enough to detect the electrical activity of a single nerve cell. By implanting these electrodes in an animal's brain, and then showing it a particular visual stimulus – like a single line at a particular angle – they can find out what nerve cells respond. Gradually, they have been able to build up a picture of how the brain interprets this type of information. But, since there are about a million nerve fibres in the optic nerve alone, and many more in the brain itself, it's a slow job.

Briefly, it seems that there are particular cells in the lateral geniculate nuclei that will only fire in response to a specific stimulus. For instance, one might fire in response to a short, vertical line in a particular part of the visual field, but not to anything else. Another cell might fire in response to a line ten degrees from vertical, in the same part of the visual field, while a third might respond only to horizontal lines in that particular part of the visual field. Because these cells will only fire in response to a particular stimulus, and a fairly simple one at that, Hubel and Wiesel called them *simple cells*.

Other cells in the lateral geniculate nuclei receive information from several different simple cells. They called these *complex cells*. For instance, a complex cell might respond to a vertical line no matter what part of the visual field it was in, because it would have connections with lots of simple cells for vertical lines. Or another complex cell might fire in response to *any* direction of line, but only in a particular part of the visual field, because it was receiving information from many simple cells concerned with that part of the visual field.

A third type of cell identified by Hubel and Wiesel received information from several different complex cells. They called these *hyper-complex cells*, and they would respond to simple patterns, or shapes, from the information they received from the complex cells. This is interesting, because it shows that simple pattern-recognition seems to be actually built-in to our visual system, from the beginning.

Their first paper on these different types of cells was published in 1968, but in 1979 Hubel and Wiesel reported some even

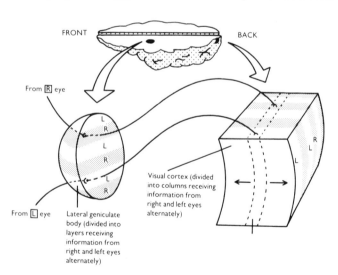

Fig. 15.4 Ocular dominance columns in the thalamus and the visual cortex

more interesting results. They found that these cells passed their message on to columns within the *visual cortex*. If you took a slice down through the visual cortex, you would find simple, complex, and hypercomplex cells dealing with similar information (like a particular horizontal line), arranged in a vertical column. And, next to that column would be another column dealing with almost the same information, but from the other eye. The columns alternated – right-eye, left-eye – throughout the visual cortex, and they showed up very clearly using some staining and photographic techniques. Hubel and Wiesel have suggested that the reason that columns from different eyes are alternated may have something to do with the binocular depth perception that I mentioned earlier. By putting the information side-by-side it may be that the brain can compare it more easily.

We can see from Hubel and Wiesel's findings, that the way the brain interprets information may have a lot to do with the actual arrangements of nerve cells within the visual cortex, but it is still very early to say definitely what those arrangements are. Vision is the sense that we know most about, probably because it is our most important sense. But we also know quite a bit about our second most important sense – hearing.

The process of hearing   Instead of light-waves, hearing deals with pressure-waves in the air. So the arrangements that the ear needs to detect those waves are quite different from the arrangements needed by the eye. But the overall purpose is still the same – to pick up information from the outside world, and to convert it into electrical messages that the brain can understand. The ear is divided into three parts, and each part has a different function. The outer ear channels the sound-waves inwards; the middle ear amplifies the vibrations so that they are large enough to be detected; and the inner ear converts the vibrations into electrical impulses, and sends them off to the brain.

The outer ear   The outside part of the ear is the pinna and the lobe – the pinna is the top part, and the lobe is the fleshy bit at the bottom. Animals like rabbits, that rely a lot on hearing, often have very large pinnas. They can often move the pinna around, so that it points towards the sound, and collects it more efficiently. Humans can't do this – the pinna of our ears is only small, and few of us can wiggle our ears. The pinna, then, collects the sound-waves and directs them inwards to the *auditory canal*. This is set into the bone of the head, and is a channel running more-or-less directly inwards. At the other end of the auditory canal is the ear-drum, known as the *tympanic membrane*.

The tympanic membrane is a piece of membrane which is

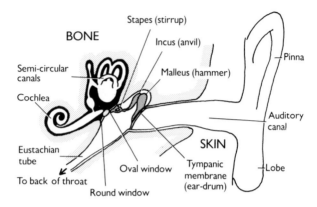

Fig. 15.5 **The structure of the ear**

stretched very tightly across the end of the auditory canal. When the pressure-waves that come along the auditory canal reach it, they make it vibrate – in the same way that an ordinary drum does when you hit it. Because the tympanic membrane has to pick up such small signals from the outside world, though, it's extremely delicate – if it was touched by a solid object like a matchstick it would break instantly. So the auditory canal manufactures ear-wax as a protective substance to catch any dirt or grit which might get into the ear.

The middle ear The tympanic membrane forms the boundary between the outer ear and the middle ear. The middle ear is a kind of amplification chamber, where the small vibrations that have been picked up by the tympanic membrane are magnified, ready for the next stage of their journey. So the middle ear consists of an air-filled chamber, which contains three small bones – the malleus, the incus, and the stapes. (These are Latin names for hammer, anvil, and stirrup – which is what these small bones look like.) The malleus bone picks up the signals from the tympanic membrane, and passes them on to the incus bone, exaggerating them a bit as it does so. The incus bone passes them on to the stapes bone, again, after amplifying them a bit. And the stapes bone passes them on to another tightly-stretched membrane on the other side of the chamber, known as the oval window.

Because the tympanic membrane is air-tight, the middle ear needs an air-tube which goes to the outside air, or it would become stagnant. So there's a small tube running from the middle ear to the back of the throat called the eustachian tube. It's in this way that air-pressure is equalised when you are at the top of a high hill, or when you go on an aeroplane – it

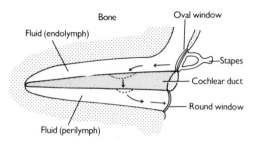

Fig. 15.6 A straightened-out view of the cochlea
As the stapes pushes in the oval window, the pressure-wave travels into the cochlear duct, vibrating the tectorial membrane. The excess pressure pushes the round window outwards

causes the 'popping' that you get in your ears. Also, this tube opens when you yawn, or when you swallow – which is why they recommend you to suck boiled sweets when your plane is taking off!

The inner ear   The oval window forms the boundary between the middle ear and the inner ear. But, because the inner ear is filled with fluid, and not with air, there is another membrane just below the oval window, known as the round window. This acts as a kind of 'safety-valve'. When the oval window pushes inwards as it vibrates, the fluid pushes the round window outwards, and if the oval window moves outwards, the round window moves inwards to balance it.

There are two sense organs in the inner ear – for hearing, which we will be looking at, and also the semi-circular canals, which are concerned with the sense of balance. The organ in the inner ear which is concerned with hearing is called the *cochlea*. It is a long tube, filled with fluid, and coiled up so that it fits into a smaller space. Inside the tube, there is a set of membranes, like a kind of 'inner tube'. These membranes run the whole length of the cochlea, and there is fluid above and below them. The fluid above the membrane is called the endolymph, and below it is called the perilymph. The endolymph is connected with the oval window, so that when the oval window pushes inwards, the fluid presses down on the membranes. In turn, they press down into the perilymph, which pushes against the round window.

This 'pushing' on the central membranes is the signal that is picked up and converted into electrical messages. Between the top membrane – the tectorial membrane – and the bottom one – the basilar membrane – there are small 'hair cells', which form a layer known as the organ of Corti. When the membranes are pushed, the hair cells are stimulated, and they trigger off an electrical message. The electrical messages are passed on to the end of the cochlea by nerve cells in the basilar membrane. When they reach the end of the cochlea, the axons of these nerve cells bunch together to form the auditory nerve, which leaves the cochlea and goes to the brain.

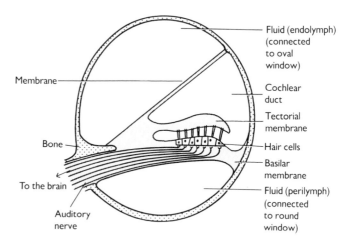

Fig. 15.7 A cross-section of the cochlea

The auditory nerve   The auditory nerve, like the optic nerve, has a kind of 'cross-over point', where the fibres from each ear join together. This is because of the way that we tell what direction a sound is coming from. Because our ears are on opposite sides of our head, a sound coming from the right will reach our right ear a fraction of a second before it reaches our left ear. And a message from the left side will reach our left ear first. Because of this we can tell what direction a sound is coming from – we compare the two messages, and can judge the direction from the slight difference in when we receive the two signals. This is known as *binaural hearing*, and it's the reason the nerve fibres need to cross over before they are decoded.

There are only two characteristics of sound that we detect: the pitch of a sound (how high or low the note is); and its volume. Volume is passed to the brain simply by the number of hair cells that fire. If the sound is very loud, more hair cells fire than if it is only faint. But the way that we code pitch so that the brain can understand it is a bit more complicated.

How pitch is coded   There are two different theories on how pitch is coded in the
in the cochlea   cochlea. One theory, known as the *place theory*, suggests that what is important is the place on the cochlea that is stimulated

by the vibrations. Von Békésy, in 1960, tested this by cutting tiny holes in the cochleas of guinea pigs, and seeing what they could hear. He found that high frequency tones seemed to stimulate the hair cells near the oval window, while lower frequency tones stimulated the hair cells at the other end of the cochlea. Unfortunately, this doesn't apply to all tones: below a certain level, the whole of the basilar membrane (and the hair cells on it) are vibrated. But for higher tones, the place theory seems to provide a reasonable explanation.

The second theory is the *frequency theory*. This suggests that hair cells fire more often if the sound is of a higher pitch – they are more frequent. It does seem to apply, at least to sounds of lower frequency. A tone of 500 Hz will produce 500 nerve impulses per second, while a tone of 2,000 Hz will produce 2,000 nerve impulses per second. So it seems that for some tones, the pitch of a sound is conveyed to the brain by the *rate* at which the nerve cells fire.

But there are limits to how much a nerve cell *can* fire in a given period of time. So it's thought that for higher-frequency sounds, which would require the nerve cells to produce too many firings per second, they work on a different principle. It is suggested that the nerve cells 'take it in turn' to fire off *volleys* of nerve impulses – different groups of fibres firing in turn – the more frequent the volleys, the higher the pitch. The volley principle is thought to apply to frequencies from 2,000 Hz up to 4,000 Hz.

As we found with the theories of colour vision, it seems likely that *both* of these theories are right to some extent. The place theory seems to account for higher tones, while the frequency theory accounts for lower tones, in general. But there seems to be quite a lot of overlapping between the theories, and there is supporting evidence of each of them.

Another thing that we find with hearing, though not with seeing, as I explained earlier, is *habituation*. I explained how the eye avoids the problem of habituation by making minute tremors and jerking movements, to make sure that the image falls on different cells in the retina all the time. But the ear can't do that, and so if we are exposed to a noise that's continuous – like the humming of a fridge – we don't notice it after a while. Our hearing will only respond to a *change* in stimulation, and so we notice when the fridge stops, but not while it's continuing. If we hear it start up again, we notice, but after that we become habituated to it. Unfortunately, though, we don't become habituated to noises like that of a pneumatic drill, because that is noise which is constantly going on and off, so our nerve cells aren't being stimulated continually, and we keep noticing it!

The other senses

Apart from sight and hearing, we have many other senses – ways of receiving information. In fact, we have more than the five 'classic' ones that used to be talked of: vision, hearing, smell, taste and touch. First of all, touch is quite a complicated sort of thing, and there are various types of information that we can receive through our skin. Secondly, we have a whole range of nerve, and nerve fibres which give us information, not about the outside world, but about *ourselves* – physical information about the position of our body, and so on. These are called the *kinaesthetic senses*, and we have already talked about one major part of them – the semi-circular canals, and balance.

In addition to the semi-circular canals, we have a network of nerve cells whose fibres run from all over our body to the brain. They give us information about our joints, and how they are angled at any time; and about whether our muscles are tense or relaxed. From these messages, we build up a picture of the way that we are standing or sitting, even though very often we aren't able to *see* ourselves. Kinaesthetic nerves also warn us when muscles are getting fatigued, or stiff, so that we are able to compensate, or do something about it, for instance, by fidgeting.

We can divide the sense of touch into four major *skin senses*. These are pressure, pain, warmth and cold. Each of these senses appears to have different receptors; nerve endings and receptors are buried throughout the skin, at varying levels. Some pain-sensitive nerves also go to the muscles and to the internal organs of the body, but most of them are concentrated on the skin surface, or just below it.

The fibres from the pain and pressure receptors pass through the thalamus in the brain, up to a particular part of the cerebral cortex, which is called the somato-sensory area. Parts of the body which are very sensitive, like the lips or the fingertips, have a much larger area of cerebral cortex for their fibres than less sensitive parts, like legs. Since there are more nerve fibres in the fingertips and the lips, they need a correspondingly larger area for the messages to be decoded and interpreted by the brain.

Our other two basic senses are the chemical senses – taste and smell. These detect the presence of particular chemical compounds, through special receptors. In the nose, the receptors are located in a spongy area in the nasal cavity, quite high up. In the mouth, the receptors are in taste buds, which are mainly found on the tongue. The nose can detect chemicals in the air, but the taste buds can only detect chemicals that have been dissolved in water – which is why we can't taste anything if the mouth is very dry. Both of these senses appear to work by recognising basic elements, and combinations of these elements. For taste, there are four: salty, sweet, bitter, and sour, and there are four different types of taste bud on different parts of the tongue, which detect them. For smell, though, there seem to be many more – perhaps nine or ten basic elements. When we consider that sound has only two that we can perceive – loudness and pitch – then we can appreciate that the world of an animal with a highly-developed sense of smell and taste must be very rich.

In humans, though the senses of smell and taste aren't so important. With training, we can improve both senses, and learn to analyse them, but it's unlikely that we would even get to be half as good as a dog. Our senses of sight and hearing are the most important ones for our contact with the outside world.

From the senses I have described in this chapter, we can see that we have a whole network of detectors and receptors, with which we can receive information from many different sources. This network is known as the *somatic nervous system*, and it is an important part of the nervous system as a whole. ('Somatic' means 'to do with the body'.) Since it is linked so closely with the central nervous system – the brain and the spinal cord – I've been unable to avoid mentioning them as well, but in the next chapter we will look at the central nervous system in more detail. Since these systems form a basic groundwork for learning, feeling, emotions, and everything else that goes to make up the human being, it's important that we have an idea of how they work, and how they are organised. The nervous system is as much a part of a human being's everyday functioning, as the way that that person was brought up; and since, in psychology, we are interested in 'what makes that person tick', then we need to know the *basic* system as well.

Summary

1 The eyeball collects light waves from the outside world, and focuses them inwards to the retina, where they are converted into electrical impulses by rod and cone cells.

2 The electrical impulses are transmitted from the retina, down the optic nerve to the optic chiasma, where some of the fibres cross; from there to the lateral geniculate nuclei, and from there to the visual area on the cerebral cortex.

3 Recent research has shown that there are specialised cells

in the cerebral cortex which decode some of the information coming in, before it passes to other parts of the brain.

4 Rod cells are used for seeing in dim light, and do not see colour, just black-and-white. Cone cells are used for more detailed vision – the fovea is made up entirely of cone cells – and see colour. There are two main colour-vision theories: the Young-Helmholtz theory, and the opponent-process theory.

5 The ear collects sound-waves from the outside world, amplifies them, and converts them into electrical impulses in the cochlea. The auditory nerve runs from the cochlea to the thalamus, and then to the auditory area on the cerebral cortex.

6 Two types of information are detected by the ear – pitch and volume. Volume appears to be transmitted by the number of nerve cells firing, while pitch appears to be the frequency of firing, and the part of the cochlea which is stimulated.

7 Other senses which we have are the kinaesthetic senses – information from muscles and joints, and information about balance from the semi-circular canals; the skin senses of pressure, pain, warmth, and cold; and the chemical senses of smell and taste.

Chapter 16

The central nervous system

As we've seen so far in this book, the study of psychology involves looking at a variety of different influences and kinds of experience. In this chapter I want to discuss the ways in which the body is able to co-ordinate and control our behaviour, and to store experiences. We began looking at this in the last chapter, by looking at the different structures that we have for collecting information from the outside world, like the visual and auditory systems. These systems are a part of the nervous system, and in the next two chapters we'll be looking at some other parts of the nervous system, and seeing how they work to influence behaviour.

Since the nervous system is very complicated, and has many different functions, it's useful to sort it into sections. We can make a general distinction between the *central nervous system*, which is concerned with the overall co-ordinating of all the different functions, and the *peripheral nervous system*, which is concerned with collecting information and sending messages to and from different parts of the body. The central nervous system consists of the brain and the spinal cord. The peripheral nervous system consists of two sections: the *somatic nervous system*, which includes sensory systems like the visual system, and which also includes the ways that we send messages to muscles for movement; and the *autonomic nervous system*, which we'll be looking at in Chapter 17.

One way of judging how highly-evolved an animal is, is by looking at how complex a nervous system it has. The most primitive animals have very simple nervous systems – a flatworm, for instance, has just a simple network of nerve fibres running throughout its body. But as animals became more complicated, and needed to be able to react to different kinds of environments and stimuli, the nervous system became more and more complex, and developed special structures to control different forms of behaviour and activity.

In order to study the nervous system, we need to know exactly how it works – how a message travels up a nerve, for instance, and what different kinds of nerve cells there are. In order to do this, we will look at one of the simplest kinds of behaviour, and see what types of cells are involved.

The reflex arc   As you'll know, if you've ever had the experience of burning yourself on a hot cooker or iron, the very first thing you do is to pull your hand away, often before you've even realised what you've done. This is a *reflex* – an automatic reaction to a stimulus which doesn't involve thinking or deciding what to do. We have other kinds of reflexes too, like the 'knee-jerk' reflex, or blinking the eyes when they feel a sudden puff of air.

A reflex is controlled by the spinal cord, and involves the action of three different types of nerve cells. Firstly, it involves the message being picked up from the skin, and passed along to the spinal cord. This is done by a *sensory neurone* (a neurone is a nerve cell). When the message arrives at the spinal cord, it is picked up and passed on by a *connector neurone*, which makes connections with several other neurones within the spinal cord. Finally, a message travels down a *motor neurone* to the muscles, to 'instruct' them to contract the muscle and move your hand, or leg.

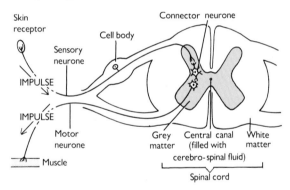

Fig. 16.1 A reflex arc

The sensory neurone   Each type of neurone is different in form, as it has a different type of job to do. A sensory neurone has a long stem, known as an *axon*, which stretches from a sense receptor in the skin all the way to the spinal cord. When it is stimulated, the sense receptor triggers off a small electrical charge, called an *impulse*, which travels up the axon by means of a chemical change happening in the membrane forming the 'skin' of the axon. At the other end, in the spinal cord, the axon divides into several branches, known as *dendrites*, which means that each sensory neurone is able to pass the message on to several different neurones in the spinal cord. The cell body of the sensory neurone (which contains the nucleus) is at the side of the axon, up near the spinal cord.

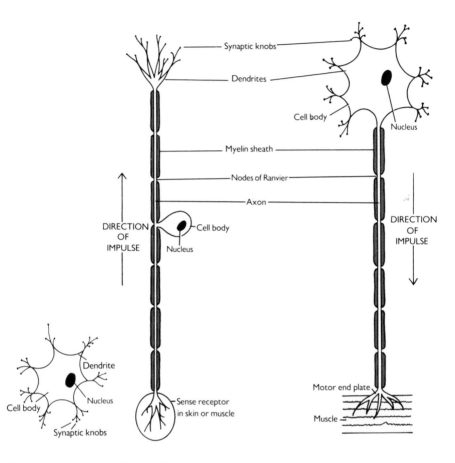

Fig. 16.3 A
connector neurone

Fig. 16.2 A sensory neurone

Fig. 16.4 A motor neurone

The connector neurone   A connector neurone does not have an axon, but instead consists of a cell body and nucleus surrounded by lots of dendrites. In this way, the connector neurone can connect with many different neurones: it can send messages on to the motor neurones, and it can also send messages up to the brain so that you know what you have just experienced.

The motor neurone   A motor neurone is very like a connector neurone at the beginning (the part that is in the spinal cord). It has a cell body surrounded by lots of dendrites, so that it can receive messages from several different connector neurones. But then, it will pass the message along the axon, out of the spinal cord to the muscle fibres. The impulse travels along the axon to the *motor end plate*, which passes the impulse on to a single muscle fibre.

As you may have guessed, it's not enough for just one single muscle fibre to be stimulated before you can move your arm, or your leg. In fact, a reflex will involve the action of many sensory, connector, and motor neurones all working together. What we call a *nerve* consists of axons from several motor or sensory neurones bunched together. A sensory (or afferent) nerve carries messages to the central nervous system, while a motor (or efferent) nerve carries messages away from the central nervous system to the muscles.

I mentioned before that the electrical impulse travels up the axon by a chemical change happening along the membrane. But obviously, if the message concerns something important, like pain, then it's a good idea if it travels as quickly as possible. For this reason, the axon is coated with fatty cells, known as Schwann cells, which wrap around it and form a kind of insulation. The chemical change can't happen where these cells are, and so the impulse has to jump along the axon to the gaps in between the *myelin sheath* (what the fatty coating is called). Each gap in the myelin sheath is called a *node of Ranvier*, and because the impulse is jumping from one node of Ranvier to the next one, it is travelling much faster than it would if it was moving continuously along the axon.

Nucleus

Axon

Schwann cell coiled round axon

Fig. 16.5 A Schwann cell

Sensory and motor neurones involved in the somatic nervous system are almost always myelinated, so that messages and reactions can be dealt with as quickly as possible. But neurones in the autonomic nervous system are not usually myelinated, as it is not so important that the message travels quickly. When we look at the brain or the spinal cord, we can see that some parts of them are whitish in colour ('white matter'), and some parts are greyish ('grey matter'). The white matter consists of myelinated nerve fibres, and the grey matter consists of cell bodies and unmyelinated nerve fibres. In the spinal cord, the grey matter is on the inside, and the white matter is on the outside, but in the brain it is the other way round, with the grey matter on the outside, and the white matter on the inside.

I said before that the message which the neurone passes on is in the form of a small electrical impulse. This is a rapid burst of electricity, triggered off in a sensory neurone by a stimulus of some kind, like heat or pressure. If the stimulus is too weak, the neurone will not fire, but if it is strong enough it will do so. So the stimulus needs to be above a certain level, known as the 'threshold of response' of the neurone.

In most of the somatic nerve system, the electrical impulse

is always the same amount – the neurone will either fire or it won't. This is known as the 'all-or-none' rule. But it has been found recently that in the brain itself the impulse can vary in strength, depending on how strong the signal is. After a neurone has just fired, there is a short period when it will not fire again, known as the *absolute refractory period*. This is followed by the *relative refractory period*, when the threshold of response is higher than usual. (The threshold of response is the amount of stimulation which the neurone needs to make it fire.) When the relative refractory period is over, the threshold of response returns to normal. So one way that the brain knows the strength of a particular stimulus, is when the neurones are firing rapidly, as only a strong stimulus will be able to trigger the neurones during the relative refractory period.

Another way that the brain is informed of the strength of a particular stimulus is when many neurones fire all at once. A strong stimulus will trigger off more neurones than a weak one does. So even though most neurones work on the all-or-none principle, the brain can still tell how strong a stimulus is.

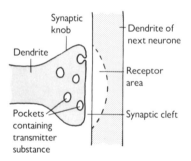

Fig. 16.6 A synapse

The synapse   Neurones have a special system for passing messages on, which allows them to react in different ways. The connection point between two neurones is known as the *synapse*. Some synapses make the next cell more likely to fire. These are known as *excitatory synapses*. But other synapses work in a different way – they make the neurone that is receiving the message *less* likely to fire. These are known as *inhibitory synapses*.

The synapse is actually a gap between two neurones. At the end of each neurone the axon divides into several branches, known as dendrites. Each dendrite ends in a small knob, called a synaptic button or synaptic knob. The button contains small 'pockets', or *vesicles*, which contain a particular chemical called a neurotransmitter. When the electrical impulse reaches the vesicles, they open and spill the neurotransmitter into the gap.

This chemical is then picked up in a special *receptor site* on the dendrite of the next neurone, and makes the next neurone either more or less likely to fire.

Although any one neurone will always contain the same neurotransmitter in its vesicles, there are many different transmitter chemicals used in the nervous system. Some of them seem to have a direct effect on how we feel – on our moods – and some of the drugs that doctors prescribe to patients who are depressed work by causing particular neurotransmitters to build up in synapses. Some poisons and nerve gases are picked up in the receptor sites at the motor end plate (which works in the same way as a synapse), so that the ordinary neurotransmitter released by the motor neurone cannot be picked up, so the muscles will not move. Curare – a paralysing poison that used to be used by South American Indian tribes for hunting – works in this way.

We can see from this, that neurones work both by electrical means, and by chemical ones. Some methods of studying the nervous system have investigated electrical activity, and some have investigated different chemicals that are involved.

Some methods of studying the CNS

One method of studying the electrical activity of nerve cells was used for Hubel and Wiesel's work on the visual system, which we looked at in the last chapter. By using minute electrodes, and inserting them into the visual cortex, they were able to measure when a single neurone was firing, or when it wasn't. From this, they could gradually build up a picture of some of the ways that our brain sorts out the information that it receives from our eyes. But since the brain has billions of neurones, and each of them makes contact with many others, building up a picture of how it works using *micro-electrode recording* is a very slow process.

Another way of studying the electrical activity of the brain is to make a general measurement of the whole brain's activity, by taking an *electro-encephalogram*, or *EEG*. This involves attaching electrodes to the scalp, and using them to record the electrical activity of the brain, as the person opens and shuts their eyes, relaxes, and performs other actions. Using EEGs, it is possible to identify people who may be likely to have epileptic fits, or to have other problems of this sort. Psychologists who have studied sleep and relaxation have learned a lot from EEGs, as the brain shows different types of electrical activity at different times. But EEGs can only really give a general picture of electrical activity in the brain – they can't tell us which parts of the brain are doing what. One psychologist described it as being a bit like standing outside a factory window and trying to guess what was happening inside, by the noises that came out.

Other methods of studying the brain have looked at the way that chemicals are operating at the synapse. By *sampling* the different chemicals involved in different forms of activity, it has been possible to find out which neurotransmitters are involved in particular pathways in the brain and nervous system. Or by *injecting* different neurotransmitters into the brain we can see what effects they have on general behaviour and functioning.

The nervous system Once we can see how individual neurones work, and how they can be grouped together to form the reflex arc, we can begin to understand how our nervous system is built up. As we saw at the beginning of this chapter, some very simple animals like the flatworm *Planaria*, have a very simple nervous system, which just consists of a ladder-like network of neurones running throughout the body. As animals evolved, however, and became more complicated, the nervous system became more and more elaborate, and able to deal with more and more complicated behaviour.

When we are studying the human nervous system, it's often useful to talk about it in terms of the oldest part, the middle part, and the most recently evolved part. As we look at the different functions of the brain, you will see that the oldest

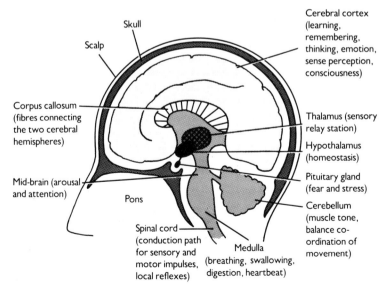

Fig. 16.7 A cross-section through the human brain

part tends to deal with basic forms of behaviour, while the more complicated types of brain activity are dealt with by more recently evolved parts of the brain.

Within the brain itself, most of the nerve cells are connector neurones, forming countless billions of connections with each other, and with the motor and sensory neurones which run up and down the spinal cord taking messages to and from different parts of the body.

The oldest part of the central nervous system consists of five main structures: the spinal cord; the medulla, or brain stem; the midbrain; the cerebellum; and the hypothalamus. We will look at each of these in turn, to see how they are involved in controlling or directing our behaviour.

The spinal cord   As we've already seen, the spinal cord is concerned with basic reflexes, such as reacting to sudden pain. Its most important function, though, is to take messages to and from the other parts of the brain – without the spinal cord we would be completely unable to co-ordinate any of our body functions. So the spinal cord is a vital link between the brain and the body.

The medulla   Towards the top end, the spinal cord seems to thicken out slightly. This part is known as the medulla, or the brain stem, and it is the beginning of the brain itself. The medulla controls basic bodily functions, such as breathing, swallowing, digestion and heartbeat. These functions are essential to us, but for the most part we tend to be unaware of them. They are also the most essential functions (apart from simple reflexes) for *any* animal, which is why the medulla was the first part of the brain to evolve. In addition, as we will see in the next chapter, the medulla and the top parts of the spinal cord co-ordinate autonomic reactions, such as fear or anger responses, although other parts of the brain are also involved.

The midbrain   This is just above the medulla, and almost a part of it. Its most important part is the reticular activating system, or RAS, which is responsible for sleep and attention. A study by French, in 1957, showed that if a sleeping cat was stimulated by a small electrode in the RAS, it would wake up gently and naturally, as if it was just rousing in the ordinary way. Cats with the RAS *ablated* (i.e. removed) would sink into a deep coma and would not wake up. Another function of the RAS seems to be to 'switch on' large areas of the cerebral cortex, the part that is involved in consciousness. It also plays a part in directing our attention – again, working together with the cerebral cortex. Some sensory information passes through the RAS on the way to the cerebral cortex.

The other part of the midbrain is known as the pons, and this consists of fibres that connect the two halves of the cerebellum. The pons also seems to be involved in controlling dreaming sleep – *lesions* (i.e. cuts) in different parts of the pons can either increase dreaming sleep in animals, or decrease it.

The cerebellum   This is a structure at the back of the brain, underneath the cerebral hemispheres. It is very wrinkled, looking a little like a cauliflower. The cerebellum is responsible for muscle tone, balance in the body (for which it receives information from the semi-circular canals in the ear), and for co-ordinating voluntary movement. When we are first learning a new skill that involves co-ordinating movements, like riding a bicycle, we find it very difficult at first, because we are using the cerebral cortex to direct each little movement – we are having to be very conscious of everything that we do. But after a while, we are able to do it 'automatically', because the new skill, and the control of each little movement, has transferred from the cerebrum to the cerebellum. The cerebellum controls most of our physical activity, although it doesn't make the *decisions* about what we should do (that's done by the cerebral cortex); it *co-ordinates* our actions and makes sure that we can do them smoothly and easily. Try watching a baby reach out to grasp something – it takes a long time for the baby to co-ordinate the different messages that it is getting from hand and eye – and yet adults do it without thinking!

One way in which we have been able to study the cerebellum, has been to look at people with *accidental injuries* to this part of the brain. We find that they often show loss of muscle control and co-ordination as a result.

The hypothalamus   This is situated just above the midbrain and just below the thalamus, as you might guess from the name ('hypo' means 'below'). Although this is quite a small structure, it is very important, because its role is to maintain *homeostasis* in the body. This is, more-or-less, when everything is functioning normally for the individual. The hypothalamus maintains homeostasis by keeping a constant check on the functioning of the body, and setting off homeostatic mechanisms if things begin to go wrong. (For instance, if you overheat you will start to sweat. Sweating is a homeostatic mechanism to cool you down.)

The hypothalamus is interesting for psychologists, because it can be involved in activating certain kinds of behaviour – like food-seeking behaviour or aggression. It has been found that lesions in a particular part of the hypothalamus will cause rats to overeat, while a lesion in another part will cause them to eat far too little. A study by Fisher (1964) showed, by injecting different chemicals into the hypothalamus, that different neurotransmitters were involved in controlling eating and drinking. So it seems that the hypothalamus has many ways of keeping the body properly regulated.

These structures represent the earliest part of the brain to develop. The more recent parts of the brain are involved in slightly more complicated forms of behaviour: instead of being mainly concerned with the basic physical functioning of the body, they deal with more complicated functions like memory or play behaviour. The two main parts of the brain which belong to the 'middle section' are the thalamus and the limbic system.

The thalamus   This has two main functions. The first is to act as a kind of 'relay station' for sensory nerve fibres that are on their way to the cerebral cortex – it channels nerve impulses to the correct areas so that they can be interpreted. The lateral geniculate nuclei, which we learned about in the last chapter as part of the visual system, are part of the thalamus. Each different sense that we possess has its own set of special nuclei in the thalamus, which acts as a first sorting system before information is sent to the cerebral cortex. The thalamus is also involved in sleep and wakefulness, and in this function it is considered to be a part of the limbic system.

The limbic system   This is a general name given to lots of small structures in the centre of the brain. The limbic system is involved in sleep and wakefulness, and it's also involved in emotional activity. Another function of the limbic system seems to be in controlling play; an important way of learning for young mammals. It also has one part – the hippocampus – that seems to be involved in storing new information in the memory. People with damage to the hippocampus are often unable to remember new information, even though they may have all their previous memories from before the accident still intact. So the limbic system is involved in quite a lot of different activities.

The cerebrum   The most recent part of the brain to evolve is the part that is the largest, and most important, in the human being – the cerebrum. It is able to direct the functioning of all the other parts of the brain, or so it seems. Because the cerebrum is so concerned with the activities in which psychologists are most interested, like learning and memory, we will be looking at it in quite a lot of detail.

The cerebrum is divided into two separate halves, which are

Fig. 16.8 A human brain

joined together by a band of fibres called the *corpus callosum*. These two halves are sometimes called the cerebral hemispheres. The part of the cerebrum that psychologists are most interested in is the *cerebral cortex*. This is the outer layer of the cerebrum. I mentioned in Chapter 2 how it is covered with grooves and fissures, because these increase its surface area, and it is on the surface that the important activities take place.

Because the cerebrum is so large, each hemisphere has been divided into four 'lobes', a system that allows us to describe more easily whereabouts on the cerebral cortex something is found. In dividing it, we use two large naturally-occurring fissures as 'boundary markers'.

On each hemisphere, there is a large fissure that goes vertically downwards from the top. This is known as the central fissure. Another large fissure runs along the side of each hemisphere – the lateral fissure.

The area of the brain that is in front of the central fissure is known as the *frontal lobe*. The area immediately underneath the lateral fissure is called the *temporal lobe*. The *parietal lobe* is the part of the brain just behind the central fissure, and the *occipital lobe* is the area at the very back of the brain.

Localisation of function in the cerebral cortex

Quite early on, it was discovered that damage or injury to certain parts of the brain could cause very specific problems for the person involved. Sir Gordon Holmes studied injured servicemen after the first world war. He found that men who had injuries from shrapnel in the very back of the head often suffered from defects of vision: they might be blind in a certain part of their visual field, but not in others. From this, he concluded that the back part of the brain was the part which was involved in interpreting visual information.

K. Lashley, in 1926, investigated whether there was a special part of the cerebral cortex concerned with learning. He taught rats how to run through a maze, and then removed a portion of their cerebral cortex, and tested them again to see if they could still run the maze. He found that, for this kind of learning, it didn't seem to matter which part of the cerebral cortex he destroyed; it was the *amount* of cortex that he destroyed that was more important. He called this the principle of equipotentiality.

Lashley concluded that most of the cerebral cortex functioned as a *whole*, and not as different parts with different purposes. He called this the 'Law of Mass Action'. Because the cortex operated as a whole, it was the amount of damage rather than the location of the damage that affected learning and memory. Learning and memory mainly seem to involve making new associations between different things, so the large areas of the cerebral cortex that didn't seem to have specific functions, but which were involved in learning were called *association cortex*.

Paul Broca, in 1861, identified an area just above the lateral fissure on the left hemisphere that seemed to control speech. He found that people who had damage to this area had trouble pronouncing words, or finding words for what they wanted to say. Another area, a bit further along from Broca's area, seemed to control how people understood what was being said to them. Investigations by Carl Wernicke, in 1874, found that people who had damage to this area seemed to have no trouble in talking, but often had trouble understanding things. By contrast, those with damage to Broca's area hadn't any trouble understanding things at all, they just had problems with speech.

As researchers investigated the brain more and more carefully, they discovered more specific areas, with particular functions, like the visual cortex. In the 1950s, W. Penfield, a brain surgeon, investigated the different experiences of patients who were having brain surgery. By stimulating the surface of the brain, while his patients were conscious (the brain has no sensory nerve endings, so it didn't hurt at all), he was able to find out from them what they were experiencing. He found that there was a 'strip' of cortex running down the central fissure, which was involved in *feelings* from different parts of the body; and another 'strip' on the opposite side of the central fissure which was concerned with *moving* different parts of the body. Other areas of the cortex concerned with senses have

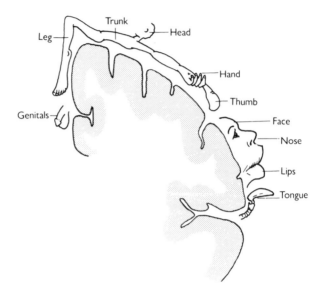

Fig. 16.9 A sensory 'homunculus'
The sensitive parts of the body are shown as larger areas on the somato-sensory cortex than less sensitive areas

been discovered, such as the olfactory cortex, which forms a strip along the bottom of the temporal lobe.

One interesting discovery about the organisation of the cerebrum, is that the two hemispheres control different sides of the body, and that each controls the *opposite* side. So the sensory and motor strips on the right hemisphere receive sensations from, and move muscles on, the left side of the body. For the other senses, though, like vision and hearing, both hemispheres are involved.

Language seems to be an ability that is localised on one hemisphere only. The language areas that have been discovered are all on the left hemisphere of the brain, while other abilities, like artistic or spatial abilities seem to be on the right hemisphere.

In all, there seem to be three areas concerned with language. *Broca's area*, which is concerned with speech; *Wernicke's area*, which is concerned with comprehension of language; and an area near the visual cortex called the *angular gyrus*. This involves translating words that we read into 'sound patterns' in the brain, so making them equivalent to the spoken words that we hear.

If we want to examine how all these areas might work

Fig. 16.10 Areas of the cerebral cortex
The language areas are found on the left cerebral hemisphere only. The other areas are found on both sides, but each side controls its opposite side in the body; e.g. the left hand and foot are controlled by the right side of the brain

together, the best way is to look at what happens if a person reads aloud from a book. At first, the information will go from the eyes to the visual cortex, as the person looks at the page. From the visual cortex, it goes to the angular gyrus, where it is converted into 'sound images'. These 'sound images' go on to Wernicke's area, where the message is understood by the person reading. From there, they go to Broca's area, where the words are formed, and from there, messages will go to the motor area, which will cause the lips and tongue to move and produce the words.

The two hemispheres of the brain are joined together by a band of fibres called the *corpus callosum*. In the 1960s, R. Sperry performed a series of studies on 'split-brain' subjects, looking at how the two different halves of the brain worked, if the corpus callosum was cut through. This was performed as an operation to help some severely epileptic patients – epilepsy is an electrical discharge which spreads through the brain, causing a 'fit'. Surgeons took this rather drastic action in some patients who were almost completely crippled by their frequent fits; the operation was an attempt to cut down the frequency of the fits.

Sperry found that the 'split-brain' subjects seemed to react as if they had two separate brains, each with slightly different abilities. If a subject saw something ᴐn the right of the visual field (so it went to the left hemisphere), they could name it, but if it was on the left of the visual field (so the message went to the right hemisphere) they could not. But if they were asked to pick it out by touch from other objects, they could do this easily. So although the right hemisphere didn't have language, it could still identify objects and solve problems.

When the left hemisphere is damaged, people often suffer from speech problems. In children, the brain eventually seems to transfer the language functions to the right hemisphere, so that they recover speech functioning. In adults, though, this does not seem to happen. But a study by S. Gooch, in 1980, showed that, in some adults suffering serious damage to the left hemisphere, if the whole left hemisphere was removed then they would recover speech functioning completely within a few months. Studies like this suggest that the localisation of different brain functions is not nearly as rigid as people have supposed in the past – the brain seems to be able to adapt to different circumstances, even in adults.

Other studies supporting this idea come from patients who have suffered strokes. These often cause loss of function to one side of the body, depending on whereabouts in the brain the stroke was. But many people seem to be able to recover the functions they had lost, if they make an effort to do so. It seems that the brain responds to *motivation*: the people who try hard are the ones who regain their functions, while those who just 'give up' and don't think it possible are the ones who suffer lasting damage.

How can we study the brain?

Electrical studies

I have already mentioned some of the methods which we have of studying the way that the brain works. The use of EEG techniques, and of micro-electrode recording methods allow us to investigate how the brain, or parts of it, are working electrically. Other studies, such as those by French and Penfield, have used *electrical stimulation* to see what happens if a particular part of the brain is activated. One problem that we have with using these methods, though, is the nature of the subjects involved.

Since it is neither possible nor ethically desirable to use normal human subjects, most researchers have used animals, and hoped that these results can be generalised to humans. Hubel and Wiesel, for instance, used cats and monkeys for their research, and so did French. Those researchers who have used human subjects, such as Penfield, have had to investigate people who were having brain surgery anyway, and it's always possible that these subjects may not have been typical (although Penfield's work does seem to be supported by studies of stroke or tumour damage in the brain).

Chemical studies

Other methods of study have concentrated on the chemicals involved in brain functioning. But again, these have mostly used animals, and animal brains may not be similar to ours. In Fisher's study of *chemical injection* into the hypothalamus, he found that the same chemical could produce totally different behaviour when injected into the same part of the hypothalamus in a rat (eating behaviour) and in a cat (aggressive behaviour). So we have no way of knowing how far our findings from animals will apply; obviously we will take more notice of studies of animals higher up the phylogenetic scale, like monkeys, but it remains a problem.

Physical or surgical studies   Some methods of study have concentrated on the physical structures and connections of the brain. *Ablation* (the removal of parts of the brain) is one way of studying function – for example in Lashley's work on intelligence. But we still do not really know what is happening. If behaviour changes as a result of removing part of the brain, we cannot tell whether that means that the particular part of the brain *controlled* the behaviour, or whether it was just *involved* in it. The cerebrum, for instance, seems to be mainly responsible for consciousness, but removing the RAS can produce unconsciousness. Since so many parts of the brain work together to produce a particular effect, we are still unsure of what it means when just one part is removed.

The use of *lesions* – cutting or damaging parts of the brain, without actually removing them – may tell us more about how different parts of the brain are normally connected; Sperry's work on 'split-brain' subjects is an example. But here again, although Sperry was working with human subjects, we have no way of knowing how typical they were; after all, they were people who had been severely epileptic for many years, and it could well be that, if the normal brain functioning is continually being interrupted by electrical discharges, brain functions may become localised in a different way to those of others. It may not be, but we cannot be sure unless we could perform the same studies on 'normal' people, which would be highly unethical.

Other facts about the brain have been discovered by using *accidental injury*. When people have damage to the brain as a result of an accident, we can try to study what they are able to do now, and compare it with what they could do before. Studies such as those by Sir Gordon Holmes, or Paul Broca, have used this method. Unfortunately, though, with many cases of accidental injury, we don't have precise enough records of what the behaviour was like before the accident for comparison. And when people know that the brain has been damaged, they often *expect* changes, and forget about similar aspects of the person's previous behaviour. So although this method is useful for very obvious results, like partial blindness, it is very limited when we are looking at more subtle effects, like personality change.

Some new methods have come into operation in recent years. Surgeons are now able to locate brain tumours, or other unusual aspects of the brain, using *tomography*. This means taking X-ray photographs of the brain from various angles, and correlating them so that a picture can be built up that will show different structures and different types of cells, when they are together as a mass. However, although this can be useful, in that we may be able to locate a tumour in a particular area, which may be having a particular effect on behaviour, it cannot show us very specific or detailed areas of the brain, or particular cells – only very general areas, which are different from their neighbouring ones.

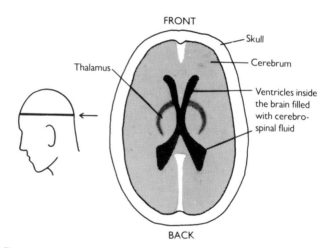

Fig. 16.11 Computerised tomogram of the head taken at the place shown on the left

Radioactive labelling is another technique that is used to study brain functioning. Certain chemicals that can pass the 'blood-brain barrier' are injected into the bloodstream, and are carried up into the brain. As the brain is supplied with thousands of small blood vessels, which carry nutrients and wastes to and from the neurones, and as neurones which are functioning need a greater blood supply than ones which aren't, we can see from scanning the brain which areas are using more blood. From this, we can build up a picture of which parts of the brain are involved in particular activities, which may help us to identify brain functions more accurately. At the moment, though, this technique suffers from the same problems as the other ones, in that it is a medical technique, and usually only used for people who are suffering some kind of brain problems – which may make them untypical.

Although all these criticisms of methods may sound very pessimistic, we are gradually building up a picture of how the brain works, and of which parts are involved in which activities. But as Gooch's study, and studies of patients recovering from strokes show, we are very far from understanding it all – especially the ways that areas of the brain can interact, and can take over new functions or recover from damage.

We have looked so far at the somatic nervous system, and at the central nervous system. In the next chapter, we will look at the part of the nervous system concerned with emotion and arousal – the autonomic nervous system.

Summary

1   The central nervous system consists of the brain and spinal cord. The peripheral nervous system includes the somatic nervous system and the autonomic nervous system.

2   The reflex arc is the simplest arrangement of three types of neurones which make up the nervous system: connector, sensory, and motor neurones.

3   Neurones connect by means of a gap called a synapse. Messages are passed across the synapse by means of a chemical transmitter substance.

4   The oldest parts of the central nervous system are the spinal cord, medulla, midbrain, cerebellum, and hypothalamus. Later the thalamus and the limbic system developed, and last the cerebrum.

5   Some parts of the cerebral cortex have specific functions, for example, sense or language. Other parts are 'association cortex' – involved with learning and memory.

6   Different ways of studying the brain are: by lesion, or damage; by ablation, or surgical removal of parts of the brain; by chemical sampling or chemical injection; by micro-electrode recording or micro-electrode stimulation; or by EEGs. Each method has its advantages and disadvantages.

Chapter 17 **Emotion**

In Chapter 15 we examined part of the somatic nervous system, which forms the way that the body receives and reacts to information from the outside world, reaching us through our senses. In the last chapter, we looked at the central nervous system, which acts as a kind of 'central control' for our activities. In this chapter, I want to look at the third division of the nervous system, which is known as the *autonomic nervous system*. The autonomic nervous system is involved in our emotional reactions and arousal.

Physiological factors in emotion

As I mentioned in the last chapter, there are some parts of the central nervous system that are also concerned with emotional behaviour – the limbic system and the hypothalamus in particular. These usually act to stimulate the autonomic nervous system into activity, and then the autonomic nervous system will act with the endocrine system to produce the emotional reaction.

The endocrine system

Since, as I've just said, the endocrine system is involved with the way that the autonomic nervous system reacts, we need to look briefly at the endocrine system as well. The endocrine system isn't a part of the nervous system. It is a separate system, consisting of special glands scattered throughout the body. These glands release substances called *hormones*, which spread through the bloodstream and serve to maintain or introduce different 'states' of the body. For instance: if a woman has just had a baby, her breasts need to be stimulated to produce milk. This is a 'state' of the body, rather than a reaction to a particular stimulus; she will carry on producing milk for as long as the baby is feeding from it. So it's an actual change in the way that her body is working. This is the kind of change that is brought about by the endocrine system. The kind of changes occurring during adolescence, when the body changes in shape and starts to function differently, are also brought about by activity within the endocrine system.

Different hormones produce very different effects. In the table, I have listed some of the main glands of the endocrine system, and some of their effects. But the hormone that we are particularly interested in in this chapter, is the one released by the adrenal gland: *adrenaline*. This is the hormone that is most involved in emotional reactions, and which is released when the autonomic nervous system is working in a particular kind of way.

Some endocrine glands and their functions	glands	*function*
	pituitary gland	Acts as 'central control' for all the other glands in the system. It also controls birth changes and lactation.
	thyroid gland	This regulates growth, and the metabolic rate of the body – how it uses energy.
	thymus gland	This regulates the body's autoimmune system – how it defends itself from illness.
	adrenal gland	involved in emotional reactions through the hormone adrenaline. It also controls blood sugar levels.
	gonads (ovaries or testes)	These glands release the sex hormones responsible for sexual development, and also secondary sexual characteristics, e.g. beards.

The hormone adrenaline, then, is the one most closely involved with emotional reactions, and which works alongside the autonomic nervous system when we are scared, angry, or in some other emotional state.

The autonomic nervous system

The autonomic nervous system consists of a series of unmyelinated nerve fibres, which run from the lower sections of the brain – the midbrain and the medulla – to various parts of the body. Because these nerve fibres don't have a myelin sheath to speed up the nerve impulse, it takes longer for us to get angry, say, than it would to pull a hand away from a hot stove. But it still is only a matter of seconds!

The system is divided into two sections – the sympathetic section and the parasympathetic section. Each of these sections has an entirely different function, which we will look at in detail.

The sympathetic section of the autonomic nervous system is the part that comes into action when the organism is threatened or frightened – it induces what Walter Cannon described as the 'emergency reaction syndrome'. It works like this: if an

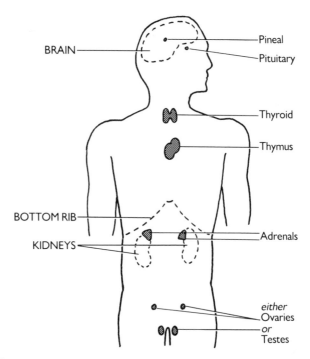

Fig. 17.1 The endocrine glands of the body

animal is frightened or threatened – if it is in danger – it has a choice of two kinds of activity. It can run away, as fast as possible; or it can attack the thing that is threatening it – 'flight or fight'. Either way, it needs to have as much power in its muscles as it can possibly manage, whether to run away swiftly, or to attack strongly. The emergency reaction is a collection of activities in the body, which all work together to achieve this.

For example: the spleen releases stored red blood cells, which will mean the blood is able to carry more oxygen; we breathe more deeply, so that more oxygen is drawn into the lungs; the bronchioles in the lung expand, so they can absorb more oxygen; the heart beats faster so the muscles receive this supply of oxygen more rapidly; the pupils dilate (so the organism can see better), and so on.

If you have ever been a passenger (or driver) in a car that has just avoided having an accident, you will have experienced this reaction. A few seconds after the driver has swerved to safety, your heart starts beating rapidly, your mouth feels dry, and you start breathing heavily. This is the emergency reaction. Although it isn't much use in a modern-day experience like

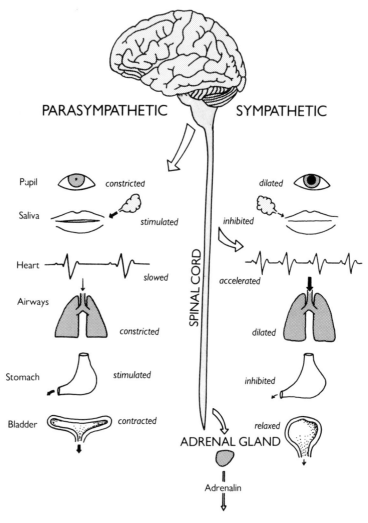

PARASYMPATHETIC   SYMPATHETIC

SPINAL CORD

Pupil   *constricted*   *dilated*

Saliva   *stimulated*   *inhibited*

Heart   *slowed*   *accelerated*

Airways   *constricted*   *dilated*

Stomach   *stimulated*   *inhibited*

Bladder   *contracted*   *relaxed*

ADRENAL GLAND

Adrenalin

Fig. 17.2 Pathways of the autonomic nervous system

that, to an animal in the wild state, it can make the difference between life and death.

The parasympathetic section of the autonomic nervous system has the opposite function. Its function is to restore and conserve the body's resources. (You will realise that the sympathetic system, by getting everything going at once, so to speak, is very wasteful of stored energy.) It causes the heartbeat to decrease, and sugar to be stored rather than converted into energy; helps the digestive processes along by stimulating salivary secretion and peristaltic action (the movement which causes food to travel along the intestine), restores breathing rate to normal, and so on. While the sympathetic section is active in emotions like fear or anger – emotions requiring energy – the parasympathetic section is active in the 'quiet' emotions like sadness or depression.

Psychological factors in emotion

In the light of all this information about the physical events connected with emotions, we may well ask ourselves the question – what, then, *is* emotion? Is it really a mental reaction to an event which we see in the outside world? Or is it just our noticing these physical reactions in our bodies and *interpreting* them as emotion? Or is it some combination of the two, or something different altogether? To answer these questions (if, indeed, we *can* answer them completely) we will look at some of the existing theories of emotion, and at some of the experiments that have been performed in this area.

The James-Lange theory of emotion

This theory was formulated by two eminent psychologists of the last century, William James and C. Lange, who both developed it independently. Observing the physical changes that emotions brought on in the body, they put forward the idea that, in fact, it is our perception of these changes that we experience as emotion. In other words, the physical reaction comes first, triggered off by an external event, and we notice this reaction and *interpret* it as the emotion we associate with those feelings. In James' words: 'We do not weep because we feel sorrow; we feel sorrow because we weep.'

If the James-Lange theory is true, then we should be able to work out different physical responses for each different emotion, as it is the physical response that enables us to recognise the emotion in the first place. In 1953, a psychologist called Ax set up an experiment to investigate this, attempting to find a difference in the 'emergency reaction' between fear and anger – two emotions involving the sympathetic nervous system, but which we experience very differently.

In the experiment he had two groups of subjects. These subjects he connected to an imposing array of wires and electrodes, which were designed to record all the physical responses that they made. For the first group, Ax arranged that they would just have been wrapped up in all the wires and electrical connections, when a technician would come into the room announcing: 'Hold it! We've just found that there's a short-circuit in the apparatus!' As you might imagine, this group was the one with which Ax wanted to study the fear reaction! For the second group, it was arranged that after they had been connected up to the recording apparatus, a technician would come into the room and begin to insult the experimenter and the subjects, so that the subjects would become angry.

Ax did find a difference between the physical reactions of the two groups of subjects. The group that had the 'fear' condition, reacted as if they had just been given injections of adrenaline; while the group in the 'anger' condition reacted as if they had been injected with adrenaline *and* noradrenaline, another hormone involved in emotions. So Ax's study did give evidence of some kind of physical difference between fear and anger, and provided some support for the James-Lange theory.

But we experience many different kinds of emotions in our lives, and also many different degrees of emotion – we might vary from being mildly irritated to being 'speechless with anger'. And, if the James-Lange theory was true, then we would need to have different physical changes for each different emotion. Although this *might* be the case, people haven't yet found these kinds of differences in emotional responses.

Cannon's theory of emotion   A different theory of emotion was put forward by the man who discovered the 'emergency reaction' of the ANS, Walter Cannon. Although he recognised that the changes in autonomic activity did occur in response to an emotional stimulus, he didn't think that this was anything to do with our *feelings* of emotion. Cannon said that the two reactions happened independently: that the stimulus had two separate effects. On the one hand, the emotion-producing stimulus resulted in the physical changes, and on the other hand, it *also* resulted in feelings of emotion – but the two didn't have anything to do with each other.

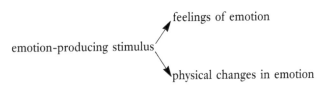

Studies by Solomon and Wynne on dogs that had had their ANS removed, seemed to support Cannon's theory. The dogs would still learn a new task to avoid an electric shock, even though they couldn't be experiencing any of the autonomic responses. But it isn't completely convincing evidence; for one thing, the dogs were very much slower to learn than ordinary dogs are. So it would appear that the ANS might be needed for a rapid response.

Another reason why this study may not provide good support for Cannon's theory, lies in the question of whether we can really take avoidance of pain to be an emotional response. Some pain-avoidance is directly controlled by the central nervous system, and the ANS may have very little to do with it, except that the pain itself can be an emotion-producing stimulus. But that doesn't necessarily mean that avoiding pain is an *emotional* reaction.

Schachter and Singer's theory of emotion

Since neither the James-Lange theory or Cannon's theory seemed to explain things thoroughly enough, two psychologists called Schachter and Singer performed a series of experiments designed to investigate just how much physiological changes *do* matter in emotions, and also how much our knowledge of what's going on is important.

In 1962, they performed experiments that involved injecting people with adrenaline, and noting how they reacted. They had three groups of subjects. One group was given an injection of adrenaline and told what it was, and the sort of reactions that they could expect from it. (A flushed face, slight tremblings, and sweaty hands). A second group was also given an adrenaline injection, but they were misinformed about the symptoms: they were told that it might give them a slight headache, or other things like that. The third group had a *placebo* – that is, they were given a harmless injection of saline solution, which wouldn't have any effect at all. So this would show up any 'imaginary' effects from being given what they thought was a drug.

Schachter and Singer told their students that it would take some time for the injection to have its full effect, and asked them to wait in a waiting room in the meantime. In the waiting room, each subject (they were tested individually) met a 'stooge', who said that he was also waiting for the second part of the experiment. The stooge was really an actor, who was instructed to act either happy, or angry. With the angry condition, he would become increasingly impatient, complaining about the experimenters and the waiting period, and eventually showing every sign of becoming really angry. With the happy condition, the stooge would appear euphoric, making jokes, and playing with paper aeroplanes.

Schachter and Singer found that the mood that their real subjects fell into matched the mood of the stooge. If the stooge was angry, the subjects would get angry; but if the stooge was euphoric, the subjects, too, would start to become happier. So it seemed from these findings, that the emotions people experience can depend on the *social* factors around them.

But another thing which Schachter and Singer found, was that the *degree* to which their subjects reacted, depended on

the injections that they had been given. The subjects who had
been given adrenaline, and misinformed about its effects,
reacted very extremely – they either became very angry, or very
happy. But the ones who had had adrenaline, and been told
what changes they could expect, didn't react so strongly, nor
did the control group who had been given the placebo
injection. So, from this, Schachter and Singer developed a
theory about how emotions seemed to depend on *both* cognitive
factors – the way that they understood their social
surroundings; and on physiological factors – the physical
changes caused by the autonomic nervous system.

From their studies, then, Schachter and Singer's theory was
developed as follows: a stimulus triggers off the physiological
response, and at the same time, the stimulus is *interpreted* in
the brain, taking into account previous experiences of similar
situations. The brain produces the actual emotion that the
subject experiences, through cognitive factors, and the ANS
produces the degree to which that emotion is felt. So emotion
is a mixture of both cognitive and physiological factors.

Further support for their theory came from a study by
Hohmann in 1966. He investigated people who had suffered
lesions to the spinal cord, thus cutting the ANS pathways. He
found that these subjects still experienced emotion, but they
didn't feel things as strongly as other people. So this would
seem to support Schachter and Singer's idea that the
physiological changes affect the degree of emotion, but not the
type of emotion which people feel.

But, as with so many studies, criticisms can be made of
Schachter and Singer's study. The first and the most serious,
is that so far nobody has been able to *replicate* their study.
When other people have tried to repeat it, they haven't had
the same results. This is serious, because if the effect that they

Schachter and Singer's theory of emotion

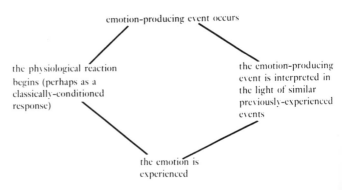

emotion-producing event occurs

the physiological reaction
begins (perhaps as a
classically-conditioned
response)

the emotion-producing
event is interpreted in
the light of similar
previously-experienced
events

the emotion is
experienced

have found is a real one, and not due to problems in the way that they controlled the study, then anyone else performing a similar experiment should get the same results. So we don't really know how far we can accept Schachter and Singer's findings as valid.

Another criticism given as a possible reason for this failure to replicate the experiment is the fact that they didn't check the moods of their subjects before they started the experiment. So it could be that that was having more effect than they thought. A third problem is that adrenaline affects different people in different ways. Some of the people that Schachter and Singer studied didn't get any particular effect from the adrenaline injection. When this happened, they were excluded from the experiment – but it could be that that was an important factor in their results.

The interaction of physiological and psychological factors

Despite these problems, it does seem to be likely that both cognitive and physiological factors play their part in the emotions that we feel. One theory argues that, in fact, we can divide the influences on emotion into three groups of factors, and that we receive information from each group. When we put all the information together, then this makes up the emotion that we experience.

The three groups of factors are: physiological factors, like the emergency reaction; stimulus factors – the actual event which has caused us to react; and cognitive factors in the form of the memories we have of previous events and experiences.

Emotions aren't necessarily the nuisance that some philosophers have found them in the past. Without the ability to become excited, or aroused, to fall in love, or to get angry, many of us wouldn't find very much in our lives at all! And although it has often been recognised that the 'nice' emotions, like joy and pleasure, are important in keeping us relaxed and balanced, it's sometimes not recognised that the other emotions can have that effect too. Many people seem to think that they should never allow themselves to get angry, and that to get annoyed with someone is some kind of failure. But people do get angry and annoyed; what's important is that we find a good way of working that anger off. Something like a good shouting match with someone, or a tennis or football match, or anything which allows the energy generated by the anger to be used, can get rid of the emotion within a few minutes; but 'bottling it up' can mean that it in fact goes on for days, or even months.

Most of us too, would say that fear is something we should avoid – surely no-one benefits from being frightened? And yet, think of fairground rides, which spin us round fast, or which take us suddenly down a steep slope – it is the fear response that is being triggered off – even though it's offset by the knowledge that we are safe really. And many people enjoy watching 'scary' films, whether about aliens on spaceships, or triffids and vampires. Again (within limits), we can sometimes get a valuable release from the sensations of fear.

Argyle and Crossland (1987) performed a study of positive emotions – ones which make us feel good, like happiness or contentment. They asked subjects to think about a series of 24 different pleasant situations, like 'spending a good social evening with friends', 'feeling overwhelmed by the beauty of nature', 'having a long hot bath', or 'being successful at work'. The subjects were asked to describe how these situations would make them feel. From this, the researchers developed 'dimensions' of emotion, which ranged from one extreme to an opposite end.

Argyle and Crossland found that there seemed to be four main dimensions for positive emotions. The first one was concerned with 'absorption', ranging from private, absorbing experiences to social experiences which weren't at all absorbing. The second dimension seemed to be to do with feelings of 'potency' – at one end there were things like sport or success at work, while the opposite end of the dimension was concerned with things like enjoying a hot bath; listening to music, and the like.

The third dimension identified by Argyle and Crossland seemed to be concerned with 'altruism'. At one end of the scale they found situations like conversations and engaging in some kind of commitment activity (like church or charity work); while at the other end they found more self-indulgent situations like receiving a valuable present or engaging in a personal hobby. The fourth dimension was described as being 'spiritual' – concerned with serious things at one extreme, like solving puzzles or enjoying nature, while the opposite end of the scale was concerned with more trivial activities, like watching a TV thriller or buying something personal for oneself.

In many ways, we know much more about the negative emotions like fear or anger than we do about the positive ones; but researchers are becoming more and more interested in positive emotions too, so hopefully we can expect this area to develop a lot more in the next few years.

Having looked at emotions, then, which are something we have inherited, along with many other abilities, from our direct ancestors, it's now time for us to look at something which, although also inherited, enables us to free ourselves from having to inherit all our behavioural patterns. Although we might learn ways of *expressing* emotions, we don't learn the emotions themselves. But there are many things which we *do* learn, and it's interesting to look at the processes by which we do this.

Summary

1 In addition to the central and somatic nervous system, there are two other systems by which the body co-ordinates and controls its activities: the endocrine system, and the autonomic nervous system.

2 The endocrine system is a set of glands that release hormones into the bloodstream. It is concerned with 'states' of the body, rather than with actions or feelings.

3 The autonomic nervous system is a set of nerves that connect with the endocrine system and with the rest of the nervous system. It has two divisions: the sympathetic division, and the parasympathetic division.

4 The sympathetic division controls the emergency 'fight or flight' reactions. The parasympathetic division is concerned with building up and restoring bodily resources.

5 The James-Lange theory of emotion states that we perceive first the physiological changes of emotion, and interpret the emotion as a result of these changes.

6 Cannon's theory of emotion states that the experience of emotion is independent of physiological sensations. Schachter and Singer's theory sees emotion as a combination of cognitive factors and physiological factors.

7 Argyle and Crossland found that positive emotions could be classified using four main dimensions: absorbtion, potency, altruism and spiritual.

8 Emotional release is a valuable part of human living – when we suppress emotions, we tend to suffer as a result. Emotions need to be channelled into acceptable outlets.

Chapter 18 Learning

Throughout this book, I have talked again and again about learning: 'We learn to talk' or 'we learn to recognise our parents', and many other examples. In this chapter, I want to look more closely at just what we mean by 'learning', and some of the ways that learning takes place.

One thing that's important to remember is that learning isn't just something that we do in school or college. People are learning all the time, even if it's just from chatting to someone at the bus stop! Some psychologists think that the drive to learn new skills and to develop new interests is one that is basic to every human being, and that we suffer badly if we aren't able to learn new things as we want to. They point to the way that so many recreational games are games of skill, which take practice to learn, like darts or video games. If people didn't like learning new things (or improving their existing skills), then, they say, these games just wouldn't be popular.

Animals, too, learn things. As we move further up the phylogenetic scale (see Chapter 2), we find more and more emphasis on learning, and less and less on fixed inherited behaviour patterns. By the time we get to mammals, learning has become a very important part of their lives.

But how do we define learning? A usual definition of learning by psychologists is as follows:

Learning is a relatively permanent change in behaviour which occurs as a result of experience.

We call it 'relatively permanent', because nobody would say that they'd learned something, if they forgot it again the next minute! But at the same time, we *do* forget things, so the 'relatively' allows for that. When we talk of a change in behaviour, we are back to the problem discussed in Chapter 1. We cannot *see* what goes on in people's minds, so we can't see what they've learned. But things that we learn usually turn up in our behaviour somewhere – even if it's only our telling a friend about it (verbal behaviour). So, in some way, our behaviour will change as a result of what we've learned, and we can call learning a 'change in behaviour'. Also, by doing this, we are putting forward a definition that includes animals as well as humans, and, as I've said, animals do learn.

Most of the early work that was done on learning was to do with the basic processes by which associations are learned. One of the first psychologists to study learning closely, in the way that we do today, was J.B. Watson, an American psychologist at the beginning of this century. Watson is sometimes called 'the Father of Behaviourism', because he argued very strongly that psychologists should only study behaviour, and not 'the mind' (see Chapter 1).

Watson held to the view that learning occurred by *association* – two things would become linked together in sequence if that sequence or association was repeated often enough. So, to learn something, it was necessary to connect it with something else, and to *repeat* (or exercise) that connection often. If this was done, the learning would take place. This became known as the *Law of Exercise*.

Pavlov and classical conditioning

At the same time as Watson was developing his *Law of Exercise*, Ivan Pavlov, the Russian physiologist, was also beginning to investigate learning. He was working on dogs, and studying their digestive systems. Therefore, he had some dogs arranged in a harness, with equipment such that he was able to measure how much saliva they produced when they were fed, and how this changed as digestion occurred. Pavlov noticed that rather than salivating when they actually started eating, the dogs would begin to salivate when they saw the assistant with the bucket of food coming near them. It was clear that they had learned to *associate* the sight of the bucket with the arrival of food. But since salivation is a *reflex*, rather than a voluntary action, Pavlov became very interested in just how reflexes could become conditioned like this. As a result of his investigations, he published the book *Conditioned Reflexes* in 1927.

This type of learning – the conditioning of reflexes such that they will occur in response to new situations – has become known as *classical conditioning* – because it is one of the first, and most basic forms of learning. What happens in classical conditioning is that everything is based on a reflex or an already established connection that the animal or person has – such as salivating when being given food, or constricting the blood vessels when the hand is placed in icy water.

On several occasions, the stimulus which elicits the response is *paired* with a completely new stimulus – like a bell or a buzzer being sounded. For instance, each time that the dog is given food, it also hears a bell.

Before conditioning has taken place, the dog will only respond to the food, and will not react to a bell ringing nearby. During conditioning, the dog hears the bell each time it is given food. By the time conditioning has finished, the new stimulus – the bell – has acquired many of the properties of the old stimulus – the food. So that, if the bell is sounded, the dog will salivate. What was previously an unlearned (unconditioned) response to the food, salivation, has become a learned (conditioned) response to the bell!

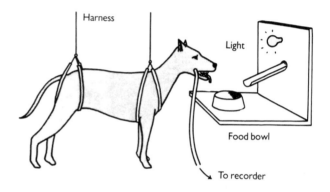

Fig. 18.1 Pavlov's study of classical conditioning
When the light shines, food is delivered to the bowl and the dog salivates. This is recorded via a tube inserted in the cheek. Eventually, the dog will salivate when the light shines even if there is no food delivered

A study by Menzies, in 1937, showed that this can work just as well with humans. The reflex was that of vasoconstriction – the constriction of the blood vessels in the skin when it is cold. (This is why your hands tend to go paler when they are very cold – it's the body's way of retaining heat by withdrawing as much of it as possible to the centre of the body.) So the *unconditioned stimulus* in his experiment was that of placing the subject's hand in a bucket of icy water, and the *unconditioned response* was vasoconstriction.

Each time the subjects had their hands placed in the water, Menzies sounded a buzzer. After several trials he found that if he sounded the buzzer, even without the icy water, the blood vessels in his subjects' hands would constrict. The *conditioned stimulus* of the buzzer was now eliciting a *conditioned response* of vasoconstriction. And this had happened simply by pairing – presenting at the same time – the unconditioned stimulus and the conditioned stimulus.

Menzies' experiment is interesting because it shows what an unconscious process classical conditioning is. We cannot deliberately control vasoconstriction, but we can learn to produce it in response to different stimuli.

Procedures of classical conditioning

Pavlov and other researchers investigated many of the procedures of classical conditioning, and found several basic 'laws' of how it works. When a form of learning is strengthened, we speak of it as being *reinforced*. Reinforcement – strengthening the learning – in classical conditioning occurs by repeating the connection between the unconditioned and the conditioned stimulus. (This is basically the same as Watson's Law of Exercise.) If the connection is never reinforced after it has been made, then eventually it will extinguish – or die out. By *extinction* of the learning, we mean that it no longer shows in the animal's (or person's) behaviour. If the previous conditioned stimulus is presented, but not with the unconditioned one, then after a while it simply will not bring about any response.

Through reinforcement and extinction in classical conditioning, we can also produce discrimination between different stimuli. If an animal has been trained – through classical conditioning – to respond to a particular bell, then it will also tend to produce that response when it hears other, similar bells. This is known as *generalisation*. The response will be strongest in response

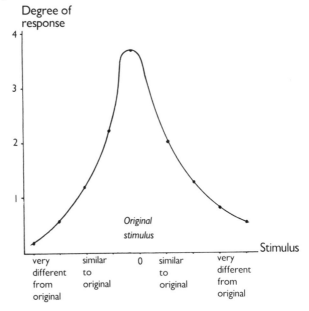

Fig. 18.2 A generalisation gradient

to a bell that is very similar to the original one, and weakest in response to a bell that is very unlike the original.

Generalisation is a natural tendency in animals and people, and does not have to be taught. But if we want to, we can train an animal or person to *discriminate* between two stimuli, by presenting one of the stimuli (say, a high-toned bell) along with the unconditioned stimulus, but not presenting anything when the lower-toned bell is sounded. Although at first the animal may generalise and respond to both bells, after sufficient training trials it will learn to respond only to the bell that is reinforced, and its response to the other bell will become extinguished.

Applications of classical conditioning

One way that findings on classical conditioning have been of direct use to people is in the treatment of certain types of psychiatric problems or disorders. Perhaps the most well-known uses of classical conditioning are the treatments that have been developed to help people with *phobias* – irrational fears that have become so strong that they interfere with the person's everyday life.

This type of treatment, which uses learning theory rather than in-depth analysis of the origins of problems and complexes, is known as *behaviour therapy*. The therapist is concerned with the actual problems the patient has at the time, and sees them as being the result of inappropriate learning. Because of this, the treatment is designed to *teach* the client more appropriate ways of behaving, so that he or she becomes able to cope better with day-to-day life.

One of the first events to suggest that phobias might develop as a result of learning came when there was a flood in Pavlov's laboratory. Several of the dogs had been trapped, and had watched the water getting closer and closer. Although they were not actually harmed by the water, they had been very alarmed, and afterwards they showed fear whenever they saw water spilt in the laboratory, even if it was only a very small amount.

Other evidence came from a study of Watson and Raynor on a small child known as 'Little Albert'. Little Albert had a pet white rat, of which he was very fond. By startling Albert with a loud noise every time he was playing with his pet, Watson and Raynor conditioned a fear response in the child, through classical conditioning. Little Albert didn't just become frightened of his pet – he would cry when he saw it – but he also *generalised* this fear to other white furry objects, like a white rabbit, and even cotton wool! We don't know whether Albert lost his fear in the end because Albert's mother understandably removed him from the hospital before Watson and Raynor had finished their experiments.

There are two main methods of treating phobias, both of which use a classical conditioning approach. The idea is, that there is a direct link between the feared object (the stimulus), and the fear which it produces (the response). The behaviour therapist aims to break this stimulus-response link, and to put a different, more suitable response in its place.

Systematic desensitisation
This technique approaches the problem by trying, gradually, to introduce a response to the feared object which is *incompatible* with or contradictory to fear. So the first thing that the therapist has to do is to train the clients in relaxation techniques – so that they learn to relax at will, and to recognise when they are relaxed and when they are not. When a client can do this, the therapist and the client draw up a list of the different situations in which the phobia happens. Some of these situations will be less extreme than others: for example, for a client with a cat phobia it might be unpleasant or disturbing to watch a film of a cat, but it wouldn't be as bad as having a cat actually in the room. So a *hierarchy* of fearful situations is drawn up, which ranges from the only-slightly-disturbing ones to the extremely-terrifying ones.

When this has been done, the therapist and the client begin at the bottom of the list, and the client learns to relax in the presence of the least frightening stimulus – while looking at a picture of a cat, say. When the client can do this successfully, every time, then they move on to the next stimulus, which might be, perhaps, a film of a cat walking around. Gradually they move up the list, making sure that the client can relax fully at each stage. It is important not to go on to another stage while the client still feels tense at a previous one, because that might reinforce the cat-fear link (or other stimulus-fear link) instead of replacing it. (It's difficult to feel frightened while you're relaxed!)

By using this technique, it is possible to get rid of a phobia, so that the client, eventually, can feel relaxed in the presence of the thing that once used to terrify them. The problem is, that it takes a long time, and is therefore very expensive. There is another, much quicker technique, which also aims to break the stimulus-fear connection, known as implosion therapy.

Implosion therapy
Implosion therapy works mainly on the grounds that extinction occurs with repeated presentation of the stimulus, if it isn't paired with the unconditioned stimulus. For many people, phobias develop as a result of a particularly frightening

experience – often forgotten. Although it would seem that they ought to extinguish naturally, as the person doesn't have the same frightening experience over and over again, in fact they do not. This would seem to be because people who have phobias tend to *avoid* the thing that they're frightened of, and so the stimulus-fear connection never gets replaced by any other reactions.

In implosion therapy, the client is continually presented with the stimulus, but with no consequences. After a period of time, the fear response tends to die away, and the person becomes calmer in the presence of the stimulus – which, of course, breaks the connection between it and fear, and allows the person to learn new responses.

One example of implosion therapy might be that of a person who has been knocked down by a car, and has developed a phobia of traffic, such that they find it very difficult even to leave the house. In some clinics, this is treated by putting the person in a room with four large wall-screens, and showing them films of cars and traffic coming towards them. At first, of course, they are very frightened by this, but after a while they calm down, and the fear reaction dies away. When this happens, and they are relatively relaxed, a new response has been substituted for the previous one of fear, and the phobia has gone.

Aversion therapy   In some forms of psychiatric treatment, the idea is not so much to cure a phobia, as actually to *create* one by using classical conditioning. This is known as aversion therapy.

This technique uses classical conditioning techniques to get someone to *avoid* things that they should not be approaching. Its main use has been with people like sex offenders, or alcoholics, or other people who experience compulsions. What aversion therapy tries to do is to link the object of the compulsion (the conditioned stimulus), with another stimulus that is highly unpleasant, such as electric shock, or vomiting (the unconditioned stimulus). Because the reaction produced by the unconditioned stimulus is unpleasant, by classical conditioning the person comes to associate the two stimuli, and so avoids them both.

An example of this is the use of a drug known as antabuse by alcoholics. This can be implanted under the skin, so that it remains active in the body over a long period of time. If the alcoholic person has a drink during that time, they instantly feel sick, and often actually are sick. Understandably, we tend to avoid food or drink which makes us sick (it's a good survival mechanism), and so this makes it easier for the person to stay off alcohol. But, through classical conditioning, antabuse works on an unconscious level as well. Because the alcohol has been linked with nausea in the past, even when the drug has worn off people will tend to avoid drink, because it has become a conditioned reaction to feel nausea in the presence of alcohol.

These are some of the ways that classical conditioning has been used to help people. But there are other forms of learning as well, which are also useful.

Operant conditioning

Thorndike's 'Law of Effect'

Perhaps the first important theorist in this field was the psychologist E. L. Thorndike. Thorndike set up a problem that he called a 'puzzle box', which he used to study learning in cats. The box was closed, but it had a door which could only be opened by performing an apparently unconnected activity, like pulling a dangling string. Thorndike watched the cats gradually learn how to get out of the box by 'trial-and-error' learning.

As the cat moved about in the box, trying to escape, sooner or later it would accidentally pull the string, and the door would open. When the cat was put into the box again, and again, the time between it being put in and finally pulling the string would gradually get shorter, until eventually the cat would pull the string as soon as it was put in the box.

From this, Thorndike developed the 'Law of Effect', which concerned the effect of the action. The reason the cat learned to pull the string, he said, was because of the *effect* of pulling the string – its release from the box. If an action had a 'good' effect for the animal or 'organism', Thorndike said, then it would be likely to be repeated – the learning was strengthened by it.

Skinner and operant conditioning

Thorndike's 'Law of Effect' was developed further by B. F. Skinner's work on 'operant conditioning' in the 1930s. This work was concerned with the 'Law of Effect', but went into a great deal more detail, and established operant conditioning as an important part of what we know of learning, and how it takes place.

Like Thorndike's 'puzzle box', Skinner developed a piece of equipment for studying learning. This is called the 'Skinner box', and is an attempt to reduce all those things that might affect learning in different ways, down to almost nothing, so that the actual learning can be studied in detail.

A Skinner box is, simply, a box. It will tend to have a metal grid floor; a food delivery chute; a lever or some kind of easily-operated switch; and usually a light. The most important features are the lever and the food delivery chute.

Lights

Food pellets

Lever

Food tray

Fig. 18.3 A Skinner box

What happens is this: a hungry animal (usually a laboratory
rat or hamster) is put into the box. Because it is hungry, it is
very active, and wanders around the box, exploring. As it
wanders, at some point it accidentally presses the lever, and a
pellet of food is delivered to the chute. Often, the rat does not
find the food immediately, but it does eventually. Very
gradually, the rat builds up a connection between pressing the
lever and getting the food reward, in the same way that
Thorndike's cats learned to let themselves out of the box.
When the animal is pressing the lever frequently, and
examining the food delivery chute after lever-pressing, then we
know that it has 'learned' the activity.

Incidentally, we do not need to talk about 'thinking' at any
point in this process. Both Thorndike's cats, and Skinner's
rats and pigeons simply learn, by trial and error, a connection
between *behaviour* (e.g. lever-pressing), and a *reward* (e.g.
food). Even worms can learn this kind of connection, so it
would be a bit silly if we used 'thoughts' to explain how the
connection was formed.

I have mentioned the fact that the food pellet, to the rat, is a
reward – because the rat is hungry. Skinner referred to this
as an example of *reinforcement*: something which strengthens
the response which we want the animal to make. In fact, this
is the definition of reinforcement – something which makes
the organism more likely to perform a certain item of
behaviour again. The food pellet made it more likely that the
rat would, eventually, press the lever again – it strengthened
the lever-pressing response. If you see a child drawing a
picture, and you praise that child, you are strengthening the
behaviour that the child is showing – that of drawing. The

child then, all other things being equal, is more likely to engage in the behaviour again, as the behaviour has been positively reinforced.

One important thing about positive reinforcement is that it has to be *immediate*, if it is to have an effect. There is no point praising a child ten minutes after it has done something you approve of; the child will be doing something else by then and your praise could easily be strengthening the wrong behaviour!

In addition to the kind of reinforcement that is a reward, there is also *negative reinforcement* as well. In negative reinforcement, behaviour is strengthened, not because the organism received something it needs, but because something unpleasant ceases as a result of that action. For example, a rat will learn to ward off an electric shock by jumping into a box when a light comes on. It isn't receiving a reward for jumping into the box, but it *is* avoiding the shock, and so the behaviour is learned. Doing your homework to avoid getting into trouble at school might be an example of learning through negative reinforcement.

As you will have noticed, negative reinforcement is *not* punishment. Punishment isn't really much help in learning at all; although it may suppress the undesired behaviour, it does not tell the person (or rat) what they *ought* to be doing instead. A child who is punished for doing something wrong, may stop doing that thing – but there's nothing to stop it going off and doing something else which is even worse. But, by using positive reinforcement, the child is being encouraged to do things right – and, while it's doing something that is approved of, then it won't be getting into trouble. Both positive and negative reinforcement, in fact, fit into Thorndike's 'Law of Effect' as they both have pleasant consequences for the individual.

Behaviour that is learned through operant conditioning can also be *extinguished*. If we stop reinforcing behaviour, then eventually it will die away. But often, we get what is known as 'spontaneous recovery', where behaviour which was thought to be extinguished suddenly reappears. For instance, a rat that learned to press a lever, and then wasn't reinforced for it, will have had its lever-pressing behaviour extinguished. But if you put it in a Skinner Box a month later, it will often start pressing the lever again spontaneously.

If we only reinforce behaviour sometimes and not always, that behaviour becomes much more strongly learned. Betting shops and one-armed bandit manufacturers are very aware of this;

people keep on gambling, because every now and then they receive a strong reinforcement – but not all the time. This 'partial reinforcement' is very resistant to extinction, as families of gamblers know, sometimes to their cost.

Ferster and Skinner investigated, in 1957, the idea of partial reinforcement, and the effect that it had on behaviour. If we want to reinforce behaviour only some of the time, we can alter two things: we can alter the time that must pass before a rat receives another food pellet, or we can alter the proportion of responses which receive reinforcement (for example, by only rewarding one lever-press in five). If we decide to use a method like this, then we say that we have decided to use a *reinforcement schedule*. Roughly speaking, the main ones are like this:

1 Fixed ratio reinforcement — the rat is reinforced according to a set pattern – for example, every fifth response, or every twentieth. A schedule of F R 6 would mean that the rat was reinforced after every sixth response.

2 Variable ratio reinforcement — the rat still receives reinforcement according to how many responses it has made, but the number may be different each time. It *averages* out to a set number, though, so a schedule of V R 6 would mean that *on average*, the rat was reinforced every sixth response.

3 Fixed interval reinforcement — a certain amount of time must pass before the rat is able to receive another reinforcement. If it presses the lever before the time is up, it does not receive any reward.

4 Variable interval reinforcement — the period of time which must pass changes each time, but *averages out* as a given period. So a schedule of V I 6 would mean that *on average*, the rat could receive reinforcement every sixth second, but the actual time would vary on each occasion.

Each of these schedules has a different effect on the animal's behaviour. The kinds of effects which they have, are on two aspects – rate of response, and extinction, or resistance to extinction.

Rate of response is the number of times the rat will press the lever in a given period; for example, it might be the number of presses per minute. *Resistance to extinction* is how many times the rat will press the lever after it has stopped receiving reinforcement. Both these measures can be used as a measure of *operant strength* – that is, how strongly the response has been learned.

Each kind of reinforcement schedule produces a slightly different effect on these two measures, after the animal has learned the response thoroughly; in other words, the operant strength depends very much on *how* the animal learned the response in the first place.

Fixed ratio reinforcement tends to produce responses which are very fast, that is, the rate of response is very high. But the rate of extinction tends also to be very fast: when the reinforcement stops, the animal stops responding very quickly.

Variable ratio reinforcement produces a very fast response rate, as does fixed ratio, but the rate of extinction is slower. The animal will tend to make many more responses after reinforcement has stopped, than it does under fixed-ratio. *Fixed interval reinforcement* produces a very slow rate of response. The rat will tend to respond only maybe once or twice per minute; but the response takes a long time to extinguish – the resistance to extinction is high. *Variable interval reinforcement* tends to produce a regular, steady response rate, and an extremely high rate of resistance to extinction – the highest of the four schedules.

It is fairly clear, then, that if we vary the way in which we provide reinforcement for a particular kind of behaviour, then this will have an effect on the time that that learning stays with us; in ordinary life, of course, neither animals nor humans tend to be reinforced *all* the time; rather, we will receive reinforcement only *some* of the time, for any one item of behaviour.

'But', you may well be thinking; 'the sort of things which human beings do are far more complicated than just pressing a lever in a box! And furthermore, it's all very well giving a food pellet to a hungry rat, but our kind of reinforcement isn't that simple, is it?'

Quite true; and I shall be looking at both these points. To take the first one: the fact that our type of behaviour tends to be far more complicated, than simply things you might do by accident, like pressing a lever in a box.

Behaviour shaping   Complicated behaviour can be accounted for in operant conditioning by behaviour shaping. This is the technique of continually changing the actual behaviour that will be reinforced, by using each new item learned as the basis for another item to be learned. For example: supposing you wanted to train a rat to salute while pressing the lever in a Skinner box. You would start off, ordinarily enough, by training the rat to press the lever in the usual way. When it had learned to do that, then you would *alter the reinforcement contingencies*. In other words, you would change what it had to do in order to be reinforced. As it pressed the lever, you would find that sometimes it held its paw down towards the ground, while at other times its paw was raised slightly. (I mean the paw which it is not using to press the lever!) So you begin to reinforce the rat *only* when its paw is raised. After a while, it is holding its paw above the ground all the time. Then, you alter the reinforcement contingencies again; this time, reinforcing only those occasions when its paw is held right up. Very soon, you have a rat which salutes each time it presses the lever.

In everyday life, we use behaviour-shaping techniques all the time. For example, supposing you took a job serving in a shop, and it was the first time you had done that kind of work. On your first day, the manageress explains what you have to do, and keeps an eye on you while you serve customers. At first, she will be tolerant if you are slow in serving, or in counting out the change. After a while, however, she will feel that you have had enough practice, and will expect you to be much faster giving change, or serving. What has happened here, is that your *reinforcement contingencies* have altered: to get reinforcement (praise) from the manageress you must *extend* the behaviour which, at first, was sufficient to get reinforcement; you must still do the first thing, but it is not enough to do it just anyhow. There are many other examples of behaviour-shaping in everyday life – the way in which an infant gradually learns table manners, for instance, or the way a child is taught to dress itself.

The question still remains about reinforcement. It is one thing to say that a hungry rat will learn because it needs food, but it is quite another to say that praise from a manageress in a shop causes the same kind of result. But there is a process, which we can demonstrate with rats, which may be how it happens in humans. This process is called *secondary reinforcement*.

We would call reinforcement which directly fills a need, like food for a hungry animal, or water for a thirsty one, *primary reinforcement*. If, though, we put a rat in a Skinner box, and we sound a noise at the same time as delivering the food pellet, when we stop the primary reinforcement, but continue the noise, the rat will continue to press the lever. It appears to be doing it, now, for the noise, and not for the food. We would say in this case that the noise has become a *secondary reinforcer*. Further, if we stop all reinforcement, so that the behaviour is allowed to extinguish, and then we restart the noise, but not the food, the rat will start lever-pressing all over again. In some ways, the noise has acquired the same reinforcing properties that the food had, and the rat responds to it in the same way.

We can use this explanation to account for some things in real life. For example, if we were asking why a certain schoolchild worked hard to get good marks from the teacher, we would account for this behaviour (working hard), by saying that the good marks *reinforced* the behaviour. And we would account for *that*, by saying that the good marks had come to be associated with the teachers' approval (like a smile, or words of praise). So the marks had acquired the same reinforcing properties as the teacher's approval.

At this point, we would find a difference between psychologists. Some would say that the teacher's approval satisfied a *primary need* in the child: that all human beings need approval from others, and will work to obtain that approval. Other psychologists might not agree, but would say that, in early infancy, the smiles or words of approval had acquired reinforcing properties, by being linked with food and cuddles from the parents. So that this would be another example of secondary reinforcement.

Either way, the concept of secondary reinforcement can be used to explain why a great many things will have an effect on behaviour, which we might not otherwise have realised.

Before we end this account of operant conditioning, there are still one or two things we should mention. One of them is *generalisation*, which you may remember from the classical conditioning section. In operant conditioning, generalisation works in much the same way. The organism will tend to 'generalise' its response to the other situations; a rat that has been trained to press the right-hand lever in a box, for example, will occasionally press the left-hand one if it is there – it has generalised the learning to include the other lever. In the same way, a child who has learned that saying 'please' when asking its parents for something meets with a pleasant response, may well generalise that to saying 'please' when speaking to other adults.

The other thing that should be mentioned, is one we have touched on in the last paragraph. The child might generalise the learning to other *adults*, but not to other children. If this were true, then we have an example of *discriminatory stimulus*. This is a signal that 'informs' the organism that the response is appropriate. For example, the rat might learn to press the lever only when the light in the box was on, and not when it was switched off. The light then provides a discriminatory stimulus for the behaviour of lever-pressing. Similarly, the child learning to say 'please' to adults, but not to other children means that the adult has become a discriminatory stimulus for the behaviour of saying 'please'.

There is an account of a horse called 'Clever Hans', which lived in Germany at the beginning of this century. This horse was apparently able to count, and to understand and solve mathematical questions. On each occasion it would answer by pawing the ground the correct number of times. How it did this was studied very carefully, as no-one would believe that it could *really* do what the trainer claimed. Eventually, what turned out to be the answer surprised even the trainer!

When a psychologist, Oskar Pfungst, investigated it, he found that the horse was expert at minute observation of its trainer's behaviour, and it responded to that. Each time it started counting, the trainer would be tense, wondering if it would still get the right answer – because *he* didn't know how it was done. When the horse reached the right number, the trainer would relax slightly, in relief. The horse detected this from the slightly different breathing movements made by the trainer, and stopped pawing the ground accordingly. The horse had become expert at detecting *discriminatory stimuli*.

In everyday life, we too respond to such signals for instance, if someone is sitting alertly, and watching us as we talk, then we know we have their attention (a positive reinforcement in most cases), and we respond to that. But the whole process is usually unconscious for both people.

Applications of operant conditioning

Socialisation

Operant conditioning has a great many applications in human behaviour. One of the main ones is one I've touched on already – the way in which children are socialised to fit into their own particular social group. In any social group, some kinds of behaviour are rewarded, while other behaviour is regarded as unacceptable. Through unconscious operant conditioning, people – especially children – come to behave in the ways that will gain approval from other people, and so they become socialised into their society.

The S-R theory of child development

The work of Pavlov and Skinner on conditioning led to a new approach to the question of how children develop. This was known as the S-R, or stimulus-response approach.

An S-R approach to child development argues that children develop as a result of the basic learning that they receive after they are born. At first, the child will be reinforced by food and affection when it behaves in ways that are approved of by its parents or caretakers. As the child matures, and becomes more active, it will spontaneously do things that seem more 'grown-up' to its parents, like trying to do up its own clothes, or putting together a more complicated speech. When this happens, the people around the child are pleased, and the behaviour is reinforced, usually by praise, which has become a *secondary reinforcer* for the child by being associated with affection or approval. By *generalising* the learning to similar situations, the child learns socially-approved ways of behaving.

In Chapter 11 I described how Skinner thought that children learned language by a process of operant conditioning and behaviour-shaping. Critics of Skinner's theory have argued that this could not explain how the child learns to construct new and original sentences, or how it may use a language rule inappropriately (like saying 'I winned the game') although it has never heard this from an adult. But supporters of the S-R approach have pointed to Harlow's work on learning sets, and said that the child could be using the learning sets that it has developed, to apply these rules or to cope with new situations. However, it would be difficult to explain some of Piaget's findings, on the way that the child's understanding of the world changes, simply by operant conditioning.

Token economy systems

Another use for operant conditioning has been the development of 'token economy' wards in psychiatric hospitals. Many long-term schizophrenics have very little idea how to act 'normally', and so in these wards, the staff deliberately reward behaviour that seems to be an attempt to behave in acceptable ways. They also use behaviour-shaping techniques to encourage appropriate kinds of behaviour. But, as I mentioned before, reinforcement isn't much good if it doesn't follow soon after the desired behaviour, so in these wards, if a patient behaves 'well', then they are immediately given a token by a member of staff. Later on, they can exchange that token for privileges, for instance being allowed to stay up late, or being able to spend their tokens in the hospital shop.

Biofeedback

In 1967, Miller and DiCara developed a new application for operant conditioning techniques. They discovered that rats could learn to control involuntary functions of their bodies, like raising or lowering their heartbeat. The way that they did this was by using rats with electrodes implanted in the 'pleasure centre' of the hypothalamus. They drugged the rats with curare, so that they were unable to move any of their voluntary muscles; but if the rats reduced their heartbeat at all while they were paralysed then they would receive a 'reward' of stimulation to the brain. The rats quickly became able to control their heartbeat, in order to obtain the reward.

This finding was an important one, because it was previously thought that operant conditioning could only be used with voluntary actions, while classical conditioning could only be used for reflexes. Miller and DiCara's study was criticised because nobody could *replicate* the results later. But it seemed to show that operant conditioning techniques could after all be used for unconscious reflexes, and the technique was applied to human beings, through the use of 'biofeedback'.

In biofeedback techniques, people are connected to a recording device, which will monitor one of their bodily functions – for instance how high their blood pressure is. The recording device will also have some way of informing the person what their blood pressure is like – either by sounding a tone when it goes over a certain level, or by putting a dial where the person can see it. When that person's blood pressure goes down to the desired level, then the person is informed of it – they have *feedback* about what they are doing.

By using this technique, people who have conditions like high blood pressure can learn to control them, without having to use drugs. At the moment, this method still isn't widely used, because the initial equipment is expensive to set up, but it is becoming more and more popular all the time, and is having considerable medical success.

Verbal conditioning of autistic children

Operant conditioning can also be used to help autistic children to communicate with other people. Autistic children are children who are completely withdrawn from human contact, and, although some of them will speak (as we saw in Chapter 11), many of them do not.

Using operant conditioning techniques, the child is rewarded at first for any sort of sound that it makes. (In a child that is not particularly interested in other people, praise is not an effective reinforcer, so they tend to be given sweets or other favourite foods as a reward.) As the child makes more and more sounds, the sounds are shaped by operant conditioning, until eventually the child only receives reinforcement for producing actual words. Later on it will be expected to connect these words into sentences, although this is more difficult to condition.

One advantage of this technique, is that the child's parents are involved, as well as the speech therapist or psychologist. If they understand how the operant conditioning process works, then they can use it at home as well as when the child is in the clinic, which means that the treatment is much more effective and less expensive.

Learning sets

In 1949, H. Harlow performed a series of experiments with monkeys, which showed that they could learn more than simple trial-and-error learning by means of operant conditioning.

Many people had objected to the idea that operant conditioning could be used to explain certain kinds of human behaviour, because, they said, quite often human beings didn't solve problems by trial-and-error, and being reinforced if they got the answer right. People also learned to solve problems sometimes by 'insight' – by seeing the relationships between different elements in a problem. And it was generally thought that this kind of more abstract learning couldn't be explained simply by operant conditioning.

Harlow looked to see if you could train monkeys to solve more abstract problems, by simply training them with operant conditioning. He wanted his monkeys to learn to solve a particular *type* of problem, not just to learn the answer to one

Fig. 18.4 Harlow's study of learning sets
The monkey must choose either the odd colour or the odd shape, depending on the background colour of the tray

problem. Harlow started out with a simple 'choice' problem. He would present a monkey with two different shapes on a tray, and it had to choose a shape. If it picked up the correct shape, there would be a raisin or peanut underneath as a reward. At first, it took the monkeys several attempts to solve this problem. But after a few different puzzles of this kind, they were able to solve it after the first attempt. In other words, they had learned to solve the type of problem. Harlow tried more and more complicated problems on these monkeys: at one time, they would be presented with a coloured tray containing three objects – two the same shape, and two the same colour – e.g. a red circle, a blue circle, and a blue square. The monkeys had learned that, if the tray was orange, they should choose the odd shape, but if the tray was green, they should choose the odd colour. When you think about it this is a pretty complicated kind of learning for just simple, trial-and-error operant conditioning!

Harlow said that these monkeys had developed what he called *learning sets*. A learning set was a way of learning how to look at and solve a particular *type* of problem. It was something that you could apply to new experiences, so that it seemed as though you had worked out the relationships between the different parts of the problem. But it was possible to develop quite complicated learning sets simply through trial-and-error learning.

Learning sets, as Harlow described them, are very similar to Piaget's schemata. And the sort of thing that Hebb was describing when he talked of phase sequences, could also mean much the same sort of thing – you learn a *way* of looking at different types of problems, so that your previous learning can be applied to new situations.

Programmed learning A special form of teaching has been developed using operant conditioning techniques, the aim being for the student to develop these kinds of learning sets. This technique is known as programmed learning. In programmed learning, the information that is to be learned has been broken down into a series of small 'frames'. In each frame, the student is required to complete a missing word, or solve a problem. As soon as they have done so, they are informed – by the answer sheet, or by the computer if they are working at a computer terminal – whether their answer is right or wrong. This feedback, the knowledge of whether they have got the answer right or not – serves as reinforcement for the student. In many programmed learning courses, the student has to complete, and get correct, about 80% of the frames; if they do so, they will go on to the next piece of work, otherwise they will go over that section again.

The important thing about programmed learning is the way that the learning happens a small step at a time, so that there is plenty of opportunity to get the right answer. Questions are designed to rest on the previously supplied information, so that students won't suddenly be faced with questions that they can't do. If they have been working steadily through the course, they should be able to get things right easily. So the right answer will provide positive reinforcement for the behaviour.
  As you can see, programmed learning is a very structured technique, in the sense that it must be possible to break the learning material down into small units and simple-answer problems. It is a technique that has been used for teaching-

by-computer, as the student can interact directly with the terminal, having 'conversations' with the computer, or the teaching machine.

Cognitive forms of learning

Discovery learning

An entirely different approach to learning in schools was put forward by J. Bruner, and several other theorists. They held the view that children learn best if they are active and involved in what they are learning. When Piaget was talking about the way that schemata developed, he stressed the importance of how the child interacted with its environment, and learned through its own experiences. Otherwise, he said, it wouldn't develop the schemata in the first place. So an alternative approach, which has been used a great deal in some schools, is discovery learning.

In this, children are encouraged to discover and work things out for themselves, instead of being taught information by their teachers (or by teaching machines). An example given by Bruner is of a group of schoolchildren who were given charts of Central America. The only information on the charts was of rivers, lakes, and other natural resources. From this, they were asked to find out, as a class, where the most important cities would be found. By discussing the question, and sharing information about where things were likely to be, the class was able to work out some ideas for where the cities would be, and only then were they allowed to look at other maps, which showed the cities on them. By this method, the children had been able to learn for themselves things such as the fact that cities grow up near to water sources, or other natural resources, like coalfields.

The difference between this method and the programmed learning method, lies in how much children are expected to find out for themselves, and how much they are expected to receive information from other people. Discovery learning works on the idea that children *like* finding things out, and that good teaching methods will use this in order to get them to learn. Programmed learning works more on the assumption that children will come to enjoy learning if they are receiving positive reinforcement for it. Both Piaget and Bruner would emphasise the discovery learning process more, in their theories, but both forms of learning may have a place. After all, the kinds of things that children are required to learn are in themselves often very different – some subjects may be better for discovery learning methods, while other subjects may be better for a programmed learning approach.

Insight learning

In 1925, W. Köhler, one of the Gestalt psychologists, investigated problem solving in chimpanzees. The Gestalt psychologists were a group of researchers who disagreed with the idea that all human behaviour could be explained by learned stimulus-response connections. Instead, they argued that some things were *holistic* in nature – that is, they were complete in themselves and couldn't be broken down into smaller units.

Köhler thought that some kinds of learning were like that. Sometimes, it was possible to learn something by having a flash of insight into the problem, and suddenly seeing what the solution was. Some psychologists call this an '*aha! experience*', because of the way that the insight comes so suddenly. In his studies with chimpanzees, Köhler showed that they, too, sometimes seemed to solve puzzles by *insight learning*.

Köhler would set problems for the chimpanzees to solve. Typically, they would involve placing a piece of fruit out of reach of the ape, but providing them with some way that the fruit could be reached, like having a stick lying around inside the cage which could be used to pull the fruit towards the bars. One study which he described was that of a male chimpanzee, named Sultan, who was trying to reach a banana which had been suspended from the ceiling, out of reach. There were several boxes in the cage, but none of them was large enough for Sultan to climb on and reach the fruit. Sultan made a couple of rather half-hearted attempts to reach the fruit by jumping up and down, and then, according to Köhler, appeared to give up, and went and sat over at the other side of the cage. But then, quite suddenly, he got up, piled one box on top of another, climbed on them and took the fruit down.

Köhler argued that this form of problem solving was very different from the trial and error involved in operant or classical conditioning. Instead, the animal seemed to have shown a *cognitive* rearrangement of the problem – it did what was necessary, as if it had suddenly realised how the boxes could be arranged. Köhler's studies showed that chimpanzees could do this with quite complex puzzles: in one variation, there would be a piece of fruit outside the bars of the cage, but the stick inside the cage would be too short to reach it. However, it could be used to pull in a longer stick which was also outside the cage, which could in turn be used to reach the fruit. This puzzle, too, was solved in the same kind of way, with the chimpanzee behaving as though it had had a sudden insight into the problem.

Insight learning can be a very enjoyable experience for people – it's fun to get that 'flash' of insight which makes everything clear. Educational methods like discovery learning aim to encourage insight learning as much as possible, by providing children with the elements to problems and allowing them to work out solutions for themselves. Although many solutions are worked out gradually by trial and error, insight learning can occur far more often with this method than it can with more traditional methods of classroom teaching.

Cognitive Maps   In 1932, Tolman performed a study which showed that cognitive learning could even apply to laboratory rats running mazes – despite the behaviourists' insistence that all they were really doing was forming connections between a stimulus and a response. Tolman's study involved a group of rats being allowed to explore a complicated maze, with no reward being given to them when they reached the end. Another group of rats was rewarded for completing the maze, and, over ten days, they learned to run through it very quickly. The 'exploration' group took quite a long time to get through the maze, and didn't get any quicker over the first ten days.

On the eleventh day, Tolman began to reward the 'exploration' group for reaching the end of the maze. Within two days they were getting through it as quickly as those which had been rewarded from the start! Tolman argued that this was because, during their explorations, they had built up a *cognitive map* – a kind of mental picture – of the maze, which they could use when they needed to. Even though their actual behaviour hadn't changed during the exploration period, they had still been learning. This became known as *latent learning* – learning which didn't show in behaviour until it was needed, but which was still happening as a result of experience.

Human beings form cognitive maps as well – we all have a kind of mental picture of our home town as the area where we live, even though this picture may have gaps in it. A study by Saarinen (1973) involved asking college students to draw maps of the college campus. In their drawings, the students tended to enlarge those parts of the campus that they were familiar with, or which were important to them; but they under-estimate the size of the buildings and areas which they didn't know very well.

Another study, by Briggs (1971), showed that we tend to under-estimate familiar distances in our cognitive maps, but we often over-estimate distances that we don't know very well – we think that they are longer than they really are. Have you ever had the experience of going somewhere for the first time and feeling as though it was a very long distance; but then getting used to the journey and finding that it really wasn't that far after all? As we become used to a journey we come to know more of the landmarks, and the distance seems to shrink.

We can see, then, that human beings and animals can learn things in many different ways. Learning is a crucial skill for human beings, and there are many forms of learning, ranging from basic associations between a stimulus and a response, to complex mental *representations* of an idea. In Chapter 8, too, we looked at Piaget's idea of the *schema*, which he suggested as another way that we come to learn things and to profit from our ordinary day-to-day experience. In the next chapter we will look at some of the more unusual forms of human experience, and the ways in which abnormal behaviour has been studied.

Summary

1 Learning is very important to everyday life in all mammals. Dependence on learning increases as we move higher up the phylogenetic scale.

2 In 1927 I. Pavlov developed the theory of classical conditioning. This is a simple, stimulus-response form of learning, in which a response is learned by a neutral stimulus being paired with a response-eliciting stimulus. Eventually the neutral stimulus acquires the ability to elicit the response.

3 B. F. Skinner developed the theory of operant conditioning, after previous work by Watson and Thorndike. Its central concept is that behaviour is strengthened through reinforcement – either positive or negative. An organism is more likely to repeat a response if it has been reinforced.

4 Both forms of learning have practical applications. Classical conditioning is used to treat phobias, and for aversion therapy. Operant conditioning is used for token economy wards, biofeedback, socialisation and programmed learning.

5 An alternative to programmed learning in education is the idea of discovery learning. This is a form of learning in which students are mainly encouraged to find things out for themselves, and it is supported by the theories of Piaget and Bruner.

6 Cognitive forms of learning include latent and insight learning, and the formation of cognitive maps and schemata.

Chapter 19

Abnormal psychology

As we go through life, we often encounter people who seem different from others, or *abnormal* in some way. Some people always seem to be extremely nervous or anxious; some seem to swing wildly from one mood to the other extreme. Occasionally, we may even meet someone who doesn't really seem to be very in touch with reality at all – they appear to live in a world of their own, and in extreme cases their behaviour may appear to be quite bizarre. People who act oddly in this way are sometimes described as being 'mentally ill' – but it isn't really illness in the normal way that we understand the word; and we don't really look at it in the same way. Many people are very nervous of people who act oddly, which means that often they can end up being avoided, and becoming socially isolated. In turn, their lack of ordinary human contact can mean that their behaviour becomes odder and odder – more and more abnormal – until they find it very difficult indeed to relate normally to other people. So the judgement that they were 'mentally ill' or 'abnormal' has become a *self-fulfilling prophecy* (see Chapter 20). The study of abnormal psychology involves looking at the possible explanations for why people come to act in an unusual or disturbing manner like this; and what kinds of therapies have been developed to help them to return to normal living.

Defining abnormality

One of the problems that we face when we are looking at abnormal psychology is just exactly what we mean if we call someone 'abnormal'. The dictionary definition simply describes it as being '*different from the norm*'; but that doesn't really help. Instead, it simply rearranges the problem – we have to start being clear about exactly what we mean by 'normal' instead. And whenever we are dealing with people, we find such a wide range of personalities and individual differences, that it's very difficult to be certain about whether a particular type of behaviour is or isn't 'normal'.

In addition, what is considered to be 'normal' behaviour can vary a great deal from one social situation to another, or between different social groups. Think of the difference between how you would be if you were sitting at home with your family, or out at a party with some friends. If you tried to act in exactly the same way at each place, people would almost certainly think that there was something a bit wrong!

The statistical approach

Another attempt to get at what we mean by 'abnormal behaviour' comes by looking at how common such behaviour is – the *statistical approach*. In 1869, Galton showed how physical characteristics, such as arm length or height, could be shown to fall into a certain pattern in terms of the way that they were distributed round the population. If enough people are measured, the same pattern seems to emerge – and that pattern always has the same shape. If we were to take all the measurements of a physical characteristic, such as the width of the upper arm; and then draw up a graph which plotted the width measurement against the number of people who had arms of each measurement, we would find that the graph would have a bell-like shape, known as the *normal distribution curve*.

Essentially, what the normal distribution curve (or Gaussian curve as it's sometimes called) means, is that for any given physical characteristic, most people will be in the middle of the range, and only a few will be at the extremes – in this example, having either very thin upper arms or extremely hefty ones. But for psychologists and statisticians, the curve has meant more than that, because it has definite mathematical properties which mean that we can use it to predict just how likely any given result is. In other words, we could take a measurement from someone's upper arm, and, if we knew just two figures from the normal distribution curve, we could tell that person just how common that measurement was – whether it happens with one in 20 people, or one in 100, or even one in 10 000. The only two figures that we would need would be the *mean*, or average score; and the *standard deviation*, which is a measure of how widely the scores are spread out on the curve.

Using the normal distribution curve, then, we can predict how frequent or uncommon a particular physical characteristic is. But Galton argued that, since mental characteristics depended on physical ones, then mental characteristics like intelligence or personality would also show a normal distribution. (Not every psychologist would agree with Galton's basic assumption that mental characteristics depend on physical ones, incidentally.) So if we are taking the statistical approach to defining abnormality, we can say that behaviour which is statistically uncommon – which doesn't happen very often – is abnormal. But the trouble with trying to define abnormality in this way, is that the definition would then include people who are uncommon, but highly regarded. Being very intelligent, for instance, or highly talented in a particular field is statistically uncommon, but wouldn't be what we mean by abnormal.

Also, there are many kinds of behaviour which are sometimes judged as representing signs of 'disturbance', but which are nonetheless quite common really. For instance: when we see someone walking along the street talking to themselves, we sometimes think that there is something 'wrong' with them. But almost everyone talks to themselves sometimes, particularly if they are alone, and the behaviour on its own doesn't really mean anything. Certainly, if we were to take the statistical approach, talking to oneself would end up classified as completely normal rather than abnormal, because it occurs so often.

In reality, of course, we wouldn't just take one kind of behaviour and base all our judgements on that. Instead, we'd take lots of other things into account. If we were to see someone who looked well-dressed and physically fit talking to themselves as they walked down the street, we would be likely to judge them differently from someone who was talking to themselves, scruffily dressed and looking unfit. We'd be more likely to conclude that the first person was preoccupied, busy or harassed, rather than mentally disturbed.

Social judgements   In practice, judgements about what behaviour is abnormal often tend to rely on social value judgements about what is acceptable in any given situation – and that can be very difficult to pin down. We see 'abnormality' as being something to do with not conforming to the appropriate social expectations, and it's when we look at the demands on people who don't know how to do this, that we realise just how sophisticated normal living is. Even very slight differences in how we act can make all the difference between whether other people feel comfortable with us or not. A slight difference in our non-verbal communication, such as not making the proper kind of eye-contact when we are talking to people, produces an effect on other people and can make them feel uneasy, or avoid contact. If there is a more serious kind of disturbance, such as the things that we say not really making much sense to other people, or showing bizarre or socially unpredictable behaviour, then other people will tend to react to it by classifying that person as 'abnormal'. Some forms of therapy have involved teaching people better social skills, on the grounds that if they can re-learn socially acceptable behaviour, their problems will become easier to control.

We can see from this that it's not always easy to pin down just what we mean by 'abnormal', and many psychiatrists and psychologists have seen it as quite a controversial concept. Most often, we judge it by whether the person concerned is upset or distressed by how they feel, and looking for help, but sometimes their behaviour is so disturbing to friends or family that they approach a doctor, clinical psychologist, social worker, or similar professional.

A clinical psychologist is a professional psychologist who works with people who are judged to be clinically disturbed. Many clinical psychologists are employed in psychiatric hospitals, and work closely with psychiatrists, psychiatric nurses and other staff there. But there are some clinical psychologists who work with other agencies, such as 'drop-in' centres or general practitioners. Clinical psychologists draw on a number of different approaches to abnormal behaviour in their work, and often use several different forms of *therapy* (treatment). We looked at one of these approaches in the last chapter, when we examined how stimulus-response learning (operant or classical conditioning) has been used to treat phobias or in aversion therapy. In other parts of this chapter, we will look at some of the other approaches which clinical psychologists use in their work.

The medical model

The most commonly-accepted approach to understanding abnormal behaviour is known as the *medical model*. This approach takes the view that people who show disturbing abnormal behaviour are mentally ill – that they have something wrong with them, like an illness, but instead of affecting their bodies, it's affecting their minds. The branch of medicine which is concerned with treating mental illness is known as *psychiatry*, and it operates mainly from the principle that an illness can be put right, or at least managed so that it doesn't get any worse, by using physical methods like drugs which affect the mind.

Drugs which affect the mind are known as *psychoactive* drugs; and their effects can range from simply reducing feelings of anxiety or panic, to producing strong feelings of being relaxed, or even euphoric. Using these kinds of drug to control or manage mental disturbance is known as *chemotherapy*. Nowadays, chemotherapy is one of the main forms of treatment used by psychiatrists, although other treatments are still in existence, like ECT (electro-convulsive therapy), which involves passing a small electric current through the brain. This produces feelings of disorientation and a temporary loss of memory by the patient, and is considered to be effective in helping to lift some kinds of depression with certain patients. However, ECT is a controversial treatment, and many professionals are opposed to its use.

Classifying mental disorders The medical model classifies mental disorders into five main groups or types. Kraepelin, in 1913, developed one of the first such classifications, and since the broad categories are still in use today, we will look at each of them in turn.

Neuroses are disorders in which the person experiences anxiety in situations which don't usually produce such a reaction. Typically, neurotics tend to cope with their anxiety by avoiding the cause of distress in thought and behaviour. This can lead to difficulties in living, such as developing phobias, or obsessive compulsions. Their behaviour may be maladaptive but it isn't bizarre or violent – often the only person who suffers is the neurotic and sometimes the immediate family. Multiple personality (often wrongly called 'schizophrenia') is usually considered to be a neurotic disorder, brought about by the person being unable to face up to having many different sides to their personality.

Personality disorders form a broad category, which can include people with paranoid personality (who believe that people are conspiring against them); obsessive personalities, with rigid thinking and an extremely close adherence to rules and regulations; schizoid personalities, who avoid reality and prefer to live in a fantasy world; and the psychopathic personality, with a complete disregard for the rights and needs of others. Psychopaths are often likeable and above average intelligence; but they are often unable to maintain personal relationships. There most distinguishing feature is that they seem to lack any kind of conscience in their dealings with others. Not all psychopaths are criminal or under psychiatric care: the worlds of entertainment, politics and big business also tend to have a fair number of psychopaths, many of whom are very successful in such careers.

Functional psychoses are more extreme problems in which the person becomes out of touch with reality, and sometimes fails to realise that there is a problem at all. Such people can end up harming themselves, or, in a very small percentage of cases, harming other people. Kraepelin distinguished two main types: schizophrenia, which involves a split between the person and reality (*not* 'split personality' as is often thought!) in which the person may experience hallucinations or delusions; and manic-depressive psychosis, which involves wild swings of mood from extreme elation to deep depression, with no control over the changes.

Organic psychoses are forms of mental illness which have been caused by some kind of disease or disorder, such as brain infections like syphilis; disorders arising from brain tumours or brain injury; illnesses which result in the degeneration of the nervous system, as happens in Huntingdons Chorea, etc.

Mental retardation was the fifth category outlined by Kraepelin, which was characterised by low IQ scores, low curiosity, and a slow response to any kind of stimulation.

These five categories form a basis for understanding the main types of mental disorder. In terms of mental illness itself, there are two main types: neurosis and psychosis. Gross (1987) compared the two types of illness like this:

Neurosis	Psychosis
Only part of the personality is affected	The whole personality is affected
Contact with reality is maintained	Contact with reality is lost
The neurotic has *insight* into the fact that there is a problem	The psychotic has no insight
Neurotic behaviour is an exaggeration of 'normal' behaviour (a *quantitative* difference)	Psychotic behaviour is different in kind from 'normal' behaviour (a *qualitative* difference)
Often begins in response to a stressful occurrence or situation	There is usually no precipitating cause
The symptoms are related to the person's personality before their illness (the *pre-morbid* personality)	The symptoms are not related to the person's pre-morbid personality
Treated mainly by psychological techniques (e.g. psychotherapy, behaviour modification etc)	Treated mainly by physical methods (e.g. chemotherapy)

DSM-III   Since Kraepelin's time the understanding of mental disorder has become much more sophisticated. There are slight variations in the system which is used in each country, but one of the most well-known diagnostic approaches is the American system known as DSM-III. (DSM is short for the *Diagnostic and Statistical Manual of Mental Disorder*, and III refers to the third edition, published in 1980.)

DSM-III has a more elaborate set of categories than Kraepelin's original five, but also moves away from the idea of simply classifying. Instead, it involves the patient being assessed in terms of five general factors, so that their disorder can be understood much more in terms of an overall picture, instead of just a type of illness. The five general factors are called axes, and are as follows:

Axis 1 Clinical syndromes – the particular problem which the patient is experiencing at the time that they come for treatment.

Axis 2 Personality disorders – the habitual ways that a person interacts with others (e.g. if they tend to be suspicious or paranoid people).

Axis 3 Medical disorders – any relevant conditions which could affect the general problem, such as high blood pressure or heart conditions.

Axis 4 Psychosocial stressors – events or situations in the person's life, which add to the stress that they are under at the time.

Axis 5 Adaptive functioning – how well the person has done over the past year on social relationships, leisure activities, work etc.

Problems of medical classification

Although these categories and factors may seem to be very clear, the actual process of diagnosing what sort of a problem somebody has, or how it ought to be treated, isn't nearly as clear-cut as it appears. Schmidt and Fonda, in 1956, arranged for two psychiatrists to diagnose 426 patients using the official diagnostic categories. They found that the psychiatrists gave widely varying diagnoses, particularly when they were concerned with schizophrenia and mental deficiency. Beck (1962) presented clinical data which was identical except for the name of the patient to psychiatrists, such that each psychiatrist received the same description on two different occasions. Beck found that the psychiatrists often used different diagnostic categories on the two occasions.

Other researchers focused on whether the diagnostic categories themselves presented a coherent picture of a disorder. Wittenborn (1951) found that patients who were classified as sharing the same diagnostic category (e.g. schizophrenic) had widely different symptoms. Bannister, in 1968 showed that it is possible for one person to have a set of symptoms of schizophrenia while another patient has a completely different set. Although they have no symptoms in common, both patients would be labelled schizophrenic.

Another problem of psychiatric classification is the way that individual behaviour is very varied and diverse; and we all experience changes in mood, attitudes etc. to some degree. In the end, the psychiatrist has to rely on clinical intuition to determine whether someone is 'sick' or not. This means that the whole business is open to unconscious value judgements on the part of the psychiatrist, and relies on their perception of what is 'normal' or what isn't.

A study by Rosenhan, in 1973 showed this very clearly. The subjects were eight 'normal' people: a psychology student, three psychologists, a paediatrician, a psychiatrist, a painter and a housewife. Each subject went to the admissions office of a mental hospital and complained of hearing voices. All the other details which they gave of how they felt or their lives were true. All of the subjects were admitted for treatment, and seven of them were diagnosed as schizophrenic. As soon as they were admitted, they stopped reporting any symptoms, and behaved normally. However, their ordinary behaviour was often regarded as evidence of abnormality by the nursing staff: one of them kept a diary, for instance, which was regarded with deep suspicion and recorded in the ward notes as 'the patient engages in writing behaviour'. The fraud was never suspected, and they were eventually (after anything from seven to 52 days) discharged with 'schizophrenia in remission' as the diagnosis.

In a follow-up study, Rosenhan informed the members of a teaching hospital about the above study, telling them that they could expect to encounter several 'false' patients over the next few months. Each member of staff was asked to rate the new patients on their likelihood of being an impostor. Although no pseudo-patients actually presented themselves, 41 out of 193 patients were alleged to be 'normal' by at least one member of staff; 23 by at least one psychiatrist; and 19 by a psychiatrist and one other person. It seems that medical staff don't find it easy to distinguish 'mental illness' from normal behaviour!

Thomas Szasz, in 1960, argued that the whole idea of 'mental illness' is a myth, used by society to cope with people who were individual and didn't conform. He argued that the criteria used to define mental illness are social ones, (like judgements about what is 'normal') rather than medical; and that the diagnostic process should be seen as an example of social labelling. If abnormal behaviour results from physical disorder in the brain, then it is a physical illness, not a 'mental' one. If, on the other hand, there is no such physical cause, then it is better to see the disorder as a 'problem in living' rather than as an illness. Such a view leads to positive attempts to foster autonomy rather than dependency on the medical profession.

In addition, Szasz said, calling abnormal behaviour an 'illness' was misleading, because physical illnesses could be treated, and pronounced cured; whereas the medical profession didn't apply the same standards to psychiatric disorder. If someone has recovered from a 'mental illness', they are not seen as cured, but as the illness being 'in remission' – implying that it could easily occur again. So it wasn't just a label based on social judgements about normality – it was one which stayed with that person throughout life!

Szasz argued that the reason why the idea of mental illness was so popular arose from four sources:

1 The strong influence of the medical professions, which did little to discourage this view of abnormal behaviour, despite being aware that their own understanding and treatments were limited.

2 The fact that seeing it as an illness leads to a reduction of ambiguity. It is difficult for people to regard 'bizarre' behaviour as valid and acceptable, if a little unusual. People tend to prefer to have clear-cut rules of behaviour, and to associate with people who stick to them.

3 Seeing such people as 'ill' makes it easier to remove unusual individuals from society, to psychiatric institutions – 'hospitals' – where they won't embarrass relatives etc.

4 The patients themselves often welcome the label of 'sick', because it reduces their responsibility for their symptoms.

Theories of schizophrenia   The debate between those who accept the medical model and those who don't has often shown itself in terms of arguments concerning the causes of particular disorders. Of these, schizophrenia is perhaps the most controversial of all.

As already stated, schizophrenia involves the person becoming withdrawn from reality, often coming out with bizarre statements and seeming to be unable to grasp what is happening around them. Proponents of the medical model argue that schizophrenia arises from physical changes in the brain, which, they say, causes the peculiar behaviour. Other theorists, notably the psychiatrist R. D. Laing, see it as resulting from environmental factors such as an intolerable home life. We will look at Laing's view more closely later on in this chapter.

One well-known view of schizophrenia is the idea that it is caused by genetic factors, inherited through a family. This view has largely been based on a famous study of identical twins by Kallman (1938), in which he produced some convincing statistics which seemed to show that schizophrenia occurred in both members of pairs of MZ (identical twins) far more frequently than in both members of pairs of DZ (fraternal) twins. Many researchers in this field, e.g. Gottesman and Shields (1982) took these findings at face value, and argued that if schizophrenia was inherited, this showed that biological factors were far more important than environmental or social factors in the development of the disorder.

Kallman's study has been severely criticised, though, for

several reasons. One of these is that his studies involved assessing members of the family not just in terms of whether or not they had been diagnosed as suffering from schizophrenia, but also in terms of whether or not family members had a 'schizoid personality'. And it was Kallman himself who decided this factor, often not even by interviewing the family members concerned (some of whom had died before the study was undertaken!), but simply by applying his 'clinical judgement'. Since Kallman believed firmly in the idea that schizophrenia was inherited, it's easy to see how this could have led to an unconscious bias in how the incomplete and sometimes anecdotal accounts of family members were assessed.

According to Marshall (1984), Kallman also altered the hospital diagnosis of schizophrenia for some of the subjects under study in such a way as to include 'suspected schizophrenia' for this MZ twin sample, although not for the DZ sample. So despite the fact that his figures are generally quoted as showing convincing evidence for the heritability of schizophrenia, the largest and most well-known study in this area can't really be taken as valid evidence at all.

A different approach to schizophrenia concentrated on the biochemical aspects of the disorder. Iversen (1979) found that schizophrenics often show very high levels of the neurotransmitter dopamine (see Chapter 15) in the limbic system. This gave rise to what has become known as the *dopamine hypothesis* of schizophrenia – that schizophrenia happens when levels of dopamine in the brain build up to an unacceptably high level. Also, one of the main drugs used to treat schizophrenia, chlorpromazine, seems to have its effect by blocking dopamine receptor sites in the brain.

However, other researchers are less certain about jumping to the conclusion that dopamine causes schizophrenia. Simply finding that two things *correlate*, or happen together, doesn't necessarily mean that one *causes* the other. Finding that high levels of dopamine go together with the behavioural disorder known as schizophrenia doesn't have to mean that dopamine causes schizophrenia – it could just as easily be the other way round, that schizophrenia causes the dopamine levels to rise. Or both of these could be symptoms produced by some other cause altogether.

As I've already mentioned, the section further on in this chapter on 'existentialist psychology' describes a third view of how schizophrenia occurs – one which emphasises a more environmental or social approach to explaining the disorder.

Alternatives to the medical model

Psychoanalysis

We looked briefly at the psychoanalytic approach to child development in Chapter 7. Freud's work was mainly devoted to understanding neurotic disturbances in adults, and he came to the conclusion that these arose through deeply-buried memories of early traumatic experiences or ideas. Because these were so deeply buried, the conscious mind was prevented from facing up to them, and they could only be identified by a trained psychoanalyst.

Psychoanalysts use a number of different methods to identify these subconscious traumas, including the analysis of slips of the tongue and dreams; and tests of free-association in which the patient hears a word and is asked to respond as quickly as possible with whatever comes to mind. From this, the nature of the deep trauma can supposedly be uncovered, and the therapist and patient can then work to develop new ways for the patient to deal with the problem.

Freud identified a number of defence mechanisms which the person's ego uses to protect itself against the 'inner threats' coming from the subconscious. Many modern psychologists consider these to be the most valuable part of Freud's work. These are some of those mechanisms.

Projection involves the person seeing their inner feelings as being held by someone else, because they couldn't admit to feeling it themselves. So, for instance, someone who was very possessive towards their partner might see it as being their partner being possessive of them instead. During psychoanalysis, the analyst deliberately remains as 'colourless' and anonymous as possible, so that the client can project deeply-buried ideas or emotions on to the therapist.

Repression is when particularly emotional memories or desires become so deeply buried that the person is unable to recall them at all. So, for instance, someone may have very deep feelings towards someone else, but be completely unaware of these feelings, because they would find it very threatening to be aware that this was how they felt.

Reaction-formation occurs when repression of a desire or wish has gone so deep that it turns into its opposite. So, for instance, someone who has deeply-buried homosexual feelings which they don't feel able to face up to may develop a reaction-formation, and become fanatically anti-homosexual instead.

People with reaction-formations of this kind tend to become very worked-up and emotional about the subject.

Rationalisation is the process by which the person finds a series of reasons to justify a more basic desire, so that what is really an emotional choice or reaction is presented as if it were the outcome of logic and reasoning.

Denial is a defence mechanism which is often found in children, and which simply involves denying that a threatening event has occurred at all. The child simply refuses to acknowledge its existence.

Regression involves moving backwards in mental time, to an earlier form of coping behaviour. Freud saw crying in frustration or distress as being a regression to infantile behaviour when other coping strategies had failed.

Although many modern psychologists disagree with many of Freud's ideas, the defence mechanisms which he identified have shown themselves to be useful in understanding some of the problems facing people which can at times lead to neurotic disorders.

Behaviour therapy   Some of the techniques used in behaviour therapy, or behaviour modification, were outlined in Chapter 18. As a general approach, behaviour therapy ignores any underlying causes of disturbed behaviour, and concentrates purely on the symptoms. It sees disturbed behaviour as being learned responses to the environment, and so, working on the principle that what is learned can be unlearned, it concentrates on teaching the person more appropriate behaviours so that they don't have the problems.

Behaviour therapy really only became popular in the 1950s, although Watson's famous study with Little Albert (see Chapter 18) took place much earlier. In 1950, Dollard and Miller showed how the main psychoanalytic principles which were in common use at the time could be re-interpreted in terms of learning theory – with the analysis being seen as the process by which the patient learned to make new responses to disturbing stimuli. B. F. Skinner's book *Science and Human Behaviour*, published in 1953, supported and developed Dollard and Millar's book; and clinical psychologists started to apply behaviour modification techniques to psychiatric patients with considerable success.

In general, the term 'behaviour therapy' is often used to refer to techniques based on classical conditioning, while 'behaviour modification' refers to techniques based on operant conditioning. They are commonly used nowadays to help people with neurotic disorders; although they are often not considered suitable for the more severe psychotic cases.

Humanistic Psychotherapy

The humanistic approach to abnormal behaviour emphasises the potential for personal growth and development which every human being has. One of the main proponents of this is Carl Rogers, who developed a theory that every human being has two basic psychological needs, which must be satisfied if that person is not to suffer psychological damage and become mentally disturbed. These two needs are:

1 The need for *self-actualisation* – in other words, the need to develop one's personal interest, skills, and abilities to the full.

2 The *need for positive regard* from other people – approval, love or respect from others.

As long as these two needs can both be satisfied to some extent, the individual doesn't face problems. Healthy personality development occurs through relationships which offer the person 'unconditional' positive regard – positive regard which they can feel sure of, regardless of the lifestyle or interests which they take up. This frees the person to explore their potential without risking the loss of their positive relationship through disapproval.

Rogers argued that his neurotic clients had had the kind of parents who always made their love conditional upon 'good behaviour'. This conveyed the message that the child wasn't really loved, and the parents would really have liked some ideal child who never misbehaved. So the child grew up striving for approval from others, and unable to develop their potential, as it might mean risking disapproval from others. Children like this also developed an unrealistically high *ideal self-concept* – the ideal which they felt they should try to live up to – which meant that they had a continuous sense of feeling 'bad' or inadequate. This formed the basis for their neurosis.

Rogers saw the role of the therapist as being to provide a relationship of unconditional positive regard, which would free the person to explore their own life-options and satisfy their need for self-actualisation. Since this was entirely centred on the client's own ideas, it became known as 'client-centred therapy'. The idea was that clients would come to know what was best for them, if they were in a relationship where they didn't have to worry about getting the therapist's approval.

This meant that the therapist would have to be an empathic

and genuine person, because it isn't possible to fake
unconditional liking for someone very convincingly. They also
need to be *non-directive*, and not tell the person what they
ought to be doing, because otherwise the client would be likely
to go along with the therapist's ideas to retain approval, instead
of developing their own plans. Rogers later argued that such
unconditional positive regard could be provided by other
people, in *encounter groups*. By meeting others face to face,
without defences, a person could feel free to explore their
potential needs in a safe environment.

A study by Butler and Haigh, in 1954, looked at how effective
client-centred therapy was. They took two groups of people
who had applied for therapy, and gave each person a test which
allowed them to measure how closely their self-image fitted
with their ideal self-image. The correlation which they obtained
(see Chapter 9) was very low indeed, at $-.01$. Another group,
of 'normal' people were tested, and their correlation between
self and ideal-self averaged out at $+.58$.

The first group of subjects received client-centred therapy
for six weeks, but the second group was asked to wait until a
therapist was available for them. When the three groups were
reassessed after six weeks, Butler and Haigh found that
although the second and third groups had stayed the same, the
first group's average correlation had risen to $+.31$, which was
quite a dramatic change. These people also said that they felt
better in themselves, and their neurotic symptoms were greatly
diminished. They were also much more practical in what they
expected of themselves.

Existentialist
Psychology
The existentialist approach to understanding abnormal
behaviour was mainly put forward by R. D. Laing, who argued
that we need to understand human beings in terms of their
everyday existence and the choices which this involves. Some
people, he argued, find themselves in situations where a retreat
from reality is in fact the only practical choice of behaviour
that they can make; and if a serious attempt is made to
understand their life, then their 'illness' makes more sense
and can be treated more appropriately.

Existentialism places a strong emphasis on the individual's
free will, and their right to choose their own alternatives or
patterns of life. Although it may be subconscious, and
disturbing for the patient, abnormal behaviour is seen as a
choice which the patient has made – a retreat into illness as a
way of escaping from an intolerable situation. The aim of
therapy is to encourage the individual to learn to feel secure
with the choices that they have made, and to act in ways that
are in tune with their 'inner' self, so that they can be less of a

victim of circumstances and more in control of their lives. Laing saw the psychiatric hospital as being the worst possible place for doing that, as patients have so little autonomy or control, and he advocated close, therapeutic communities as a more practical alternative. The most famous one of these is one which he founded himself, known as Kingsley Hall.

Laing's ideas had originated from work by Bateson (1956), who showed that some families seemed to be 'schizophrenogenic' – in other words, they seemed to produce schizophrenia in their family members, by placing them under continuous psychological pressure. Bateson identified the 'double-bind' – the situation where all courses of action were deemed wrong, and criticised or punished. Those family members who became schizophrenic, Bateson showed, tended to experience double-binds as a normal part of the family life. So schizophrenia was seen as being a comprehensible reaction to an intolerable life situation, understandable in its own context.

Family therapy   Partly as a result of Laing's work, a new approach to therapy emerged which sees the person in the context of their family. The idea behind family therapy is that often, the member of the family who is being 'difficult' or 'disturbed' is simply being used as a scapegoat for the tensions and problems of all the family members. By treating one person as 'ill' in this way, they don't need to face up to or admit their own feelings of anger, hostility or aggression towards other family members.

Family therapists see each family as a working system, with the behaviour of each member of the family affecting everyone else. They see families as being capable of adjusting to new circumstances, and sorting out their own problems once they can recognise what these are. This means that much of the work of a family therapist is concerned with teaching family members how to recognise unspoken messages and signals from each other, and how to provide feedback for one another so that future misunderstandings can be avoided or dealt with in a less tense manner.

    Family therapy has been criticised by some psychologists as making too many assumptions about what a 'normal' family is. Critics argue that by ignoring individual or class differences, family therapists try to fit everyone into the same pattern. But most modern family therapists are aware of this as a difficulty, and wouldn't attempt to enforce rigid views of how people should act on their clients.

There are many other areas covered by abnormal psychology, which we don't have space to go into here. In the next chapter, we'll be looking at how social influences can affect how we behave, where, as with abnormal psychology, we find the debate about the most important factors are physical or social ones.

Summary   1 It is difficult to define what we mean by 'abnormal', because individual behaviour varies so widely.

2 The medical model sees abnormal behaviour as resulting from physiological disturbance in the brain, as if the person were 'mentally ill'.

3 Mental disorders have been classified into five kinds: neuroses, personality disorders, functional psychoses, organic psychoses, and mental retardation.

4 DSM-III represents a popular modern approach to diagnosing mental illness. It assesses patients in terms of clinical syndromes, personality disorders, medical disorders, psychosocial stressors, and adaptive functioning.

5 Psychiatric classification has been criticised as being too vague, and as unable to distinguish between normal and abnormal behaviour.

6 Theories of schizophrenia range from those which ascribe it to genetic or neurochemical causes, to those which see it as arising from family interactions.

7 Some alternatives to the medical model include psychoanalysis, behaviour therapy, humanistic psychology, existentialist psychology, and family therapy.

Chapter 20 **Social pressure**

In the last chapter, I talked of the way that other people's reactions and responses can affect our mental health. It seems that the quotation 'no man is an island' is true – all of us are affected to some degree by what others do, or by how they react to what we do. Social pressure is something that is quite important to us as human beings, and is with us all the time, without our even noticing it particularly.

When I say 'social pressure', it sounds as if I am talking about being *forced* to do something, perhaps against your will. But social pressure can be much more gentle and invisible than that. We all like to be accepted by other people – even if we don't go out of our way to seek such acceptance – and often quite unconsciously we will try to go along with things that they say.

Conformity

Sherif's study

An experiment by Sherif, in 1935, showed how this sort of thing can happen, how people tend to *conform* to other people's ideas, when they know what those ideas are. Sherif used a phenomenon known as the 'autokinetic effect'. If you sit in a completely dark room – so dark that you can't see anything at all – and are then shown a pin-point of light, that pin-point of light will appear to move about, even though it's completely still. That's the autokinetic effect. Sherif asked people to estimate how much the point of light moved in inches. The answers that they gave were very different, ranging from one to seven inches. Each person, though, tended to make the same kind of judgement whenever they were tested: if someone estimated four inches in one test, in the next test their answer would also be about four inches. And if a subject had estimated the movement as seven inches, then their judgement would also be about seven inches. So they were quite *consistent* in their judgements.

These were the results that Sherif got when people were tested on their own. When they sat in the room with other people, however, the results were completely different. Instead of producing a wide variety of judgements, they now tended to go along with each other – even though they hadn't been told to agree at all. Where previously their judgements had ranged from one to seven inches, now they all estimated the movement to be around four to five inches.

Sherif said that this showed that people will always tend to conform. Rather than make an independent judgement, they will come to a 'group agreement' about things, and go by that.

There are problems with this conclusion, though. The first is that Sherif had told his subjects that he was going to move the light. Because of this, the subjects thought that they were trying to solve a problem that had a *right answer*, and so they were concerned to find that answer. If they weren't sure of the effect – don't forget, in a dark room you haven't got a background to measure it up against – then they might easily just choose the middle judgement as the most likely, or they might agree with the person who sounded most definite. Although that would be conformity – because they all agreed on a conclusion – it would only show that when people are unsure, they give weight to other people's views. It wouldn't show that people tended to conform to others in any other situation.

Following these criticisms, two other experiments were conducted along the same lines, but with a more definite kind of measure. Since the autokinetic effect is an illusion anyway, it is not possible to measure it at all, or to say that someone is right and someone else is wrong. So what was needed was an experiment where there was clearly a right answer and a wrong answer; this would test whether the subject would conform with the group then.

Asch's study of conformity The first experiment was set by S. Asch, in 1951. He used a simple test, where subjects were shown a line, and asked which of three lines on a test card it matched. The lines were clearly different in length, and when tested on their own, none of

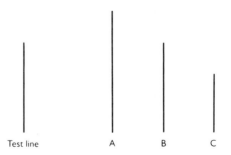

Test line   A   B   C

Fig. 20.1 The lines used in Asch's study

Asch's subjects had the least difficulty in giving the right answers.

For the group experiment, Asch used six 'stooges', who were primed beforehand to give certain answers. The subject and the six stooges sat around a table, so arranged that the 'real' subject was sixth to speak. So, before the 'real' subject gave his judgement on whether the line was the same as line A, B, or C on the sample card, he had already heard five of the others give their judgements. (Incidentally, the subject had been told that he was taking part in an experiment in perception.) For the first couple of trials (each trial consisted of showing a line, and asking for the judgement on it), the stooges gave the right answer. I shall quote from Asch's paper for what happened next:

> on the third trial, there is an unexpected disturbance. One person near the end of the group disagrees with all the others in his selection of the matching line. He looks surprised, indeed incredulous, about the disagreement. On the following trial he disagrees again, while the others remain unanimous in their choice. The dissenter becomes more and more worried and hesitant as the disagreement continues in succeeding trials . . .

Every now and then, the stooges would give the right answer, so that the subject wouldn't suspect that they were in collusion, but sometimes they would all give the same wrong answer in a quite definite manner.

The experimental set-up left people with two choices: they could go along with the majority verdict – denying the evidence of their own eyes – or they could keep on with their own independent judgements – going against everyone else. Asch found that thirty-two per cent of his subjects conformed with the majority opinion all the time – against the evidence of their senses. Another forty-two per cent conformed with the group *some* of the time, but also sometimes made their own judgements as well. Since the test was so easy, and the right answer so clear, this result was quite surprising, but does show the power of group pressure quite convincingly.

Asch performed several variations of his experiment, trying to find out which things were important in getting someone to conform to other views. He found out that the number of people was important: if a subject was only confronted with one other person, who gave a different view, then the subject would tend to keep his own judgement. If there were *two* others, then the subjects started to accept the wrong answer on fourteen per cent of the trials. And if there were three or

more, the results were the same as the ones given above –
seventy-four per cent conformed at least sometimes.
Interestingly, above three it didn't make a great deal of
difference how many there were in the group – the same effect
was achieved.

What *did* make a difference, though, was whether the stooges
were unanimous or not. If just *one* person disagreed with the
majority, then the power of the majority verdict was reduced
to a quarter. So instead of seventy-four per cent the
compliance went down to eighteen per cent – it seems that just
one person was enough, even if they didn't actually agree with
the subject! When Asch set things up so that one person agreed
with the subject for some of the trials, but then switched to
going along with the majority, the subject resisted the group
pressure while the 'confederate' was with him, but then, when
'on his own', reached the same levels of compliance as if he
had never had an ally.

Although Asch's findings were repeated quite often in the years
after they were made, a more recent study, by Perrin and
Spencer in 1980, suggested that this high level of conformity
might be a 'child of its time'. They replicated the original
experiments which Asch had performed, with a wide number
of undergraduate students. (Asch's original subjects had been
students.) Because Asch's experiment was so well known, they
took care to choose their subjects from disciplines like
chemistry, or engineering, where they weren't likely to have
heard of it. Also, after the experiment, they asked the students
if they had heard of his experiment before, and left out those
who had from their results.
    When they had completed their study, they found that the
students just hadn't conformed in the same way as Asch's
students. In fact, a subject conformed to the majority verdict
on only one trial out of 396. Although their subjects had been
just as agitated by the different judgements of the stooges as
the previous ones had, they nonetheless stuck to their own
judgements and didn't go along with the majority.
    Asch (and Perrin and Spencer) attributed this finding to a
change in social expectations in the student populations over
the thirty years. Students were no longer as uncritical towards
their tutors and their teaching as they had been, and the social
pressure on students to conform was less. Nowadays, people
may be expected to rely on their own judgements quite a lot
more than they were in 1951. Asch had always explained his
findings in terms of the pressures that are around in society,
so he was quite prepared to accept that if society changes, then
the levels of conformity in a study like this would change too.

However, Doms and Avermaet (1981) reported that, unlike Perrin and Spencer, they did find that Asch's study still works today. One thing that they pointed out was that engineering students and students from other scientific disciplines, may be particularly inclined to view accurate measurement as important, and so they may give the correct judgements because of this, although wishing to conform with the others.

Crutchfield's study   An experiment similar to Asch's was performed by R. Crutchfield in 1954. He set up a situation where subjects had to choose the right answer from a set of very obvious and easy problems. Unlike Asch, though, he didn't sit his subjects in the same room as the stooges. Instead, they sat in cubicles on their own, but with an array of lights which supposedly showed what other people had answered. (The lights were 'fixed', of course.) It was possible, Crutchfield thought, that Asch's results had been caused by the *physical presence* of the other people. With his experiment, there wasn't the same kind of personal contact, only a more abstract knowledge of what other people had said, shown through the light-display. (Each subject was told that he was the last to answer, so he 'knew' what everyone else had said.)

Fig. 20.2 **Crutchfield's shapes.** *Which has the largest surface area?*

Crutchfield found a slightly lower level of conformity in his experiment than Asch had found – supporting the hypothesis that it was influenced by other people's physical presence. But, given the simple nature of the problems, the level he found was still considerable, at forty-six per cent. None of the subjects had any difficulty with the problem when asked to do it on their own, afterwards.

Crutchfield also found the same sort of effect when opinions were being expressed. His subjects were all military men, and when asked privately, they all said that they thought they would make good leaders; but when asked in the experimental situation whether they agreed with the statement 'I doubt whether I would make a good leader', thirty-seven per cent of them agreed!

Another finding of Crutchfield's was that, if the problem was made more difficult, conformity increased. This would support what we were saying about Sherif's experiment: when people are unsure of the answers, they are more likely to accept other people's opinions than when they know what the answer is.

However, when we're looking at these experiments, it's important to make a distinction between *compliance* – going along with the others; and *internalisation* – actually agreeing with the others. When Asch talked to his subjects after the experiment, many of them were very concerned to explain *why* they had gone along with the majority (or why they hadn't!). Most of them said that they 'hadn't wanted to spoil the results of the perception experiment', and so had gone along with the others. Only a few of them had reached the conclusion that they were wrong and the others were right. These were the ones who would be said to have internalised the judgement: they had accepted it as being true. Most of the subjects, though, only complied, and didn't internalise the judgements; they suspected that the others were suffering from an optical illusion, or were 'sheep' following the first one.

It's important for us to be clear about this difference, because it would be a mistake to think that people who go along with the majority always do so because they agree with it. In our society, as in most others, we tend to avoid quarrelling, and disagreements; where a decision doesn't seem to be very important, we often don't think it's worth it to disagree with someone else. So although we don't internalise the agreement, we still don't openly disagree with it – that is, we *comply* with it.

Obedience The real question, though, is how far will we go in this compliance? As I said before, we may easily go along with others when something isn't really important, for the sake of avoiding 'trouble' or argument. But what about when something *is* important? Will we go along with others then? An experiment by S. Milgram, in 1963, was set up to investigate this question. First of all, he asked many people about what they thought would happen if someone, as part of a psychological experiment, was asked to give another person a set of increasingly strong electrical shocks. Would they do it, or wouldn't they? If they did, what level of shock would they go up to? All the people who were asked said similar things; the subjects wouldn't go beyond quite a low shock level; they would refuse to give any more than a low level of shock. All were agreed that less than three per cent of subjects would go to the most extreme shock level – people would stop the experiment well before that.

Milgram then proceeded with the experiment. He advertised for subjects in a local paper, saying that they would be paid to take part in an experiment. When they arrived at the laboratory, they were told that, simply by turning up, they had earned the money, no matter what happened now. (This was to make sure that subjects weren't just doing it for the money.) They were then introduced to another person, and told that they would both take part in a learning experiment – one would be teacher, and the other learner. They drew names from a hat to see who would be which, but in fact the lots were rigged. Both slips of paper said 'teacher', but the other man (who was an actor) said his said 'learner', and was treated accordingly. In this way, the subjects didn't suspect that the experiment wasn't just a simple learning one.

The learner, with the subject looking on, was taken into the next room, and strapped into a chair. Electrodes were attached to his wrists, and the subject was told that they were connected to a shock generator in the next room. (In fact, they were dummies.) The teacher was then put in front of the shock generator, which had a long row of switches, each of which was labelled for a different level of shock. The labels went up by 15 volts each time, until they reached 450 volts. They were also labelled: 'slight shock; moderate shock; strong shock; very strong shock; intense shock; extreme intensity shock; danger; severe shock'; and finally just 'XXX'. So the subjects were well informed about the nature of the 'shock' that they were giving to the learner.

Fig. 20.3 Milgram's study of obedience

The learning task that they were supposed to be doing was a word-pair one. The teacher would read out a word, and then four possible words which might be paired with it. The learner pressed a button for the answer he chose (A, B, C, or D), which lit up a panel on the teacher's console. If the answer was wrong, the teacher had to give an electric shock – and it had to be increased one step (15 volts) each time. In fact, the wrong answers were all prearranged, as were the learner's reaction to the shock. When the shock level reached 300 volts, the learner started to bang on the wall – he had made some vocal complaints before then – but after that he didn't do anything at all. The subjects were told, by the experimenter, to treat no answer at all as if it were a wrong answer; that is, to carry on shocking the subject even though they didn't get a reply to the question, and, of course, increasing the voltage each time.

Milgram's results surprised everyone: instead of the less-than-three per cent who had been predicted to go as far as 450 volts, 62.5% did! And *all* the subjects who took part in the experiments went as far as 300 volts – the point at which the learner banged on the wall. (This was immediately before the 'extreme intensity shock' level.) Despite the fact that our society gives such strong objections to administering violence to others, *most* of Milgram's subjects were prepared to do that to an extreme level. And all of them would do that to one degree or another.

Milgram puts his findings in the context of the concentration camps of the Second World War. He points out that most of the atrocities that were carried out, were done by ordinary people following orders. It was the habit of *obedience*, even to orders going against conscience, which made the atrocities possible. Even if the orders were given by insane people, they were carried out by soldiers and camp guards, and, before people were taken to the camps, by ordinary German people, who would throw stones at Jewish people in the streets, and damage their houses. And it was the same question – of whether people would obey an instruction even when it went against their own conscience – that Milgram was investigating in this set of experiments.

Factors influencing obedience

It must not be thought that Milgram's subjects were all 'latent sadists' – they were not. Throughout the experiment people objected to what they were being asked to do, arguing with the experimenter, and expressing worry about what the learner was experiencing. But very few of them actually got out of the chair, and refused to do any more. When the experimenter said things like: 'The experiment requires that you continue', or 'You have no other choice – you must go on', they went on with the experiment, even though reluctantly. But many were highly disturbed by what they were doing, and, even when they found out that the learner was well and unhurt, they were shocked at their own behaviour: 'I'd never have thought I could do that!'

There were in fact, several things built in to the experiment that made it very difficult for them to stop. One of those was the 'prods' used by the experimenter: 'It is absolutely essential that you continue', and so on. If the subjects wanted to know about responsibility, the experimenter would claim responsibility for the experiment.

Another factor was that the amount of shock they had to give was only increased by a little bit each time. This, actually, made it difficult for the subjects to choose a cut-off point – 315 volts isn't *very* different from 300 volts, and they'd already given 300 volts! So, on each occasion, it was only a small change from the previous time.

The fact that they had drawn lots to see who would be teacher and who learner was another thing that made it more difficult for the subjects to object. As far as they were concerned, it could just as easily have been *them* receiving the shocks, and not giving them.

The learner being in a different room also made a difference. When Milgram repeated the experiment with the learner in the same room as the subject, compliance dropped to forty per cent, which is nonetheless still quite high.

Another possible reason why people were so compliant, Milgram thought, might be because he conducted the experiment at Yale University, where people would expect to find scientists who (a) knew what they were doing; and (b) were responsible. Because of this, he conducted another set of the same experiments, in a seedy set of offices in the centre of the city. Compliance dropped slightly – to fifty per cent – but that is still high, when you think of what it implies about ordinary people.

When Milgram set up a slightly different version of the experiment, where subjects didn't actually press the button themselves, to give the learner the shock, but instead pressed a switch which enabled someone else to give the shock, compliance with the experimenter's request went right up to more than ninety per cent. It seems that, since they didn't actually administer the shock themselves, they didn't feel the responsibility as much either, even though they were the people who made the shock possible.

It is clear from these experiments that, when asked to do so, people will do things that go strongly against their consciences, even though they object at the time. These results weren't just found in America, either. Even in completely different countries, like Norway, the same results were found. So we are talking about a pretty powerful social pressure, which people would go along with, even though they disagreed, and even though they could always have walked out of the experiment.

In looking for things that would affect the results, Milgram did find one that had quite a strong influence. If the experimenter wasn't actually in the room when the instructions were given – if he gave the orders by telephone instead – the subject's level of compliance dropped right down to almost zero. Instead of pressing the button, they would only pretend to, or would press the button for a much lower level of shock than the one they were supposed to give. So the physical presence of someone in authority made all the difference.

Milgram linked this to our reactions to people in authority, in general. We do tend to obey people who are in authority – teachers, policemen, and so on – indeed, we are trained to do so from when we are quite young. And we also, very often, have the belief that the person in authority knows what they are doing; has been trained for a special job, and often wears a uniform to symbolise their position. Although Milgram's experimenter didn't have any *real* authority – the subjects could have 'disobeyed' at any time, without any bad consequences at all – he did have a calm and detached manner, a uniform (a grey lab. coat), and – perhaps most important of all – seemed to know what was going on, and to be aware of possible consequences. All these things served to make him quite a convincing figure of authority, who commanded reluctant obedience from the subjects.

Support for this theory comes from the fact that the subjects were told, if they asked, that the experimenter claimed all responsibility for what was going on. Once they had had that reassurance, many of the subjects were visibly relieved. Even though they continued to argue, they didn't do so as strongly as they had before. The experimenter was the 'expert', and so they were able to feel less personally responsible for their actions.

Social roles
In the last chapter, I talked about 'roles' in terms of the way that the roles that an individual plays in life become a part of that individual's self-concept, and influence the person's development. Milgram's experiments show us an entirely different side to social roles – the way in which a role can influence the behaviour of other people – to an alarming degree.

Throughout Milgram's experiments, the experimenter played his part in a very impersonal kind of way. In order that it wouldn't be his personality which caused the effects, everything he said was written down beforehand, and he always used a neutral tone of voice. In this way, Milgram made sure that it wasn't just that the experimenter was an unusually friendly, or persuasive kind of person, as the real person didn't show through at all. Milgram's subjects reacted to the role that the experimenter had, and not to the man himself.

We can see from that, that the position of the experimenter – wearing a lab. coat, and directing (or appearing to direct the experiment – was enough to generate, or to create, *expectations* about that person. In other words, the role the experimenter played led the others in the experiment to decide things about him; for instance that he 'knew what he was doing', or that he was 'responsible and intelligent'. And because they had that set of expectations, the subjects in the experiment went on to do what he asked them.

Any social role which we play in life will tend to generate a similar set of expectations. Not the same expectations for each role – but different people playing the same role will be expected to have things in common with each other. Any doctor, for instance, will be expected to be relatively pleasant, but not too friendly, to dress respectably, and so on. No doctor would be expected to be found busking with a guitar on a street corner. Similarly, we wouldn't expect to go into the doctor's surgery, and find him or her in tears, saying 'I can't stand it any more!' Although we would probably find it quite difficult to list them, we do have very clear ideas about how someone in a certain role should behave, even though we may only become aware of them when those rules are broken.

In 1973, Haney, Banks and Zimbardo demonstrated just how strong our ideas about roles and role behaviour are. By drawing lots (genuine ones this time) from a pool of subjects, he sorted them into two groups. They were to be an imitation of prisoners and guards in a mock jail: one group was to act the part of guards, while the others acted the part of prisoners. The subjects weren't told how to behave, simply the parts they were to play, prisoner or guard. How they acted these roles was up to them.

After five days, Zimbardo had to stop the experiment. The guards were so clear in their ideas of how prison guards behaved, and so strict with the prisoners, that they wouldn't allow them any rights at all, and often treated them in a humiliating fashion. Although they never used physical violence, they would do things like lining them up and making them count in sequence, with each prisoner saying a number in turn, and not letting them stop until they had said the numbers perfectly in time. When one of the prisoners went on hunger-strike, they locked him in a small closet. The other prisoners were told that they could get him out simply by each of them giving up a blanket (it wasn't cold at all), but by then they were so concerned with their own 'survival' that they thought of the hunger-striker as a 'trouble-maker' and wouldn't help him!

The people who were playing the guards had a very clear idea of just what the role of guard involved. (In fact, it was much stricter than most real prison guards.) By acting that role, they showed how they understood it – and how powerful their expectations were. Similarly once the prisoners had realised that the guards were acting the role out fully, they also adopted the kind of behaviour which they considered appropriate to their role as prisoners. They were anxious not to antagonise the guards – that's why they called the other one a 'trouble-maker' – and wanted just to 'get by' as well as they could. The guards hadn't just got a clear idea of their own role *themselves* but they had also generated *expectations* about themselves from the prisoners.

In part, it could easily have been the prisoners' expectations which helped the experiment to become as extreme as it did. By acting in appeasing ways, they would have strengthened the guards' ideas of their own power, and so caused their behaviour to become more bullying. Of course, it wasn't just that – the guards were well able to become bullying anyway – but the mixture of their own understanding of the role, and the prisoners' expectations, would have been a circular trap, from which they wouldn't have been able to get out. (Several of the guards said afterwards that they had hated what they were doing.) As I said before, roles don't just influence our own behaviour, but they also cause others to have expectations about what we are likely to do.

The self-fulfilling
prophecy

These expectations are very often powerful in influencing our behaviour in all sorts of ways. Sometimes we can get into a kind of circle, where people expect something of us, we try to live up to it, and that strengthens what they expect. For example: supposing a woman has friends who think that she is really witty, and often makes amusing remarks. Because that is their expectation of her, they expect her to make a witty remark when any occasion arises. Because she knows that that is what they expect, she tries hard to think of one, and comes out with a fairly witty remark. But, since she has made another one, her friends' belief that she really is witty is strengthened. They now have 'proof' that they were right. So next time, they'll expect her to say something witty again, and the whole process will repeat itself. But notice that the circle is being kept up as much by the friends' expectations, as by the individual's behaviour. And as the reputation is strengthened, the cycle is reinforced – even if she says something which isn't really funny, the friends will make allowances, and still expect her to be amusing the next time. In fact, the whole cycle *might* have even started off accidentally. She might just have said something – once – which her friends found funny, and the whole thing could go on from there.

When we get a cycle like this one, we call it a *self-fulfilling prophecy*. In this case, the friends have made a prophecy – that X is witty – and by their behaviour to X they have made that prophecy come true.

In 1966, R. Rosenthal performed an experiment which demonstrated just how powerful an influence expectations can have. He used laboratory rats, which had been carefully matched for their abilities, at least in things like running through mazes. The rats were allocated to students, who were told to teach their rats (each student had five rats) to run a particular maze – that is, to take the quickest route through a series of turns and junctions, to reach the goal-box at the end of the maze (where there was food for the rats).

Half the students were told that their rats had been specially bred to be good at running mazes, that they were the result of careful selection and parentage. The other half were told that their rats could be expected, for genetic reasons, to be very poor at maze-learning. When the students proceeded to teach their rats to run through the maze, the self-fulfilling prophecy came true – the rats that were supposed to be 'maze-bright' actually did better than the rats who were supposed to be 'maze-dull'. Some of the 'maze-dull' rats wouldn't even budge from the starting point of the maze. And yet they had all been similar to start with.

On examining these results, Rosenthal found that the students who expected their rats to be bright actually treated them differently to the students whose rats were supposed to be dull. They handled them more, and treated them more gently, and were far more enthusiastic about the whole experiment. The students with the dull rats hadn't liked their rats at all, while those with the bright rats had liked theirs. The difference in handling had made a dramatic difference in the way that the rats performed.

In 1968, Rosenthal and Jacobson performed an experiment to see if that same self-fulfilling prophecy would also work in schools. They used a fairly average school in a middle-sized American city, and told teachers there that they were testing the validity of a new test designed to predict intellectual gain in children. In fact, they used a fairly standard intelligence test. By random means, they chose some children from the school who were to be called 'spurters'; in fact these children were no different from their fellows in class, in terms of their work or test results. The teachers were told – as if in casual conversation – that these were children who could be expected to show unusual intellectual gains in the next year. Apart from the teachers being told this, no other experimental treatment was used: the children weren't singled out in front of their classmates, or even spoken to by the experimenters. So the control group of the experiment was the other children in the class; the teachers hadn't been told anything about them at all.

By the end of the year, the 'spurters' had shown considerable changes in their academic work. Their results on schoolwork tests were compared with the results from the year before, and a very strong change showed that by comparison with the other children in their class, they actually had improved. On looking for explanations for this result, Rosenthal and Jacobson found that it *wasn't* just that teachers *talked* to these students more, as they expected, but that their whole attitude – tones of voice, touch, attention – was the thing that seemed to have made a difference to the children. This is quite an important finding, as we tend to be unconscious of these kind of signals; it would be much harder for a teacher to control that kind of influence, than to control something like the length of time spent talking to the children.

Rosenthal and Jacobson found that, in the year of the experiment, it was younger children who showed the most gains; but in the follow-up year, which was the year after that, the older children showed more lasting effects than younger ones did. They thought that this might be because the younger children had had changes of teachers, and were more dependent on their teachers' reactions, while the older ones, although initially not so easily influenced, had been able to keep up the improved performance once they had absorbed it into their self-concept. So after a while, they didn't *need* the teachers' encouragement, while the younger ones did.

This experiment has quite strong implications for schools. For instance, if a child comes from a background in a slum area, teachers may well not expect it to do particularly well at school, and may *communicate* that expectation to the child. So a self-fulfilling prophecy would be set up. The teachers would expect the child to be dull at lessons, so they wouldn't give encouragement and help as much as they would to a child they thought more capable, and so the child would fall behind the others. Once it had fallen behind the others, this would be 'proof' that it really *was* dull – at least, it would be proof to the teachers – and so their expectations and treatment of the child as dull would continue. And, because this happens on an unconscious level, it's a particularly difficult circle to break – you can't stop yourself doing something if you don't know that you *are* doing it.

Personal inferences of self

Often, we come to *infer* traits in ourselves, from our behaviour. The sentence: 'This is my second sandwich – I must have been hungrier than I thought' is the sort of thing I mean. Although we receive messages from our bodies, like hunger, we may still accept that we might not have had the full picture, and our actual behaviour serves to put us right! But this sort of thing can also happen with other non-physical traits.

An experiment with adults, by Freedman and Fraser, investigated this kind of thing. They asked suburban housewives to sign a petition concerned with promoting safe driving. Since this was a relatively trivial request, many of the housewives agreed to sign it. Freedman and Fraser thought that, then, they would *infer* that they were the kind of people who agreed to this kind of request, or supported this kind of cause. Because of this inference, these housewives would be more likely to agree to a further request than ones who hadn't been asked to sign the petition. Accordingly, two weeks later, a second person went round and asked them to display a large, ugly sign on their lawns: 'Keep California Beautiful'. About half of the women who had signed the petition agreed to the request, compared with only seventeen per cent of the women who were only asked to display the sign but hadn't been asked to sign the petition. So, Freedman and Fraser said, the housewives had drawn conclusions about *themselves*, from their own behaviour. (The ones who refused to sign the petition would probably have inferred that they weren't that kind of person, but Freedman and Fraser didn't look into that.) Snynder and Cunningham did, though, in 1975, and got just those results. This kind of 'foot-in-the-door' technique is one of the ways that people can influence others, without the person being influenced realising it.

Factors influencing the self-concept

M. Argyle described, in 1969, four main factors that affect the way an individual's self-concept develops, and is maintained in day-to-day living. These four factors are: other people's reactions; comparisons which we make with other people; the roles we play in life; and the identifications which we make. We will look at each of these four factors in turn.

Other people's reactions

We tend to notice the way that other people react, and to respond. In the chapter on non-verbal communication, we saw how people can react in many different ways – consciously and unconsciously; and how we interpret these signals as a kind of message which tells us something about the way we are affecting that person. For example: if we are talking to someone, and they are looking out of the window and appearing thoroughly bored while we are doing so, then we receive and interpret the message that we are being dull, and boring – or at least, that they aren't interested in what we are saying. If people reacted that way *every* time we started to talk, then we would tend to form an image of ourselves as 'a boring person'. Similarly, if the people we were with sat forward and looked interested each time we opened our mouths, then we'd probably come to think of ourselves as 'interesting people'. Other people's reactions are very important in the process of developing the self-concept, through a form of operant conditioning. If the people we are with obviously approve of something we do – like making jokes – then we come to do it more and more, and we develop, at the same time, an image of ourselves as a 'joker'.

However, it isn't just anyone's reaction which has that effect. It doesn't really make a great deal of difference to us what the stranger in the bus-queue thinks of us – whether we're kind, or nasty. It is our *significant others* who will make most difference to us in the long run. If we're learning to play tennis, for instance, it doesn't really matter to us that a friend who can't play thinks we're doing all right. It's the opinion of the person teaching us that matters – only people who, we feel, are expert in this area will count as 'significant others'. But their reactions are likely to make a lot of difference to us, and will affect whether we develop an image of ourself as 'a good tennis player' or not.

Comparisons with other people

We are constantly comparing ourselves with other people. If we think of ourselves as tall, we mean by comparison with other people around us; if we think we are clever, we really mean more clever than the other people we have met. We don't really have any way of assessing 'tall', or 'clever' *except* by comparing ourselves with other people: after all, if *any* of us were suddenly transplanted back in time to the middle ages, we'd be huge – most people then were only about four to five feet tall! But someone who is 5ft 4ins tall in our society is only average, perhaps even a bit on the small side (or very small if they're male).

Many studies show that people want to get information about others – we like to see how we 'measure up'. We use this kind of information to make more accurate self-evaluations about any particular area of skill that we have, or about our personality traits. We might not think of ourselves as particularly generous, for instance, but if we discover that, although we regularly donate money to charity, the other people we know do not, then we would be likely to revise our self-image, and start thinking of ourselves as generous after all! We might think of ourselves as young, and then find that most of the people we know are very much younger than ourselves. With that information, we'd be likely to change our self-image, and start to think of ourselves as older. By making these comparisons, we affect our self-image, and gradually adjust it.

As with other people's reactions, though, it's important *who* we compare ourselves with. If we were just learning to play darts, we wouldn't compare ourselves with the national champions, to see how we measure up, as we'd expect them to be very much better than ourselves. In the same way, we wouldn't compare ourselves with someone who had never held a dart in their life (or not after we'd played for a short while, anyway). We'd expect them to be much worse than we were. The person we would use for comparison would be someone like ourselves, or perhaps someone a little bit better than ourselves, because then we would know if we were making progress, by eventually beating them. We need someone similar with whom to compare ourselves.

This group of people is known as a *reference group*, because it's the group of people to which we *refer*, in order to make comparisons. Members of our reference group aren't necessarily personal friends – they might be the 'experts' that I talked of earlier – those people who we use to set standards for ourselves. Sometimes this is someone who isn't very close to us at all, perhaps someone whom we admire at work, for instance.

In addition to the reference group – which may consist of different people for the different kinds of things that we do – we also have our *peer group*. This is the group of people that we socialise with, that we see as being 'like ourselves'. If you're a teenager, then your peer group will tend to be those other people of your own age, whom you think that you have most in common with; if you're a full-time housewife, then your peer group will usually be those other full-time housewives you know and meet. Our peer group is important, because it sets standards for us: we learn from our peers the kind of behaviour which is expected of us, and how we should go about things.

Roles   The various roles that we play in our lives have quite an effect on our self-concept. A role is a name that we give to a whole set of behaviour that goes with a certain kind of place in society. For example: when we have children, we become parents. From then on, we will tend to adopt a parental role towards our children: we will act towards them in the way that we think

that parents ought to act, we will look after them in the way
that we consider that parents should look after their children,
and so on. But these acts which we use in our role as parents
are different from the kind of things we would do in the role
of bus conductor, for instance (if that happened to be our job).
Bus-conducting requires a different *set* of behaviour from us
– although it may still be the same person as both a bus
conductor and a parent. Each person, in life, plays many
different roles: as parent, as neighbour, as husband or wife, as
friend, and so on.

Each role incorporates a set of role-behaviour, which we
must adopt when we take on that role. For instance, if someone
starts a job at a factory, there will be certain kinds of behaviour
that are not acceptable to the other people working there,
while other kinds of behaviour will be expected. 'Crawling' to
the boss may be the sort of thing that generates social
disapproval, while sitting with one's work-mates in the canteen
may be expected at lunchtime. An individual quickly adopts
the correct role behaviour, and 'fits in' with the rest.

The different roles we adopt become a part of our self-concept.
In 1960, a study by M. Kuhn was performed on people at
different ages. He asked his subjects to provide twenty different
answers to the question 'Who am I?', and found that seven-
year olds tended to include only a few statements relating to
role (like sister, schoolchild, and so on), while university
students tended to produce about ten role statements out of
the twenty. One of the reasons for this might be that we
actually have many more roles as we grow up – we might
belong to more clubs or organisations, have more decided
political views, and so on. But we also tend to become more
conscious of them, as well.

Our role can be very powerful in determining how other people
see us. If I were to wear the uniform of a traffic warden, in a
town street, it is unlikely that people would notice much other
than the uniform; they wouldn't be concerned with the person
wearing the uniform. People react similarly to different people
wearing a doctor's coat in a hospital – the role of doctor is
more important than the individual person. And the doctor,
too, is expected to behave in a 'professional manner' – people
would object if a doctor started to behave like a bus conductor!

E. Goffman said, in 1959, that when we take on a new role
– for instance, the one required by a job – we adopt a kind of
'mask' at first, and we try to behave in the way that the role
demands. But as we get used to the job, and used to the role
behaviour, the 'mask' becomes more and more a part of
ourselves, and we come to *think* of ourselves as 'a nurse', or

'a typist', or 'a tea-maker'. So we adjust ourselves to fit the
role and incorporate the role into our self-concept.

Identification with   In Chapter 5, we talked about identification in terms of the
others   ways that children come to adopt sex-roles, and other forms
of behaviour. We tend to take 'models', and by trying to copy
what they do, we can come to feel like them. This doesn't just
happen in childhood. An adult, too, will often take a 'model',
and eventually come to identify with that model. An adult who
has joined a new club, for instance, will often use one of the
established club members as a 'model', and behave in similar
ways. Later on, that person may well come to 'feel like', or
identify with the established club member.

We only adopt models who we feel are already, in some way,
similar to ourselves: an experiment by Stotland, Zander and
others found that boys reacted differently to the same talk,
from someone claiming to be a deep-sea diver, depending on
whether the speaker emphasised similarities with them – 'I
come from a small town like this', or differences – 'I was
brought up in a large city'. More of the boys who heard the
first type of talk, where the 'diver' emphasised similarities, said
that they would like to be deep-sea divers when they grew up.
The researchers also found that it was the boys whose self-
esteem was lowest that made such ready identifications – by
considering themselves to be like the 'diver' they could boost
their own self-confidence.

Summary   1 People tend to conform to what others have said, if they are
aware of others' judgements.

2 Conformity is greater when others are physically present,
than when they are apart, although people will still conform
if apart.

3 Some experiments have shown that people will conform even
against their own judgements.

4 There is a difference between compliance – going along with
the group for the sake of avoiding argument, but still
retaining one's own opinions privately – and internalisation,
which means fully accepting the views of the group.

5 Milgram's experiments showed that people will obey others,
even when obedience causes them to act against their own
conscience and harm another person.

6 Milgram's results link with our behaviour to people in certain
roles. Roles generate a set of expectations about others, and
we expect the people in the roles to conform to those
expectations.

7 People's expectations about others can become a self-fulfilling prophecy – the individual lives up to the expectations, and so the expectations are reinforced – thus causing the person to live up to them even more.

8 People often infer things about themselves from their behaviour. This may affect their subsequent actions.

9 Argyle described four main factors which influence the self-concept: other people's reactions, comparisons with others, roles, and identifications.

Chapter 21

Social perception

In the last chapter we looked at some of the psychological mechanisms which are involved when we interact with other people. Our inclinations to conform and to go along with other people are important features of social interaction. But there's more to it than that, because social interaction is affected by more than just the immediate situation that we are in. We saw in the last chapter how important *expectations* are in directing how we respond to other people. Expectations are cognitive – they are to do with what we are thinking and how we understand the situation. There are a number of other aspects of social cognition, which we will look at in this chapter.

Forming impressions of others

The first time you meet someone, you form an impression of what they are like. Almost unconsciously you will pick up information from the way that they dress, their gestures and facial expressions, and the kinds of things that they say and do. We looked at how we react to some of these kinds of signals in Chapter 12, because signals like dress, posture and facial expression are all part of the way that we communicate, non-verbally, to other people. But there are cognitive aspects to how we form impressions of other people, as well. We don't just meet new people as if we knew nothing whatsoever about them: we look for information which can tell us something about what type of person they are, and how they might be likely to react to us, and we form an instant impression of what they are like, on the basis of that information. Of course, jumping to conclusions like this means that we are often completely wrong, but that doesn't seem to stop us doing it!

Implicit personality theory

One of the factors which is involved in the way that we form impressions of other people is the way that we seem to use unconscious, or implicit, theories about human personality. We naturally expect some personality traits to go together, so that if someone has one characteristic, we expect them to have several others as well.

Kelley (1950) performed a study in which a group of students was given a description of a visiting lecturer. As part of the background information that they were given, the description included the words intelligent, skilful, industrious, determined, practical and cautious. But half the students also had the word 'warm' included in the description, while the other half had the description 'cold'. Once the lecture was over, those students who stayed behind to talk to the visiting lecturer afterwards were the ones who had received the word 'warm' in their descriptions – the others did not approach the lecturer. It seemed that the description 'warm' or 'cold' had been taken to include a number of other personality characteristics, like being prepared to spend time talking to students, friendliness, and patience.

These *implicit personality theories* aren't just about personality traits. We also make judgements about people from their occupations. When Maier (1955) performed a study which involved giving personality descriptions much like the ones in Kelley's experiment, but including an occupational description of the person as either someone who worked for a trade union or someone who was a manager of a small company, the judgements which the subjects made were very different. It seemed that the subjects took it for granted that people with different occupations would have different personalities.

Stereotyping Implicit personality theories are also linked which is how we tend to stereotype other people. *Stereotyping* is when we fit someone into a category and completely disregard anything individual about them – we just assume that everyone who fits into that category is the same.

Gahagan (1984) asked subjects to read a description of someone's experiences during a single week. Later, they were tested to see what they remembered of the description. Then each of the subjects was given some extra information about that person. One group of subjects was told that she had just started up a lesbian relationship (a relationship with another woman); another group was told that she had just started a heterosexual relationship (a relationship with a man); and a third group were just given neutral information, which didn't refer to any relationships at all.

Gahagan found that when the subjects were tested again on what they remembered from the passage, they remembered different bits from it, (even though they didn't see the passage again). And the bits they remembered or forgot fitted with their stereotypes – for example, the group who were told that the woman had just started a lesbian relationship did not remember that they had been told that she had dated boys when she was younger, although subjects in the other two groups did. Their stereotypes of lesbians had affected what those subjects remembered and what they forgot.

Harari and McDavid (1973) asked teachers about how well they expected children to perform at school. They found that the teachers tended to stereotype the children by their names: children with very popular names were expected to do less well than those with less common ones. More importantly, though, this also affected how the children's work was marked: Harari and McDavid found that the teachers gave children with 'positive' names higher marks than those with 'negative' names. Because they expected those children to do less well, they noticed their mistakes more and didn't make as many allowances for them.

We can see, then, that stereotypes can be very important in determining how people respond to others. Holding a particular social stereotype means that we treat people as if they were all the same, and ignore their individual personalities. What is often referred to as the 'women's movement' developed because of the way that stereotypes about women meant that women were not seen as individuals, and were treated as if they were all the same. Although this attitude is one which is gradually dying out, it is still apparent among some groups, like older people and some literary personalities. A number of studies have shown how the media often acts to create and reinforce *gender stereotypes* of one sort or another.

Perhaps the most extreme outcomes of stereotyping can be seen in some of the *ethnic stereotypes* held by racists, which have at times caused the deaths of millions of people. Ethnic stereotyping is when everyone who belongs to a particular ethnic category – like, say, Caribbean, white European, or Pakistani categories – is assumed to be the same as everyone else belonging to that category. The fact that everyone is different, with their own personalities, talents and abilities, is completely ignored. It is this type of stereotyping which underlies racism, and has contributed to the vicious and unjust behaviour generated by racist movements. We will be looking at some of the other mechanisms involved in this type of prejudice later on in this chapter.

Primacy effects Another, rather less dramatic, factor which is involved when we are first forming an impression of someone else is the way that our first contact with them is the one which sticks in our minds. This is known as the *primacy effect*, and it applies to many types of information, ranging from simply remembering numbers in a list that's been read out, to judgements of whether a defendant in court was guilty or not. We take much more notice of the very first information that we receive, than we do of later information. Which is, of course, why it's so important to dress well and smile if you're going for an interview – the interviewers are likely to be influenced by their very first impressions of you, and if that is of someone scruffy or surly, you're not very likely to get the job!

Pennington (1982) asked subjects to read a summary of a rape trial. Once they had read it, they were asked to decide whether the defendant in the trial was guilty or innocent. One group of subjects was given an account of the trial in which the defendant's evidence was given first, but the other group were given an account in which the prosecution's evidence came first. When they were asked to make a decision, the subjects who had heard the defendant's evidence first were much more likely to say that the man was innocent than the subjects who had heard the prosecution's case first. In each case, the information which they had heard first had coloured how they had received the remaining information, and affected the decision which they had made.

In a study by Luchins (1959) subjects were asked to read a description of someone called 'Jim'. There were two paragraphs in the description, one describing Jim being sociable with others – chatting with friends and arranging to meet them after college, and the other describing Jim as reserved and quiet – crossing the street to avoid someone, and having a solitary drink in a candy store. One group of subjects was given the paragraph with the sociable description first, and the other second; another group of subjects was given the two paragraphs the other way round. Although they had both had the same information altogether, when they were asked to describe what Jim was probably like, the subjects drew on the information in the first paragraphs they had read. The first group described Jim as an extraverted and outgoing person, while those in the second group thought he was generally introverted and quiet.

We can see, then, that our first impressions of other people can be affected by a number of different factors, which may have nothing at all to do with what that person is really like. People often like to believe that they can 'size people up' very quickly, but more often than not we find that our first impressions were completely wrong, because they were based on our own expectations, stereotypes and implicit personality theories and not on what the actual person was like. But, as we saw in Chapter 13, we're also very good at changing what we remember to fit in with what we believe, so it is very easy to forget that you thought of someone very differently when you first met them.

Scripts, schemata and explanations

In Chapter 13, we saw how psychologists use the idea of the *schema* to describe the set of memories, plans and actions associated with particular kinds of circumstances or events, and in Chapter 12 we looked at how the *anticipatory schemata* which we develop can influence our perception. In Chapter 8, we saw how Piaget viewed the formation of schemata as the basis for all cognitive development. Schemata are an important part of our social perception too, since it is our understanding of what is going on that forms the basis for our social actions.

Scripts

There seem to be four main types of social schemata. The first of these is the social script. Another name for scripts is *event schemata* – they are pre-set, shared plans for things that are likely to happen. Schank and Abelson (1977) discussed how, a lot of what we do in everyday living, is routine and planned out, much like the script of a play. All the people who take part in a given episode have an unconscious knowledge of the scripts, which are carried out in a routine, completely automatic manner.

The classic example of a social script is what happens when you go to a restaurant. There is a definite sequence of things that happen, and everyone implicitly understands that they have to happen in the proper order. You'd be a bit confused, for instance, if a waiter asked you if you wanted coffee immediately after your starter course, or if the bill was presented at the beginning of the meal. Schank and Abelson (1977) argued that we are so used to our social scripts that we only actually become aware of them when they are broken in some way.

Role-schemata

Another type of schema is the *role-schema*. This is a type of schema which contains information about social roles — the sort of actions and behaviours which are associated with them, and how they link with others. As you can see, role-schemata are often closely linked with social scripts, and it is sometimes a bit artificial to try to draw a hard and fast distinction between them. But, essentially, role-schemata are concerned with what is expected of an individual person, while scripts are to do with the interactions between different people in different settings. Hamilton (1981) argued that role-schemata are the basic cognitive mechanisms involved in stereotyping. That doesn't mean that they are the same thing, though. What it means is that we get an idea about what people are like from the role-schema, and then, if we are stereotyping, we make that rigid and inflexible, denying that anyone can perform the same role and be any different.

Person-schemata

As we get to know them, we also develop schemata about individual people. The *person-schema* is the cognitive structure which allows you to represent that person to yourself – not just as a factual description of what they are like, but also including all the 'human' aspects – your interactions with them, the quality of the relationships you have with them and they have with other people, the sorts of things that they like, and so on. It is your person-schema which you are using, for example, if you are trying to find the 'right' birthday present for someone – you draw on all of your knowledge about that particular person, and look for a gift which fits with that. And, of course, the better we know somebody, the deeper and richer our person-schema of them becomes.

Self-schemata   We also, of course, develop schemata about ourselves, and these come into play when we are making plans or deciding what we would like to do. The *self-schema* is closely linked with the self-concept, which we looked at in the last chapter; but it also includes other aspects of how we see ourselves, like predictions about the sorts of things that we are likely to enjoy, or our personal ideas of how well we are likely to do something.

Beliefs about how good we are at doing things – about our personal competences – are known as *self-efficacy beliefs*. Bandura (1989) argued that self-efficacy beliefs are an important part of human motivation: if we believe that we are good at doing something, or that we will get better if we practise, then we will tend to try harder than if we perceive ourselves as being incompetent – if our self-efficacy beliefs are low in that area.

Collins (1982) showed that, regardless of their actual ability, children with high self-efficacy beliefs with regard to doing arithmetic solved problems more quickly, and were more prepared to go over them a second time and correct them if they were wrong. Children who had low self-efficacy beliefs about arithmetic – in other words, who thought that there was nothing they could do about how well they did – didn't put any effort in, and so didn't improve. Bandura (1989) argued that it is often a good thing if our self-efficacy beliefs are actually higher than our achievements would suggest, because that way we will aim high and try harder, so we actually tend to achieve more in the long run.

Many modern researchers are beginning to see the concept of self-efficacy as being more useful than the general idea of self-esteem which we looked at in the last chapter, since self-esteem isn't always the same in all situations. The same person can have high self-confidence on one area – like, say, in playing sport – but very low self-confidence in another – like, say, interacting socially with other people of the same age. So to talk about levels of self-esteem as if they were all the same can be very misleading. If we see it in terms of self-efficacy beliefs, it is easier to understand, because we can see how one person can have high self-efficacy beliefs in one area but not in another.

Attributions   One of the most interesting things about social cognition is the way that we give reasons for why things happen. This is known as *attribution*. Attribution is closely linked with the question of scripts and schemata, because a lot of the time when we give explanations for things we are drawing on socially-accepted ideas and assumptions. In this section, we will look at two different approaches to attribution theory.

Covariance   Kelley (1973) argued that the process of making a causal
theory   attribution depends on three main factors. The first of these is *consensus* – whether other people do that sort of thing as well. The second is *distinctiveness* – whether our reactions to that thing are different from our reactions to similar things. And the third is *consistency* – whether we always react in the same way.

These three factors might be a bit clearer if we look at a real example. Say I found out that my friend Lorna uses Ecover washing up liquid. The first factor would be whether it had high consistency – whether she always used it. And if I were looking for a reason for her buying Ecover, I would take this into account. But I would also take into account whether most other people use Ecover as well (high consensus), and whether Lorna uses other ecologically-sensitive household products too (low distinctiveness). And that would form the basis for my attribution about the reason for her behaviour.

For example: if I found that Lorna's use of Ecover showed low consensus, low distinctiveness, but high consistency, I would come to the conclusion that she uses it because she has a personal commitment to ecological issues. But if it showed high consistency, high consensus and high distinctiveness (in other words, she always buys it, so do other people, but she doesn't buy other ecologically-sensitive products) then I would come to the conclusion that it was something to do with the target of the attribution – that Ecover as a brand was particularly good. And if her behaviour showed low consistency, high distinctiveness and low consensus (she hadn't bought it before, she doesn't buy other ecologically-sensitive products, and other people don't buy it) then I would probably come to the conclusion that there must have been something special about that occasion – perhaps there was a special offer, or something.

The process of analysing consistency, consensus and distinctiveness outlined by Kelley (1973) is known as *covariance*. But covariance theory has been quite seriously criticised, because it presents the process of making attributions as if they were simply a matter of processing information, without applying our wider social knowledge. Lalljee (1981) argued that explanations are always given for a reason, and what counts as a reason differs depending on what it is that needs to be explained. Explanations are social in nature, and don't just depend on the immediate situation.

For example, if you were to find that someone goes for a walk at 6 o'clock in the evening, you might accept 'he always does it' as an adequate reason. But it wouldn't be an adequate reason for why they went for a walk at 4 o'clock every morning – that behaviour would be so different from what is normally accepted that we would require a different type of explanation. In the same way, we wouldn't accept consistency, consensus and distinctiveness factors as adequate explanation for why someone stole a car. So the information-processing approach which covariance theory adopts isn't really sufficient for us to understand how we explain human behaviour.

Correspondent inferences

Another approach to attribution is known as *correspondent inference theory*. Jones and Davis (1965) proposed that what is important when we are trying to explain someone else's behaviour is whether we think they did it deliberately or not. There are factors which may encourage us to think an act was deliberate. If we do think it was deliberate, we then assume that there was something about that person which made them do it. But if we think it was accidental, we generally assume that there was something about the situation that they were in which made them act that way. So the inference which we make about that action corresponds to our judgement about whether the act was intentional or not.

Hedonic relevance

One of the things which affects whether we are likely to think that an act was deliberate is whether its consequences for us are pleasant or unpleasant, or just neutral. If someone does something which has a pleasant or unpleasant consequence, we are likely to see it as deliberate. If it doesn't affect us, we are likely to see it as accidental. If there is a change in the TV scheduling so that you are unable to watch your favourite programme, you're more likely to think that 'they' have done it deliberately than if it only affects something you don't want to watch. This is known as the *hedonic relevance* of the act. Jones and Davis also showed that we are more likely to judge acts as deliberate if they affect us personally, and if they are socially undesirable in some way.

The fundamental attribution error

One of the outcomes of making inferences in this way is that we become very likely to judge other people's behaviour differently from the way that we judge our own. Effectively, we are much more likely to make *dispositional attributions* (seeing the act as occurring because of someone's personality or nature) when we are judging other people's behaviour than we are when we are judging what we ourselves have done – so this means that we often see other people's behaviour as more deliberate than it really was. But we tend to make situational attributions when we are judging our own behaviour – seeing it as coming from the pressures or demands of the situation that we are in.

There are differences, though, in the types of *dispositional attributions* which we make. For instance, if we concluded that someone was 'clumsy', we would certainly be making a dispositional attribution – but that doesn't necessarily mean that we would see what they did as being deliberate. Eiser (1983) suggested that the distinction between situational and dispositional attributions is really only an important one when we see the person as having had some kind of choice in the matter, and not if the consequences are accidental.

But we often see people as having had more choice than they really did. Jones and Harris (1967) asked people to give a talk on racial segregation to an audience. The audience were then asked to judge whether the person believed what they had said, or not. Despite the fact that they had all been told that the speakers had had no choice in their topic – in other words, that it was the situation which was producing their behaviour – the audience made dispositional attributions about why the speakers were saying what they did.

In part, that may have been because the talks were concerned with unpopular views. Jones and Davis (1965) showed that when people act in the way that we expect, we are more likely to make situational attributions; but if they act in a way that is socially different, we are likely to attribute it to their personality or character. You wouldn't see the need to explain why someone turned up on time for a meal in a restaurant – the situation itself would be enough to explain that. But if they were half-an-hour late, you would expect an explanation, and if it didn't seem to be good enough you would be inclined to think that it was something to do with them – maybe they were generally late, or had no respect for punctuality.

The tendency to attribute our own behaviour to situational causes and other people's to dispositional ones is known as the *fundamental attribution error*. It seems that we are particularly likely to make this error when we are directly comparing ourselves with other people. Nisbett et al. (1973) asked male students to write a paragraph about why they had chosen their course at college, and then to write a similar paragraph about why their best friend had chosen the course. The researchers found that the students made situational attributions about themselves ('my course will help me to get a good job'), but dispositional attributions about their friends ('he's good at maths').

Changing attributions

Guimond and Palmer (1990) showed that we can change our style of attribution with experience. They looked at the explanations which students gave for poverty and unemployment comparing first year students studying social science, commerce and engineering. There were no differences between the groups. But by the end of the first year, the students showed significant differences in the types of attributions which they made. The social science students were much more likely to make situational attributions for unemployment and poverty, while the engineering and commerce students made dispositional ones, seeing unemployed people as lazy or stupid.

We can see from this that our previous knowledge is important in making attributions. Kulik (1983) showed that if we see someone's behaviour as different from what we would have expected, given our knowledge of that person's disposition, then we will tend to make situational attributions. If I knew that one of my students is normally hard-working and successful, I would look for a situational explanation for why she failed a particular exam. As Lalljee (1981) pointed out, we have to bear in mind the social context and prior social knowledge involved in making the attribution.

Social representations

In recent years there has been an increasing amount of interest in shared social explanations. In any society, some assumptions and explanations are more generally-held than others. That is a part of what makes societies and cultures different. These assumptions are often concerned with why life is like it is, and why people are like they are. For example, British society tends to assume that people who commit criminal acts do so because they are 'that sort of person' – in other words, because they have a criminal character or personality. This means that the prison system doesn't receive very good funding for rehabilitation programmes, because British society as a whole tends to assume that people don't change, and so it sees spending money like that as being a waste of time. But although it is very strong in Britain, this belief is not shared as strongly by many other countries. In Belgium, for instance, there is much more money made available for criminal rehabilitation programmes because there the accepted social belief is that criminals can be trained and re-educated to become socially useful members of society.

In a sense, this is like the difference between the situational and dispositional attributions, which we looked at in the last section. But it is more than that, because these beliefs are not just held by isolated individuals – they are generally shared by members of that society, and so they influence social policy and cultural practice. These shared social beliefs are known as *social representations*. Moscovici (1984) argued that social representations serve an important function in society, because they provide us with explanations for why things happen and why life is like it is. So they are important in reinforcing social values and assumptions.

Social representations don't just reinforce social values, though: as we saw in the description of the prison systems, they also affect what people do. Herzlich (1973) showed how the theory which a doctor holds about illnesses will make all the difference to how that doctor treats their patient. If the doctor mainly believes that illnesses comes from physical causes, they will treat their patient very differently from a doctor who believes that psychological factors like stress or loneliness are the cause of many people's medical problems. Our theories about human beings and the nature of reality directly influence what we do, and these theories are not just ones which we develop individually – they are often ones which we have picked up because they are shared by our whole society.

As times change, so do social representations. Jodelet (1984) showed how views of what constitutes an 'ideal body' for women have changed considerably during this century, and Fischler (1980) showed how changes in social representations of what an acceptable diet is like have also changed. In each of these studies, the psychologists showed how social changes (like the influence of consumerism, the women's movement, or the availability of convenience 'fast-food') have influenced the changes in social beliefs.

Di Giacomo (1980) studied a student protest movement, which failed because most of the students had ignored the student leaders. When the social representations being applied by the ordinary students were compared with those of the student leaders, Di Giacomo found that they had very little in common. For example, the student leaders would talk of 'student–worker solidarity', but the ordinary students couldn't see that students and workers had anything in common at all – they saw the two as being quite different. So the protest movement failed, because the two groups were just talking past each other, and not communicating on the same wavelength at all!

Investigating social   Analysing social representations is not an easy task, although
representations   there are a number of different ways that they can be identified.
Di Giacomo studied the social representations of the students

by asking them to provide *free-associations* to particular words connected with the protest. The words were obtained by interviewing key figures beforehand. Other researchers have analysed the images and metaphors used by the media or by people describing events; others have analysed interviews with people in order to identify the opinions and explanations that they provide.

Some psychologists have looked at whether the attributions which people make may reveal underlying social representations. Hayes (1992) asked employees in two small companies to talk about their work, and found that there were differences between the companies in the types of explanations which people gave, which seemed to reflect differences in the general assumptions and beliefs of the company as a whole.

Bond and Hewstone (1988) asked students in Britain and Hong Kong to explain what was happening in Hong Kong at that time – a time of considerable political change. The attributions showed a number of systematic differences between the two groups in things like how much the two groups disliked change, and how satisfied they were with things as they stood. These differences were very apparent in the explanations which they made, and it is possible that they were revealing underlying differences in social representations.

How social representations develop

According to Moscovici, social representations develop by making unfamiliar ideas into familiar ones. They do this in two ways. Firstly, by *anchoring* ideas so that they are firmly based in a familar context, and have their own 'place' among other social beliefs. The idea becomes named and classified, and therefore seems to be more acceptable. The second mechanism is *objectification*. While an idea is just abstract, it is sometimes a bit hard for people to grasp; but if it can be made to seem like a real object, by using some kind of metaphor, then it becomes easier for people to accept. For example, when scientists were simply talking about changes in the atmosphere as a result of pollution, it was difficult for them to get journalists to talk about these concepts in the media. But once someone produced the metaphor of the 'greenhouse effect', this resistance disappeared – the metaphor produced an image which people could understand, and the greenhouse effect became a social representation shared by a much larger number of people.

Other researchers have shown how social representations, or popular beliefs, have changed over time. Moscovici (1961) traced the way that Freud's psychoanalytic theory became socially accepted in French society, moving from a theory which was only held by a restricted number of experts into one which was widely used as an explanation for why society is like it is. In the process, it went through a number of *transformations*, as psychoanalytic ideas became fitted to popular assumptions. Similarly, Moscovici and Hewstone (1983) showed how Sperry's research into split brains which we looked at in Chapter 16 had changed as it became generally known, until it was eventually used as an explanation for all sorts of things, including the idea that modern society is too technological and inhuman (because it supposedly favours left-hemisphere dominant people over the more intuitive right-hemisphere dominant individuals).

So how do social representations change? Moscovici (1984) argued that we don't just accept social beliefs uncritically. We develop them through conversations with other people, and in those conversations we adapt them to fit with our own personal ways of seeing the world. They change, gradually, as people negotiate their own versions of these beliefs through conversation. Moscovici (1984) suggested that there is a central core, which he called the *'figurative nucleus'* in each social representation. This is connected with reality by peripheral elements, which contain metaphors and images to help people make connections between the central belief and their everyday experiences. Flament (1988) suggested that social representations change as the changes in the peripheral elements slowly feed back to the figurative nucleus.

We can see, then, that the process of explaining why people do what they do doesn't just involve individual attributions; it also involves looking at the shared assumptions and beliefs in our culture, society, and social groups.

Attitudes and prejudice

A different aspect of social cognition which has attracted a lot of attention from psychologists is the study of *attitudes*. As a general rule, when we talk about attitudes in everyday life, we are referring to mental states which mean that we are pre-disposed to act in certain kinds of ways rather than others. So, for example, we assume that someone who has a positive attitude towards, say, environmental organisations, would be more likely to contribute to such organisations when they were having a fund-raising day than someone who didn't hold the same attitudes.

We can change our attitudes too. Sometimes, as we learn more about a topic, we change our beliefs and assumptions about it; although at other times it doesn't seem to matter how much more we learn, we still hold to the same views. Fishbein and Ajzen (1975) argued that, actually, there is quite a difference between attitudes and beliefs. Beliefs, they said, are simply neutral statements which we hold as being true. But attitudes are rather different, because they contain an emotional dimension as well.

Eiser (1983) argued that we have to look very carefully at the words which people use if we want to tell the difference between statements which are about attitudes and statements which are about beliefs: if someone is describing an attitude, they will generally use words which are *emotionally loaded* – which carry some kind *of evaluation*, over and above the simple description. But when people are just describing beliefs, they tend to use language which is much more objective and neutral.

Rokeach (1973) argued that attitudes aren't just different from beliefs, they're also different from *values*. We each have personal values, which are consistent, personal assumptions that underlie how we think, and have to do with principles about right and wrong or social desirability. We use values as standards, for our own behaviour as well as other people's, and because of that they do have quite an influence on our attitudes, but they are not the same thing. An underlying value can provide the direction for an attitude – environmentalist attitudes may come from underlying values about respect for the natural world, for example – but attitudes are much more specific, and some of them may have a much looser relationship to underlying values.

Smith, Bruner and White (1964) described attitudes as having three different functions. One of these is *object appraisal*: attitudes provide guidance for us in terms of how we should react to events or objects. This is built up through our past experience: for example, if you have been scratched by a cat in the past, developing a negative attitude towards cats will mean that you will tend to avoid them in the future, and so avoid getting scratched again. The attitude guides your behaviour in such as way as to make sure that you don't have to go through the same unpleasant experience again.

Social adjustment is the second function of attitudes which Smith, Bruner and White identified, and this is concerned with the way that attitudes serve social functions, as well as helping us to learn from our experiences. We find it easier to mix with other people when they hold similar views to us: Smith, Bruner and White believed that attitudes serve an important function as a kind of 'social glue', binding people together into cohesive groups. Holding an attitude similar to those held by your friends is one way of saying that you are like them – and conversely, holding an attitude which is exactly the opposite of someone you don't like is a way of making it clear just how different you are.

The third function of an attitude is *externalisation*. This is to do with the way that our own unconscious motives or inner states influence how we interact with the world – on a cognitive level as well as on a behavioural one. Often, our attitudes are unconsciously expressing some kind of inner conflict or uncertainty: for example, someone who has lacked warm and friendly family relationships may hold sceptical attitudes about the value of close families. Externalisation is the unconscious matching up of unconscious motivations or inner states with something that is going on in the wider society. So an external object or event becomes treated as if it were relevant to an internal problem.

Each of these three functions, according to Smith, Bruner and White, is involved in why we hold the complete set of attitudes that we do, although, of course, that doesn't mean that all the attitudes that we hold always involve all three of them. But this can explain why it is sometimes too hard to change people's attitudes. If an attitude is serving so many different functions, then they are not going to be abandoned lightly. And yet, progress in society often depends on people being prepared to change their attitudes and adjust to new developments and situations. So we need to look very carefully at how we go about changing attitudes.

Attitude change

Smith, Bruner and White (1964) argued that there are four conditions which help in attitude change. Firstly, people will change their attitudes more easily if they only have to change a little bit at a time, and not everything all at once – since attitudes can serve such an important function, we need time to adjust to changing them. People will also change their attitudes more easily if the attitudes concerned are relatively minor for them, and not a central part of their psychological functioning. People are also more able to change their attitudes when they are calm and relaxed than if they are anxious, because when we are tense, stressed or anxious we tend to hold on to familiar things. But when we are more relaxed we are more able to experiment with new ideas. And fourthly, the amount of information which people have available is important – if we know about lots of different ways of looking at the same issues, we are less likely to hold rigidly to our own attitudes.

Advertising and attitude dimensions

One important feature of most theories of attitude change is that we have to be *motivated* to do it. If we have no reason to change our attitudes, and do not want to, then, mostly, we're not likely to bother. But in our modern consumer society, a vast industry has grown up around the idea that it is possible to change people's attitudes without them even being particularly interested in having them changed: the advertising industry. For the most part, advertisers are rarely demanding immediate change in behaviour – they don't expect us to rush out and buy a chocolate bar the minute the advert comes on the TV. Instead, they are mostly trying to generate a positive attitude towards the product, so that when we do feel slightly hungry, or want something to eat, it is that chocolate bar that we think of, rather than anything else.

One way that advertisers do this is by using the different *dimensions* of an attitude. Attitudes are generally considered to have three different dimensions: the cognitive, affective, and conative (or behavioural) dimensions. The *cognitive dimension* is the reasoned one – the aspect of an attitude which is concerned with beliefs and explanations. If we hold a particular attitude, we can usually give an explanation for why we hold it, and for why we think it is important. And some advertisements are clearly tackling our attitudes from that point of view – they give you lots of reasons why you should buy, say, that particular car, or that particular newspaper.

Other advertisements, though, are doing nothing of the kind. Instead, they are drawing on the *affective* dimension of our attitudes – the dimension which is concerned with feelings and emotions. Advertisements which present attractive role-images and lifestyles that we might want to aim for, or those which are designed to make us feel sentimental by showing cuddly puppies or cute children, or those which amuse and entertain us, are all advertisements which are trying to persuade us into a positive attitude by concentrating on the affective dimension.

A third group of advertisements tends to concentrate on the *behavioural* dimension – attempting to persuade us that we should act, directly. Advertisements which show people, say, choosing the product from a supermarket shelf and buying it are designed to persuade us to act in the same way. The 'hard-sell' adverts which fast food outlets show to people walking past them are also focused on the behavioural dimension – they want people to act, immediately, and go and purchase their food.

Of course, most adverts use a combination of all of these things, and apply very sophisticated uses of colours, photography, animations, and so on. You may find it interesting to look at the advertisements that you see around you and work out whether each one particularly focuses on the cognitive, affective or behavioural dimensions of an attitude, or whether it is drawing on a combination of them. Although most of us like to believe that we aren't particularly affected by adverts, it's clear that we are – if nothing else, advertisers wouldn't be spending so many millions of pounds on advertising campaigns if they didn't work. And part of the reason for that is the way that they tap in, subtly, to our pre-existing attitudes.

Cognitive dissonance   Another factor that motivates us to change our attitudes is to do with *cognitive balance*. We like to believe that our attitudes and beliefs are consistent – that they are balanced and equal and don't contradict one another. Heider (1944) proposed that if we become aware that two of our attitudes are unbalanced, we become uneasy – it creates a state of tension – and we are likely to change our attitudes to reduce that tension. So, for example, if I like Sally and I also like John, but Sally really dislikes John, I might feel a cognitive imbalance, especially if I believe that Sally and I generally see people in pretty much the same way. So I would probably change my attitude towards John to reduce the conflict, and perhaps decide that I didn't like him all that much after all.

Notice, though, that this would only be the case if I already valued Sally's opinion. Mower-White (1977) showed that we are only really bothered about cognitive balance if it affects people who we are personally concerned about. Mower-White asked people to make decisions about how pleasant or unpleasant it would be if they were in a situation like the one I have just described (e.g. 'Sue likes Jill, Jill likes Karen, Karen doesn't like Sue'). Sometimes, the situation was presented as if it directly referred to the subject – using 'you' to describe one of the people. At other times, it was presented as if it only concerned other people. Mower-White found that if an unbalanced situation seemed to refer directly to the subject, they were likely to rate it as much more unpleasant than if it was about other people. They didn't really mind unbalanced situations when they only concerned other people.

Festinger (1957) argued that it is when we find that two of our attitudes directly contradict one another that we are most likely to change one of them. Having contradictory beliefs or attitudes produces what Festinger called *cognitive dissonance*, and this produces tension. So we try to reduce the dissonance in some way – either by changing our attitudes so that they fit better with each other, or by adding extra beliefs or attitudes so that the apparent contradiction isn't important. In the example which I gave earlier, I might cope with the dissonance produced by the fact that Sally didn't like John by saying to myself that Sally didn't like John because she has never liked people with moustaches, and John has a moustache. In that way, I could explain Sally's dislike to myself by adding an extra belief. Because this belief explained why Sally and myself would think differently, it would reduce the dissonance.

Festinger and Carlsmith (1959) performed a study of cognitive dissonance, in which they asked subjects to perform an extremely dull task, putting pegs into holes in a board and turning them from time to time. This lasted for a whole hour – it was deliberately designed to be as boring as possible, and it succeeded! All of the subjects told the experimenters at the end that they had found it tedious. But then, they were asked to introduce the next subject to the task, and to tell them that it had been fun and interesting. All of the subjects were paid to do this, but some were paid what was then a fairly high amount, $20, while others were only paid $1 – far too small a payment to make it worthwhile.

Later, the experimenters asked the subjects again how they had found the task. Those who had been paid $20 had not changed their attitudes at all – they still thought that the task had been extremely boring. But the other group, who had only been paid $1, had changed. Although they didn't exactly rate the task as thrilling, their judgements were different from what they had said the first time they had been asked, in that they said that they had found it moderately enjoyable. Festinger and Carlsmith explained this result as being an attempt by these subjects to reduce cognitive dissonance. Being paid just one dollar wasn't enough to make it worthwhile lying to other people about the task, and so they had changed their attitudes to imply that perhaps something of what they had said had been true. The group who had been paid $20, on the other hand, didn't need to change their attitudes, because they could justify their lying simply by saying that they had done it for the money.

Festinger, Riecken and Schachter (1956) performed a famous field study — a kind of 'natural experiment'. This was a study of a religious cult, who believed that a large American city was about to be destroyed by a huge flood – all except for the cult members, who would be rescued by a flying saucer. On the day before the flood was due, the members of this cult sold their possessions and waited at the top of a hill outside the city. Festinger, Riecken and Schachter joined them as participant observers. They were interested in finding out how the cult members would respond when the prediction didn't come true, because that would give them some serious cognitive dissonance – they had, after all, sold all their possessions on the strength of this!

When the flood failed to come, the reaction of the cult members was very interesting. Rather than admit that they might have been wrong, they concluded that it was the way that they had acted which had saved the city – their prayers and sacrifices (of their possessions) had been heard by God, who had relented. Festinger saw this as a classic example of attitude change through adding extra beliefs to reduce cognitive dissonance.

We can see from this that people with strong feelings on an issue often resist information which will contradict their beliefs. Festinger showed that they will protect their beliefs in three ways:

1 Discrediting the person, newspaper or other source of the information, so that they are viewed as unreliable or untruthful.
2 Re-analysing the information so that it's seen as having different implications – as the cult members did when they saw the continued existence of the city as an example of how effective their prayers had been.
3 Choosing to notice only those bits of information which fit with what they already think, and ignoring the rest.

By using these strategies, people can often avoid facing up to things which might cause them to re-think their attitudes. You might like to look out for these strategies in the conversations which you hear around you!

Attitudes and behaviour

It's easy to assume that holding a certain type of attitude automatically means that we are likely to act in a certain type of way. But, in fact, this doesn't always seem to be the case. In one famous study, LaPière (1934) showed that people often act quite differently from the attitudes which they say they had. LaPière was investigating attitudes at a time when anti-Chinese prejudice was very strong in the United States, and he and a Chinese couple travelled all over the States, visiting over 200 hotels and restaurants altogether. They only encountered one case of prejudice, in all the visits. But when they returned home, LaPière wrote to the places which they had visited, and asked them if they were prepared to receive Chinese guests. Out of the 200 hotels and restaurants 47% replied to the letter, and in the replies 92% said that they did not accept Chinese people. So the attitudes which the hotel and restaurant owners were saying they had were not at all the same as the behaviour which they had actually shown.

However, Ajzen (1988) argued that this doesn't necessarily mean that attitudes and behaviour are different. Often, when we ask for someone's attitudes, we are asking about very general trends, but if we are expecting them to refuse to serve someone in a restaurant, we are asking them to do something very specific concerning those particular people rather than Chinese people in general. Moreover, refusing to serve customers may directly contradict a different set of attitudes, like the idea of service to the customer as the way to make the business successful. So Ajzen sees it as a bit simplistic to assume that LaPière's study showed a situation where attitudes and behaviour were contradicting one another – there are differences in the scope of the attitude and the behaviour (general or specific), as well as additional beliefs which may be involved.

In 1980, Ajzen and Fishbein produced a theory about how

attitudes and behaviour are linked, known as the *theory of reasoned action*. They argued that people's intentions – how they plan to behave – come from two sources: the first being the attitudes that they hold, and the second being social pressures. For example, we saw in the last chapter what a powerful force the pressure to conform to other people can be, and this is a factor which we don't ignore when we are planning what we are going to do. There are other social factors, too. For the most part, Ajzen and Fishbein argued, people tend to act in a consistent and reasoned way, working out the likely consequences of their actions and deciding whether or not to do them on that basis. They express this when they are talking about what they intend to do. But they also take into account their existing attitudes, as well. So intentions are a combination of predictions about social pressures, and attitudes, which explains why attitudes and behaviour may not always end up as being the same thing.

Prejudice

The study by LaPière which we looked at before was concerned with a particular type of social attitude – racial prejudice. A prejudice is a pre-set, rigid attitude, which tends to be very resistant to change – people who are prejudiced often adopt all the strategies which Festinger identified, in refusing to accept information which might contradict their attitude. Regrettably, prejudices against particular social groups are all too common in modern society – the most common are racial prejudice (*racism*), gender prejudice (*sexism*), and prejudice against old people (*ageism*). Even in mild forms, these kinds of prejudice lead to insulting and hurtful behaviour towards people in their groups – in extreme forms, they can lead directly to murder and even genocide.

Theories of prejudice

As you can probably see, prejudice is closely linked with the process of stereotyping which we looked at earlier in this chapter. People who are racially prejudiced, for instance, tend to see all black people as being the same, and to ignore or discount information which shows them that this is not true. There have been a number of explanations put forward for why this type of prejudice occurs – why people who in other respects seem to be ordinary, pleasant individuals seem to be able to hold attitudes which are so directly hostile and insulting to other people.

One of the earliest explanations for social prejudice focused on *social norms* as an explanation. In some societies, levels of racism are higher than others, and, in this context, people may adopt racist attitudes simply as conformity to the majority. For example, anti-Semitic (anti-Jewish) attitudes were much more common in England before the Second World War than they are now, and books from that period often reflect this. Although anti-Semitic attitudes do still exist, they tend mainly to come from either right-wing political extremists or older people – partly because the horrors of the Nazi concentration camps showed just exactly what the logical consequences of such attitudes were, partly because racist attention shifted to black ethnic groups, but mostly because the social norms have changed. Expressing anti-Semitic attitudes or telling anti-Semitic jokes is no longer seen as socially acceptable behaviour by society.

Pettigrew (1958) argued that it is cultural and social ideas about socially acceptable behaviour which both produce and maintain prejudice. Pettigrew visited eight towns in the United States, four in the north and four in the south – where racist attitudes are very much more common. All of the subjects were given personality tests, and Pettigrew also made notes on racial prejudices which they revealed. Although there were no differences in personality between the northern and southern towns, there were very strong differences in the levels of racism, reflecting the very different social norms in the two parts of America.

Scapegoating   Another explanation which has been suggested for prejudice is that people take out their own frustrations on others – they make them into *scapegoats*, in much the same way as someone who has had a hard day at college or work takes it out on members of their own family. This theory has been used to explain a number of observations about prejudice, and in particular why social prejudices like racism increase at times of economic hardship. The idea is that when we feel personally threatened, we look around for someone to blame.

Some experimental evidence that feeling threatened may increase racial prejudice came from a study by Weatherley, in 1961. In this study, subjects were first asked to complete a questionnaire which identified anti-Semitic attitudes. Then they were asked to complete a different questionnaire, and while they were doing it they were subjected to a number of insulting remarks designed to lower their self-esteem. Another group, heard just as many remarks, but these were not personal or insulting ones. Then the subjects were asked to look at a series of pictures and tell a story associated with each one. Some of the pictures had distinctively Jewish themes, and Weatherley found that the subjects who had been insulted revealed more anti-Semitic attitudes in their stories than the others, and also more than they had shown when they had completed the first questionnaire. It seemed that the experience of being threatened had increased their preparedness to express racist attitudes.

The authoritarian personality

After the Second World War, Adorno conducted a number of interviews with people who held extreme right-wing political beliefs. He showed how some of these people seemed to be particularly inclined to show extreme racism, and are also very hostile and punitive in their attitudes towards people who challenge social conventions or are different from 'normal'. These people tend to be very rigid in their ideas, and to be highly intolerant of ambiguities – they like things to be clear-cut and simple. Adorno et al. (1950) described this type of personality as the *authoritarian personality*.

Adorno attributed the development of the authoritarian personality to the way that these people had been brought up. They tended to come from rigidly disciplinarian homes, with cold, authoritarian parents who never allowed their children to express their opinions, or to show resentment if they were unfairly treated. Adorno argued that this meant that the anger which the child felt at how it was being treated had to be rigidly suppressed, producing a psychological state where the person just had to support authority figures, because otherwise their suppressed aggression might burst out uncontrollably. This, Adorno argued, was why they didn't like ambiguities or tolerance – because it might lead to a situation which led them to question authority.

The rigid thought-patterns which these experiences produced meant that these people found it very hard to change their opinions about almost anything. In 1948, Rokeach tested a number of highly authoritarian subjects on puzzles of mental set, like the ones which we looked at in Chapter 13. They found it much harder than most people to switch to a new way of seeing a puzzle, or to adapt their thinking to new circumstances – even though they could see that their existing approaches weren't really adequate. Rokeach thought this might explain why such people often cling rigidly to old-fashioned solutions to social problems ('bring back hanging', etc.). Even though they know that these will not solve the current problems, they are not able to adjust their thinking.

Although at first Adorno et al. believed that the authoritarian personality tended to be only right-wing, politically, in 1960 Rokeach showed that some people with extreme left-wing political beliefs could sometimes be equally rigid. Since these people were equally rigid, but naturally didn't hold exactly the same sets of beliefs as the right-wingers, Rokeach concluded that what it was really about was whether the person was open-minded or closed-minded and dogmatic about things. As a result of this, Rokeach called the personality type which they were describing *dogmatism*, rather than authoritarianism. But the syndrome was very similar indeed: both groups tended to glorify authority figures, and see them as unquestionably right in all respects; and both groups were equally rigid and intolerant in their attitudes towards people who were different.

Sherif's realistic Sherif proposed that prejudice develops when two groups really
conflict theory are in conflict with one another, because they are both competing for the same thing. In 1961, Sherif et al. studied how competition between groups can develop into prejudice. They were studying a group of boys who were attending a summer camp. The boys were divided into two groups, who were staying in different huts. At first, each group didn't know of the other's existence; but they met after the boys had been together in their groups for a few days. Then, the camp organisers set up a series of competitions between the two groups of boys. Very quickly, the boys developed a strong team spirit, with one group calling themselves the 'Bulldogs' and the other the 'Red Devils', and this rapidly developed into a strong hostility between the two groups. Each group saw members of their team as 'brave' and 'tough', while the others were seen as unpleasant and sneaky. On some occasions, the rivalry between the two became quite bitter, and this persisted even when the boys were working alongside members of the other group on minor tasks.

Sherif interpreted this prejudice as developing because both groups were competing for the same resources – only one group could win in the competitions. This conflict between the two groups had escalated into a powerful 'in-group'/'out-group' rivalry, which showed every sign of becoming a full-scale prejudice.

A similar source of prejudice develops when one group has privileges and the other doesn't. Aronson and Osherow (1980) reported an experiment conducted by a school-teacher, who told the class one morning that, for that day, the children with brown eyes were the 'ruling class', and would have extra privileges. As the experiment progressed, the blue-eyed children began to show the effects of being the underdogs. They became depressed, did less well at their work, and some of them became very angry and frustrated. The brown-eyed children, on the other hand, became aggressive and arrogant towards the others who had to sit at the back of the class, wait at the end of lines, and had less time for free play. The next day, the groups were reversed, so that the blue-eyed children were the 'ruling class', and the same kinds of effects began to appear again, but in reverse. The competition for privileges had produced the prejudice, and the apparent personality changes showed how powerful social discrimination and prejudice could be.

Social identification   Another explanation for prejudice was put forward by Tajfel and Turner in 1979. This explanation comes from social identity theory, and it is all to do with how people categorise the world. The essence of social identity theory is that people don't just see themselves as individuals, they also see themselves as belonging to social groups and categories, and this group membership is an important part of our feelings of identity – who we are.

Tajfel and Turner showed that simply belonging to one group as opposed to another seems to be enough to produce intergroup discrimination – a tendency for people to favour members of their own group as opposed to people in other groups. Billig and Tajfel (1973) showed that this was such a powerful tendency that it would happen even if subjects had been divided into groups quite randomly, by tossing a coin. When subjects were put into groups like this and then asked to perform a task which involves awarding points to other people, they favoured members of their own group above others.

The type of laboratory study used by Billig and Tajfel is known as a *minimal group experiment*, because the basis of belonging to the group is so trivial – just the toss of a coin. But Tajfel and Turner (1979) suggested that a similar process of intergroup discrimination was happening with large-scale social prejudices. Since it seemed that just belonging to a group was enough to favour it, and to discriminate against members of different groups, Tajfel and Turner argued that membership of one social category could be enough to produce hostility towards others.

Such intergroup hostility wouldn't just happen randomly, though – it wouldn't be directed at just any group. Since real social groups happen in the real world, there are differences in how they are perceived – some groups are more prestigious than others. It carries more social status to be a doctor, for instance, than to be a factory worker. And one important feature of identifying with your social group, according to Tajfel and Turner, is that you should be able to gain a positive self-esteem from it – in other words, you should be able to feel proud of belonging to your group.

For the high-status groups in society, that isn't a problem, of course; and nor is it for many lower-status groups, since a group can often command pride and self-respect regardless of its social status. But sometimes a group which feels its social standing to be threatened will perceive another group as direct rivals or competitors and become actively hostile. This means that racism, for instance, is likely to become strongest at times of economic recession. Since work is an important source of self-respect and social identification, unemployment becomes a threat to the social group, and ethnic groups are seen or scapegoated as the source of that threat.

Tajfel (1969) also argued that groups try to justify their prejudiced attitudes, by providing explanations for them. Social groups tend to develop shared beliefs which make it seem as though their bigotry is simply being reasonable. Van Dijk (1987) studied the strategies which racists use in conversations to make it seem as though they are not really being racist at all. One set of strategies uses 'credibility-enhancing moves' – statements which are designed to imply that the person has had special experiences which means that they know what they are talking about, whereas other people, who might oppose them, are really just being naïve and gullible.

Another set of strategies which Van Dijk identified is 'positive self-presentation' – 'I'm not racist myself, but . . . '. In other words, the person would disclaim being racist but still give reasons for disliking the minority group in question – like, for example, that they were unfairly favoured. In this way, the racist would make it seem as though their attitudes weren't really prejudice, but were based on social concern. The third strategy which Van Dijk identified was 'negative other-presentation', in which the racist would describe how unpleasantly the group in question acted – that they didn't take care of their children properly, or that their homes were unclean and uncared for.

Using these kinds of strategies in everyday conversation, Van Dijk argued, makes it more difficult for ordinary people, who are not racists, to challenge what is being said, because they made it appear that the racist attitudes are socially acceptable. But they are most powerful because they are hidden – if you can identify them when they are happening, it becomes easier to oppose the racist views. I have always admired the technique of a friend of mine, who, when she was talking with a racist making these nasty insinuations, would say, as if puzzled, 'I don't know what you mean', and continue saying that she didn't understand until they were forced to come right out with their racist beliefs. By making them expose their attitudes in this way, my friend was able to show – very politely and without getting hostile or upset – that the strategies which they were using in conversation were really just that – strategies, and not the apparently socially acceptable arguments that they might have seemed to be.

Reducing prejudice

Prejudice may be a type of attitude, but it seems to be one which is harder to change than other kinds of attitudes – perhaps because of some of the underlying psychological mechanisms that we have just been looking at. Since an important part of prejudice is stereotyping – ignoring the things about people which make them special and individual, and seeing all members of that group as the same – reducing prejudice involves setting up a situation where people are seen as individuals, rather than just being seen as members of their social groups. Cook (1978) argued that there are five conditions which need to be met if prejudice is to be reduced.

Equal status   The first of these conditions is that the people concerned should have equal status. If one group in society has a much lower status than another, that will encourage stereotyping and discrimination. It's unlikely, for example, that prejudice could be significantly reduced in a society where all high-status and executive positions were held by whites, and black people only had menial jobs. In such a situation, the society itself is showing racist values. Systems of 'positive discrimination' are designed to help black people to overcome racism in job interviews and career opportunities, and so to take a greater share in the higher-status jobs of society. As more people become visibly successful in this way, it becomes harder for racists to stereotype black people as a group, as if everyone were the same.

Personal contact   The second of these conditions is that it must be possible for people from different groups to meet. If they never have any contact, then almost by definition they will be likely to stereotype each other, because they won't have the knowledge of individuals and personalities which show how people are different. At one point, it was thought that this alone might be enough to reduce prejudice. Deutsch and Collins, in 1951, showed how black and white housewives who were living in the same apartment building gradually became more friendly, and showed less racial prejudice. But a similar group of people in housing which was racially segregated did not show any such reduction in prejudice.

The trouble, though, is that personal contact on its own doesn't seem to be enough, because racially prejudiced people often just make exceptions for the people that they know personally, yet still think that 'the others' are all the same. Secord and Backman (1974) showed that increasing contact between black and white people at work reduces those aspects of prejudice which are related to their work, but doesn't seem to affect the rest of their attitudes.

Contact with non-   A third condition for reducing prejudice is that people need to
stereotypical   have contact with members of the social group who don't fit
individuals   into the stereotype. In any group, there are wide differences between people, and this naturally means that some people will almost fit the stereotype, while others will be completely

different from it. In order for prejudice to be reduced, the person needs to get to know something of the range of personalities within a group, and at least to have direct evidence that the people in that group are not all the same.

Social support   The fourth condition for reducing prejudice is that there needs to be some social support for doing so. On an individual level, the person needs to have at least someone else who agrees with their point of view – family, or friends, or perhaps a committed social group like the Anti-Nazi-League. If everyone that the person has contact with is racist, it is unlikely that a single individual will reduce their own levels of prejudice.

This is true of reducing prejudice on a wider social scale as well. There have been many individuals, throughout history, who have broken free of the racist ideas of their time, and related to people as individuals. The famous Victorian biologist Thomas Henry Huxley, for example, began his career accepting the racist views of his society, and some of his early writing reflects that. But as he grew older he recognised these views as coming from ignorance and prejudice, and rejected them. But although he was a very influential person in many respects, and spoke out frequently, his personal views made little difference to his society as a whole. Serious attempts to combat racism on a social level didn't really begin to happen until after Nazi Germany had shown the horrific consequences of such beliefs, and after black and other ethnic groups became more assertive about their rights. Before that, there was little social support for reducing racism, and so individual attempts were often unsuccessful.

Co-operative   The fifth condition for reducing prejudice is that people should
interaction   have some opportunity to do something together, co-operatively. In the study by Sherif et al. (1961) which I described earlier, the prejudice between the two teams continued very strongly, until the point where all the boys had to co-operate to get a stuck lorry out of some mud. The joint effort proved to be a turning point in getting the two groups friendly to one another – because they had co-operated, and possibly also because they had been successful in that co-operation, the other group had, for a while, been seen as 'us' instead of 'them', and this led to greatly increased friendship between them.

Cook (1978) showed that meeting all five of these conditions can produce a reduction in prejudice in even very severely prejudiced people. One possible explanation for this is that the factors tackle several different aspects of the attitude simultaneously – cognitive aspects, to do with the person's individual judgement about the situation, and social aspects, to do with social norms and social interactions.

Summary 1 Research into impression-formation has looked at how implicit personality theories, stereotyping, and primacy effects can affect how we perceive other people when we meet them.

2 There are roughly four types of schema: scripts, or shared ideas about acceptable sequences of action; role-schemata; person-schemata; and self-schemata, which include self-efficacy beliefs.

3 Types of attribution theory include the covariance model, which emphasises distinctiveness, consensus and consistency in making attributions, and correspondent inference theory, which can lead to the fundamental attribution error.

4 Social representations are the shared explanations and beliefs held in society. They serve to anchor and familiarise new sorts of knowledge, and change over time as people negotiate acceptable explanations in conversation with one another.

5 Attitude studies have shown how the cognitive behavioural and affective dimensions of attitudes can be linked with advertising, and have investigated factors, such as cognitive dissonance, which can lead to attitude change.

6 Theories put forward to explain prejudice include prejudice as a social norm, scapegoating, the authoritarian personality, the realistic conflict theory, and social identification.

7 Prejudice can be effectively reduced if five conditions are met. These involve: equal status, personal contact, contact with non-stereotypical individuals, social support, and opportunities for co-operative interaction.

Chapter 22

Work

What *is* work anyway? We all think we know perfectly well what we mean when we talk of work, but, like 'personality', and so many other concepts that we use all the time, it's a difficult thing to define. If we said, for instance, that work was something we did for pay, then that would imply that such things as housework, or looking after children, *weren't* work – and very few housewives would be prepared to agree with us there. Or if we said that work is something we do because we *have* to – to earn money, or to maintain a comfortable living environment, and so on – then that cuts out all the people who work because they *want* to, and enjoy their work. Clearly, any definition is going to lead us into difficulties somewhere along the line. Perhaps it would be better to talk of work as we all understand the term, but bearing in mind that there can be many different forms of work, and many different attitudes towards it.

Why do people work?

The question 'Why do people work?' is an important one for the psychology of work. Without knowing the answer to this question, we aren't likely to be able to account for the ways that people behave when they're at work, or the ways that they will interpret their experiences. One of the first theories put forward in answer to this question may easily have been the first to spring to your mind when you started reading this paragraph: that people work both because they are rewarded (financially) for doing so, and to avoid the consequences (financial) of *not* working – not having enough money.

Taylor's theory of work

This was the view held, in 1911, by F. W. Taylor, who was probably the first person to introduce a systematic approach to work, and efficiency. Perhaps he is best known as the father of the 'time and motion study' – ways of developing the most efficient use of energy and time, in any given work task. Taylor's first experiment along these lines was with labourers loading pig-iron into railway trucks. On average, each man loaded about twelve and a half tons of pig-iron a day, but as he watched them working, Taylor became convinced that they could handle much more, if they went about it in the most efficient way. He approached a certain labourer, and got him to agree to work exactly as he was told – lifting when he was told to lift; resting when he was told to rest, and so on – and promised him that this would gain him more pay. By the end of the day, this particular labourer had loaded forty seven and a half tons of pig-iron.

This approach to work became popular, and time-and-motion study systems are still used in industry, to set the rates for piece work. But this approach is often not popular with workers; not because it makes them work harder, necessarily, but because it removes any *personal* involvement in the job. If everyone is required to act in an identical fashion, and to repeat these identical movements, people tend to feel that they are being treated, not as human beings, but as machines, which they resent strongly.

It is apparent from the resentment that people show when faced with an approach to their work like Taylor's, that we need a different explanation for why people work. If, as Taylor thought, people work for rewards, i.e. pay, then they should welcome an opportunity to earn more money, such as is provided by Taylor's time-and-motion work. The fact that they don't necessarily welcome this opportunity shows that economic factors can't be enough to explain work motivation.

McGregor's theory of work

A completely different view of why people work has been put forward by D. McGregor, in 1960. He says that people work, not for economic reasons (although these can be contributing factors, of course), but because they have a natural desire to work – to perform socially useful tasks, and to contribute to their society and social groupings. In the normal run of things, people *like* their work; when they don't, the fault is to be found in the working environment and economic conditions, not in the worker.

McGregor said that employers, managers, and other industrial experts held two main theories about why people work. Theory X, as he called it, was that people were mainly concerned with the money that they were earning; that if it wasn't for the money they wouldn't be working at all; and that for this reason people had to be *made* to work hard, as they would get away with as little as possible if they could. Theory Y put forward a different picture of the person at work, that people will tend to seek responsibility and achievement at work, and unless their work is so unpleasant or meaningless that they become alienated from it, they will tend to work hard anyway. As we will see later, Theory Y seems to provide a much better explanation for some of the findings about social influences at work. But Theory X still seems to be quite commonly held by some managers and employers.

Since the industrial revolution, the kinds of things we think of as 'work' have changed enormously. Before then, most work tended to be either agricultural, or, if it was concerned with manufacturing things, the manufacturing was done by craftsmen, who went through the whole process from beginning to end, and could thus see clearly what they had been making. They were able to take pride in the finished product, in a way that isn't as possible with the factory system for manufacturing. And, in agricultural work too, the end result of labour is clearly visible as the year progresses. When the factory system became established as the general rule, however, people started doing only a small part of the whole manufacturing process as their share, and not the whole thing. In a small factory, the sense of what the work is *for* – what is being made – still isn't lost, but in a large factory, people can come to regard what they do as being separate from the other tasks, and cannot relate the particular job they do to the finished product. Modern clerical work, too, can often seem meaningless and repetitive, when people are simply doing the same fairly simple task day after day.

Because of these factors, it is easy for people to become *alienated* from their work, in a way that they weren't before the industrial revolution. By alienation, I mean that they feel that they have no control over their work, that it's meaningless to them, and that they don't consider their work to be an important part of their lives – it's just something which they do to make their 'real' lives possible. Where previously, working was just a part of living, now it's separated off, for many people, and they feel it hasn't anything to do with them, personally.

This side of working life wasn't considered at all by the traditional management and factory-owners of the nineteenth century – in fact, sometimes it still isn't really taken into account in some old-fashioned factories even nowadays. But it is an important part of working life, as I hope this section will show.

Factors affecting the individual at work
The old kind of industrial management, and industrial psychology too, laid a very strong emphasis on the *individual* at work, and examined the kinds of things likely to interfere with efficient work, and what sort of conditions would assist the individual to function more effectively. In a sense, this approach had progressed from an extreme 'economic' approach, such as the one that we were talking of earlier, because it did recognise that paying more money wasn't always enough. On the other hand, though, it was still, like Taylor's time-and-motion work, concerned with improving the *efficiency*

of the individual as a 'working unit'. The studies conducted from this approach have told us a great deal about the *optimal* working conditions for people, in terms of such things as noise-level, dust, and so on. We will look at some of the findings of these studies in more detail.

Arousal and stress   With any of these environmental factors, one of the ways in which they affect performance is their effect on the *arousal* level of the individual. 'Arousal' is the general word used to describe how 'keyed up' a person might be – whether it's from excitement, anger, fright or nervousness, or simply happiness. Whatever the cause is, it can affect how well we perform certain tasks, and it will do so according to a particular pattern, which is known as the *Yerkes-Dodson Law*.

Fig. 22.1 The Yerkes-Dodson Law
(a) *Graph for a simple task* (b) *Graph for a complicated task*

The Yerkes-Dodson Law states that, if you draw up a graph of how much arousal an individual is experiencing (along the bottom line), against their performance, it will show an inverted U shape. So that when arousal is very low, performance will be very low too. (After all, if you're half-asleep you don't do very well at anything, do you?) But if arousal is very *high*, performance is also low – like when you become too angry to argue with someone, or when you are over-excited. The best level of arousal – the *optimum* level – is in between those two extremes. So the highest point on the graph – the time when performance is best – is when arousal is fairly, but not very, high.

The optimal arousal level for work will be different for different kinds of jobs. If the task is a complex one, then arousal tends to be lower than if it is only a simple repetitive task. But with any work, if the level of arousal gets too high (or too low), then it will tend to reduce effective performance.

So anything that can increase arousal – such as continuous noise – may affect how well people work.

Noise   There is an optimal noise level for humans in a working environment, which is one that is not so quiet that any sudden sound will distract attention, but not so loud that it is impossible to communicate with the person next to you. Most research findings suggest that if the noise level rises above ninety decibels, then performance will decrease; it will encourage lapses in attention, and irritation. (A busy street would be about seventy decibels; a large lorry twenty five feet away would be about ninety decibels). If noise of more than ninety decibels is continuous, there is a strong risk of hearing damage resulting.

Of course, we always measure noise levels against the existing background: if we were in a ninety decibel environment, a five-second burst of eighty decibels would seem quiet, and might be a relief; while if the background noise was only fifty decibels, then an eighty decibel burst would be loud, and might well make a different sort of effect on our work. In fact, eighty-decibel bursts of sound (in a quieter background) have been shown to have a different effect, depending on the task which was being performed. For simple tasks, they can improve performance, while they seem to decrease performance when people are engaged in complex tasks. This can be linked-in with the Yerkes-Dodson Law that we looked at earlier – up to a point, arousal improves performance, but after that it impairs it. The optimal point for improved performance with arousal, if you remember, was set at a higher level of arousal when we were talking of simple tasks, than it was when we were talking of complex tasks.

The frequency or the harmonics of a noise can also be disturbing in a work situation, even when the actual decibel level isn't very high. A high screeching noise can be much more disturbing than a louder humming. Certain frequencies seem to trigger off arousal systems more easily than others in human beings. However, different people tend to respond in different ways; one person might be driven to distraction by the sound of someone drilling through metal in a workshop, while another person might not mind it at all. And someone who minded it at first, might become used to it during the course of the working day. Because there are so many individual differences in this area, it's difficult to make general statements about which kinds of noise are disturbing, and which aren't.

Lighting   Lighting, too, is one of the factors affecting the working environment. It can be quite difficult to strike the balance between a harsh glare, which lets employees engaged in detailed work see clearly what they are doing, (but which also encourages headaches and dazzle), and the alternative of a lighting too dim to allow them to see properly, which would mean that they would work inefficiently, and also suffer from eyestrain. Recently, some firms have started offering planned lighting systems to factories and offices, which use controlled spotlighting to ensure well-lit working areas without over-lighting the rest of the working area.

The optimal illumination for a task, in addition to depending on whether the work is finely detailed (which would require brighter lighting) or not, also depends on how much light the materials themselves reflect. Paper, for instance, reflects far more light than dark wood does, and so a level of lighting high enough for people dealing with paper would probably not be bright enough for someone working with wood, or with coal. Any extreme of lighting level – either too dim or too bright – tends to decrease productivity, and to increase discontentment.

Temperature   Environmental temperature can also have a considerable effect on the individual's performance at work. As with lighting and noise, there are very wide individual variations in the optimal level of work. If it's too high, performance will decrease, and people may well become inattentive and sleepy; while if it is too low, performance will fall off as well. If the person is doing heavy, physical work they will be generating their own body-heat, and so the optimum temperature for them will be lower than if they are sitting relatively still at a desk, or at a work bench.

We also have our own built-in temperature regulator, which comes into play when we are too hot – sweating. As the sweat evaporates, it cools us down; heat is needed for the evaporation process. Because of this, if we are in an atmosphere which is humid, or steamy, we will tend to feel hotter than we do if the atmosphere is just as hot, but if it is dry heat, the sweat we produce evaporates more quickly than in damp heat, or humidity, and so we don't feel so uncomfortable. So ventilation, to prevent the build-up of humidity, is quite important for a good working environment.

Time of day   The time of day, too, is important in terms of how effectively we work. Human beings all seem to have a kind of 'body clock', which causes us to function differently according to what time of day it is. Our body has certain rhythms, which work in a twenty-four-hour cycle, and mean that we have some periods during twenty-four hours when we will work very efficiently, and some periods when, if we did work, we wouldn't be working well at all. These rhythms are called *circadian rhythms*, or *diurnal rhythms*, and they can affect our behaviour very strongly.

Very young infants don't have a developed circadian rhythm. They alternate between short periods of sleep, and shorter periods of wakefulness; a newborn infant averages about eight hours waking and sixteen hours sleep in twenty-four hours. As the child grows, however, and becomes more accustomed to patterns in its life, the many short periods of sleep become combined into one long one, at night, and one shorter one in the afternoon, which tends to be abandoned when the child reaches kindergarten age. By the time we are adult, we have become adjusted to a pattern of about sixteen hours waking and eight hours sleeping out of twenty-four.

Our waking hours aren't by any means all the same, though. At some times of day, we are distinctly more 'awake' than others – just before we go to bed, for instance, isn't the best time to start a lively activity needing total concentration – although we would handle it quite easily if it were in the middle of the day. Interestingly, this pattern of times when we are alert, and times when we are less so, also coincides with the changes in our body temperature which occur during the course of the day. Our body temperature rises steadily from when we wake in the morning, until it reaches a peak somewhere between midday and six-o'clock. (Those people who always feel their best in the evening, tend to peak in the afternoon, while the 'early risers' have peaks about noon.) After it has reached its peak, it falls off steadily, and reaches its lowest point at the time of least activity – between 2 and 6 a.m.

This doesn't necessarily mean that raised body temperature *causes* increased activity; we don't get this result when the body temperature is artificially raised. The two are *correlated*, but may easily both be caused by something quite different. 'Jet lag' arises when we move too quickly from one time zone into another, because our systems haven't had time to adjust to the new times gradually, as they would if we travelled on a boat, say. We feel uncomfortable, sick, and often have headaches and temperatures until we have adjusted properly. For most people, since the effect wears off after a few days, this isn't really serious, but for people whose job means that they must travel round a great deal, it can become a serious problem, as they find themselves moving into new time zones before their bodies have yet adjusted to the previous one.

This effect of circadian rhythms on work performance, however, isn't a very common one, as most of us don't have those kinds of jobs. The most common way that circadian rhythms affect work performance, in our society, concerns people on shift work. The normal working day – from 8 or 9 until 5 or 6 p.m. – means that we are at work at our most efficient times, when our bodies are most alert and able to cope. People on permanent night shift are often able to shift their diurnal rhythm onto a different cycle, so that their lowest period happens during the daytime, and their peak about 4 or 5 a.m., particularly if they can have quiet during the daytime.

Some factories, though, run alternating shift systems, where workers will not be on permanent nights, but instead will have a period on days, followed by a period on nights; or perhaps a 6 a.m. to 2 p.m. shift, for one week, then a 2 p.m. to 10 p.m. shift week, followed by a week on 'nights'. Although this system may make the most efficient use of *equipment* – since the machines aren't switched off at night – it certainly doesn't make the most efficient use of the *people* employed there. Since they are changing their daily rhythms all the time, they are not working at their optimal times. Similarly, nurses and people working in residential institutions who do shift work, don't have the conditions for their times of peak alertness to be used fully at work.

Herzberg's theory of
job satisfaction

For some people, though, their job is such that they are prepared to put up with conditions of this kind, in the interests of job satisfaction. In nursing, for instance, the hospital must be staffed at all times, so they accept the hours, and continue with the nursing work rather than go into a job with more conventional working hours, but a very tedious daily routine. A study by F. Herzberg, in 1959, put forward the view that there were two main kinds of factors affecting job satisfaction: *motivators*, and *hygiene factors*. By 'motivators', Herzberg meant such things as the recognition that a person was doing a good job; the feelings of achievement that an individual received from the job; the prospects for promotion; or the nature of the work itself. By 'hygiene factors', he meant such things as working conditions (noise, dust etc); the attitude of the supervisors and their duties; managerial policies (did they tell the workforce what was going on?); and co-workers. Herzberg thought that it was motivators that were mainly responsible for job satisfaction, while it was the hygiene factors that mainly accounted for dissatisfaction with the job.

If the hygiene factors at a person's work are good, then workers won't be as dissatisfied as they would be if they were bad, but that isn't the same as actually liking their work or feeling a sense of job satisfaction. It's the motivators, the intrinsic factors in the work, which affect how much people like their jobs and how much satisfaction they obtain from it. (But even if the motivators were really good, if the hygiene factors were very bad the person could still become dissatisfied.)

Many investigators have found this to be an over-simple view, however. A study by Cummings and El Salmi, in 1968, showed that it wasn't *that* easy to separate the two. From results obtained by questionnaires, it appeared that *both* hygiene factors and motivators contributed to satisfaction and dissatisfaction. Other studies, particularly one by King, in 1970, have shown that job satisfaction may be correlated with *both* factors, not simply with motivators as Herzberg claimed.

Maslow's theory of motivation at work

A popular view of motivation for working was put forward by Maslow in 1954. While his was a general view of human personality, it has been thought of as having particular relevance to the study of human work, and in particular to questions of job satisfaction and dissatisfaction. Briefly, Maslow considers that people have certain *needs*, which can be organised into a pyramid-type hierarchy. Once the bottom layer of the pyramid is satisfied, then the next layer becomes all-important to the human being; once that layer is satisfied, the layer above it becomes the most important 'force' 'driving' people on. At any given time, it is the lowest layer that still hasn't been satisfied, which is the important drive for the individual. The 'basic needs' talked of by Maslow are physiological ones like hunger and thirst; when those are satisfied, the individual moves on to 'higher needs', like self-confidence, and competence. At the very top of human needs, according to Maslow, is self-actualisation – using *all* one's potential to the full, and being totally fulfilled as a result.

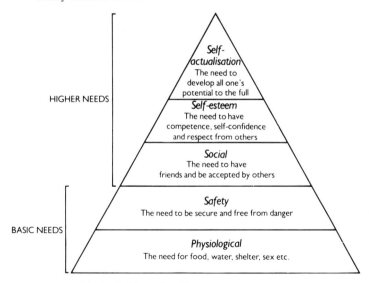

Fig. 22.2 Maslow's hierarchy of needs
Lower needs must be satisfied before the next level becomes important in motivating the individual

Maslow's hierarchy can be broadly divided into five layers. The bottom layer is of *physiological needs*: the need for water, food, sex, and other basic drives. Once this is satisfied, the individual will need to satisfy *safety needs* for security in their day-to-day life. The third layer is *social needs*: the need to affiliate with other people, and to have friends and acquaintances. When these needs are satisfied, according to Maslow, the individual becomes more concerned with satisfying *esteem needs*: to be competent and recognised as such. Only when all four levels are satisfied will the individual move to the highest level of *self-actualisation*, where developing one's potential as fully as possible becomes the most important thing.

Many psychologists disagree with Maslow's approach. They claim that a person may still be concerned with such issues as a quest for beauty, or self-confidence, even though a basic need remains unfulfilled, for example, even if they are perpetually hungry. But it has been a very popular theory in industrial psychology, as an explanation – or a means of looking at – people and their reactions to their work. At least Maslow's theory does put forward the view that people may, in some circumstances, be *self-motivating*, and can't simply be manipulated by more pay, or the fear of unemployment, as Taylor's theory implied.

Social influences at work

This later approach, as shown by the theories of people like Maslow and Herzberg, getting away from Taylor's materialistic view of people, began to develop as a result of a series of experiments at the Hawthorne works of the Western Electric Company in Chicago, between 1924 and 1927. These experiments were performed by Elton Mayo, with his associates Roethlisberger and Dickson. The experiments showed clearly that the old view of people at work just wasn't enough to explain what was going on on the factory floor.

It all started with an experiment – the first one that they ran – on lighting levels in the workshop. This had been fixed on as the most likely cause of the great deal of dissatisfaction among the work-force, which was otherwise puzzling, as the management were quite progressive, and the employees had recreation facilities, pension and sickness schemes, and other welfare benefits from working there.

Roethlisberger and Dickson selected a part of the workshop, and divided its employees into two groups. One group received improved lighting conditions and their output went up, apparently supporting the idea that it was lighting that was hindering the efficiency of the workers on that floor. But, completely unexpectedly, the output of the control group went up, too! Puzzled, the experimenters tried *lowering* the lighting levels, until eventually they reached a stage where the light was only the same as bright moonlight, but still output went up! Obviously, whatever was happening here wasn't much to do with lighting levels, as output seemed to go up in both groups no matter what they did. It became apparent that they would have to set up even more experiments to find out just what *was* happening, and what the mysterious factor was which caused output to go up no matter what they did.

Accordingly, they performed another experiment with a group of girls who assembled small, complicated parts for telephone relays. At the beginning of the experiment, each girl was producing, on average, 2,400 relays a week. By the end of the experiment, each girl was producing about 3,000 relays a week.

First of all, they tried putting the girls on piece-work (where they were paid a certain amount for each part they made). Output increased. Then they introduced five-minute tea-breaks, in the morning and afternoon. Output increased again. The tea-breaks were extended to ten minutes; again output increased. They tried dismissing the girls half-an-hour early, and again output went up. It seemed that, no matter *what* they did, it improved their productivity – except for one occasion, when they tried giving them six five-minute tea-breaks during the day, and the girls complained that they were being distracted by constantly having to break off what they were doing.

During all these changes, someone sat with the girls as they worked, keeping them informed about what was going on, and listening to the suggestions they made. Because of this, the girls felt that (a) someone was interested in them, and thought that their job was worth studying, (b) that they were being listened to, and (c) – most important of all – that they were being treated as responsible adults, who had clear roles, and could be given considerable freedom of movement (which amounts to trust really – the girls felt that they were being trusted not to abuse that freedom). As a result of this, the girls *became* more responsible and trustworthy, maintaining discipline within their own work-group, without orders or discipline having to come from a higher authority. And, importantly for management, by the end of the experiment, when they had reverted to the original conditions of work, their output was the highest it had ever been.

Interest from management   Feeling that people are taking an interest in you and your work can be beneficial, even without the increased responsibility and trust that the telephone relay girls experienced. Roethlisberger and Dickson tried setting up a situation where every employee was interviewed, and encouraged to talk about anything they wanted, to do with the factory. One worker, who had spent all the time complaining about the factory canteen, came along to the researchers a week later and thanked them for getting such an improvement in the canteen's food – although the researchers hadn't done anything about the complaint at all! It seems that simply being listened to was enough to make that worker feel more at ease, and so the complaint disappeared. This sort of result appeared quite often and the interviews had a generally good effect on the morale of the factory.

The working group   As a result of the way that these experiments turned out, people started to become very much more interested in the *social* side of work. It had become apparent that the old way, concentrating on each individual and the working environment, was no longer an approach that accounted for what went on, if, indeed, it ever had been. Who you work with, and how well you get on with them, and what sort of relationships you have with your supervisors, are just as important. So it was the *working group* that now became the focus of attention.

Mayo investigated one department of the Hawthorne plant, which was known as the 'bank-wiring room', and which had been noted for having a strong group feeling. The job was to attach wires to pieces of apparatus. Of the fourteen men employed there, nine attached the wires, three soldered them, and two were inspectors. Mayo discovered that there was a very strong 'code' in the room, which related to behaviour at work, and which was strictly enforced by the group.

Roughly, this code could be boiled down to four parts:

1 You shouldn't work too hard – 'rate-busting' isn't approved of.
2 You shouldn't 'slack' over your work – do your share.
3 You shouldn't 'snitch' to a supervisor about a colleague – telling a supervisor anything which gets a work-mate into trouble is 'snitching'.
4 If you are in a position of authority, you shouldn't act officiously – 'pulling rank' isn't approved of.

This code may well be familiar to many people. In a sense, it's the 'school code' which features in schools and school-stories. Most working groups that stay together develop a set of rules like that, which will tend to establish what is expected of people, and also to protect them against individual antagonism. In the case of the back-wiring room at the Hawthorne plant, this set of rules was creating a situation where, no matter what the management did, the work-rate remained constant – they wouldn't increase production, but they didn't decrease it either.

This sort of observation is important, because it shows how unrealistic it can be to approach these sort of problems from an individual level only. Because it is the working *group* which sets these norms, they can only be changed by approaching the group – talking to individual workers isn't going to do any good at all.

Leadership and leadership styles

Another aspect of the working group studied by Mayo and his associates, was that of group leadership. This issue became clearer as a result of some studies of aircraft factories in Southern California (1943). Partly because of the pressure from people leaving the army and going into industry, these factories had a very high turnover of workers; they would come and work for a short while, and then leave. One particular workshop, however, had a very low labour turnover, and also a very high production record. Mayo and his colleagues decided to study the social relations in this workshop, to see what it was that made this difference.

It turned out to be a mixture of the kind of things we have already talked about, and of the leader of the group. The foreman of the department, being busy, and also knowing that this group could be relied on, very rarely came to visit it; the floor supervisor, for the same reasons, only popped in once or twice a day. The group had its own, 'natural' leader, who handled all problems with employees as they came up – or referred them to a higher authority if he couldn't solve them – and who had a definite procedure for introducing new people to the work. New people were introduced to the other people working in that section, and placed with someone they seemed likely to get on with. When they had seen what work was done by their section, they were taken along to the end of the assembly line, to see how the part made in their section fitted into the finished aircraft.

In this way, new people coming to work in that section were given a sense of belonging to the group, as quickly as possible. Also, by then being taken to the end of the assembly line, they could see their work in *context*, so it didn't just seem a meaningless, repetitive activity. Because the group leader didn't have any *official* position in the factory, he was able to concentrate on the group and its problems, while the foreman was too busy to be able to spare the time. And, largely because of this leader, the group worked well, and was trusted by the supervisors; this, as we have seen, tends to lead to people becoming more trustworthy.

Most work groups tend to have some kind of informal leader – someone who might not have an official position, but is, nonetheless, looked on as someone to bring troubles to, or who sorts out problems. Because their position is informal, and has arisen through the way their work-mates regard them, they will often tend to be people who are concerned about others, and who are able to sort out problems when they come up. Someone who couldn't live up to the position wouldn't get into it in the first place. Formal leaders, though, are another matter. Because supervisors and foremen tend to be selected by management, and not by their work-mates, they can quite often be inadequate at their jobs – certainly in terms of getting the trust and confidence of people in their department, and of being able to sort out problems when they arise.

A study at the Prudential Insurance Company in Michigan compared supervisors whose departments produced above-average work, and those whose departments' work was only up to standard. They found that, in general, supervisors whose departments produced high output levels tended to be very much more concerned with the employees, than with production as such, and more confident in their own position as supervisors. If the employees had a supervisor breathing down their necks, then the tension showed in worse relationships with their department, and lower production. And, interestingly, the supervisors who took the 'production is all that matters' attitude did *worse* than the ones who concentrated on human relations running smoothly. Because these latter departments were more harmonious, they also had higher production.

The study by Lewin, Lippitt and White, which we looked at in the chapter on child-rearing styles, also has its implications for industry. Companies with a very authoritarian style of leadership don't tend to produce such consistent results, or such high morale among the workforce, as do companies with a democratic approach, which treat their employees as responsible adults. Consulting the workforce on changes – or at least informing them that they are going to take place – is vital for the smooth running of industry.

Consultation An example of this was reported by D. Robertson, of Unilever Ltd. They had decided to replace the old lighting in one of the drawing offices with fluorescent units. Immediately the change was made, the men started to complain about the lighting, saying that it was giving them eyestrain, and headaches. They even presented a petition to management saying that they couldn't continue their work because of the awkward lighting in the room. Once all the group had been consulted, and other problems discussed, the men settled down happily with the new lighting. But the whole problem could easily have been avoided by informing the men, *beforehand*, that the change was going to take place. Because they felt that they weren't being considered, and they had other grievances as well, the new lighting became a sort of scapegoat for all the other issues.

It is apparent from Mayo's studies, and from the studies of other people in this field, that the social side of life in industry is very important, and has 'spin-offs' for production and efficiency, too. While the physical environment does make a difference, it isn't by any means as important as the social factor.

Argyle's theory of work
Perhaps the most important thing to emerge from all these studies was the idea that people aren't simply controlled by money. Michael Argyle, in 1972, said that the reasons why people work can be divided into three main types:

1 The first set of reasons were *economic*. People can afford a more satisfying lifestyle if they are bringing home a regular income. It would be silly to think that money has nothing to do with why people work, but it isn't the only reason.

2 The second type of reasons were those to do with getting *intrinsic satisfaction* out of a job. Having a job where you can develop a sense of competence is just as important in manual work as it is in professional jobs. But having *any* job is better than having no job at all – as we can see from the way that people react when they're unemployed. (We'll be looking at this more closely later on.) So any job provides us with some kind of status, and helps us to get a higher level of self-esteem.

3 The third set of reasons were *social* factors – the kinds of things we've been looking at with the Hawthorne experiment. Most women who return to work after bringing up children say that their main reason for doing so, is to get the company of other adults. For many individuals, the social side of work⁾is by far the most important of the reasons why they do work.

Summary
1 Early industrial psychologists were concerned with the individual at work, and with identifying the environmental factors which would hinder or aid the individual.

2 Other theories, about working motivation, were put forward. Herzberg said that there are two different types of factors; motivators and hygiene factors.

3 Maslow put forward a hierarchy of individual needs, which he said was important for understanding work.

4 Studies at the Hawthorne factory in the 1920s indicated that social factors were more important than people had previously thought.

5 Norms for group behaviour can be quickly established, and the working group is very important to how people work. Leadership can also make a great deal of difference.

6 Information flow through the company makes a difference too. If people are informed about what is going on, and treated as responsible, then they tend to act responsibly.

7 Argyle identified three important factors which should be taken into account when trying to understand people's reasons for working: economic factors; intrinsic satisfaction factors; and social factors.

Chapter 23

Environmental psychology

Environmental psychology is the study of how human beings are affected by their surroundings. It looks at the many different ways in which environments can affect our reactions to others, the way that we live and our general emotional state. In this chapter, we'll be looking at three main areas of environmental psychology, beginning with a general look at people and their environment, and then going on to look at the way in which the environment can produce stress of one kind or another. Finally, we'll be looking at how the presence of other people can affect our behaviour – other people are part of our environment too!

Shouksmith (1988) described three distinguishing features of the environment, in terms of how it can affect human behaviour:

1 The environment is a restricting force: an environment tends to allow only a limited choice of possible behaviour. Sometimes this is obvious – we can see clearly that someone in a prison environment, for instance, doesn't have much option in what they can do; nor does someone in hospital. But all environments restrict behaviour to some extent: you couldn't go jogging or playing sports in the living room (unless it was unusually large); nor would you be likely to settle down for an evening's conversation with a friend in the middle of a field! Although usually we don't notice it, most everyday environments restrict our behaviour quite a lot: what's possible for a housewife who is tied to the home with a baby or a small child is very limited; and workplaces or classrooms also limit behaviour quite a lot.

2 The environment also produces behaviour. If you think about it, you act very differently in a social environment with your friends from the way you do at work, or in school or college. Although this is probably partly because you are mixing with different people, it is also because the environment itself influences how you act. It's hard to be bubbly and cheerful if you are sitting in a bleak hospital waiting-room; even if you were quite happy when you first walked in the door,

the odds are that after a while you'd be feeling much more
subdued. Most work places directly affect people's
behaviour. Production line workers in factories, for instance,
are often quiet and unenthusiastic at work, even though at
home they may be bright and happy.

3 The environment also acts as a motivating force: sometimes
it directly encourages us to try out different kinds of
behaviour. We all recognise this when we think about going
away for a holiday – we know that taking ourselves right
away from our everyday environment and into somewhere
different will mean that we start acting differently, and
showing different sides of our personality. People often go
to great lengths to be in one environment rather than
another – they may travel quite long distances to work rather
than live close by it; or they may deliberately go short of
money to live in an area which suits them.

These three characteristics of the environment are important
ones, because they show that the way we act isn't separate from
our environment at all. Instead, our behaviour is often directly
influenced by the type of environment that we live in, and how
it's organised.

People and their environment

Personal space

In Chapter 12 we saw that personal space can be an important
way of signalling attitudes: we tend to sit or stand closer to
people we like, than to people who are strangers, or whom we
dislike. Hall (1966) referred to this as *proxemics*, and argued
that personal space was an important factor in the ways in
which human beings interacted with one another. Because of
this, it forms an important part of environmental psychology.

Hall argued that personal space could be divided roughly into
four zones which varied from one culture to another, but which
in England, Europe and the United States could be defined
roughly as follows:

1 **Intimate** (0–18 inches) – the kind of distance normally
reserved only for lovers, very close family (such as mother
and child), or very close friends.

2 **Personal** (18 inches–4 feet) – the kind of distance
maintained by friends, or family members.

3 **Social** (4–12 feet) – the distance which would be maintained
for something like a business conversation, or a discussion
with someone you didn't know very well.

4 **Public** (12–25 feet) – the distance you would usually find
at public meetings and ceremonies, such as between a
speaker and an audience.

Although these categories are useful in giving us a general picture of how space is used, they can often be a bit misleading, because they seem to be presenting hard and fast distinctions when really one category can merge into another. If you think of yourself and your best friend when you're together, you'll probably find that you use a number of different distances, depending on lots of other factors, like what's happening at the time and how much space there is available anyway.

There are large cultural variations within these categories as well: Jourard (1966) performed a study which involved observing couples while they sat at pavement cafés, and counting the number of times they made body-contact (usually by touching hands). He found that London had the lowest number per hour, with no contacts at all between couples, whereas couples in Puerto Rico had an average of 180 contacts per hour – quite a difference!

Although there are variations between cultures and situations, people often have a very clear idea of what the 'right' kind of distance is for any given situation. Garfinkel (1964) performed a series of studies in which he deliberately broke the accepted social conventions, such as by sitting closer to someone than usual. He found that people reacted to this very strongly, often becoming bewildered, embarrassed or trying to avoid the intruder.

Territoriality   In a sense, our personal space forms a kind of 'portable territory' that we carry round with us. Altman (1975) identified three types of territories: primary, secondary and public. *Primary territories* are those which are private, restricted to the owner and carefully guarded against intruders, like someone's home, or, within a family or shared household, their bedroom. *Secondary territories* are more open to other people, but are still not entirely available to all – like, say, a classroom or a local youth club. *Public territories*, on the other hand, are open to just about anyone for temporary occupation, such as phone boxes, bus seats or park benches.

When we settle for a while in a public territory, we often 'adopt' that place as a temporary territory, often using **markers** like shopping bags or newspapers to stop other people coming too close. A study by Sommer (1969) looked at how students protected their territory when they were studying in a library. One strategy was for the student to sit as far away from anyone else as possible, which was a way of signalling that they wanted to be left alone. The second, more popular strategy, was for students to set up 'barriers', using books, coats or bags, which stopped people coming too close.

Felipe and Sommer (1966) performed a study which involved deliberately sitting too close to people working in libraries. They found that, out of 80 subjects, only one of them asked for more space in so many words. The others all signalled their discomfort in other ways: some of them left the library or moved to another working area, others used clothing or books to build a physical barrier, and some used body posture, turning away from others or wrapping their arms protectively round their work to signal their wish to be undisturbed.

Some researchers in the past saw the human tendency to protect territories as an innate, biological one: Ardrey (1966) argued that the drive which people had to maintain territories was a basic drive of the same kind as is found in many birds or fish, which will select an area and then drive off all intruders. However, this kind of territoriality in animals is usually linked with protecting an area which will give that animal and its young enough food to live on, without competition from other members of the same species, whereas territoriality in humans is much more flexible and complex than that.

Also, if the drive for territoriality were inherited, it would, as we saw in Chapter 2, be *stereotyped* – the same in all human beings. But territoriality varies a great deal from one person to another, and from one culture to another. Some people are happy living in large households, whether it is with family members or unrelated people; others like to live on their own. Some people can work happily in libraries side by side with others, while other people feel that they can't concentrate at all if there's anyone else around.

Privacy The concept of privacy is an important one for environmental psychology, although it's very difficult to define. Many people feel that they have a right to their privacy, but privacy can take a number of different forms. For some people, it means being entirely alone, but for most people it means only associating with a few, carefully-selected or very well-known individuals. Lee (1976) defines privacy as: 'a condition of optimal access by others to the self (or group)'.

Although this definition might seem to be a bit vague, it allows for the idea that privacy can vary but will usually form some kind of intermediate level between too much and too little contact with other people. And only the individual can judge that!

There are several ways by which people can protect their privacy. We have already looked at one way: the use of boundary markers in public territories. But we can use other signals too, like the use of posture by Felipe and Sommer's subjects when their privacy was invaded in the library. Alternatively, we may use direct sanctions: scolding someone or even, in extreme cases, slapping them if they invade our personal privacy too far!

To protect privacy in a secondary territory, we can use a number of different techniques. For instance, a group may signal that a particular table in the students' canteen is 'theirs' by marking it with personal possessions, or by one or two of the group sitting at it to 'guard' it from intruders. Or someone may choose to maintain their individual privacy by selecting a seat which is isolated from the rest, and which also restricts the amount of possible *eye-contact*. In this way, people can often make sure that they remain quite private even though they are surrounded by other people. In fact, many people who suffer from loneliness are unconsciously giving out signals of this kind: when they are with other people their behaviour implies that they don't want any contact with anyone else, even though this may not be how they are feeling at all!

Privacy in primary territories tends to be maintained very carefully, often by physical barriers such as fences and locks. Even visitors, who have been invited into the private territory of a house, are usually only allowed access to certain areas: the livingroom, bathroom, and sometimes the kitchen are usually open to visitors, but bedrooms tend to be strictly private and this is usually signalled by closed doors. This protecting of privacy can be so important that, for many people, the upsetting aspects of a house burglary come more from the knowledge that their primary territory has been invaded than from their material losses.

Defensible space In 1972, Newman produced a paper which gave the results of a comparison of 100 different housing projects in New York, and looked at the incidence of crime which was reported in them. Newman found, overall, that the largest types of buildings were associated with the highest crime rates; and that those parts of the buildings which were public areas, but were nonetheless usually closed-in, like lifts and stairwells, were the parts in which most crime took place.

   Newman suggested that crime rates were strongly influenced by the nature of the physical environment – that there were certain kinds of buildings and housing developments which produced more crime than others simply because of the way they had been designed. In particular, he argued that a housing development must present *defensible space* – space which is arranged in such a way that crime is difficult and people can look after their neighbourhood. He argued that there were four main factors which needed to be considered when designing a housing development or similar type of environment:

1 *Territory:* there should be particular areas or zones which people see as belonging directly to them, such as individual gardens or entrances. If an area belongs to no-one in particular, then it will become neglected and is likely to be vandalised but if people feel that a certain area is their own, then they are more likely to look after it and protect it.

2 *Surveillance:* some areas in traditional housing developments have a large number of areas, like stair-wells or passageways, which are not overlooked, so that nobody can see what's going on in them. But if developments were designed so that people could see what was going on easily, allowing intruders or unusual events to be easily identified, then crimes like vandalism or assault would be less likely to happen.

3 *Image:* a building can look secure, or it can look as though it would be easy to commit crimes in. The type of image a building projects will affect how likely it is that **opportunistic crimes** will take place there. (Opportunistic crimes are ones which haven't been elaborately planned in advance, but simply take place when an opportunity presents itself. Most burglaries, for instance, are opportunistic: the burglar comes across an empty house or an open window, and takes advantage of the opportunity that is being offered.)

4 *Milieu:* the general area which surrounds the development also needs to be designed in such a way that it is safe and presents adequate surveillance. There's not much point having a well-designed housing development which has to be reached by passing along dark, narrow roadways which leave people vulnerable to crime. Defensible space needs to provide safe and easy access to the wider world as well as to provide a secure and pleasant environment for its residents when they are indoors.

Newman thought that if housing developers and town planners gave more thought to designing with people and defensible space in mind, then the amount of urban crime could be reduced considerably. The areas with the worst crime rates are usually inner-city or urban housing developments, which tend to have large areas which belong to no-one in particular and are difficult for people to oversee, so they present very easy targets for opportunistic crime. Newman argued that if these areas were re-designed, with much more attention paid to defensible space, then the people who lived in those areas would develop a feeling of shared responsibility for their community. People would come to know and recognise one another, and they would be more likely to keep an eye on strangers and to protect their public areas. Newman argued that this would have the effect of reducing a number of different crimes – mainly vandalism, but also theft, assault and mugging.

One problem with Newman's theory, though, is that at first he phrased it as if defensible space could present a complete answer to social problems, without looking at other causes of crime. Other studies identified other social factors: for instance a study by Wilson, in London during 1978 found that the number of children in any given area seemed to be the most important factor influencing vandalism; but if two areas each had relatively few children, then the one which had more 'defensible space' would suffer less from vandalism than the other one.

In 1976 Newman revised his ideas and pointed out that although defensible space did make a difference to the overall crime rate, other characteristics of an area were more decisive, such as how poor people were, and what proportion of residents were unemployed or receiving state benefits. Areas of extreme poverty always tend to have very high crime rates, and although good area design might be helpful in reducing these a little, unless the basic social problems can be resolved then such measures can only ever have limited success.

Stress   Our environment can affect us in a number of different ways. It can help us to feel uplifted and serene, as we might after a visit to somewhere particularly peaceful or beautiful; it can contribute to a feeling of tension and anxiety, as in a crowded city street; or it can help us to feel relaxed and cheerful, as in a favourite pub or social club, or in the livingroom at home. Our moods and feelings are caused by lots of different factors all working together, and the environment that we are in can sometimes be one of the most important factors although often we don't notice what an effect it's having.

Because of this, environmental psychologists are interested in the *stress* that people are experiencing. People nowadays often live under quite a lot of pressure, and this can sometimes affect their health, as well as their reactions to the other people around them. Stress is a general term to describe this pressure and the ways in which people respond to it. Stress itself has been defined in at least three different ways. One set of definitions concentrates on how the body reacts when faced with stressful situations; another definition emphasises the

stimuli in the person's life which produce stress; and a third
set of definitions concentrates on how people cope with
stressful events. We will look at each of these three in turn.

Stress as a response   In 1956, Selye found that prolonged stress produces a special
physiological reaction, which he called the *general adaptation
syndrome*, or *GAS*. The general adaptation syndrome has three
distinct stages, beginning with the alarm response, or the 'fight
or flight' reaction. (We looked at this in detail in Chapter 17.)
The alarm response involves the release of large amounts of
adrenaline into the bloodstream, which keeps the body alert
and ready for action by affecting the heartrate, blood pressure,
and other systems of the body. If the stressful situation is
something which demands immediate, short-term activity, like
fighting off an attack or running away, then the energy
produced by the alarm reaction is used, and afterwards the
system returns to normal. But if it's constantly triggered off by
worrying events which don't require physical action – like the
upset of a divorce or long-term worries about money; then it
goes into the second stage.

Selye's second stage has been described as the *stage of
resistance*. The body continues to produce large amounts of
adrenaline, but the obvious alarm symptoms seem to die down
– the heartrate goes back to normal, and the person isn't so
obviously affected. Usually, it means that they have found some
way of *coping* with the problems. But the high levels of
adrenaline mean that they will react very strongly to the slightest
extra strain – people in the general adaptation syndrome are
often very 'jumpy' and nervous.

If the stress continues, and the coping strategies don't really
succeed in holding off the pressure, then eventually the whole
system will *collapse* – the third stage of the GAS. Often, this
happens through physical illness: stress reactions use up a lot
of the body's resources, so the body can't devote the same
amount of effort to fighting off disease and illness. Seligman
(1970) showed how continued stress affects our physical
resistance to illness and disease, so that we are more likely to
catch colds, 'flu, and more serious illnesses when we are under
long-term pressure.

Brady (1958) performed a study in which he placed pairs of
monkeys in stressful situations. Each of the monkeys was
strapped into a chair and given electric shocks at intervals. One
monkey from each pair was given a button which it could press
to stop the electric shocks; but the other monkey had no button,
although it received exactly the same shocks. (This is known
as a 'yoked control' – the experiment is arranged so that
whatever happens to the experimental animal automatically

happens to the control one, as if they were 'yoked' or linked together.) By the end of the experiment, the 'executive' monkeys – the ones which had been able to do something to stop the shocks – had developed stomach ulcers, but the control monkeys hadn't. Brady considered that this was because the 'executive' monkeys had experienced more stress, since they could stop the shocks by their own actions, whereas the control monkeys couldn't do anything about them.

From Brady's results, people began to look at how stressful work could produce illnesses. At first, people concentrated on the nature of the job itself, but very quickly psychologists found that only certain people seemed to develop problems, while others didn't seem to be affected at all. In 1974, Friedman and Rosenman published the results of a survey of people with heart disease. Like stomach ulcers, this is often thought of as a 'stress-related illness', and Friedman and Rosenman found it correlated with personality. Some types of people are far more likely to develop heart disease than others, even others doing the same kind of work. Friedman and Rosenman named the heart-attack-prone people *Type A*, and those who didn't develop such disorders *Type B*. They found that the two groups showed strong differences in their general behaviour and attitudes to work.

Type A people tend to be very intense, and are often very ambitious, although they can be vague about exactly what they're aiming for. They are usually very quick to react, and very alert; and they are easily irritated with other people and intolerant or impatient when things are going more slowly than they would like. They are very competitive, and find it hard to allow other people to work at a slower pace, or do things in a different way. By contrast, Type B people often work just as hard as Type As, but they have a much more relaxed attitude to their work; dealing with problems as they arise without worrying about the future, and delegating things to other people without feeling a constant need to supervise them. They also find it much easier to relax when they are away from work – when they go home they can forget about it, and relax, while the Type A individual finds it hard to 'switch off' mentally.

There have been many other studies which have shown a connection between stress and illness, and the ailments which stress can produce range from ulcers and heart attacks, to diabetes, migraines, asthma and skin rashes, dyspepsia and diarrhoea and many others. Also, by generally lowering the body's fitness, stress can make other medical conditions worse: for instance, people carrying the HIV virus have to be careful of additional stress because AIDS seems to develop mainly when the body's resistance to illness is low, and people who keep themselves very healthy can often delay the onset of the illness, sometimes for many years. As we'll be seeing later in this chapter, if we can develop positive *coping* mechanisms, we can reduce the stress that we experience quite considerably.

Source of environmental stress   Our senses are continually taking in information from the world around us, even when we don't realise that we are doing it. In Chapter 15, we saw how we can become *habituated* to a particular stimulus, so that we don't really notice it – like the way that we don't notice a fridge which 'hums' until it suddenly switches itself off and we realise that things have gone quiet. But we can tell from that silence that we have been unconsciously aware of the background noise all the time – if we weren't, then we wouldn't miss it once it stopped. Most of us live with continual background noise, from traffic, machinery and household equipment, which can represent one course of slight but continual stress.

Loud noise, though, is a far more obvious source of stress. People who live under aeroplane flight paths, or near to busy motorways, often need to alter their houses so that they will keep out noise better; and when an existing airport begins to take larger planes, those living under the flight path can sometimes obtain special financial support to help them to reduce this new source of stress. Continued loud noise at work has been shown to cause deafness, and in many cases can produce quite a high level of stress.

Poulton (1976) showed that the kinds of job which were most affected by noise were skilled tasks, those which involved the person working very quickly, and jobs which required a high level of concentration. Noise at work affects a person's general level of arousal – so that their autonomic nervous system is active, making them feel 'keyed up' and often irritable. It also interferes with a person's ability to communicate with other people around them, which adds to the amount of stress that they experience.

But all noise isn't equally irritating – after all, lots of people experience extremely loud noise at concerts and discos without getting upset. Even with unpleasant noise, if we have some kind of choice about the noise we experience it can reduce stress quite considerably. Glass and Singer (1972) performed a study in which subjects heard a loud and unpleasant noise at intervals. One group of subjects were provided with a way of stopping the noise, by pressing a button, although they were asked not to do it unless they really felt that they needed to, and in fact, none of them did. The second group had no way of stopping the noise at all. When they were given a set of problems to do later, the experimental group (the ones who could have stopped the noise if they'd wanted to) performed

much better than the second group – it seemed that they had
been much less disturbed by it.

Other features of the environment, like lighting and
temperature, can produce stress if they are inappropriate for
the work. As we saw in the last chapter, this is often connected
with the *Yerkes-Dodson law* of arousal: if we are working in an
environment which isn't suitable for what we are doing, then
our work is likely to suffer; and the more unsuitable it is, the
less effectively we work. This is particularly true of temperature
– you probably know how hard it is to stay alert and
concentrating when you're in a hot, stuffy environment!

Temperature can also have a strong effect on people's
moods. Baron (1972) performed a series of studies
investigating how different temperatures could affect levels of
aggression. They found that people were most likely to be
aggressive when the temperature was moderately hot, but if it
was extremely hot aggression tended to be much less. A study
by Baron and Ransberger (1978) looked at weather records
and cases of riots or civil disturbance in America, to find out
if this relationship was also true for large-scale outbreaks of
aggression. They found that riots were most likely to happen
when the temperature was in the low to mid-eighties
(Fahrenheit), and were unlikely in weather which was either
much hotter or much cooler.

Pollution is another source of stress in the environment. It can
affect our general levels of health, and place a significant strain
on the body's resources. Pollution not only produces physical
effects, like increased rates of skin and lung cancer, it also
affects people psychologically. Rotton et al (1978) showed that
increased amounts of air pollution resulted in people reporting
that they felt less happy, and also meant that they rated other
people and objects more negatively.

Individual sources of pollution, like cigarette smoke, can also
produce quite strong reactions. Bleda and Sandman (1977)
showed that non-smokers who are often exposed to cigarette
smoke by being married to heavy smokers are much more
likely to contract lung cancer than those who are married to
non-smokers. They also found that cigarette smoke could
produce depression and anxiety in non-smokers; and that in
general people who didn't smoke disliked people who did.

Earlier on, we saw how architecture and the design of housing
estates can affect a person's reaction to what's around them,
and this in itself can sometimes be another source of stress.
It's clear that environments can affect behaviour considerably:
Bornstein and Bornstein (1976) performed an observational

study of how rapidly people walk along the streets, and found that people who live in cities tend to walk faster than those who live in towns.

Herzog et al (1982) showed that the features of cities that people found most pleasant were settings that included natural features, like trees, grass and water, and architecture which was distinctive and in harmony with its surroundings. They also found that people found old, untidy settings like factories and alleyways to be the most unpleasant features of cities.

Coping with stressful events

In the next chapter, we'll be looking at the ways that different life-events can produce stress, and in particular at the work of Holmes and Rahe, who developed a scale by which the seriousness of particular events could be compared.

One of the key ideas in this field was proposed by Rotter, in 1966. He argued that what was important wasn't the actual stressors themselves, but how the person felt about them and, in particular, whether the person felt that they had some kind of control over them or not. As we saw with the Glass and Singer study earlier, if people can control the stressful stimuli around them, they don't feel as stressed as they do when events are out of their control; and Rotter felt that this is the most important factor in dealing with stressful experiences.

Rotter felt that people tend to adopt general beliefs about the world and how it works which often add up to a general belief about the *locus of control*. He performed a questionnaire study which involved asking people about these beliefs by asking them to choose between pairs of statements. Some of the statements reflected a general belief that things are influenced mainly by people themselves (e.g. 'What happens to me is my own doing'), and some of them reflected the idea that external factors are to blame for what happens to people (e.g. 'Many of the unhappy things in people's lives are due partly to bad luck').

Rotter found that people are often very consistent in their attitudes: in particular, they tend to have either an *external* or an *internal* locus of control. People with an internal locus of control can deal with sources of stress much more positively than people who have an external one. For example: if someone believes that success in examinations comes from working hard through the course, revising effectively and making sure that they arrive for the examination in good condition (e.g. well-rested and unhurried), then, although they will be working hard as the exam approaches, their stress levels will be within manageable limits. But someone who feels that exam success comes mainly from 'luck' will become increasingly anxious as the exam approaches, because all the time that they are revising, they have a nagging worry that it could all be for nothing.

Because of this, they experience a great deal of stress and anxiety as the exam approaches – sometimes to the point of being quite panic-stricken when the exam comes around.

Locus of control can also explain why people who are experiencing the same amount of stress can deal with it very differently. Some people – those with an external locus of control – can develop a kind of 'victim mentality', where they see themselves as being pretty well helpless and unable to do anything about their lives. Seligman (1975) drew parallels between this and some experimental work he had done with animals. In one series of studies, he compared a set of animals who had been given random electric shocks with a set who hadn't had the experience. While the experimental animals were receiving the electric shocks, they had been unable to avoid them – they were effectively helpless. Later on, they were put into a new experimental situation where the shocks were signalled by a light, and they could avoid the shocks by jumping into a different part of the cage. The control animals, who hadn't had the shocks the first time, learned to do this very quickly, but the experimental ones didn't learn to avoid the shocks in the new condition – they just remained passive.

Seligman called this *learned helplessness*: the animals had previously learned that there was nothing they could do, so now they did nothing, even though the situation was different. Seligman also thought that there was a strong parallel between this and human depression, which is also characterised by people being passive and not doing anything to get themselves out of stressful situations. Having an internal locus of control and believing that you can do something about your situation can be the main influence in how effectively people cope with stress.

Bystanders and crowds

One major source of stress in modern society comes from the sheer numbers of other people that we encounter. In small, rural communities, the people we meet during the course of daily life are usually well-known and familiar. In modern industrial society, however, we encounter strangers all the time: a walk down a busy city street can mean encountering literally hundreds of strangers in just a short space of time.

Coming into contact with so many strangers is bound to produce some stress. Earlier on in this chapter, we saw how people have very clear ideas about personal space, and how we feel uncomfortable if a stranger comes too close – but in a crowd our personal space is continually being violated. If it's a dense crowd, we may even end up in physical contact with strangers, being pushed or jostled. Speeded-up film of people walking along busy shopping streets shows how we often perform quite complicated manoeuvres to avoid body-contact with others – weaving in and out of groups of people as we go along the pavement.

Eye-contact, as we've seen, is a powerful signal of either intimacy or aggression, which means that we need to be very careful about making eye-contact with strangers. Advertisements in lifts and underground trains are located very high up, because passengers look upwards to avoid accidently making eye-contact with each other, and people are often embarrassed when they accidentally catch another's eye. Although all this happens quite unconsciously, being part of a crowd can be a considerable source of stress.

Population density   A well-known study by Calhoun, in 1962, showed how crowding could produce aggressive behaviour in animals. He placed a number of rats in a large enclosure, provided them with plenty of food and water, and allowed them to breed freely. As each generation of rats matured, the environment became more and more crowded, and the rats' behaviour began to change. They became very aggressive towards one another, with serious fights becoming commonplace. Mother rats began to neglect their offspring, and it was not uncommon for young rats to be killed. Some rats even became cannibals, eating young rat pups, although there was no shortage of conventional food; and many of the rats became physically ill.

There have been several studies showing that crowding among human beings also results in increased aggression – although not, fortunately, to the level shown by Calhoun's rats! Loo (1979) performed an observational study of pre-school children in a day nursery, and found that the more children there were, the more aggressive behaviour and verbal bad temper was shown. McCain et al (1980) examined prison conditions and found that the more overcrowded the prison, the greater the likelihood of disturbance and riots by the inmates; they also found that suicide and illness rates increased.

Kelley (1982) performed a study of 175 American cities and found that the density of population (the number of people living in a given area) correlated strongly with the amount of crime in that area; in other words, the more people there were, the more crime there was. The crimes concerned ranged from murders and rapes to car thefts and robberies. Interestingly, this happened no matter what type of residential area it was. Although there was generally less crime in some areas, it still increased as the population size increased.

A study of crowd behaviour in America was performed by Mann (1981), who examined how crowds react to a person threatening to commit suicide by jumping off a high building. American crowds often behave very cruelly to these people, shouting taunts like 'jump', or other kinds of insult. Mann found that this was much more likely to happen with large crowds – particularly crowds of over 300 people; and in the summer months rather than the winter ones. In addition, Mann found that most of this 'baiting' took place under cover of darkness – possibly because the people shouting the insults were far less likely to be identified.

Deindividuation Being a member of a crowd forms a kind of *deindividuation* – the person isn't seen as an individual, but as someone who is anonymous and can't be distinguished from anyone else. In this kind of situation people often behave quite differently from the way they behave on their own. In Chapter 20 we saw how the 'guards' in Zimbardo's Stanford Prison experiment acted in ways that were completely different from their own personalities, simply because they felt that they had to act out a definite social role, in which their own personal likes and dislikes didn't count. They had become deindividuated – they didn't see themselves as individuals any more.

Another study by Zimbardo (1970) illustrated how powerful deindividuation could be. He asked female subjects to deliver electric shocks to other women who were supposed to be taking part in a learning experiment. Half of the women were deindividuated – they wore anonymous clothing (laboratory coats) and hoods which entirely covered their faces. Also, during the experiment, they were never spoken to individually, only as a group. The other half of the subjects wore their own clothes, no masks, and were treated individually by the experimenter. When they were asked to give the electric shocks, the deindividuated women gave much stronger shocks than the individual women – on average, twice as strong. It seems that being anonymous can mean that we pay less attention to our individual values and consciences, so that we become more punitive and aggressive.

Other researchers, though, have questioned these findings. Jones and Downing (1979) argued that the particular costume worn by the women in this study was one which would encourage a more aggressive attitude, because it resembled the uniform of the racist Ku Klux Klan organisation. When they performed a similar study, but including other costumes, they found that the results were not as strong. When the women were dressed as nurses, for instance, they gave fewer electric shocks than the control group. So although researchers are agreed that deindividuation does have strong effects on people, they don't always have to be negative ones. In general, it seems to reduce our self-awareness, which can often mean that we act more on impulse than we would do normally.

Bystander intervention

Living among strangers, in towns and cities, can sometimes present a problem of what to do when we see some kind of event or emergency. There have been cases reported in the newspapers of people being attacked – and even killed – in front of witnesses who didn't do anything to help the victim. At other times, though, perfect strangers will stop and help people who are in difficulties, and psychologists have investigated why people will help on some occasions but not on others.

Our *definition of the situation* can be important for the way in which we react in an emergency. Latane and Darley (1968) invited male college students along to an interview. They were asked to wait in a small waiting room, either on their own or with other people. After a short while, smoke began to come through an air vent on the wall, as if there was a fire in the next room, and the subjects were observed through a one-way mirror to see how they would react. Latane and Darley found that 75 per cent of subjects who were waiting on their own reported the smoke within two minutes of it starting, but if there were other people present, they were less likely to report it. When the subject was waiting with two other people, only 13 per cent of them reported the smoke within six minutes – despite the fact that the room was filled with smoke by then! It seemed that the fact that the other people weren't reacting to the smoke meant that the subjects saw the situation as being not particularly serious.

If we see someone fall down in the street, the way we define the situation can make a considerable difference. We may react one way if we think that the person has been drinking, for instance, and a different way if we think that they are ill or disabled. But even so, we may still be prepared to be helpful. In a study by Piliavin et al (1969) a man appeared to collapse in the New York subway, and observers noted whether or not anyone went to help. In one condition the man carried a cane, implying that he was blind, and Piliavin et al found that he was helped 95 per cent of the time. When he was obviously smelling of alcohol and appeared to be drunk, he was still helped 50 per cent of the time. So even though our definitions of the situation are important, they don't necessarily mean that we will refuse to help out.

Whether we will help or not often seems to be affected by whether there are other people around. This produces a kind of *diffusion of responsibility* – if there are other people around, people think that someone else could just as well go and help. Often, bystanders seem to produce a kind of *pluralistic ignorance*, in which they all define the situation as being not important enough for someone to need help. Latane and Rodin (1969) staged an experiment in which subjects heard a female experimenter in the next room climb on to a chair to reach the top shelf of a bookcase, and fall to the floor. The experimenter cried for help, saying that she couldn't get up because her ankle was injured; and the subjects were observed to see if they would offer assistance. Again, the important factor was whether the subject was alone or not: if they were on their own, 70 per cent of the subjects went to help the experimenter, but if there was someone else in the testing room with them only 40 per cent went to help. When they were asked later why they hadn't helped, they said that they had decided that it wasn't serious – a kind of pluralistic ignorance based on the fact that the others in the room weren't reacting either.

If a situation is at all ambiguous, people are often more reluctant to help – possibly because they are worried about making themselves look silly. In a study by Darley and Latane (1968), subjects were placed in individual cubicles and told that they would be part of a private, anonymous discussion about the personal problems of college students. In order to avoid embarrassment, the discussion would be held via an intercom, with each person speaking in turn for two minutes. Unknown to the subject, all of the other voices were tape-recordings, but during the 'discussion', one of the other 'participants' appeared to be having an epileptic fit. (They had previously mentioned that they sometimes had problems that way.) In this case, there was no question about the emergency of the situation, and subjects were observed to see if they would report it.

When they thought that they were the only other person participating, then the subjects reported the emergency 87 per cent of the time. If there were two other voices in the experiment, then 62 per cent of the subjects reported it – which is much higher than the more ambiguous experimental situations described in the earlier studies. And even if there were five other voices, 31 per cent of the subjects reported the incident. So it seems that although the presence of other people does make a difference, if a situation is clear and unambiguous, people will be more ready to help than if they feel that they could be mistaken.

Overall, then, it seems that some of the most important factors involved in determining whether or not we will go and help someone in difficulties are: how we define the situation, whether or not we are on our own and whether or not the situation is ambiguous. But we should remember, perhaps, that some people are always prepared to go and help other people – and researchers have also found that just knowing about these studies makes people more prepared to help other people when help is needed. In the same way that knowing about the Milgram studies makes people less likely to act cruelly just because they are told to, knowing why some people help and some don't seems to encourage us to be helpful towards others. In the next chapter, we'll be looking at some of the major events and transitions which happen to us as we go through life, and at how these can affect us.

Summary

1 The environment can affect behaviour in a number of ways. Personal space and territoriality are important in how people respond to their environments.

2 Newman showed how designing housing estates with defensible space in mind could reduce crime rates significantly.

3 Long-term stress produces a general adaptation syndrome, which can have serious effects on people's health.

4 Many features of the environment can produce stress, including noise, temperature and pollution.

5 People with an internal locus of control can cope with stressful events more effectively than those with an external one.

6 Crowding and deindividuation can reduce self-awareness, resulting in people behaving more aggressively towards one another.

7 Bystanders are more likely to help other people if they are on their own, and if the situation is clear and unambiguous.

Chapter 24 **Life-changes**

In Chapter 22 I talked about a very important part of our
everyday lives: work, and the things that influence us at work.
In this chapter, I want to go on to look at other important
aspects of our lives, and the ways that we react to them.
Throughout life, we encounter a series of changes – changes
like leaving school and going to work, or becoming parents,
or growing old. We have to learn to adjust to and cope with
them, and to incorporate the new roles into our self-concept,
as a part of our experience, or of ourselves.

Locus of control   When we are adjusting to, or coping with, some kind of major
change like the ones which I have just mentioned, there is one
main factor affecting the way that we do it. This factor is
whether we feel that the change is under our control, or not.
For example: if someone has wanted to be a nurse, has stayed
at school to get the necessary qualifications, and has gained a
place at a training hospital, then they will tend to regard the
change in their lives – the transition from school to work –
very positively. Because it is what they *wanted*, they've taken
steps to make sure that they get there, and, to a large extent,
the whole process has been controlled by that person. By
contrast, if someone leaves school with no particular idea about
what they want to do, and finally, after drifting for a while, gets
pushed into an unskilled factory job by, say, other members of
the family, then they aren't likely to react to their change – the
new job – in the same way as the trainee nurse. At no point
has that person actually had *control* – or felt that they had
control – over what he or she is doing, and this will make a
large difference to how he or she copes with the work – whether
they find it enjoyable, or boring; or whether they become
resigned to it easily.

Of course, it's not always possible for someone to feel that
they have control over their life-changes; very often they
haven't! The person I mentioned above, who left school with
no clear idea of what he or she wanted to do, might think that
way because they wouldn't be *able* to go into nursing, because
of not doing well at school, and not being able to take the
necessary exams. If that was the case, and nursing had been

what they really wanted to do, then they might well feel that events were not under control and that they actually hadn't got any choice about what they were going to to.

Perception of events   In a lot of ways, it's not what actually happens which matters, but what the person perceives to be happening. If you don't know that a certain option is open to you, then how can you choose that option? For example: someone might not want to do any of the jobs that are open to them when they leave school, because all the jobs seem to be unappealing and nothing to do with their real interests, which are painting and photography. If that person doesn't know that it's possible to get a job connected with photography – as an assistant in a studio; or even just working in a camera shop – then they're likely to drift into a job they don't like, and find boring. But if they're aware of those possibilities, then they are more likely to go for one of those kind of jobs, and to feel that they have had more say in what they ended up doing.

Interestingly, our feelings of control over our lives are strongly linked with superstition. In societies where people feel that they haven't much control, there is often a very strong belief in 'luck', and charms and omens. Where people feel that what comes to them has come as a result of their own efforts, there tends to be much less superstitious belief. For example: village life under the feudal system was largely agricultural, and therefore very subject to the weather. Because there was no way that people could control whether they had a good harvest, or a bad one, a whole series of elaborate rituals and superstitions developed. Partly, of course, these were serious, often quite sensible, attempts to understand the world around them; but partly, too, they resulted from the lack of control which people felt they had over their lives. And, of course, in a sense these superstitions gave people the control that they felt was lacking from their lives. If you know that cold iron above the door stops fairies from coming in and souring the milk, and you then put an iron horse-shoe over the door, then you have actually done something about it – you've controlled the situation, by obeying the rules. Although it's easy for us to scoff at that sort of thing, it did have its uses – but they were mainly psychological.

The activity is a central part of this control, which is why so many superstitions involve the performance of rituals. People like to be involved in things that concern them – they don't like things to be done for them, with their having no say in it at all. The nursing student I talked of earlier has been active in getting to the chosen career (by taking the school exams, and so on), so the achievement is through merit, not just drifting. By being active in our own life-decisions, we increase our sense of competence, and our self-confidence. Without our personal involvement, we are just floundering. If we were pushed into a career, without feeling that we had any choice in it at all, then we'd be much less likely to adjust happily to it – not necessarily because we are 'contrary', but because our own feelings of competence and self-respect would have been undermined. Fortunately, most people who go into a career as a result of family expectations or other pressures, usually come to the conclusion that they want that career anyway, so they come to regain personal control over the situation.

Changes throughout life

Leaving school

Making the transition from school to work can depend on what kind of work people are going into. For someone going into a professional career, like medicine or law, the transition is very gradual. When they leave school, they go on to university, and, for example in the case of medical students, they make a gradual changeover from being a 'student' to being a 'doctor' throughout their course years. According to Argyle (1967), only thirty-one per cent of medical students see themselves as doctors in their first year of training, while by the fourth year eighty-three per cent do. Since medical training is a mixture of course-work and practical experience, the transition between education and work is only made very gradually. By contrast, someone who leaves school at 16, and goes to work in a factory has a very sudden and abrupt change. Very often, working has almost nothing in common with school-life (except that it takes place during the day-time, for the first two years at least). People who get apprenticeships, or similar arrangements, have a slightly less sudden change, since they spend a day a week in college, on 'day release', but it is still very different from full-time schooling.

These changes include a different set of attitudes, both from the people around the school-leaver, and from the school-leaver personally. Where before, the discipline and authority structures were *imposed* – it is the law that says one must attend school until the age of sixteen – and not really open to question, the school-leaver who has just started work finds a different set of constraints, and must shift from (for example) attending daily as a legal obligation, to attending daily to earn money. Perhaps the difference is a wider awareness of consequences which may arise if rules are not followed: insubordination may lead to the sack, rather than to a detention. Also, of course, becoming financially independent is an important factor in developing self-esteem, for many young people.

Margaret Mead, in her book *Coming of Age in Samoa*, shows how adolescence and the change-over from childhood to adulthood is very different in other societies. In Samoa, there isn't the same sort of sudden break that we have in our society, between the period of little or no responsibility and adult-type work, to a time of almost complete adoption of adult work roles and responsibilities. Rather, the child adopts adult-type roles from a very early age; from about five years old the child will start to copy and help with adult tasks. As it grows older, it simply adopts more and more of the adult work, until by the time it comes of age it is working fully as an adult of that society. In this way, people in Samoa don't find adolescence, and the period of role-change, nearly as stressful as Western teenagers do; there are no sudden changes, but just a gradual transition from childhood to adulthood.

Unemployment and redundancy

One of the reasons young people find unemployment so demoralising, is because it is something over which they have so little control. Adolescence tends to be a time when people are trying to identify which areas of their life are under control anyway, and to find that one does not even have the opportunity to work for a living can be a serious blow to a young person. At a time when self-confidence is not usually at its highest, to be told 'you're no use to us' is something many people find extremely difficult to handle.

Unemployment and redundancy can have serious effects on the individual, no matter what age he or she might be. According to J. Brown (1954), people have a strong need for status and useful function (we touched on this in the last section). When someone is made redundant, that need is denied; they are effectively being told that they are not needed or wanted, and that the work they can do is no longer useful to their employers. The demoralising effect that this has on people is strong, and serious – and, if the period of unemployment becomes a lengthy one, can become very long-lasting indeed, in that the individual may take a great deal of time to repair this blow to their self-esteem.

Unemployment tends to produce a two-stage reaction from people. When they first become unemployed, they are very active, trying all sorts of possible sources of work. When the society is providing a fair number of jobs, many people will find replacement work within a couple of weeks, and so they don't suffer the long-term effects of unemployment at all. At a time of economic recession, however, when replacement jobs are scarce, and redundancies common, the unemployed person finds it very much harder to get a replacement job.

After several weeks of active searching, they begin to become depressed and demoralised. After so many rejections, they feel that it isn't worthwhile bothering – they won't manage to get a job anyway. And so they don't bother any more, and the unemployed period goes on.

Very often, too, the loss of confidence that accompanies unemployment affects the individual's family life, and leads to personal problems. Sometimes, the individual's personal problems can get to the point where they feel that the *last* thing they need is a job – they've enough on their plate without that as well! But, according to Eisenberg and Lazarsfeld, in 1938, this last reaction is, or appears to be, less common than simply sinking into depression and lethargy. Furthermore, such feelings quickly disappear when a person finally does get work.

In our society women tend to be less affected by redundancy than men. The reasons for this are thought to lie in the different up-bringings that men and women receive: men have a stronger emphasis on the importance of their work to provide for the home, while women even now have the option of a marriage with the emphasis on children and domestic life. There is some recent evidence that these sex-differences are becoming less strong – current school-leavers of both sexes seem to suffer the effects of unemployment just as seriously, although it is a bit early yet for us to come to any strong conclusions on this question.

In the next chapter, we'll be looking at the effects of a slightly different form of unemployment – what happens to people when they grow old and retire from work completely.

Marriage   Another major change that most people experience at some point in their lives, is adjusting to married life. A study by Holmes and Rahe, in 1967, pointed out that for most people adjustment to marriage meant a complete readjustment in almost every area of their lives. The changes, though, were most obvious in the social sphere. From the moment they got married, Holmes and Rahe said, the individual was expected to change from regarding their 'outside' social life as being the most important, to having to concentrate on their domestic social life. Home relationships are now regarded as being much more important than any relationship outside the home.

This extreme change seems to be stronger for women than it is for men, mainly because women have been brought up to expect marriage to be very fulfilling and important to them, and also because it is regarded as more acceptable for men to have friends outside the home, and relationships through their work. Because society expects women to find their main satisfaction in their relationships with their husbands, many women find it very difficult to form outside relationships with other people, and often they even lose their previous friends from the days before they married.

A study of young married couples by Lowenthal, Thurnher and Chiriboga, mentioned that many of them had expressed uncertainty about getting married, in the first few months after the event. They wondered if they had done the right thing, and were very inclined to daydream about previous social relationships and encounters. As the first year progressed, however, they became more settled, and developed a greater sense of commitment to the marriage, and their partner. As a result of this growing commitment, they began to feel more certain of each other, and became more able to express disagreements, and to have arguments when these were necessary. All the couples who described this process expressed relief that they had reached this stage; the previous phase, where they hadn't been able to argue or express dissatisfaction had been quite a strain for them.

We might, perhaps, expect a difference in this kind of transition, between couples who have married from home – and so are more adjusted to the give-and-take of family life – and those who have lived independently for some time, and may not be so ready to adjust to other people's idiosyncracies. But it seems likely that the same *processes* will occur, even if the degree to which they go is different. All the couples in the Lowenthal study said that over the first year of marriage, one of the most important changes was that they had become more sensitive to the emotional needs of their partner. This, they felt, had been a major factor in the 'settling down' of their marriages. They tended to be very optimistic about the future, and to expect their marriages to continue to improve.

Parenthood   For many couples, adjusting to each other after getting married is immediately followed by another major adjustment – parenthood. There is some evidence that marital breakdowns are less likely to happen between couples who have waited for a couple of years before having children, compared with couples who have started a family immediately after getting married. It seems likely that this results from the need to adjust to one's partner having been overshadowed by the new baby, leaving misunderstandings and false impressions not sorted out, which may cause trouble later on.

The transition to parenthood is a gradual one for most people – although looking back it often seems to have happened very quickly. But the nine months of pregnancy serve as a valuable adjusting time, when things are planned, and talked over, and prepared for the new baby. And once the baby is born, the

kinds of demands which it makes are, at first, mainly caretaking ones, and playing, or interactive ones. The
'responsibilities' of parenthood only develop gradually, and
change with each stage that the child reaches – from simple,
physical responsibilities, to later concerns with the child's
moral and social development. Because of this gradual
transition in the kind of parenting which the child requires,
the parents themselves tend to change gradually, in response
to their own duties and responsibilities, and to adopt a
different outlook on such aspects of society as 'teenagers', or
'pop music'. It's often not until they look back, on their own
early marriage, that they realise how much they have changed
over the years.

One of the biggest problems people find in first adjusting to
parenthood, is the difference between what they have come to
expect the baby to be like, and what it actually is like! Our
society is full of advertisements showing mothers with happy,
gurgling, contented babies – not a care in the world! The
mother is obviously happy, and enjoying her baby's company,
and the baby is relaxed and smiling. From this, many people
are led to build up a picture of 'motherhood', which implies
that this is how motherhood should be, and what they are
entitled to expect from their baby. Then, all of a sudden, they
are faced with a baby that is fractious, and cries for no apparent
reason; catches snuffly colds or develops rashes; or wakes up
often in the middle of the night. Many young mothers don't
realise that their baby is the normal one, and see themselves
as having 'failed' because they aren't like the relaxed contented
mother in the advert. It's difficult to be relaxed and contented
when you've been up five or six times in the night with a yelling
infant. In earlier times, when young mothers tended to live very
near *their* mothers, this wasn't such a problem, as they always
had someone they could turn to for advice and reassurance;
nowadays, when many people move far away from their parents,
many young parents find themselves alone with these worries
and stresses, and a large part of the function of baby clinics is
to reassure mothers that they and their babies are *not* failures,
but quite normal.

Conflicts like this, between expectations and reality, happen at
other times of life too. Often we find a major conflict at the
time of retirement, for men. They are happily looking forward
to a relaxed life, where they can follow hobbies, and potter
around; but faced with the reality, they can rapidly become
bored and dissatisfied. The relaxed life turns into an empty

one, with nothing much to do to fill the day, and little purpose to it.

Bereavement   For many people, one of the most serious life-changes is the death of someone very close to them – a parent, or a marriage partner. A study by Colin Murray Parkes, in 1972, looked at the ways that people react to this kind of loss, and how they learn to live with it.

Parkes interviewed people who had lost a husband or wife, at varying intervals after their loss. His subjects were referred to him by their doctors, and it was emphasised to them that they did not have to join in the study. Gradually Parkes found a pattern beginning to emerge, of three stages of grief.

The first stage Parkes described was a period of numbness, that people felt when they first heard the news of their spouse's death. Often they would make comments like: 'It just doesn't seem real – I keep expecting to wake up soon.' This period would last for several hours, and in many cases for several days. It seems as though it does take time for such bad news to 'sink in'.

The second stage that people went through was a period which Parkes called 'pining'. One of the characteristics of this stage was a strong sense of the other person's absence, and a tendency to search for him or her, in familiar places, or to look for their face in a crowd. Although many of Parkes' subjects were aware of how useless this behaviour was, they would still do it; often they would say: 'I just can't help myself – I keep expecting that they'll turn up.' Parkes found this to be strikingly similar to the searching behaviour that many animals show if they lose a mate, even though they may have seen the mate's dead body. He considers that this may be evidence of some kind of biological reaction, perhaps one that we inherit and share with other animals.

The third stage that Parkes outlines seemed to happen when the 'searching' had finished, and it was all too obvious that the missing person would not appear again. At this point the bereaved person would tend to become very depressed, and listless, and their grief would be felt most acutely. Parkes also pointed out that grief is not felt in the same way all the time, but comes and goes in 'pangs', or waves of intensity. He said that it reaches its peak, usually, about five to fourteen days after bereavement, although it may not ease off for some time. After a while, though, these pangs become less frequent, but can be easily triggered off by little things, like finding an old photograph.

Many people experience feelings of guilt or of self-reproach after the death of their spouse, even in circumstances which might not seem to warrant it. One woman Parkes interviewed had cared for her husband throughout his illness for a year, but felt guilty because she had lost her temper with him about a week before he died. Although they had made it up, and she had been forgiven by him, she still felt as if it were a 'punishment' for her not being able to cope.

Also, many newly-bereaved people become very irritable and quarrelsome with others. Often they have quarrels with old friends, or with relatives who 'don't understand'. Parkes attributed this to part of the reaction to bereavement, and says that this is something which would-be helpers should recognise, and should make allowances for.

In some of Parkes subjects, their reactions to their bereavement had been so extreme that they had had to seek psychiatric help. These individuals were not typical, and Parkes conducted a special study to try to find out what factors might be involved in this kind of case. One of the main things he found was that these people had often had a very delayed reaction to the bereavement – the period of numbness had extended for very much longer than usual. When they eventually did 'break down', their grief appeared to be very much more intense, and to last for much longer than that of more normal individuals. These were people who would carry on mourning for a dead husband or wife for several years, where most others were gradually beginning to readjust their lives and to cope with things by the end of a year.

Another factor that seemed important in whether grief reactions became extreme enough to need treatment, was whether the person had felt able to express their emotion or not. Those who had 'bottled it up', and refused to cry, or to 'break down', seemed to be much more likely to need treatment in the long run than those who had been able to cry, or in other ways express how they felt (like by talking about it to a friend).

Parkes found an important difference in people's reactions, depending on whether they had been prepared for the death or not. Those who had expected it, or who had worried about such things, seemed to be able to cope with their loss more than those who experienced it as a complete shock. But that isn't to say that they didn't feel any grief when the bereavement finally came. Also, for some people who knew that their spouse was going to die, but had been asked to keep the news from them, this had presented extra strain, as they had to pretend that nothing was wrong when they visited the person.

A study by John Hinton, in 1967, on dying, showed that for many people who were dying in hospital, not being told had simply given them another burden. Often, Hinton said, they knew that they were dying anyway, and would have liked to be able to talk about it, but the insistence of other people that they would recover prevented them. Of course, everyone is different, and there are some people who don't want to know such things, but Hinton found that many would have preferred to be able to come to terms with death openly, by talking about it with other people. Some hospitals have tried this approach with some terminally-ill patients, and have found it to be quite rewarding and successful.

As far as helping bereaved people is concerned, Parkes suggests that it is most useful for friends and relatives just to be around, and to help with the practical details, like looking after children or arranging the funeral. The bereaved person may well need assistance, but often friends will tend to 'avoid intruding', and so leave the bereaved person alone at a time when help is most useful. Also, of course, the irritability which I mentioned before may put some people off. But Parkes' subjects said that they had appreciated those people who were around, and who had visited them during this period, even if they hadn't shown it at the time.

Also, of course, the bereaved person eventually has to develop a social life again, and finds it difficult to visit people who haven't been seen since the bereavement. Recovery from a serious event like the loss of a partner takes some time, and isn't the sort of thing you can just 'snap out of', but it does happen, and people begin to form a new life, with new social roles and interactions. But Parkes emphasises that, for most people, this happens gradually, and in small stages. Most of his subjects had adapted to their new life by about a year after the death (although it was common for a wave of grief to occur around the anniversary date).

Nowadays several organisations have been formed to help people cope with severe grief. Often they have been formed by people who have themselves experienced such bereavement, and who wish to help others through this difficult period. In Britain, one of the more well-known is Cruse, the Organisation for Widows and their Children. Also, the Samaritans do a great deal of counselling for people who are learning to cope with such a loss. But many people still have to depend on friends, relatives, clergymen, or perhaps their local doctor, for any help or advice.

Stressful life-events In 1967, Holmes and Rahe published a study of the effects which major life-changes can have on people's health. They looked at medical case histories and conducted interviews with people to identify which kinds of event people found stressful, and how serious they considered the stress to be. From this, they developed a list, which ranged from fairly trivial events to ones which were considered to be very stressful indeed. Since marriage is a life-change which is fairly common, but

The Holmes and Rahe Stressful Life-events Scale

Death of marriage partner	100
Divorce	73
Marital separation	65
Prison sentence	63
Death of parent, or close family member	63
Personal injury or illness	53
Marriage	50
Being sacked from work	47
Marital reconciliation	45
Retirement	45
Change in health of family member	44
Pregnancy	40
Sex difficulties	39
Gain of new family member	39
Business readjustment	39
Change in financial state	38
Death of close friend	37
Change to a different kind of work	36
Foreclosure of mortgage	30
Change in work responsibilities	29
Son or daughter leaving home	29
Trouble with in-laws	29
Outstanding personal achievement	28
Spouse begins or stops work	26
Begin or end school/college	26
Change in living conditions	25
Change in personal habits	24
Trouble with boss at work	23
Moving house	20
Change of school/college	20
Change of recreation	19
Change of social activities	18
Change in sleeping habits	16
Change in eating habits	15
Holiday	13
Christmas	12
Minor breaches of the law	11

also involves a considerable amount of change and adjustment, they assigned it a value of 50 on the scale; and the most stressful event of all – the death of a marriage partner – was given a value of 100. Each other life-event was given a numerical value depending on the subjects' ratings of its severity.

Holmes and Rahe found that when people were asked to count up their total points for, say, the previous year, the amount that they scored often correlated very closely with that person's physical and emotional health. Subjects whose total scores were over 300 points in a given year were very likely to become ill during the next year; and those whose score amounted to between 200 and 300 were likely to develop health problems.

Holmes and Rahe attributed these findings to the effort which we have to make in coping with stressful events. As we saw in the last chapter, stress can be very physically demanding, so it's not really surprising that people who have experienced large amounts of stress end up below par physically. For most people, though, the amount of stress which they face with each life-change is well within the amount that they can cope with positively.

Erikson's 'whole-life' theory of development

Most theories of psychological development only cover the changes which happen during childhood, but Erik Erikson has developed a theory that spans the whole course of our lives. Throughout our lives, says Erikson, we go through a series of stages, and at each stage we have different conflicts and problems which we must resolve successfully. Erikson outlines eight of these stages, and the conflicts which go with them:

Stage 1   **Trust vs. Mistrust**
In this stage, the infant has to learn to trust others, and to trust in its world. Since it has been born, it has experienced discomfort and loss, which might lead it to become very distrustful. If it is provided with comfort and satisfaction during its infancy, it will develop a more trusting attitude, which will help it to develop further.

Stage 2   **Autonomy vs. Doubt**
The infant is gradually learning that it can control and direct its behaviour. This gives it a growing sense of autonomy. At the same time, though, it is very confined and limited in what it can do, and this gives it an element of self-doubt and shame, which will inhibit it. The infant has to develop its sense of autonomy despite these restrictions.

Stage 3 **Initiative vs. Guilt**
The child is developing, both socially and physically. Gradually, it is being asked to take responsibility for more and more in its life (e.g. pets, bedroom tidying, toys etc.). This gives the child a developing sense of initiative – it is becoming more and more able to make decisions and to take action. But this increasing responsibility may, instead, just bring feelings of doubt and guilt, rather than initiative.

Stage 4 **Industry vs. Inferiority**
As it develops the child is meeting more and more challenges. If it is able to meet those challenges, and to overcome them, then it is likely to enjoy learning, and to become industrious. On the other hand, if it meets with failure and gives up, or if it just opts for the easy route of avoiding challenges, then it may develop a sense of inferiority, which may lead it to avoid further challenges.

Stage 5 **Identity vs. Role confusion**
This is the problem facing the adolescent. Many adolescents face a considerable number of role-changes, like the transition from school to work, different relationships with their peer group, and so on. At the same time, they are experiencing considerable physical changes. So the danger is that they may become 'lost' in this period of confusion. The main task of the adolescent is to develop a sense of identity, or a consistent self-concept.

Stage 6 **Intimacy vs. Isolation**
Fully intimate relationships with other people cannot be developed until the sense of self-identity problem has been resolved. The task of the young adult, then, is to develop such intimate relationships with others, or with another.

Stage 7 **Generativity vs. Stagnation**
The mature adult may lead a life concerned with productive activities, like rearing children, or producing effective work strategies, and occupational achievements. On the other hand, he or she may simply allow themselves to stagnate, and not to do much at all with their lives.

Stage 8 **Integrity vs. Despair**
As old age becomes a reality, the individual develops an increasing awareness of approaching death, which is often triggered off by retirement, or by a decline in health. The crucial task of old age is to evaluate the achievements made during life, and to affirm that one's life has been meaningful, and not simply futile.

As you can probably see, each of Erikson's stages follows on from the previous ones. If an early problem is not successfully resolved, then it can lead to difficulty with later ones – for example, if the basic trust versus mistrust problem was not sorted out, then someone could find it very hard to develop an intimate relationship in adulthood. Erikson follows the psychoanalytic approach, in that he places a lot of importance on the early years, for the adult personality, but he does not neglect the fact that we are constantly developing throughout our lives too.

Summary

1 The way that people perceive events is an important factor in how they cope with life-changes.

2 Change from school to work is an important transition. For some it takes place more gradually than for others.

3 Unemployment and redundancy present strong blows to an individual's self-esteem. There appears to be a two-stage reaction to unemployment: *(a)* a period of intense job-hunting, followed by *(b)* a period of depression and lethargy.

4 Adjusting to marriage is another important life-change. Married couples go through stages in adjusting to one another. Usually by the end of the first year they have become more sensitive to one another, and have become able to disagree without feeling guilty.

5 Parenthood is another major adjustment. Unrealistic expectations from advertising and TV have to be coped with.

6 Parkes identified three stages in reaction to bereavement: numbness; pining (which often involves a kind of searching); and depression. Many factors affect the way that people cope with their bereavement.

7 Holmes and Rahe identified a scale of stressful life-events, which has been useful in predicting the onset of stress-related disorder.

8 Erikson has put forward a whole-life theory of human development, going from birth to old-age. There are eight stages, and at each stage the individual has a different conflict to come to terms with, which needs to be resolved successfully.

Chapter 25 Ageing

One of the biggest problems we face when we start to talk about the aged in our society, is that of defining what we mean exactly by the term 'old', or 'ageing'. As with intelligence, we all have a good idea of what we mean, but actually bringing that into a formal definition is another question entirely. In many different ways a formal definition may not be quite enough to explain exactly what we mean.

Defining 'old' One of these ways is the problem of individual differences. People are widely different in their physical ageing – some are noticeably 'old' at fifty, while others may still not look particularly 'old' when they are getting close to seventy! Some of these differences seem to be inherited: certainly, people with long-lived parents and grandparents tend to live active, healthy lives for longer than those with short-lived parents and grandparents. But this is only a general trend – so many other things can affect our health and development that it would be ridiculous to predict very definitely from that. For example: it would not matter how long-lived your parents were, if you have lived all your life on an inadequate diet which provided little in the way of necessary proteins and vitamins. In those circumstances you would not be likely to reach a 'ripe and healthy old age'. So we can't really take innate factors in ageing for granted, as they will be working along with environmental experiences.

These individual differences mean that it is not very practical to take a set age as a definition of 'old'. If, for instance, we tried to say 'People who are over sixty are old', then we would immediately have the problem of the many people in our society who are active, still working and energetic at sixty-plus. Because of our definition, we would have to include them as 'old', and yet I doubt that they would have been the people that we originally meant when we started talking about 'old people'. So we need to look for a better way of defining what we mean by 'old'.

Retirement has been another way that people have attempted to define 'old people'. Some researchers have adopted the view

that people who are retired are 'old', and so this is enough of
a definition. By looking at retired people, we can see what 'old
people' are like. The problem with this is that many people
work until a compulsory retirement age, and then they have
no choice but to retire. So there we may find just the same
problems as if we had set a fixed age.

Retirement also presents problems, in that there are some
people in our society who are in certain kinds of work, where
they do not have a retiring age. Professions like the law,
medicine, Parliament, etc. do not require their members to
retire at a certain age – they can carry on working as long as
they feel inclined to. So it isn't uncommon to find doctors,
judges, or MPs who are well over seventy, but are still working.
This is made even more difficult by the fact that these
professions (and most of the others where you don't have a set
retiring age) are middle-class occupations. So instead of simply
looking at people who are retired, you might find that you were
instead looking at certain *groups* of people who were retired –
not 'old people' in general at all.

The real trouble is that 'old' is a *relative* concept, which doesn't
have any particular meaning in itself. What we really mean
when we talk about old people is people who are *older* than
most members of society. In other words, we can only really
define what we mean by old people by comparing them with
other people. After all, in the sixteenth century you were
considered 'old' by the time you got to thirty-five! As the length
of time that people live grows longer, through better health
care and living conditions, so also what we mean by 'old'
changes.

Physical changes with ageing

For many people, it is the physical effects of ageing which they
think of, when they think of the old. There is a stereotype of
the old person as being toothless, wrinkled, and balding – in
short, rather like some kind of medieval witch or wizard. But
if you think of the old people you know, it's almost certain that
some of them aren't like that at all; many old people are active,
keep their own teeth and hair, and retain quite a lot of their
strength. So it's clear that there is a lot of individual difference
in the way that people change physically as they grow older.

One thing that does happen is that the skin becomes wrinkled
– losing some of its natural elasticity – and often eyesight or
hearing may become weaker. But, in our society, these changes
can be easily compensated for, by wearing glasses, or hearing
aids. So it isn't such a problem for the old person, except that
they know that they used to be able to do better, and may find
it depressing at times. We only find *serious* physical changes,

of the sort that actually interfere with how someone can manage, in very old people. In these cases, there can be a loss in overall brain weight of up to twenty per cent, and an old person may lose up to twenty-five per cent of muscle strength. However, since we don't often use all our strength, this means that they can manage most ordinary things around the home, but that they just don't have the stamina for long effort. The heart, too, will frequently become less powerful; again, it can operate perfectly well for ordinary tasks, but not for sustained effort.

Old people can also experience 'strokes' – momentary interruption of the blood supply to a part of the brain. This can result in paralysis, and interference with speech production (although not often with their ability to understand other people's speech). But the one thing that is very noticeable about recovery from strokes is the way that *effort* and *motivation* affect it. People who really try to recover, and who believe that they will be able to do so, often get full functioning back after a stroke, although it does take some time. But those who just accept it as part of growing old, and don't try hard, tend not to recover at all – or only slightly. It seems as though the highly-motivated people are recapturing control over the bit of the brain that was affected, simply by sustained effort. So it is clear that how we think may also affect our physical development.

Psychological changes with ageing

Many researchers have concentrated on the way that skills and abilities change as we get older. In particular, they have been interested in the way that changes in ability may affect an older worker's performance at work, particularly factory work.

Performance on simple tasks

A paper by Miles, in 1931, showed how performance changes at simple tasks as we get older. In general the tasks that Miles used were mechanical ones – like starting a clock, picking up a pencil and putting it in a hole, then stopping the clock again. Another task was turning the handle of a light drill. Miles showed that on many of these sorts of tasks, the peak performance came from people aged about thirty, and then there was a steady decline with age. The older people got, the fewer times they could perform the task in one minute.

Many other researchers made similar findings. Perhaps the best-known of all these is Welford's, in 1958. Welford had a deliberate policy of testing subjects to the *limit* of their abilities, rather than trying just to see if they could manage a particular task. He reasoned that many of the things people are asked to do are well within their abilities; they don't have to try very

428 A FIRST COURSE IN PSYCHOLOGY

hard to do them. But if you tested people to their limit, then you might be able to detect changes that wouldn't normally be particularly noticeable.

Memory One of the changes Welford found was that older people seemed to be much more vulnerable to interference in their short-term memory abilities. *Short-term memory* (STM) is the kind of memory you use when you have just looked up a telephone number: you keep it in your mind, perhaps repeating it over and over again, until you have finished dialling it. But then you forget it – it has only stayed in your mind for a few seconds. If the number turns out to be engaged, and you have to ring again, then very often you have to look up the number again too – it hasn't been stored in your long-term memory like your own telephone number, or all the other things you remember. Short-term memory can be easily interfered with by distractions. If you are about to dial a number that you've just looked up, and someone asks you a question, often you find that you have forgotten the number. Because your mind was distracted for a moment, it has vanished from your short-term memory. Welford found that this was more likely to happen with older people. Although it can happen with younger ones too, they seemed to be more successful at shutting out other noises and messages while they were concentrating.

This decline in STM can be important in the area of learning new skills, at work or at home. If you are trying to learn a new task, very often people will tell you what to do, and then you try to do it yourself. This means that you have to carry their instructions in your head – in your short-term memory – while you attempt to carry them out. If your STM is constantly being interfered with, by distractions, then you will find it much harder to learn to do the new task. So, from Welford's findings, many people thought that it would be difficult to re-train older workers when they needed to learn new methods and activities.

Reaction time and decision-making Another thing which Welford found older people did less well on was reaction time – the time it takes you to react to a new stimulus, like pressing a button as soon as you see a light, or hear a noise. But he did not find it was because older people were slower at moving; instead he found that they took more time to *decide* to move when they received the stimulus. So it was the decision time that was increased.

Looking further, Welford found that in many cases, older people tended to take longer to make decisions than younger people, and again this could influence their work. In the sort of job where they had to make rapid decisions and act on them

immediately, then possibly older workers would find this to be
an increasing problem.

Welford did stress, however, that these effects were not
noticeable in everyday life; that they had only been discovered
because they had tested individuals to the very limit of their
ability. With most kinds of work, he said, people operated well
within their abilities, and so older individuals had no problems
at all. He identified five possible effects that could arise from
decline as a result of ageing:

1 Performance fails completely – the job becomes more than
   the individual can manage.
2 The individual can still work, but not so efficiently as before.
3 The individual adjusts to their changed abilities, and still
   works efficiently even though they are not as able as they
   were.
4 No loss in performance – the job is still well within capacity
   and the older person can do it as well as ever.
5 The individual is aware of the decline in ability, and so tries
   hard to overcome it. By doing so, it can end up that the
   older worker does even better than they did before. (This is
   known as *over-compensation*.)

Many of the declines in ability that occur as the result of ageing
are compensated for. Failing eyesight can be adjusted by
spectacles, and deafness may be coped with by using a hearing
aid. The tendency of the body to stiffen with age may be
avoided by careful attention to diet and exercise. Many of the
distractions and stresses that disturb an older worker could be
avoided by improving working conditions, as well. So these are
not really permanent and lasting problems.

Experience   Perhaps the main advantage an older worker can have over a
younger one is the development of memory strategies and a
store of previously-learned skills. This can mean that the older
worker can actually be *better* at some kinds of work than
younger workers are – it's not all the other way round!
   Bromley pointed out, in 1966, that in any task where they
have to draw on previous experience, older workers show a
strong advantage over younger ones. The kind of tasks where
they did badly were the abstract, 'context-free' tasks, where
they did not relate the skill to everyday life. It seemed that, for
the most part, older workers were compensating for their
decline in STM and decision-time on abstract tasks, by using
strategies gained from their previous experience in other areas.

Training older   In view of these findings about the abilities of older people,
workers   some researchers thought that perhaps it would be possible to

develop new retraining methods for use with older people. The main researcher in this field at first was E. Belbin who developed methods of retraining for older workers that did not rely so much on short-term memory, but more on the person seeing for themselves exactly what needed to be done. This emphasised the *context* of the task much more, and didn't require so much resistance to distraction as the ordinary teaching methods. According to Belbin, in 1958, there were three main problems presented by ordinary teaching:

1 Understanding long and complicated verbal instructions. When you are first learning something new, it is often difficult to grasp the first instructions, because you don't yet know how they are applied. In other words, you can't see them *in context*.
2 Translating instructions into actions. This presents a difficulty because it involves holding the instructions in short-term memory while attempting to convert them into actions at the same time.
3 'Unlearning' your mistakes. When you are first learning something it is very easy to start to do it 'wrong', or awkwardly. Later on when you want to improve, you have to forget those first habits and relearn new ones. For a lot of people this is the most difficult of all.

The method Belbin devised involved preventing all of these difficulties from happening. For example: one of their experiments concerned training people in a wool mill to mend cloth that had not been woven properly. Instead of following the traditional method for training Belbin used special cloth, woven from very thick thread. Because this was so large, it was very easy to see the pattern of the weave, and to identify any errors that had been made. By working on this, the trainees could see exactly what they were doing, and could learn the correct techniques easily. When they had done that, they moved on to working with ordinary cloth, but using a magnifying glass so that they could also see that very clearly. Then, when they were used to that they discarded the magnifying glasses. By this time, they were working correctly, and were able to mend several different types of weaves.

Belbin compared the results of this method with people learning by the older, traditional way of sitting next to an experienced mender who would explain what needed to be done. They also compared the older people learning by the new method, with school-leavers – some of whom had learnt by the traditional method, and some of whom learned by the new method. In all cases, the older workers using the new method were much quicker to learn than the fifteen-year-olds. They had reached a good standard after only about twenty hours instruction, while the school-leavers took between three and ten weeks to reach the same level, even if they, too, were being given the new teaching method. So the Belbin studies were able to show quite clearly that older workers were *not* slower to learn, or not worth retraining, as some of the early studies had implied.

A more recent paper by Welford, in 1976, has indicated that what seems to impede performance in old people is not so much their being unable to perform the various tests, but that they are not particularly willing to. He has come to the conclusion that performance and ability do not so much depend on people's physical and mental capacities, as they do on their willingness to use these capacities to the full. This might perhaps explain Bromley's findings, that old people do better on tasks which make sense to them than on meaningless, context-free tasks. Perhaps they are just not as prepared to co-operate on these sort of problems as young people!

Intelligence   Many people have tried to find out whether people become less intelligent when they get older. In part, we have already been dealing with this question, since learning new skills is unquestionably a part of intelligence. But there are other aspects of it, too. If we take intelligence as measured by intelligence tests, then straightaway we have a problem. As we saw in the section on intelligence testing, IQ scores are a kind of comparison between an individual's abilities, and those of other people of the same age. So if intelligence really did decline with age, and decline in the same way with everyone, then you wouldn't be able to tell that from an IQ score! Since the measurement of your IQ is standardised by comparison with other people of your age, then if your IQ had gone down with age, theirs would have done too. So it would come out exactly the same as it was before. Fortunately, though, people don't age at the same rate, and there are lots of individual differences, so we can still use IQ scores to some extent.

The early studies which looked at IQ and age were very alarming. They showed a clear decline in IQ as people got older; it appeared that your intelligence started getting less as soon as you were past your twenties. So people thought that there must be a very serious problem with old people not being very 'bright'. Fortunately, however, these findings aren't quite as definite as they appeared. They had been obtained by taking a *cross-section* of age groups; comparing the IQ scores of people who were twenty, thirty, forty etc. The problem with this is that these people have all grown up in different ways, and at different times, so it is not really valid to compare them. For example: people who were sixty in 1950 would have grown up and gone to school at the very end of the last century, while those who were twenty would have gone to school in the 1930s. Education methods have changed a great deal over those years. So has the amount of time spent at school, and the kinds of examination taken. So it is not really surprising to find such a difference in their intelligence test scores, is it?

More recent studies have shown a very different picture. In 1966 Burns reported on a longitudinal study of teachers, which had started in the 1920s. The same people had been given intelligence tests when they were twenty-two and again when they were fifty-six. On average, their IQs were seven points *higher* when they were fifty-six than when they were twenty-two. So it seems that there is not such a serious decline in ageing and intelligence as had been thought.

Another discovery Burns made was that practice and experience makes a difference to how well our intelligence is maintained. He divided the group of teachers into two sets: those who taught arts subjects and those who taught sciences. The arts teachers showed an increase in scores for verbal abilities, while the science teachers showed an increase in numerical and diagrammatical skills. So it seems that they had improved in those areas in which they had been working most.

Although there isn't a steady decline of intelligence and skills with ageing, as was previously thought, some recent studies have shown that there is some sort of decline that sets in just before people die. It appears that people retain their skills and abilities quite well, but that there is a decrease in ability and skill which first starts to show about five years before death. From then, the person gradually deteriorates until they eventually become weak and die. But in our society, people live for very long periods – it is not uncommon to meet people still fit and active at eighty, and as capable as they ever have been. It would appear that a lot of the old studies had such pessimistic results about old people's abilities because they mixed together those who were fit and healthy, with those who were leading up to their final years of life.

The social side of ageing

Many theories about the social side of ageing have concentrated on the changes that seem to happen once people retire. We live in a society containing many old or elderly individuals, and yet, in our day-to-day lives, we don't usually have much contact with people over sixty. Most of us will have relatives who are over retiring age, and may perhaps know one or two other people, but this isn't many, when you think of just how many pensioners we have in our society.

To a large extent, our society seems to be divided up into age-layers, where people mix mostly with people of roughly their own age. This hasn't always been the case; in most earlier times, there was much less interaction with just one age group, and people would mix with others of all ages. But in our modern society, the tendency is to seek the company of one's peer group, whether that is other adolescents, other young married couples, other middle-aged couples, or other elderly people. It is odd to find someone of thirty-five whose social group is mainly individuals of twenty-three, for instance.

We can find in this some explanation for the fact that we don't meet many old people; we can also point out that if we are thirty, we don't usually meet many teenagers either. But although we might not actually *meet* many teenagers, we are still aware of the teenagers in our society. We still see them, in the streets, or on the bus. In general, old people don't seem to be quite so visible: we don't see many old people around (although we do see some, of course). But not nearly as many as we should, given the numbers in society. It appears that when people retire, they often don't just stop working, but they also don't participate in society so much, and this is something which some researchers have concentrated on, as a possible explanation of the changes that happen to people when they get old.

Disengagement theory   Cummings and Henry put forward a theory of ageing, in 1961, which concentrated on the way that old people seem to withdraw from society. Until they retire, most people's lives are centred around their work and their social life. When they do retire, they no longer have their work, and their social life becomes increasingly difficult to maintain, partly perhaps because of reduced incomes, and partly because their friends are often still at work. So, gradually, these people have less and less of a social life.

Also, people who have retired have far fewer 'social roles' in their lives than they had before. Where before, they not only had their family roles, but also roles at work, now they are left with only those roles which relate to family. So Cummings and Henry pointed out that the retired person is just not as involved with society as before.

Another factor about retirement is the way that many people feel about receiving money for doing nothing. If you have been accustomed all your life to working for your living – to being economically active, and earning your money – it is often difficult to get used to the idea that you are receiving money for nothing. Many old people describe feeling really guilty when they first draw their pension – they say it makes them feel a fraud. But also, receiving the pension is giving that person another message – that they are no longer economically useful to society. People are aware that working is important to the economy of the country as a whole, but now they are being told that there is nothing more they can contribute. This makes many old people feel socially useless.

All these things go together, according to Cummings and Henry, to encourage the old person to 'disengage' from society – to withdraw, and to become less involved than they were before. At the same time, society is withdrawing from the person; there is less and less for old people to get involved in, and to make them feel important to society. So Cummings and Henry said that the old person and society *mutually* withdraw from one another.

As old people disengage from society, they become less and less involved with other people, and become increasingly isolated. This becomes accentuated by their increasing ill-health as well. Some researchers regarded this as a way of gradually preparing for death, and some have even suggested that it may be innate – that we might be preprogrammed to disengage from society once we retire. Other research however, has shown that perhaps disengagement is not quite as inevitable as it appeared from Cummings and Henry's theory, because some old people do not seem to disengage from society, but instead appear to become *more* involved and active once they retire.

Activity theory

Havighurst, in 1964, put forward an alternative view of the ageing process. He said that those individuals who adjusted most successfully to old age were the ones who didn't withdraw from society, but who kept up their levels of activities, finding new things to do as they gave up their work.

In particular, Havighurst thought it was important for an old person to keep up their 'role count' – in other words, to make sure that they always had lots of different social roles. If they lost roles through leaving work, then they should find more through new hobbies and activities which would bring them into contact with other people and interests. The people who did keep up their role count, according to Havighurst, would be the ones who adjusted most successfully, and enjoyed their retirement years.

This model is very much the one that has been adopted by organisations like *Age Concern*, who regard it as very important that people coming up to retirement should start to direct themselves towards the new things that they can do. Many places are now putting on pre-retirement courses, which are intended to encourage people approaching retirement to think constructively about these kinds of alternatives.

However, neither of these theories can be thought of as providing the final answer to the question of what people who are retired should be doing. It appears to depend very much on the individual; some people find disengagement a good strategy when they retire, and enjoy the freedom from responsibility that it brings; other people find that activity is the better strategy. People are individuals, and what suits one person may well be totally the wrong thing for another.

J. Dyson criticised, in 1980, both these approaches to old age. Although they may well be right as far as they go, she points out that neither really takes much account of the more mundane social reasons which might limit an individual's choices. Both activity theory and disengagement seem to be providing a *prescriptive* approach – they are saying what people *ought* to be doing at this time in their lives. But for many people, factors like low incomes or poor health may actually prevent them from having this choice; if you are tied to the house, then your opportunities for getting out and increasing your role count are limited before you start.

Social exchange theory
Dyson has suggested that it may be more useful to see the process of adjusting to retirement as being the development of a sort of contract between the individual and society. This idea was first put forward by J. Dowd, in 1975, who suggested that an individual agrees to give up certain things that they have been used to, when they retire. In exchange, they receive other things from society, which act as a kind of inducement.

For example, Dowd suggested that people give up their place in the workforce, as an economically active member of society; and their political and social involvement in society. In exchange, they receive increased leisure time, money (in the form of a pension), and an 'honourable discharge' from the obligation to work. This is put as a kind of contract, in that certain inducements are offered, in exchange for certain kinds of behaviour.

Dowd pointed out that this is not a 'forced' contract – there is nothing to prevent an individual refusing to withdraw from society, or political activity – but it works by social pressure. There are *expectations* in society that an old person will act in certain kinds of ways. As we've seen in previous sections, social pressure can be very powerful.

So how do old people feel about this? Dowd suggested that most old people feel that it isn't really a fair exchange, but don't feel that there is anything they can do about it. However, Dyson suggests that, when asked, most people will admit that it is a fair exchange – but often they will also say that they don't feel it is right for them *personally*. So because they see it as being just themselves, and not wrong for most other old people, they are not as likely to try to challenge it. Although many old people don't feel that their situation is much fun, you still don't often find them organised into protest groups to try to change it!

We have looked at three very different ways of regarding old people and their social lives. Disengagement theory puts forward a picture of the old person as withdrawing and becoming more and more isolated from society, until eventually they reach death. Activity theory puts forward a much brighter picture – that what people should be doing is becoming more and more involved with things, and developing new interests and hobbies. Social exchange theory tries to show how people *feel* about the process of change that happens to them when they retire.

As with so many other things, it would be silly to try to say that one of these theories is right and that the others are wrong. People vary widely in their needs: for some people activity is the best kind of strategy, while for others disengagement is the better option. But by being aware of each of these theories, we may be able to get a clearer picture of what does happen after we retire, and what sort of choices people do have in front of them. Taken all in all, it would seem that the picture modern psychology has of old age and ageing is not nearly as gloomy as perhaps the accepted social view would lead us to believe.

Summary

1 One of the biggest problems in talking about old people is defining what we mean by 'old'. There are so many individual and social differences that it is difficult to draw the line at any particular point.

2 Many researchers studied what people were capable of as they aged. Welford adopted a strategy of testing people to the limit of their abilities, to show up changes better.

3 Welford found old people to be less efficient at reaction-time tests, and short-term memory. But they could compensate for this from their previous experience.

4 Belbin developed new training methods, which showed that older people could be just as quick to develop new skills as younger individuals – if they were taught appropriately.

5 Older studies seemed to show that people got less intelligent as they grew older. But more recent, longitudinal studies, showed that this was not necessarily true.

6 Cummings and Henry suggested that old people went

through an inevitable process of disengagement from society, after retirement.

7 Havighurst suggested that the people who adapted best to retirement were those who took up new activities and maintained their role count.

8 Dyson suggested that people see retirement as a kind of social exchange, where they give up some things in exchange for other privileges. She suggested that they see it as a fair exchange, even if they don't think it's right for them personally.

Glossary

Abnormal	Unusual, or different from the norm.
Absolute refractory period	The period immediately after a nerve cell has fired.
Accommodation	One of the two ways in which schemata develop. New information forces the schema to adjust and change in order to absorb it.
Achievement motivation	The need to be successful in things which are attempted.
Affectionless psychopathy	A state in which the person has, or appears to have, no social conscience, and no relationships with others.
AH group tests	A series of pencil and paper intelligence tests designed be administered to a large group of people at the same time. There are different AH tests for different ranges of intelligence.
Alienation	A feeling of being separate and cut-off from one's work – seeing it as something impersonal and irrelevant to one's own individual needs or desires.
All-or-none principle	A nerve cell either fires by an amount which is always the same, or not at all.
Anal stage	Freud's second psycho-sexual stage, in which the libido is focused on the anus, and this is the child's main source of pleasure.
Anthropometric	Concerned with measuring the human being ('metric' = measurement; 'anthropo' = to do with human beings).
Arousal	Any form of excitement of the nervous system – e.g. anger, fear, extreme happiness.
Assimilation	One of the two ways in which schemata develop. New information is absorbed into the schema, without changing it.
Association	The connection of one thing with another.
Attribution	The process of giving reasons for why things happen.
Auditory stimulation	Sounds that an animal will notice or respond to.
Authoritarianism	A personality state which involves very rigid approaches to discipline, extreme hostility to social deviants, and a very intolerant, 'black and white' view of right and wrong.
Autism	A psychological disorder suffered by some children, in which they withdraw from human contact and reality.

Autokinetic effect	A visual illusion, in which a stationary spot of light in a dark room appears to move.
Autonomic reactions	Reactions of the body which are not under conscious control, such as heartbeat, sweating, or blood pressure.
Autonomous morality stage	Kohlberg's third stage of moral development. Acts are judged in terms of the morality of the underlying rules or principles of behaviour.
Aversion therapy	A form of behaviour therapy designed to make patients avoid certain things.
Behaviour	Anything which a person or an animal does – an activity, or a response of some kind.
Behaviour shaping	The systematic reinforcement of small bits of behaviour to produce complicated behaviour.
Behaviour therapy	An approach to treating psychiatric problems – it consists of teaching patients how to learn new forms of behaviour which will help them to cope.
Binocular disparity	The difference between the pictures received by one individual's two eyes.
Biofeedback	A method of learning to control one's autonomic responses through operant conditioning.
Case study	A detailed study of one, or just a few, individuals rather than a study of a large group.
Cephalo-caudal	'Head to tail' – the top parts of the body become co-ordinated before the lower parts.
Challenging play	Play which the child has to make some kind of effort with.
Chemotherapy	Treating medical or psychiatric problems by giving drugs.
Circadian/diurnal rhythms	24-hour-biological rhythms.
Classical conditioning	A basic form of association learning.
Cloning	Growing new animals or plants artificially from a few cells from one parent plant or animal.
Cognition	Mental processes. Cognition includes the processes of perception, memory, thinking, reasoning, language, and some types of learning.
Cognitive development	The way that a child's thinking changes as the child grows older – intellectual development.
Cognitive maps	Mental images about where things are. People develop cognitive maps as they get to know a town or an institution; rats develop one as they explore experiential mazes.
Collapse	The third stage of Selye's long-term stress reaction, in which the system cannot sustain the effort needed to cope with stress any more, and the person becomes physically or mentally ill.

Compliance	Doing what others are doing, or what is expected, while retaining personal reservations about it.
Concrete operational stage	Piaget's third stage of intellectual development.
Conditioned reflexes	Reflexes which are produced in response to a new, learned stimulus.
Conservation	The recognition that volume, number, or other properties stay the same, even if their arrangement is altered.
Conventional morality stage	Kohlberg's second stage of moral development. Acts are judged by the intentions which underly them.
Convergent thinking	Thinking which is directed towards getting a single 'right' answer to a problem, concentrating on strict logic, and ruling out creative or intuitive thinking.
Correlation	Co-variance, or how two measurements may vary together, without one actually causing the other to change. In a positive correlation, when one of the items or measurement is great, so is the other; in a negative correlation, when one is great the other is small, and vice versa.
Correlation coefficient	A number which describes how much two measures vary together.
Correspondent inference theory	An approach to understanding how people judge whether an act is deliberate or not – which looks at how they infer that the act came from dispositional or situational causes.
Covariance theory	An approach to understanding how people judge whether an act was deliberate or not by looking at three aspects of the situation: consensus (whether other people do it too); consistency (whether that person always does it); and distinctiveness (whether they act that way in similar circumstances or not).
Critical period	A time when a certain form of learning must occur if it is to happen at all.
Cross-modal transfer	Using information obtained through one sense to understand the experience of another sense.
Cross-sectional study	A study which looks at differences in development over time by taking a cross section of people of different ages and comparing them.
Decentring	Being able to see things from someone else's point of view.
Defensible space	Living areas in which territories are clearly defined, and vandalism is discouraged because public areas are clearly visible.
Deindividuation	Losing one's personal identity, and becoming simply a 'faceless' member of a crowd or group.
Depth	Distance.

Diffusion of responsibility	The sharing out of responsibility, so that everyone feels that other people present are equally to blame, or equally responsible for what happens.
Discovery learning	A method of learning by finding explanations for oneself, rather than being given them by a teacher.
Discriminatory stimulus	A stimulus which informs the organism when the response is appropriate.
Disengagement	A theory of ageing which states that old people systematically cut themselves off from society when they retire.
Divergent thinking	Thinking which is intuitive or creative, often involving non-logical 'leaps' or sudden ideas.
Dizygotic (DZ) twins	Twins which are fraternal – that is, related to each other in the same way that ordinary siblings are.
Dogmatism	A type of rigid personality similar to authoritarianism, but one which can be left-wing too (authoritarianism is always right-wing). Like authoritarianism, it includes intolerance of those who differ from the established view, a rigid 'black and white' approach to issues, and an extreme and personal categorising of 'us and them'.
Dominant genes	Genes which always affect the phenotype if they are present, even if their opposing pair would give a contradictory instruction.
Double-blind control	When both the subjects and the person dealing with the subjects (the experimenter) are unaware of the aim of the study.
Dramatic play	Play which involves acting out events or stories.
Ego	The part of the personality which is in direct contact with reality – the conscious self.
Egocentricity	The child's initial understanding of the world, according to Piaget, as being completely centred around itself.
Egocentric speech	When a young child keeps up a spoken commentary on what's going on, but doesn't seem to be talking to anyone in particular.
Ego-defence mechanisms	Methods which the subconscious mind uses to protect the ego from various types of threat.
Electro-encephalogram (EEG)	A technique for measuring the overall electrical activity of the brain by electrodes placed on the scalp.
Empiricist	A person who believes that development occurs mainly as a result of environmental influences.
Enactive representation	Coding memories as if they were movements or muscle actions, so that things are remembered on the basis of how they feel to the body.
Ethology	The study of either human or animal behaviour in the natural environment.
Eugenics	The idea of breeding together ideal types of human beings to produce 'perfect' people – e.g. highly

intelligent ones and preventing imperfect types from breeding.

Experimenter effects When the experimenter unconsciously influences the results of the experiment or study.

External locus of control The belief that what happens to you isn't something which you can help, but occurs because of outside circumstances, like society or fate.

Eye contact Looking at someone else's eyes when they are looking at yours.

Feedback Receiving information about the effects of an action.

Fixed action patterns Inherited behaviour patterns which, because they are inherited, do not change no matter how often they are repeated.

Formal operational stage Piaget's fourth stage of intellectual development.

Free association Saying the first thing that comes into one's head, in response to a word suggested by someone else.

Frequency theory A theory of pitch perception which says that pitch is coded by the rate (or frequency) at which the cells fire.

Functional fixedness The state of being unable to think of any other use for an object except the one that is conventional.

General adaptation syndrome (GAS) The three-stage response to long-term stress outlined by Selye.

General ('g') factor Overall intelligence which is applied to all situations.

Generalisation Applying one particular learned association to more than one situation.

Genetics The study of inheritance, through the actions of genes and chromosomes.

Genotype The total genetic characteristics which an individual possesses in their chromosomes, and which they may pass on to the next generation.

Grey matter Masses of unmyelinated (unsheathed) nerve fibres and cell bodies packed together.

GSR Galvanic skin resistance – the slight but detectable increase in electrical conductivity of the skin which is caused by sweating in response to stress or tension.

Habituation The process of getting used to a continual stimulus, so that nerve cells don't register it any more and the person doesn't notice it.

Homeostasis A state of the body in which all the main functions are balanced and a constant internal environment is maintained.

Hygiene factors Factors which affect the individual at work because they are concerned with material conditions and circumstances of the work.

Hypothesis	An idea about what may happen, or be happening, if a particular theory is true.
Iconic representation	Coding memories as if they were pictures, so that things are 'visualised' in memory.
Id	The part of the personality which contains strong impulses, desires, and emotions.
Idiographic	Describing ('graphic') the individual ('idio'). The term idiographic is particularly used to describe those personality tests which are concerned with looking in detail at the characteristics of the single person, and not with comparing that person with other members of the population.
Implosion therapy (or 'flooding')	A form of behaviour therapy used to treat phobias.
Imprinting	A form of attachment, whereby a young animal develops a bond with its mother.
Independent-measures design	When each condition of a study involves a different set of subjects.
Innate releasing mechanisms (IRMs)	'Triggers', or rapid switching mechanisms, which produce inherited behaviour in response to a particular environmental stimulus.
Insight learning	Learning which takes place as a result of making a sudden mental connection and seeing the solution all at once, as opposed to more gradual forms of learning in which the solution is arrived at a little bit at a time, like trial and error learning.
Intelligence A	The potential intelligence which we could develop if our environment was absolutely perfect from the moment we were conceived – genetic intelligence.
Intelligence B	The unknown proportion of intelligence A which is actually developed through interaction with the environment.
Intelligence C	The unknown proportion of intelligence B which can be measured by IQ tests.
Internalisation	Doing what others are doing, or what is expected, because of a belief that it is correct.
Internal locus of control	The belief that what happens to you is largely a result of your own efforts, or at least can be influenced by them.
Introspection	Looking 'inwards' to analyse one's own mental state.
Involuntary communication	Giving information to others accidentally.
Kinaesthetic senses	Senses to do with feelings within the body.
Language acquisition device (LAD)	An innate mechanism, suggested by Chomsky, which gives children a genetic ability to pick up language rapidly, by recognising its 'deep structure'.
Law of effect	A principle of learning, that behaviour which brings about pleasant consequences is likely to be repeated.

Law of exercise	A principle of learning, that learned associations are strengthened through repetition.
Learned helplessness	Failing to deal with or avoid unpleasant situations which could easily be changed, because of previous experience with other situations.
Learning set	A general principle or concept which has been derived by trial and error, but can be applied to new learning.
Libido	Internal energy responsible for pleasurable sensations, and which, according to Freud, directs human behaviour.
Locus of control	The general belief that a person has about why things happen to them: whether they come largely from that person's own efforts, or whether they come from outside sources.
Longitudinal study	A study which examines changes over a period of time, by following up the same individuals over a long period.
Make-believe play	Play which involves the child using its imagination to pretend about places, people or objects.
Markers	Objects which are used to mark out a territory, such as a coat placed over the back of a chair to signal that the seat is 'taken'.
Mastery play	Play which involves developing skills of some kind.
Maternal deprivation	When a child does not have any contact with the mother.
Maturation	Development which occurs as a result of genetic influences showing as the animal or plant becomes older.
Mean	The arithmetic average of a set of numbers.
Medical model	The approach to disturbed behaviour which holds that the person has something physically wrong with them – that they are sick.
Meiosis	The division of cells for reproduction in such a way that each reproductive cell has only half the usual number of chromosomes, and must fuse with another reproductive cell to grow into a whole plant or animal.
Micro-electrode recording	A technique for recording when single nerve cells are firing.
Mitosis	The division of cells in such a way that each chromosome is copied in each new cell.
Modelling	Providing someone to be imitated.
Monocular depth cues	Clues the brain uses to work out how far away things are, even if only seen through one eye.
Monotropy	A special attachment formed by babies with just one other person, which is different from other relationships.
Monozygotic (MZ) twins	Twins who are genetically identical.
Motivators	Factors at work which, according to Herzberg, encourage individuals to work for their own personal satisfaction in some way.

Motor skills	Physical skills, to do with movement and co-ordination.
Nativist	A person who believes that development occurs mainly as a result of genetic influences.
Nature/nurture debate	The question of whether a particular kind of development happens because of learning and the environment, or because of inheritance and biological maturation.
Neonate studies	Studies of new-born babies.
Nomothetic	A term which is used to describe those psychometric tests which are designed to assess how normal or typical someone is, by comparing their scores with what would normally be expected of members of that population.
Non-verbal communication (NVC)	Passing information to others, consciously or unconsciously, without using language.
Normal distribution curve	A bell-shaped pattern on a graph, in which most scores come near the centre point, and fewer and fewer tail out to the extremes.
Object concept	The idea that objects have a lasting existence, which continues even if you are not paying attention to them.
Observational learning	Learning through watching how others behave.
Operant conditioning	Learning through the effects of an action or set of actions.
Operant strength	The extent to which a certain association has been learned through operant conditioning.
Opponent-process theory	A theory of colour vision which says that different cone cells respond to red/green, blue/yellow, or light/dark.
Opportunistic crime	Crimes which take place on the spur of the moment because the opportunity presents itself – they are not planned in advance.
Optimum level	The best possible level, taking into account all the various influencing factors.
Oral stage	Freud's first psycho-sexual stage, in which the libido is focused on the mouth, and this is the child's main source of pleasure.
Over-compensation	Correcting a failing skill so thoroughly that it actually becomes better than before.
Pairing	Putting one thing with another.
Partial reinforcement	Presenting reinforcements in such a way that not every response made is reinforced.
Participant observation	When the observer joins in as a fully participating member of the group being observed.
Peer group	People who are like ourselves – e.g. the same age.
Perception	Making sense of the information we receive through our sense organs (touch, vision, smell etc.).
Personal constructs	Individual ways of making sense of the world, which have been developed on the basis of experience. Personal

construct theorists argue that getting to understand the personal constructs which someone applies to make sense of their experience is essential for effective psychotherapy, as well as for effective interaction in day to day living.

Personal space An area round the individual, which is the distance they prefer to keep from unknown others.

Phallic stage Freud's third psycho-sexual stage, in which the libido is focused on the genitals, and the child develops Oedipus or Electra complexes which must be resolved.

Phenotype The genetic characteristics which individuals actually develop as they grow and mature.

Phobia An irrational fear which is so strong that it interferes with day-to-day life.

Phylogenetic scale A scale of evolutionary development which tells us roughly how closely related to humans various animals are.

Pilomotor response A response which consists of hair standing on end.

Placebo A harmless substance given instead of a drug, without the subject or patient being aware that it is ineffective.

Place theory A theory of pitch perception which says that pitch is coded by the place of the hair cells on the cochlea (coiled structure in inner ear).

Play face A special facial expression which both chimpanzees and human beings use, which signals that the person is playing, and shouldn't be taken seriously.

Play therapy A method of treating disturbed children by encouraging them to play freely, and to express their worries through play.

Pleasure principle The id's demands that its impulses be satisfied immediately – that gratification of desires is the most important thing.

Pluralistic ignorance The way that people in a group tend to mislead each other about how serious the situation is.

Polygenic Caused by the actions of any genes working together.

Polygraph A machine often used to measure stress or anxiety – and therefore sometimes as a 'lie-detector' – which works by measuring many ('poly') different physical indicators that the person is under stress, such as blood pressure, pulse rate, heart rate, and GSR.

Population norms A set of scores for a particular population (e.g. females aged 18–24) which establishes the normal range of scores for that population on a particular psychometric test or measure.

Prejudice A fixed, pre-set attitude, usually negative and hostile, and usually applied to members of a particular social category.

Pre-moral stage	Kohlberg's first stage of moral development. Acts are judged purely by their consequences.
Pre-operational stage	Piaget's second stage of cognitive development.
Primacy effect	The way that the first things you encounter make more of an impression than later ones do. So, for example, we are more likely to remember the first items in a list, or the first impression which someone made on us.
Primary territories	Personal areas which are owned and private, like someone's bedroom.
Proxemics	The study of how people use space and distance to convey social information, like how friendly they are with someone.
Proximo-distal	'Near to far' – the central parts of the body become co-ordinated before the outer parts.
Psychiatry	The branch of medicine which is concerned with those who behave oddly or show psychological disturbances.
Psychoactive drugs	Drugs which directly affect how someone's mind works, eg by making them less anxious or more alert.
Psychoanalyst	Someone who attempts to understand the human mind by using techniques and theories derived from the ideas of Freud and his followers.
Psycho-dynamic theory	The psychoanalytic view of adult personality as keeping a flexible balance between the different demands of the id, the ego, and the superego.
Psychology	The scientific study of experience and behaviour. Psychology draws together systematic studies of experience and behaviour using a wide range of methods, and focuses on many different angles and levels of experience.
Psychometric tests	Instruments which are designed to measure mental characteristics like intelligence, ability or aptitudes.
Public territories	Areas which can be occupied by anyone for a while, like seats in shopping centres, or telephone boxes.
Random sample	A sample chosen in such a way that any member of the relevant population is equally likely to be selected.
Rate of response	The frequency with which a response is made in a particular period of time.
Reality principle	The ego's insistence that impulses must be satisfied in a realistic way, which will not produce social or internal problems.
Recessive genes	Genes which would not affect the phenotype unless paired with another gene of the same type. If paired with a dominant gene they would not show in that individual, but they might be passed on to another generation.

Recidivism	Repeated breaking of the law resulting in court cases.
Reference group	Those others with whom we make comparisons, in order to assess our own behaviour.
Reinforcement	Something which strengthens a learned association.
Reinforcement schedule	A specific method of administering partial reinforcement.
Relative refractory period	A period after the absolute refractory period, when the cell will only fire in response to a very strong stimulus.
Repeated-measures design	When each condition of a study involves the same set of subjects.
Replicable experiment	An experiment which can be repeated and which, given the same conditions, will produce the same results.
Representative sample	A set of subjects which is typical of the whole population of subjects who could have been used in the study.
Resistance to extinction	The length of time an organism will continue to respond after reinforcement has ceased.
Retinal image	The pattern of light which falls on the retina of the eye, through the pupil.
Retrospective study	A study which attempts to discover influences on development by looking back over a period of time.
Role count	The number of social roles which an individual plays in society – eg mother, bus passenger, worker etc.
Rule-bound play	A type of play described by Piaget, in which the child's actions are confined by an agreed set of rules. These may be organised by adults or developed by children themselves.
Schema (pl. schemata)	A set of ideas, memories and deductions which is used to direct and control behaviour in new situations as well as in familiar ones.
Secondary territories	Areas which are used by many people and not 'owned' by anyone in particular, but which are open to the public.
Selective placement	The matching of an adoptive child to a home which is similar to the one it has come from as far as possible.
Self-actualisation	The development of one's whole potential.
Self-concept	The complete set of ideas which individuals hold about themselves.
Self-esteem	The evaluative aspects of the self-concept.
Self-fulfilling prophecy	A statement which comes true simply because it has been made.
Self-image	The descriptive aspects of the self-concept.
Senile dementia	A form of mental illness which particularly affects old people, in which they become very confused as to where they are and what is happening, and may appear to be irrational. This is also sometimes known as Alzheimer's syndrome.
Sensitive period	A time in which certain forms of learning are most likely to occur.

Sensitive responsiveness	The ability to notice and to react to the small messages with which a baby signals what it wants.
Sensori-motor stage	Piaget's first stage of cognitive development.
Shape constancy	The recognition that an object remains the same shape even if it is seen from different angles.
Short-term memory (STM)	Immediate memory, which only lasts for a few seconds – eg the sort of memory which is used to retain a telephone number for the few seconds it takes to dial it.
Sibling rivalry	Competition or jealousy between brothers and/or sisters for their mother's affection.
Simple play	Play for its own sake, which doesn't involve any particular challenges to the child.
Single-blind control	When the subjects in a study are unaware of the aim or purpose of that study.
Size constancy	Recognition that an object remains the same size, even though the size of the retinal image differs according to how far away it is.
Socialisation	The process by which a person comes to behave in the ways that society requires.
Social learning	Learning through interaction with others in society.
Social privation	Having no contact at all with any others.
Somatic nervous system	The part of the nervous system concerned with sending or receiving information from the body.
Specific ('s') factor	The particular intelligence is applied to certain problems, such as mathematical reasoning, or like vocabulary.
S-R theory	Stimulus-Response theory – using either Classical or Operant conditioning to explain behaviour.
(S-R) theory of child development	An approach to understanding child development in which the main emphasis of study is on the child learning specific behavioural responses to specific stimuli.
Stage of resistance	The second stage of adaptation to long-term stress, in which the body is fighting off the effects of the shock, and trying to cope with the increased pressure.
Standard deviation	A measure used in statistics to describe how varied a set of scores are – how common it is for any given score to be very different from the average. If it is usual for scores to be very varied, the set of scores is said to have a high standard deviation.
Standardised instructions	When each subject in a study receives exactly the same (word-for-word) instructions from the experimenter. These are prearranged.
Standardised procedures	When each subject in a study experiences exactly the same, prearranged, events as other subjects.
Status envy	Being jealous of someone because they have higher rank or more power, or are more important.
Stereotyped	Exactly the same each time that it occurs.

Stratified, or quota sampling	When the sample, or set of subjects, is chosen in such a way that each different type of subject in the population is represented.
Super-ego	The part of the personality which is concerned with morality, conscience and duty, according to Freud.
Symbolic play	Play in which objects or areas are used as symbols for other things – the child pretends, for instance, that a sofa is a doll's bed.
Symbolic representation	The coding of memories by using symbols to 'represent' them mentally.
Tactile stimulation	Touch that an animal will notice or respond to.
Therapy	Treatment for some kind of problem or disorder.
Threshold of response	The smallest amount of stimulation needed to trigger the firing of a nerve cell.
Time and motion study	A technique used to assess piece-work rates in factories, by examining the physical movements involved and seeing how they may be made most efficiently.
Token economy systems	A method of teaching 'normal' behaviour to long-term psychiatric patients through behaviour shaping.
Transgenerational transmission	When an effect appears to arise from genetic influences, but has really come from environmental influences on the mother before birth.
Two-factor theory of intelligence	The idea that any intelligent behaviour is brought about by two different aspects of intelligence working together.
Type A people	People who are tense and ambitious in their approach to work, and at risk of getting heart disease.
Type B people	People who are relaxed and easy-going in their approach to work, although they may still work hard. Type B people are unlikely to develop heart disease.
Visual field dependence/ independence	Strong reliance on the information we receive through our eyes, or the ability to manage without it.
Visual stimulation	Sights that an animal will notice or respond to.
Volley principle	Hair cells taking it in turns to fire, thus producing a more rapid burst of signals than a single cell could manage.
White matter	Masses of myelinated (encased in fatty sheath) nerve fibres packed together.
X and Y chromosomes	Chromosomes which carry the genes affecting gender. Women have two X chromosomes, while men have one X and one Y chromosome.
Yerkes-Dodson Law	A principle expressing the relationship between arousal and achievement.
Young-Helmholtz theory	A theory of colour vision which says that different cone cells respond to the three primary colours of red, blue and green.

Academic
References

Abernathy, E. M. (1940) The effect of changed environmental conditions upon the results of college examinations. *Journal of Psychology*, **10**, 293–301.

Adorno, T. W., Frenkel-Brunswik, G., Levinson, D. J. and Sanford, R. N. (1950) *The Authoritarian Personality*. New York: Harper.

Ahrens, S. R. (1954) Beitrage zur entwicklung des physiognomie und mimikerkennes. (Contributions on the development of physiognomy and mimicry recognition). *Zeitschrift für Experimentelle und Angewandte Psychologie*, **2**, 412–454.

Ainsworth, M. D. S. (1967) *Infancy in Uganda: Infant Care and the Growth of Love*. Baltimore: Johns Hopkins Press.

Ajzen, I. (1988) *Attitudes, Personality and Behaviour*. Milton Keynes: Open University Press.

Ajzen, I. and Fishbein, M. (1980) *Understanding Attitudes and Predicting Social Behaviour*. Englewood Cliffs, NJ: Prentice-Hall.

Altman, I. (1975) *The Environment and Social Behaviour*. Monterey, CA: Brooks/Cole.

Andrew, R. J. (1965) The origins of facial expressions. *Scientific American*, **213**, 88–94.

Annis, R. C. and Frost, B. (1973) Human visual ecology and orientation anisotropies in acuity. *Science*, **182**, 729–731.

Archer, J. (1986) Ethical issues in psychobiological research on animals. *Bulletin of the British Psychological Society*, **39**, 361–364.

Ardrey, R. (1966) *The Territorial Imperative*. London: Collins.

Argyle, M. (1967) *The Psychology of Interpersonal Behaviour*. Harmondsworth: Penguin.

Argyle, M. (1969) *Social Interaction*. London: Methuen.

Argyle, M. (1972) *The Social Psychology of Work*. Harmondsworth: Penguin.

Argyle, M., Alkema, F. and Gilmour, R. (1971) The communication of friendly and hostile attitudes by verbal and non-verbal signals. *European Journal of Social Psychology*, **1**, 385–402.

Argyle, M. and Crossland, J. (1987) The dimensions of positive emotions. *British Journal of Social Psychology*, **26**, 127–137.

Argyle, M. and Dean, J. (1965) Eye contact, distance and affiliation. *Sociometry*, **28**, 289–304.

Aronson, E. and Osherow, N. (1980) Co-operation, prosocial behaviour, and academic performance: experiments in the desegregated classroom. In: L. Bickerman (ed) *Applied Social Psychology Annual*. Beverly Hills, CA: Sage.

Asch, S. E. (1951) Effects of group pressure on the modification and distortion of judgements. In: H. Guetzkow (ed) *Groups, Leadership & Men*. Pittsburgh: Carnegie Press.

Atkinson, R. C. (1975) Mnemotechnics in second-language learning. *American Psychologist*, **30**, 821–828.

Atkinson, R. C. and Shiffrin, R. M. (1977) Human memory: a proposed system and its control processes. In: G. H. Bower (ed) *Human Memory: Basic Processes.* New York: Academic Press.

Ax, A. F. (1953) Physiological differentiation of emotional states. *Psychosomatic Medicine,* **15**, 433–442.

Axline, V. (1971) *Dibs: In Search of Self.* Harmondsworth: Penguin.

Ballard, R. (1983) Personal communication.

Bandura, A. (1989) Perceived self-agency in the exercise of personal agency. *The Psychologist,* **2(10)**, 411–424.

Bandura, A., Ross, D. and Ross, S. (1963) Imitation of film mediated aggressive models. *Journal of Abnormal and Social Psychology,* **66**, 3–11.

Bandura, A. and Walters, R. H. (1963) *Social Learning and Personality Development.* New York: Holt, Rinehart and Winston.

Bard, B. and Sachs, J. (1977) Language acquisition patterns in two normal children of deaf parents. Paper presented to the 2nd Annual Boston University Conference on Language Acquisition, October 1977.

Baron, R. A. (1972) Aggression as a function of ambient temperature and prior anger arousal. *Journal of Personality and Social Psychology,* **21**, 183–189.

Baron, R. A. and Ransberger, V. M. (1978) Ambient temperature and the occurrence of collective violence: the 'long hot summer' revisited. *Journal of Personality and Social Psychology,* **36**, 351–360.

Bartlett, F. C. (1932) *Remembering.* London: Cambridge University Press.

Bateson, G. (1956) The message 'this is play'. In: B. Schaffner (ed) *Group Processes: Transactions of the Second Conference.* New York: Josiah Macy Foundation.

Bateson, G., Jackson, D. D., Haley, J. and Weakland, J. (1956) Towards a theory of schizophrenia. *Behavioural Science,* **1**, 251–264.

Baumrind, D. (1967) Child-care practices anteceding three patterns of preschool behaviour. *Genetic Psychology Monographs,* **75**, 43–88.

Bekerian, D. A. and Baddeley, A. D. (1980) Saturation advertising and the repetition effect. *Journal of Verbal Learning & Verbal Behaviour,* **19**, 17–25.

Von Békésy, G. (1960) *Experiments in Hearing.* New York: McGraw-Hill.

Belbin, E. (1958) Methods of training older workers. *Ergonomics,* **1**, 207–221.

Billig, M. and Tajfel, H. (1973) Social categorisation and similarity in intergroup behaviour. *European Journal of Social Psychology,* **3**, 27–52.

Binet, A. and Simon, T. (1911) *A Method of Measuring the Development of the Intelligence of Young Children.* Lincoln, IL.: Courier Co.

Blakemore, C. and Cooper, J. F. (1970) Development of the brain depends on the visual environment. *Nature,* **228**, 477–478.

Bleda, P. R. and Sandman, P. H. (1977) In smoke's way: socio-emotional reactions to another's smoking. *Journal of Applied Psychology,* **62**, 452–458.

Bond, M. H. and Hewstone, M. (1988) Social identity theory and the perception of intergroup relations in Hong Kong. *International Journal of Intercultural Relations,* **12(2)**, 153–170.

de Bono, E. (1977) *Lateral Thinking.* Harmondsworth: Penguin.

Bornstein, M. H. and Bornstein, H. G. (1976) Cities fast paced. *Rocky Mountain News,* 19th February 1976.

Bower, G. H. (1969) Chunks as interference units in free recall. *Journal of Verbal Learning & Verbal Behaviour,* **8**, 610–613.

Bower, G. H. (1981) Mood and memory. *American Psychologist,* **36**, 129–148.

Bower, G. H. and Karlin, M. B. (1974) Depth of processing pictures of faces and recognition memory. *Journal of Experimental Psychology,* **103**, 751–757.

Bower, T. G. R. (1966) The visual world of infants. *Scientific American*, **215(6)**, 80–92.

Bowlby, J. (1946) *Forty-Four Juvenile Thieves: Their Characters and Home Life*. Baillère, Tindall and Cox.

Bowlby, J. (1951) *Child Care and the Growth of Love*. Harmondsworth: Penguin.

Bowlby, J. (1951) *Maternal Care and Mental Health*. Geneva: World Health Organisation.

Bowlby, J. (1956) The effects of mother-child separation: a follow-up study. *British Journal of Medical Psychology*, **29**, 211–247.

Bowlby, J. (1958) The nature of the child's tie to his mother. *International Journal of Psychoanalysis*, **39**, 350–373.

Brady, J. P. (1958) Ulcers in 'executive' monkeys. *Scientific American*, **199**, 95–100.

Briggs, R. (1971) Urban cognitive distances. Unpublished doctoral dissertation, Ohio State University, cited in Matlin, M. (1983) *Cognition*. New York: Holt, Rinehart and Winston.

Broadhurst, P. L. (1960) Experiments in psychogenetics. In: H. J. Eysenck (ed) *Experiments in Personality*, Vol I. London: Routledge and Kegan Paul.

Broca, P. (1861) Remarques sur le siège de la faculté du langage articulé suivees d'une observation d'aphemie. *Bulletin de la Société Anatomique* (Paris), **6**, 330–357.

Bromley, D. (1966) *The Psychology of Human Ageing*. Harmondsworth: Penguin.

Bronfenbrenner, U. (1973) *Two Worlds of Childhood: US and USSR*. New York: Pocket Books.

Bronson, G. W. (1972) Infants reactions to unfamiliar persons and novel objects. *Monographs of the Society for Research in Child Development*, **37(3)**, Serial No. 148.

Brooks, P. Preston (1984) *The Anatomy of Intelligence*. London: Today's World Publications.

Brown, G. W. and Harris, T. (1978) *Social Origins of Depression: A Study in Psychiatric Disorder in Women*. London: Tavistock.

Brown, J. A. C. (1954) *The Social Psychology of Industry*. Harmondsworth: Penguin.

Brown, R. (1973) *A First Language*. London: Allen and Unwin.

Brown, R. and Kulik, J. (1977) Flashbulb Memories. Cognition, **(5)**, 73–99.

Bruner, J. S. (1961) The conditions of creativity. In: H. E. Gruber et al. (eds) *Contemporary Approaches to Creative Thinking*. New York: Atherton.

Bruner, J. S. (1964) The course of cognitive growth. *American Psychologist*, **19**, 1–15.

Bruner, J. S. (1975) The ontogenesis of speech acts. *Journal of Child Language*, **3**, 255–287.

Bruner, J. S., Goodnow, J. J. and Austin, G. A. (1956) *A Study of Thinking*. New York: Wiley.

Bruner, J. S. and Kenney, H. (1966) The development of the concepts of order and proportion in children. In: J. S. Bruner et al. (eds) *Studies in Cognitive Growth*. New York: Wiley.

Bruner, J. S. and Minturn, A. L. (1955) Perceptual identification and perceptual organisation. *Journal of General Psychology*, **53**, 21–8.

Bryant, B., Harris, M. and Newton, D. (1980) *Children and Minders*. London: Grant McIntyre.

Burns, R. B. (1966) Age and mental ability. *British Journal of Educational Psychology*, **36**, 116.

Burt, C. (1955) The evidence for the concept of intelligence. *British Journal of Educational Psychology*, **25**, 158–177.

Butler, J. M. and Haigh, G. V. (1954) Changes in the relation between self-concept and ideal concepts consequent on client-centred counselling. In: C. R. Rogers and R. F.

Dymond (eds) *Psychotherapy and Personality Change*. Chicago: University of Chicago Press.

Calhoun, J. B. (1962) Population density and social pathology. *Scientific American*, **206(3)**, 139–148.

Cannon, W. B. (1929) *Bodily Changes in Pain, Hunger, Fear and Rage*. New York: Appleton.

Cattell, R. B. (1946) *Description and Measurement of Personality*. New York: World Book Company.

Cheyney, D. and Seyfarth, E. (1980) Vervet monkeys give the alarm. *New Scientist*, September 1980.

Chomsky, N. (1959) A review of B. F. Skinner's 'verbal behaviour'. *Language*, **35**, 26–58.

Chomsky, N. (1965) *Aspects of the Theory of Syntax*. Cambridge, MA.: MIT Press.

Clarke, A. D. B. (1968) Learning and human development – the 42nd Maudsley lecture. *British Journal of Psychiatry*, **114**, 164–177.

Cohen, D. (1987) *The Development of Play*. London: Croom Helm.

Collins, A. M. and Quillian, M. R. (1972) Experiments on semantic memory and language comprehension. In: L. W. Gregg (ed) *Cognition in Learning and Memory*. New York: Wiley.

Collins, J. L. (1982) Self-efficacy and ability in achievement behavior. Cited in A. Bandura: perceived self-agency in the exercise of personal agency. *The Psychologist*, **2(10)**, 411–424.

Conrad, R. (1964) Acoustic confusion in immediate memory. *British Journal of Psychology*, **55**, 75–84.

Cook, M. (1978) *Perceiving Others*. London: Routledge.

Craik, I. F. M. and Lockhart, R. S. (1972) Levels of processing: a framework for memory research. *Journal of Verbal Learning & Verbal Behaviour*, **11**, 671–684.

Cravioto, J. and DeLicardie, E. R. (1978) Nutrition, mental development and learning. In: F. Falkner and J. M. Tanner (eds) *Human Growth Vol. 3: Neurobiology and Nutrition*. New York: Plenum.

Crutchfield, R. S. (1954) A new technique for measuring individual differences in conformity to group judgement. *Proceedings of the Invitational Conference on Testing Problems*, 1954, 69–74.

Cumming, E. and Henry, W. E. (1961) *Growing Old*. New York: Basic Books.

Cummings, L. L. and El Salmi, A. M. (1970) The impact of role diversity, job level and organisational size on managerial satisfaction. *Administrative Science Quarterly*, **15**, 1–10.

Curtiss, S. (1977) *Genie*. New York: Academic Press.

Darley, J. M. and Latané, B. (1968) Bystander intervention in emergencies: diffusion of responsibility. *Journal of Personality and Social Psychology*, **8**, 377–383.

Darwin, C. (1859) *The Origin of Species*. London: John Murray.

Davitz, J. R. and Davitz, L. (1959) Correlates of accuracy in the communication of feelings. *Journal of Communication*, **9**, 110–117.

Dennis, W. (1960) Causes of retardation among institutional children: Iran. *Journal of Genetic Psychology*, **96**, 47–59.

Dennis, W. and Dennis, M. G. (1940) The effect of cradling practices upon the onset of walking in Hopi children. *Journal of Genetic Psychology*, **56**, 77–86.

Deutsch, M. and Collins, M. E. (1951) *Interracial Housing: a Psychological Evaluation of a Social Experiment*. Minneapolis: University of Minneapolis Press.

van Dijk, T. A. (1987) *Communicating Racism: Ethnic Prejudice in Thought and Action*. Newbury Park, CA: Sage.

Dollard, J. and Miller, N. E. (1950) *Personality and Psychotherapy: An Analysis in Terms of Learning, Thinking and Culture.* New York: McGraw-Hill.

Doms, M. and Avermaet, E. van (1981) The conformity effect: a timeless phenomenon? *Bulletin of the British Psychological Society,* **34,** 383–5.

Donaldson, M. (1978) *Children's Minds.* London: Fontana.

Douglas, J. W. B. and Turner, R. K. (1970) The association of anxiety provoking events in early childhood with enuresis. *Proceedings of the Fifth International Scientific Meeting of the International Epidemiology Association.* Savremena Adinistracija, Belgrade.

Dowd, J. J. (1975) Ageing as exchange: a preface to theory. *Journal of Gerontology,* **30,** 584–594.

Durkin, D. (1959) Children's concepts of justice: a comparison with Piaget's data. *Child Development,* **30,** 59–67.

Dyson, J. (1980) Sociopolitical influences on retirement research. *Bulletin of the British Psychological Society,* **33,** 128–130.

Ebbinghaus, H. (1885) *Memory: a Contribution to Experimental Psychology Refurbished,* 1964. New York: Dover.

Eisenberg, P. and Lazarsfeld, P. F. (1938) The psychological effects of unemployment. *Psychological Bulletin,* **35,** 358–390.

Eiser, J. R. (1983) From attributions to behaviour. In: M. Hewstone (ed) *Attribution Theory: Social and Functional Extensions.* Oxford: Basil Blackwell.

Erikson, E. H. (1965) *Childhood and Society,* 2nd edn. Harmondsworth: Penguin.

Eysenck, H. J. (1947) *Dimensions of Personality.* London: Routledge.

Eysenck, H. J. (1965) The effects of psychotherapy. *International Journal of Psychiatry,* **1,** 99–142.

Fantz, R. L. (1961) The origins of form perception. *Scientific American,* **204,** 66–72.

Fein, G. (1975) A transformational analysis of pretending. *Developmental Psychology,* **11,** 291–296.

Felipe, N. J. and Sommer, R. (1966) Invasions of personal space. *Social Problems,* **14,** 206–214.

Ferster, C. B. and Skinner, B. F. (1957) *Schedules of Reinforcement.* New York: Appleton Century Crofts.

Festinger, L. (1957) *A Theory of Cognitive Dissonance.* Evanston, IL: Row, Peterson.

Festinger, L. and Carlsmith, L. M. (1959) Cognitive consequences of forced compliance. *Journal of Abnormal & Social Psychology,* **58,** 203–210.

Festinger, L., Riecken, H. W. and Schachter, S. (1956) *When Prophecy Fails.* Minneapolis: University of Minneapolis Press.

Fischler, C. (1980) Food habits, social change and the nature/culture dilemma. *Social Science Information,* **19,** 937–953.

Fishbein, M. and Ajzen, I. (1975) *Attitude Intention and Behaviour: An Introduction to Theory and Research.* Reading, MA: Addison Wesley.

Fisher, A. E. (1964) Chemical stimulation of the brain. *Scientific American,* **210(6),** 60–68.

Flament, C. (1988) Praktyka i poznawcze reprezentacje spoleczne. (Practical activity and social cognitive representations – English abstract). *Przeglad Psychologiczny,* **31,** 221–228.

Freedman, J. L. and Fraser, S. C. (1966) Compliance without pressure: the foot-in-the-door technique. *Journal of Personality and Social Psychology,* **2,** 195–202.

Freeman, D. (1983) *Margaret Mead and Samoa.* Harmondsworth: Penguin.

French, J. D. (1957) The reticular formation. *Scientific American,* **196(6),** 54–60.

Freud, A. (1946) *The Ego and the Mechanisms of Defence.* London: Hogarth Press.

Freud, A. and Dann, S. (1951) An experiment in group upbringing. *Psychoanalytic Studies of Childhood*, **6**, 127–168.

Freud, S. (1901) The psychopathology of everyday life. Republished 1953. In: J. Strachey (ed) *The Standard Edition of the Complete Psychological Works of Sigmund Freud Vol 6*. London: Hogarth.

Freud, S. (1909) Analysis of a phobia in a five-year-old boy. In: J. Strachey (ed) *The Standard Edition of the Complete Psychological Works of Sigmund Freud Vol 10*. London: Hogarth.

Friedman, M. and Rosenman, R. H. (1974) *Type A Behaviour*. New York: Knopf.

Gahagan, J. (1984) *Social Interaction and its Management*. London: Methuen.

Galton, F. (1869) Classification of men according to their natural gifts. In: J. J. Jenkins and D. G. Paterson *Studies in Individual Differences*, 1961. New York: Appleton Century Crofts.

Galton, F. (1884) *Hereditary Genius*. New York: Appleton.

Galton, F. (1888) Co-relations and their measurement, chiefly from anthropometric data. In: J. J. Jenkins and D. G. Paterson *Studies in Individual Differences*, 1961. New York: Appleton Century Crofts.

Gardner, R. A. and Gardner, B. T. (1969) Teaching sign language to a chimpanzee. *Science*, **165**, 664–672.

Garfinkel, H. (1967) *Studies in Ethnomethodology*. Englewood Cliffs, NJ: Prentice-Hall.

Garland, C. and White, S. (1980) *Children and Day Nurseries*. London: Grant McIntyre.

Garvey, C. (1977) *Play*. London: Fontana/Open Books.

Gesell, A. (1929) Maturation and infant behaviour patterns. *Psychological Review*, **36**, 307–319.

Ghiselin, B. (1952) *The Creative Process*. Berkeley: University of California Press.

Di Giacomo, J.-P. (1980) Intergroup alliances and rejections within a protest movement (analysis of the social representations). *European Journal of Social Psychology*, **10**, 329–344.

Gibson, E. J. and Walk, R. D. (1960) The visual cliff. *Scientific American*, **202**, 64–71.

Gillie, O. (1976) *Sunday Times*, 24th October 1976, London.

Glass, D. C. and Singer, J. L. (1972) Behavioural after effects of unpredictable and uncontrollable aversive events. *American Scientist*, **80**, 457–465.

Glucksberg, S. (1962) The influence of strength of drive on functional fixedness and perceptual recognition. *Journal of Experimental Psychology*, **63**, 36–41.

Goddard, H. H. (1913) The Binet tests in relation to immigration. *Journal of Psycho-Asthenics*, **18**, 105–107.

Goffman, E. (1959) *The Presentation of Self in Everyday Life*. New York: Anchor.

Goldfarb, W. (1943) Infant rearing and problem behaviour. *American Journal of Orthopsychiatry*, **13**, 249–265.

Golomb, C. (1977) The role of substitution in pretence and puzzle games. *British Journal of Educational Psychology*, **47**, 175–186.

Gooch, S. (1980) Right brain, left brain. *New Scientist*, 11 September, 790–792.

Gottesman, I. I. and Shields, J. (1982) *Schizophrenia: The Epigenetic Puzzle*. Cambridge: Cambridge University Press.

Gray, J. A. (1985) A whole and its parts: behaviour, the brain, cognition and emotion. *Bulletin of the British Psychological Society*, **38**, 99–112.

Gregory, R. L. (1963) Distortion of visual space as inappropriate constancy scaling. *Nature*, **119**, 678.

Gregory, R. L. and Wallace, J. G. (1963) Recovery from early blindness: a case study. *Experimental Psychology Society Monographs*, No. 2.

Guilford, J. P. (1967) *The Nature of Human Intelligence*. New York: McGraw-Hill.

Guimond, S. and Palmer, D. L. (1990) Types of academic training and causal attributions for social problems. *European Journal of Social Psychology*, **20(1)**, 61–75.

Guiton, P. (1966) Early experience and sexual object choice in the Brown Leghorn. *Animal Behaviour*, **14**, 534–538.

Hailman, J. P. (1969) How an instinct is learned. *Scientific American*, **221**, 98–106.

Hall, E. T. (1966) *The Hidden Dimension*. New York: Doubleday.

Hamilton, D. L. (1981) *Cognitive Processes in Stereotyping and Intergroup Behaviour*. Hillsdale, NJ: Erlbaum.

Haney, C., Banks, W. C. and Zimbardo, P. G. (1973) Interpersonal dynamics in a simulated prison. *International Journal of Criminology and Penology*, **1**, 69–79.

Harari, H. and McDavid, J. W. (1973) Name stereotypes and teacher's expectations. *Journal of Educational Psychology*, **65**, 222–225.

Harlow, H. F. (1949) The formation of learning sets. *Psychological Review*, **56**, 51–65.

Harlow, H. F. (1959) Love in infant monkeys. *Scientific American*, **200**, 64–74.

Harlow, H. F. and Harlow, M. K. (1962) Social deprivation in monkeys. *Scientific American*, **207(5)**, 136–146.

Harris, J. E. and Sunderland, A. (1981) Effects of age and instruction on an everyday memory questionnaire. Paper presented to the British Psychological Society Cognitive Psychology Section Conference, Plymouth.

Havighurst, R. J. (1964) Flexibility and the social roles of the retired. *American Journal of Sociology*, **59**, 309–311.

Hayes, N. J. (1992) *Social Identity, Social Representations and Organisational Culture*. Unpublished doctoral dissertation. CNAA/Huddersfield Polytechnic.

Hebb, D. O. (1949) *The Organisation of Behaviour*. New York: Wiley.

Heider, F. (1944) Social perception and phenomenal causality. *Psychological Review*, **51**, 358–374.

Heim, A. (1970) *Intelligence and Personality*. Harmondsworth: Penguin.

Held, R. and Hein, A. (1963) Movement-produced stimulation in the development of visually-guided behaviour. *Journal of Comparative and Physiological Psychology*, **56**, 607–613.

Herzberg, F., Mausner, B., Peterson, R. and Capwell, D. F. (1957) *Job Attitudes: Review of Research and Opinions*. Pittsburgh, PA.: Psychological Service of Pittsburgh.

Herzlich, C. (1973) *Health and Illness: A Social–Psychological Analysis*. London: Academic Press.

Herzog, T. R., Kaplan, S. and Kaplan, R. (1982) The prediction of preference for unfamiliar urban places. *Population and Environment*, **5**, 43–58.

Hess, E. H. (1956) Space perception in the chick. *Scientific American*, **195**, 71–80.

Hess, E. H. (1958) 'Imprinting' in animals. *Scientific American*, **198(3)**, 81–90.

Hess, E. H. (1965) Attitude and pupil size. *Scientific American*, **212**, 46–54.

Hess, E. H. (1972) 'Imprinting' in a natural laboratory. *Scientific American*, **227(2)**, 24–31.

Hill, W. F. (1963) *Learning*. London: Methuen.

Hinton, J. (1967) *Dying*. Harmondsworth: Penguin.

Hohmann, G. W. (1966) Some effects of spinal cord lesions on experienced emotional feelings. *Psychophysiology*, **3**, 143–156.

Holmes, D. S. (1974) Investigation of repressions: differential recall of material experimentally or naturally associated with ego threat. *Psychological Bulletin*, **81**, 632–653.

Holmes, G. (1919) Disturbances of vision by cerebral lesions. *British Journal of Ophthalmics*, **1**.

Holmes, T. H. and Rahe, R. H. (1967) The social readjustment rating scale. *Journal of Psychosomatic Research*, **11**, 213–218.

Hubel, D. H. and Wiesel, T. N. (1968) Receptive fields and functional architecture of monkey striate cortex. *Journal of Physiology*, **195**, 215–243.

Hubel, D. H. and Wiesel, T. N. (1979) Brain mechanisms of vision. *Scientific American*, **241(3)**, 150–162.

Hudson, L. (1966) *Contrary Imaginations*. Harmondsworth: Penguin.

Hughes, M. (1975) Egocentricity in children. Unpublished PhD thesis, Edinburgh University, cited in M. Donaldson *Children's Minds*. London: Fontana.

Hutt, C. (1966) Exploration and play in children. *Symposia of the Zoological Society of London*, **18**, 61–81.

Iverson, L. L. (1979) The chemistry of the brain. *Scientific American*, **241**, 118–129.

Jaffe, J., Stern, D. L. and Peery, J. C. (1973) 'Conversational' complexity of gaze behaviour in pre-linguistic human development. *Journal of Psycholinguistic Research*, **2**, 321–330.

Jaffe, P. G. and Katz, A. N. (1975) Attenuating anterograde amnesia in Korsakoff's psychosis. *Journal of Abnormal Psychology*, **84**, 559–562.

James, W. (1884) What is an emotion? *Mind*, **19**, 188–205.

James, W. (1890) *Principles of Psychology*. New York: Henry Holt.

Janis, I. L. (1972) *Victims of Groupthink*. Boston: Houghton Mifflin.

Jensen, A. R. (1969) How much can we boost IQ and scholastic achievement? *Harvard Educational Review*, **33**, 1–123.

Jodelet, D. (1984) The representation of the body and its transformations. In: R. M. Farr and S. Moscovici *Social Representations*. Cambridge: Cambridge University Press.

Jones, E. E. and Davis, K. E. (1965) From acts to dispositions: the attribution process in person perception. In: L. Berkowitz (ed) *Advances in Experimental Social Psychology* 2. New York: Academic Press.

Jones, E. E. and Harris, V. A. (1967) The attribution of attitudes. *Journal of Experimental Social Psychology*, **3**, 1–24.

Jones, E. E., Rock, L., Shaver, K. G. Goethels, G. R. and Ward, L. M. (1968) Pattern of performance and ability attribution: an unexpected primacy effect. *Journal of Personality and Social Psychology*, **9**, 317–340.

Jones, R. D. and Downing, L. L. (1979) Deindividuation and valence of cues: effects on prosocial and antisocial behaviour. *Journal of Personality and Social Psychology*, **37**, 1532–1538.

Jourard, S. M. (1966) An exploratory study of body accessibility. *British Journal of Social and Clinical Psychology*, **5**, 221–231.

Jung, C. G. (1964) *Man and His Symbols*. New York: Doubleday.

Kallman, F. J. (1938) *The Genetics of Schizophrenia*. New York: J. J. Augustin.

Kamin, L. J. (1974) *The Science and Politics of IQ*. Potomac, MD: Lawrence Erlbaum Associates.

Kelley, H. H. (1950) The warm–cold variable in first impressions of persons. *Journal of Personality and Social Psychology*, **18**, 431–439.

Kelley, H. H. (1973) The process of causal attribution. *American Psychologist*, **28**, 107–128.

Kelley, K. (1982) Population size or density inflects eight social indices. Unpublished manuscript, University of New York at Albany, cited in: R. A. Baron and D.

Byrne (1984) *Social Psychology: Understanding Human Interaction*, 4th edn. Boston: Allyn and Bacon.

Kellett, D. and Morris, I. (1992) The predictive validity of a tailor made aptitude test. *Selection and Development Review*, **8(2)**, 3–5.

Kelly, G. A. (1955) *The Psychology of Personal Constructs*. New York: W. W. Norton.

Kendon, A. (1967) Some functions of gaze direction in social interaction. *Acta Psychologica*, **26**, 22–63.

King, N. (1970) Clarification and evaluation of the two-factor theory of job satisfaction. *Psychological Bulletin*, **74**, 18–31.

Kohlberg, L. (1963) Development of children's orientation towards a moral order. Part 1, sequence in the development of moral thought. *Vita Humana*, **6**, 11–36.

Kohler, I. (1962) Experiments with goggles. *Scientific American*, Offprint No. 465.

Köhler, W. (1925) *The Mentality of Apes*. New York: Harcourt Brace.

Koluchova, J. (1976) Severe deprivation in twins: a case study. In: A. M. Clarke and A. D. B. Clarke *Early Experience: Myth and Evidence*. London: Open Books.

Kraepelin, E. (1913) *Psychiatry*, 8th edn. Leipzig: Thieme.

Kral, V. A. (1978) Benign senile forgetfulness. In: R. Katzman et al. (eds) *Alzheimer's Disease: Senile Dementia and Relating Disorders*. New York: Raven Press.

Kuhlman, C. (1960) Visual imagery in children. Unpublished doctoral dissertation, Harvard University. Cited in J. S. Bruner et al. *Studies in Cognitive Growth*. New York: Wiley.

Kuhn, M. H. (1960) Self attitudes by age, sex and professional training. *Sociological Quarterly*, **1**, 39–55.

Kulik, J. A. (1983) Confirmatory attribution and the perpetuation of social beliefs. *Journal of Personality and Social Psychology*, **44**, 1171–1181.

Labov, W. (1972) The logic of nonstandard English. In: V. Lee (ed) (1979) *Language Development*. London: Croom Helm/Open University.

Laing, R. D. (1960) *The Divided Self*. Harmondsworth: Penguin.

Lalljee, M. (1981) Attribution theory and the analysis of explanations. In: C. Antaki (ed) *The Psychology of Ordinary Explanations of Social Behaviour*. London: Academic Press.

Lange, C. (1885) The emotions (trans. I. A. Haupt). In: K. Dunlap (ed) *The Emotions*. Baltimore: Williams and Wilkins 1922.

LaPière, R. T. (1934) Attitudes versus actions. *Social Forces*, **13**, 230–237.

Lashley, K. (1926) Studies of cerebral function in learning: VII. The relation between cerebral mass, learning and retention. *Journal of Comparative Neurology*, **41**, 1–48.

Latané, B. and Darley, J. M. (1968) Group inhibition of bystander intervention in emergencies. *Journal of Personality and Social Psychology*, **10**, 215–221.

Latané, B. and Rodin, J. (1969) A lady in distress: inhibiting effects of friends and strangers on bystander intervention. *Journal of Experimental and Social Psychology*, **5**, 189–202.

Lazar, I. and Darlington, R. (1982) Leasting effects of early education: a report from the consortium of longitudinal studies. *Monographs of the Society for Research into Child Development*, **33**.

Lee, J. A. (1976) *The Colours of Love*. New York: Bantam.

Lenneberg, E. H. (1967) *Biological Foundations of Language*. New York: Wiley.

Levine, S. (1960) Stimulation in infancy. *Scientific American*, **202**, 81–86.

Lewin, K., Lippitt, R. and White, R. K. (1939) Patterns of aggressive behaviour in artificially created social climates. *Journal of Social Psychology*, **10**, 271–299.

Linton, M. (1982) Transformations of memory in everyday life. In: U. Neisser (ed) *Memory Observed: Remembering in Natural Contexts*. San Francisco: Freeman.

Loftus, G. R. and Loftus, E. F. (1975) *Human Memory: The Processing of Information*. New York: Halsted Press.

Loo, C. M. (1979) A factor analytic approach to the study of spatial density effects on preschoolers. *Journal of Population*, **2**, 47–68.

Lorenz, K. Z. (1950) The comparative method in studying innate behaviour patterns. *Symposia of the Society for Experimental Biology*, **4**, 221–268.

Lorenz, K. Z. (1958) The evolution of behaviour. *Scientific American*, **199(6)**, 67–78.

Lorenz, K. Z. (1970) *Studies in Animal and Human Behaviour*, Vol. **1**. London: Methuen.

Lowe, M. (1975) The development of representational play in children. *Journal of Child Psychology and Psychiatry*, **16**, 33–47.

Lowenthal, M. F., Thurnher, M. and Chiriboga, D. (1975) *Four Stages of Life*. San Francisco: Jossey-Bass.

Luchins, A. S. (1942) Mechanisation in problem-solving. *Psychological Monographs*, **54**, No. 248.

Luchins, A. S. (1959) Primacy-recency in impression formation. In: C. I. Hovland (ed) *The Order of Presentation in Persuasion*. New Haven, CT: Yale University Press.

Mackinnon, D. W. (1938) Violation of prohibitions. In: H. W. Murray (ed) *Exploration in Personality*. Oxford: Oxford University Press.

Mahl, G. F. (1963) The lexical and linguistic levels in the expression of emotions. In: P. H. Knapp (ed) *Expression of the Emotions in Man*. New York: International Universities Press.

Maier, N. R. F. (1955) *Psychology in Industry*. New York: McGraw-Hill.

Malinowski, B. (1927) *Sex and Repression in Savage Society*. New York: Harcourt Brace Jovanovich.

Mann, L. (1981) The baiting crowd in episodes of threatened suicide. *Journal of Personality and Social Psychology*, **41**, 703–709.

Marler, P. R. and Tamura, M. (1964) Culturally transmitted patterns of vocal behaviour in sparrows. *Science*, **146**, 1483–1486.

Marshall, J. R. (1984) The genetics of schizophrenia revisited. *Bulletin of the British Psychological Society*, **37**, 177–181.

Maslow, A. H. (1954) *Motivation and Personality*. New York: Harper.

Mayo, E. (1933) *The Human Problems of an Industrial Civilisation*. London: Macmillan.

McGarrigle, J. and Donaldson, M. (1974) Conservation accidents. *Cognition*, **3**, 341–350.

McGregor, D. (1960) *The Human Side of Enterprise*. New York: McGraw-Hill.

Mead, M. (1928) *Coming of Age in Samoa*. New York: Morrow.

Mead, M. (1962) *Male and Female*. Harmondsworth: Penguin.

Mehrabian, A. (1972) *Nonverbal Communication*. New York: Aldine-Atherton.

Menzies, R. (1937) Conditioned vasomotor responses in human subjects. *Journal of Psychology*, **4**, 75–120.

Miles, W. R. (1931) Measurement of certain human abilities throughout lifespan. *Proceedings of the National Academy of Science*, **17**, 627–633.

Milgram, S. (1963) Behavioural study of obedience. *Journal of Abnormal Psychology*, **67**, 371–378.

Miller, G. A. (1956) The magical number seven, plus or minus two: some limits on our capacity for processing information. *Psychological Review*, **63**, 81–97.

Morris, P. E., Gruneberg, M. M., Sykes, R. N. and Merrick, A. (1981) Football knowledge and the acquisition of new results. *British Journal of Psychology*, **72**, 479–483.

Moscovici, S. (1961) *La Psychoanalyse: Son Image et Son Public*. Paris: Presses Universitaires de France.

Moscovici, S. (1984) The phenomenon of social representations. In: R. M. Farr and S. Moscovici (eds) *Social Representations*. Cambridge: Cambridge University Press.

Moscovici, S. and Hewstone, M. (1983) Social representations and social explanations: from the 'naive' to the 'amateur' scientist. In: M. Hewstone (ed) *Attribution Theory: Social and Functional Extensions*. Oxford: Blackwell.

Mower-White, C. J. (1977) A limitation of balance theory: the effects of identification with a member of the triad. *European Journal of Social Psychology*, **7**, 11–116.

Neisser, U. (1976) *Cognition and Reality: Principles and Implications of Cognitive Psychology*. San Francisco: W. H. Freeman.

Newman, H. H., Freeman, F. N. and Holzinger, K. J. (1937) *Twins: A Study of Heredity and Environment*. Chicago: University of Chicago Press.

Newman, O. (1972) *Defensible Space: Crime Prevention Through Urban Design*. New York: Macmillan.

Newman, O. (1976) *Design Guidelines for Creating Defensible Space*. National Institute of Law Enforcement and Criminal Justice, United States Department of Justice, Washington.

Newson, J. and Newson, E. (1968) *Four Years Old in an Urban Community*. London: Allen and Unwin.

Nisbett, R. E., Caputo, C., Legant, P. and Marcek, J. (1973) Behaviour as seen by the actor and as seen by the observer. *Journal of Personality and Social Psychology*, **27**, 157–164.

Opie, I., and Opie, P. (1959) *The Lore and Language of Schoolchildren*. Oxford: Oxford University Press.

Osgood, C. E. (1966) Dimensionality of the semantic space for communication via facial expression. *Scandinavian Journal of Psychology*, **7**, 1–30.

Parkes, C. M. (1972) *Bereavement*. Harmondsworth: Penguin.

Parten, M. (1933) Social play among pre-school children. *Journal of Abnormal and Social Psychology*, **28**, 136–147.

Patterson, F. (1979) Conversations with a gorilla. *National Geographic*, **154**, 438–465.

Patton, R. G. and Gardner, L. I. (1963) *Growth Failure in Maternal Deprivation*. London: C. C. Thomas.

Pavlov, I. P. (1927) *Conditioned Reflexes: An Investigation of the Physiological Activity of the Cerebal Cortex*. New York: Dover.

Penfield, W. (1959) The interpretive cortex. *Science*, **129**, 1719–1725.

Pennington, D. C. (1982) Witnesses and their testimony: the effects of ordering on juror verdicts. *Journal of Applied Social Psychology*, **12**, 318–333.

Perrin, S. and Spencer, C. (1980) The Asch effect: a child of its time? *Bulletin of the British Psychological Society*, **32**, 405–406.

Pettigrew, T. F. (1958) Personality and sociocultural factors in intergroup attitudes: a cross-national comparison. *Journal of Conflict Resolution*, **2**, 29–42.

Pfungst, O. (1912) Zur Psychologie der Affe. *Bericht Über Kongress für Experimentelle Psychologie*, **5**, 200–205.

Piaget, J. (1932) *The Moral Judgement of the Child*. London: Routledge and Kegan Paul.

Piaget, J. (1952) *Play, Dreams and Imitation in Childhood*. London: Routledge.

Piaget, J. (1952) *The Origins of Intelligence in Children*. New York: International Universities Press.

Piliavin, I. M., Rodin, J. and Piliavin, J. A. (1969) Good samaritanism: an underground phenomenon? *Journal of Personality and Social Psychology*, **13**, 289–299.

Poulton, E. C. (1976) Continuous noise interferes with work by masking auditory feedback and inner speech. *Applied Ergonomics*, **7**, 79–84.

Power, M. J., Ashe, P., Fchoenberg, E. and Sorrey, E. C. (1974) Delinquency and family. *British Journal of Social Work*, **4**, 13–38.

Premack, D. (1983) Animal cognition. *Annual Review of Psychology*, **34**, 351–362.

Pringle, M. L. K. and Bossio, V. (1960) Early prolonged separations and emotional adjustment. *Journal of Child Psychology and Psychiatry*, **1**, 37–48.

Pritchard, R. M. (1961) Stabilised images on the retina. *Scientific American*, **204(6)**, 72–78.

Riesen, A. H. (1950) Arrested vision. *Scientific American*, **183**, 16–20.

Riesen, A. H. (1966) Sensory deprivation. In: E. Stellar and J. M. Sprague (eds) *Progress in Physiological Psychology*. New York: Academic Press.

Roethlisberger, F. J. and Dickson, W. G. (1939) *Management and the Worker*. Cambridge, MA.: Harvard University Press.

Rogers, C. R. (1961) *On Becoming a Person: A Therapists View of Psychotherapy*. London: Constable.

Rokeach, M. (1948) Generalised mental rigidity as a factor in ethnocentrism. *Journal of Abnormal and Social Psychology*, **43**, 259–278.

Rokeach, M. (1960) *The Open and Closed Mind*. New York: Basic Books.

Rokeach, M. (1973) *The Nature of Human Values*. New York: Free Press.

Rosch, E. H. (1973) Natural categories. *Cognitive Psychology*, **4**, 328–250.

Rosch, E. H., Mervis, C. B., Gray, W. D., Johnson, D. M. and Boyes-Braem, P. (1976) Basic objects in natural categories. *Cognitive Psychology*, **8**, 382–439.

Rose, S. A. and Blank, M. (1974) The potency of context in children's cognition: an illustration through conservation. *Child Development*, **45**, 499–502.

Rose, S., Kamin, L. J. and Lewontin, R. C. (1984) *Not in Our Genes: Biology, Ideology and Human Nature*. Harmondsworth: Penguin.

Rosen, B. C. and D'Andrade, R. (1959) The psychosocial origins of achievement motivation. *Sociometry*, **22**, 185–218.

Rosenhan, D. L. (1973) On being sane in insane places. *Science*, **179**, 250–258.

Rosenthal, R. and Fode, K. L. (1963) The effect of experimenter bias on the performance of the albino rat. *Behavioural Science*, **8**, 183–189.

Rosenthal, R. and Jacobsen, L. (1968) *Pygmalion in the Classroom: Teacher Expectations and Pupil Intellectual Development*. New York: Holt, Rinehart and Winston.

Rosenzweig, M. R. and Bennett, E. L. (1976) Enriched environments: facts, factors and fantasies. In: J. L. McGaugh and L. Petrinovitch (eds) *Knowing, Thinking and Believing*. New York: Plenum.

Ross, H. S. and Goldman, B. D. (1977) Infants' sociability towards strangers. *Child Development*, **48**, 638–642.

Rothbart, K. and Maccoby, E. E. (1966) Parents differential reactions to sons and daughters. *Journal of Personality and Social Psychology*, **4**, 237–243.

Rotter, J. B. (1966) Generalised expectancies for internal versus external control of reinforcement. *Psychological Monographs*, **80**, No. 609.

Rotton, J., Frey, J., Barry, T., Milligan, M. and Fitzpatrick, M. (1979) The air pollution experience and physical aggression. *Journal of Applied Social Psychology*, **9**, 397–412.

Rubin, K. H., Maioni, T. L. and Hornung, M. (1976) Free play behaviours in middle- and lower-class preschoolers. Parten and Piaget revisited. *Child Development*, **47**, 414–419.

Rutter, M. (1972) *Maternal Deprivation Reassessed*. Harmondsworth: Penguin.

Rutter, M. (1979) Maternal deprivation 1971–1978: new findings, new concepts, new approaches. *Child Development*, **50**, 283–305.

Saarinen, T. F. (1973) The use of projective techniques in geographic research. In: W. H. Ittelson (ed) *Environment and Cognition*. New York: Seminar Press.

Sacks, O. (1985) *The Man Who Mistook his Wife for a Hat*. London: Picador.

Scarr, S. and Weinberg, R. A. (1978) Attitudes, interests and IQ. *Human Nature*, **1**, 29–36.

Schachter, S. and Singer, J. E. (1962) Cognitive, social and physiological determinants of emotional state. *Psychological Review*, **69**, 379–399.

Schaffer, H. R. and Emerson, P. E. (1964) The development of social attachments in infancy. *Monographs of Social Research in Child Development*, **29**, No. 94.

Schank, R. and Abelson, R. (1977) *Scripts, Plans, Goals and Understanding: An Enquiry into Human Knowledge*. Hillsdale, NJ: Erlbaum.

Sears, R. R., Maccoby, E. E. and Levin, H. (1957) *Patterns of Child Rearing*. Evanston, IL.: Row Peterson.

Secord, P. F. and Backman, C. W. (1974) *Social Psychology* 2nd edn. Tokyo: McGraw-Hill.

Segall, M. H., Campbell, D. T. and Herskowits, M. J. (1963) *The Influence of Culture on Visual Perception*. New York: Bobs-Merrill.

Seligman, M. E. P. (1970) On the generality of the laws of learning. *Psychological Review*, **77**, 406–418.

Seligman, M. E. P. (1975) *Helplessness: On Depression, Development and Death*. San Francisco: Freeman.

Selye, H. (1956) *The Stress of Life*. New York: McGraw-Hill.

von Senden, M. (1932) *Space and Sight*. London: Methuen/Free Press.

Sherif, M. (1935) A study of some social factors in perception. *Archives of Psychology*, **27**, No. 187.

Sherif, M., Harvey, O. J., White, B. J., Hood, W. R. and Sherif, C. W. (1961) *Intergroup Conflict and Co-operation: the Robbers Cave Experiment*. Norman, OK: University of Oklahoma Press.

Shields, J. (1962) *Monozygotic Twins Brought Up Apart and Brought Together*. London: Oxford University Press.

Shouksmith et al. (1988) *Introducing Psychology*. London: Longman.

Singer, P. (1976) *Animal Liberation*. London: Cape.

Skeels, H. M. (1966) Adult status of children with contrasting early life experiences. *Monographs of the Society for Research into Child Development*, **31**, 1–56.

Skeels, H. M. and Dye, H. B. (1939) A study of the effects of differential stimulation on mentally retarded children. *Proceedings of the American Association on Mental Deficiency*, **44**, 114–136.

Skeels, H. M. (1966) Adult status of children with contrasting early life-experiences. *Monographs of Social Research in Child Development*, **31**.

Skinner, B. F. (1938) *The Behaviour of Organisms*. New York: Appleton Century Crofts.

Skinner, B. F. (1953) *Science and Human Behaviour*. New York: Macmillan.

Skinner, B. F. (1957) *Verbal Behaviour*. New York: Appleton Century Crofts.

Skodak, M. and Skeels, H. M. (1949) A final follow-up study of one hundred adopted children. *Journal of Genetic Psychology*, **75**, 85–125.

Sluckin, W. (1964) *Imprinting and Early Learning*. London: Methuen.

Smith, C. and Lloyd, B. Maternal behaviour and perceived sex of infant revisited. *Child Development*, **49**, 1263–1265.

Smith, M. B., Bruner, J. S. and White, R. W. (1964) Opinions and personality. In: J. Murphy et al. (eds) *Dialogues and Debates in Social Psychology*, 1984. London: Erlbaum.

Snyder, M. and Cunningham, M. R. (1975) To comply or not to comply: testing the self-perception explanation of the 'foot-in-the-door' phenomenon. *Journal of Personality and Social Psychology*, **31**, 64–67.

Solley, C. M. and Haigh, G. (1958) A note to Santa Claus. *TPR The Menninger Foundation*, **18(3)**, 4–5.

Solomon, R. L. and Wynne, L. C. (1950) Avoidance conditioning in normal dogs and in dogs deprived of normal autonomic functioning. *American Psychologist*, **5**, 264.

Sommer, R. (1969) *Personal Space*. Englewood Cliffs, NJ: Prentice-Hall.

Spearman, C. (1904) General intelligence objectively determined and measured. *American Journal of Psychology*, **15**, 201–293.

Sperry, R. W. (1982) Some effects of disconnecting the cerebral hemispheres. *Science*, **217**, 1223–1226.

Spitz, R. A. (1945) Hospitalism: an inquiry into the genesis of psychiatric conditions in early childhood. *Psychoanalytic Studies of Childhood*, **1**, 53–74.

Stern, D. (1978) *The First Relationship: Infant and Mother*. London: Fontana.

Sternberg, R. J. (1985) *Beyond IQ: A Triarchic Theory of Human Intelligence*. Cambridge: Cambridge University Press.

Stotland, E., Thorley, S., Thomas, R. E., Cohen, A. R. and Zander, A. (1957) The effects of group expectation and self-esteem upon self-evaluation. *Journal of Abnormal and Social Psychology*, **54**, 55–63.

Strathern, M. (1983) *Mead, Freeman and Samoa*. The Times Review of Books, July 1983.

Stratton, G. M. (1897) Vision without inversion of the retinal image. *Psychological Review*, **4**, 341–360 and 463–481.

Sylva, K. D., Roy, C. and Painter, M. (1980) *Childwatching at Playgroup and Nursery School*. London: Grant McIntyre.

Szasz, T. S. (1960) The myth of mental illness. *American Psychologist*, 15, 113–118.

Tajfel, H. (1969) Cognitive aspects of prejudice. *Journal of Social Issues*, 25(4), 79–97.

Tajfel, H. and Turner, J. C. (1979) An integrative theory of intergroup conflict. In: W. G. Austin and S. Worchel (eds) *The Social Psychology of Intergroup Relations*. Monterey, CA: Brooks/Cole.

Tanner, J. M. (1971) Sequence, tempo and individual variation in the growth and development of boys and girls aged twelve to sixteen. *Daedalus*, 100, 907–930.

Tapp, J. L. and Levine, F. J. (1972) Compliance from kindergarten to college: a speculative research note. *Journal of Adolescence and Youth*, 1, 233–249.

Taylor, F. W. (1911) *The Principles of Scientific Management*. New York: Harper and Row.

Thorndike, E. L. (1911) *Animal Intelligence: Experimental Studies*. New York: Macmillan.

Thurstone, L. L. (1938) *Primary Mental Abilities*. Chicago, IL.: The University of Chicago Press.

Tinbergen, N. (1951) *The Study of Instinct*. Oxford: Oxford University Press.

Tizard, B. (1974) IQ and race. *Nature*, 247, 316.

Tizard, B. (1977) *Adoption: A Second Chance*. London: Open Books.

Tizard, B. and Hodges, J. (1978) The effect of early institutional rearing on the development of eight-year-old children. *Journal of Child Psychology and Psychiatry*, 12, 99–118.

Tizard, B. and Rees, J. (1974) A comparison of the effects of adoption, restoration to the natural mother and continued institutionalisation on the cognitive development of four-year-old children. *Child Development*, 45, 92–99.

Tolman, E. C. (1932) *Purposive Behaviour in Animals and Men*. New York: Century.

Trasler, G. (1960) *In Place of Parents: A Study of Foster Care*. London: Routledge and Kegan Paul.

Tulving, E. (1972) Episodic and semantic memory. In: E. Tulving and W. Donaldson (eds) *Organisation of Memory*. New York: Academic Press.

Tulving, E. and Pearlstone, Z. (1966) Availability versus accessibility of information in memory for words. *Journal of Verbal Learning and Verbal Behaviour*, 5, 381–391.

Turnbull, C. M. (1961) *The Forest People*. New York: Simon and Schuster.

Tyler, L. E. (1965) *The Psychology of Human Differences*. New York: Appleton Century Crofts.

Valentine, C. W. (1942) *The Early Life of the Child*. London: Methuen.

Vernon, P. E. (1950) *The Structure of Human Abilities*. London: Methuen.

De Villiers, J. and De Villiers, P. (1978) *Early Language*. London: Fontana.

Vygotsky, L. S. (1962) *Thought and Language*. Cambridge, MA.: MIT Press.

Wason, P. C. (1968) Reasoning about a rule. *The Quarterly Journal of Experimental Psychology*, 20, 273–281.

Wason, P. C. and Johnson-Laird, P. N. (1970) A conflict between selecting and evaluating information in an inferential task. *British Journal of Psychology*, 61, 509–515.

Watson, J. B. (1903) *Animal Education*. Chicago, IL: The University of Chicago Press.

Watson, J. B. (1913) Psychology from the standpoint of a behaviourist. *Psychological Review*, **20**, 158–177.

Watson, J. B. and Rayner, R. (1920) Conditioned emotional reactions. *Journal of Experimental Psychology*, **3(1)**, 1–14.

Weatherley, D. (1961) Anti-semitism and the expression of fantasy aggression. *Journal of Abnormal and Social Psychology*, **62**, 454–457.

Weiskrantz, L. (1980) Varieties of residual experience. *Quarterly Journal of Experimental Psychology*, **32**, 365–386.

Welford, A. T. (1958) *Ageing and Human Skill*. Oxford: Oxford University Press.

Welford, A. T. (1976) Motivation, capacity, learning and age. *International Journal of Aging and Human Development*, **7**, 189–199.

Wernicke, C. (1874) *Der aphasiche symptomenkomplex*. Breslau: Cohn und Weigart.

White, B. L. (1971) *Human Infants: Experience and Psychological Development*. Englewood Cliffs, NJ: Prentice-Hall.

Whiting, J. W. M. (1962) Resource mediation and learning by identification. In: I. Iscoe and H. W. Stevenson (eds) *Personality Development in Young Children*. Texas: University of Texas Press.

Williams, M. D. and Hollan, J. D. (1981) The process of retrieval from very long-term memory. *Cognitive Science*, **5**, 87–119.

Wilson, S. (1978) Vandalism and 'defensible space' on London housing estates. In: R. V. G. Clarke (ed) *Tackling Vandalism*. London: HMSO.

Winterbottom, M. (1953) The sources of achievement motivation in mothers' attitudes towards independence training. In: D. McClelland et al. (eds) *The Achievement Motive*. New York: Appleton Century Crofts.

Witkin, H. A. et al. (1962) *Psychological Differentiation*. New York: Wiley.

Wittenborn, J. (1951) Symptom patterns in a group of mental hospital patients *Journal of Consulting Psychology*, **15**, 290–302.

Wolff, P. (1969) The natural history of crying and other vocalisations in early infancy. In: B. M. Foss (ed) *Determinants of Infant Behaviour IV*. London: Methuen.

Wundt, W. (1896) *Grundriss der Psychologie*. Leipzig: Engelmann.

Yarnell, P. R. and Lynch, S. (1973) The ding: amnesic states in football trauma. *Neurology*, **23**, 196–197.

Zimbardo, P. G. (1970) The human choice: individuation, reason and order versus deindividuation, impulse and chaos. In: W. J. Arnold and D. Levine (eds) *Nebraska Symposium on Motivation 1969*. Lincoln: University of Nebraska Press.

Index